CRISIS BY DESIGN

CRISIS BY DESIGN

EMERGENCY POWERS AND COLONIAL LEGALITY IN PUERTO RICO

JOSE ATILES

STANFORD UNIVERSITY PRESS
Stanford, California

Stanford University Press
Stanford, California

Printed in the United States of America on acid-free, archival-quality paper

Library of Congress Cataloging-in-Publication Data
Names: Atiles, Jose, author.
Title: Crisis by design : emergency powers and colonial legacy in Puerto Rico / Jose Atiles.
Description: Stanford, California : Stanford University Press, 2024. | Includes bibliographical references and index.
Identifiers: LCCN 2024028628 (print) | LCCN 2024028629 (ebook) | ISBN 9781503640597 (cloth) | ISBN 9781503641174 (paperback) | ISBN 9781503641181 (ebook)
Subjects: LCSH: Emergency management—Law and legislation—Puerto Rico. | Disaster relief—Law and legislation—Puerto Rico. | Law—Political aspects—Puerto Rico. | Crises—Political aspects—Puerto Rico. | Puerto Rico—Colonial influence. | Puerto Rico—Politics and government—21st century. | Puerto Rico—Relations—United States. | United States—Relations—Puerto Rico.
Classification: LCC KGV2060 .A98 2024 (print) | LCC KGV2060 (ebook) | DDC 342.7295/062—dc23/eng/20240625
LC record available at https://lccn.loc.gov/2024028628
LC ebook record available at https://lccn.loc.gov/2024028629

Cover design: Lindy Kasler
Cover art: Shutterstock

For Mateo

CONTENTS

TABLES

ACKNOWLEDGMENTS

This book is the result of the ties of solidarity that bind together colonial subjects and their allies amid a permanent colonial multilayered crisis. To acknowledge these ties is to recognize that this book is the result of acts of solidarity and ruptures with neoliberal rationalities. *Crisis by Design* could not have come to fruition without the generosity of all my interviewees, who graciously shared their time and insights into their experiences, understanding, and legal practices. I extend my heartfelt gratitude to Cecille Blondet, Rolando Emmanuelli, Mari Mari Narváez, Denis Márquez, José B. Márquez, Adi Martínez-Roman, Carla Minet, Carlos Ramos Hernández, Oscar Serrano, Luis José Torres, among other interviewees that took the time to share their knowledge and experiences. I am thankful to Issel Masses, whose support and collaboration through projects and initiatives at Sembrando Sentido were invaluable. Issel's guidance was instrumental in navigating the transparency network and understanding elements of the Puerto Rican colonial governance.

This book received generous support from various funding institutions and research centers. At the University of Illinois Urbana-Champaign (UIUC), I received institutional support and funding from the Humanities Research Institute 2020 Inaugural Summer Faculty Research Fellowship, the Campus Research Board 2022 Funding Initiative for Multiracial Democracy

(Scholarship Award), and the 2022 Humanities Teaching Release Time. The College of Liberal Arts and Sciences, along with the dean's offices, provided an emergency grant to study the sociolegal impact of Hurricane Fiona in Puerto Rico in 2022, as well as the 2023 COVID-19 Revitalization Fellowship.

Similarly, the Unit for Criticism and Interpretative Theory generously awarded me the 2023 Critical Book Labs, facilitating a manuscript workshop. My sincere thanks go to Dede Fairchild Ruggles and the Unit staff for organizing the workshop, and to Anna Maria Marshall, Jessica Greenberg, Mónica Jiménez, and Sebastian León for their participation and insightful feedback. The early reading of this manuscript by Anna, Jessica, Mónica, and Sebastian, coupled with their systemic revisions and insightful engagement, significantly enhances its quality and opens it to broader interdisciplinary scholarship.

I am grateful for the support and intellectual companionship of the Office of Research Advising and Project Development (RAPD), particularly Maria Gillombardo, whose dedication significantly improved my book proposal and grant applications. Special thanks also to Andrew Greenlee, Michael Silvers, Cynthia Oliver, Carol Symes, and Shelley Weinberg, and colleagues in the First Book Writing Group for their invaluable feedback and support. I extend my gratitude to Craig Willse who read earlier versions of this manuscript and provided feedback and edits to my work.

I would also like to express my gratitude for the supportive community at UIUC, especially among my colleagues in the Department of Sociology: Asef Bayat, Cynthia Buckley, Brian Dill, Zsuzsa Gille, Isak Ladegaard, Anna Maria Marshall, Reuben May, Ruby Mendenhall, Ghassan Moussawi, Matthew Soener, and Daniel Steward. I extend my gratitude to Rebecca Hill Riley and all the sociology staff who have made our lives at this institution easier. I am also thankful to the graduate students in the Department of Sociology whose intellectual engagement and teaching support kept me going during the writing of this manuscript—especially, to my research assistants Musa Hamideh and Maya Rodríguez-Reyes, who played a crucial role in completing this book in a timely manner.

Furthermore, I want to express my appreciation to colleagues in the Departments of Latina/Latino Studies and Political Science, the College of Law, the Center for Latin American and Caribbean Studies, the Center for Global Studies, the Center for Social & Behavioral Science, and the Global Studies Program. Special thanks are due to Robert M. Lawless and Jennifer K. Robbennolt for their unwavering support and encouragement in pursuing sociolegal research across the UIUC campus.

Since my arrival at UIUC, I have been fortunate to find support within the Latinx, Latin American, and Puerto Rican communities, who have generously supported and nourished me, both figuratively and literally. I am deeply thankful to Nikolai Alvarado, Janett Barragán, David Cisneros, Nic Flores, Ángel García, Jose de la Garza, Jesann Gonzalez, Marina Moscoso, Alisa Ortiz, Omar Pérez, Andrea Pimentel, Mónica Rivera, Gilberto Rosas, Gisela Sin, Antonio Sotomayor, and Ariam Torres. I am also grateful to Billy Huff, Sue K. Lee, and Lindsay Russell who welcomed me and made me part of their community.

Outside UIUC, this book received significant support from various institutions. The idea for this book was conceived in 2015 primarily as a study of the Puerto Rican economic and financial crisis. For this endeavor, I received financial support through a postdoctoral fellowship from the Portuguese Foundation for Science and Technology (FCT) and the Center for Social Studies at the University of Coimbra, Portugal. In the aftermath of Hurricane María, I received additional financial support from the Latino and Latina Studies program at Northwestern University, through their generous grant for Puerto Rican Scholars affected by Hurricane María. This grant, along with Frances Aparicio's solidarity, opened doors to a series of life-changing opportunities. Following the receipt of this grant, I taught for a semester at the University of Massachusetts, Amherst (UMass), within the Legal Studies Program and the Department of Political Science. This opportunity was made possible by the efforts of Roberto Alejandro and Agustin Lao Montes, who generously facilitated the presence of Puerto Rican scholars affected by Hurricane María at their institution. Agustin and Roberto's kindness, generosity, and solidarity not only kept me going but also helped me find my place in academia.

During my time in the Legal Studies Program, I was fortunate to encounter supportive colleagues who assisted in my transition to UMass and continued to offer support even after my departure. I am grateful to Paul Collins Jr. and his family, who have been supporting me since day one and continue to do so consistently. Additionally, during my time at UMass, I received support from the Center for Latin America, Caribbean, and Latino Studies, as well as from Laura Valdiviezo. I also extend my gratitude to Guillermo Irizarry at the University of Connecticut, Storrs, for his guidance, mentorship, and friendship.

Portions of this book were presented at talks and workshops both nationally and internationally, including at the Center for Global Cooperation Research, University of Duisburg-Essen, Germany; the National University of La Plata, Argentina; the Corruption in the Global South Research Consortium; the Center for Latin American and Caribbean Studies at UIUC; the ISCTE in Lisbon, Portugal; the Center for Latin American, Latinx, and Caribbean Studies at UMass; the University of Texas, Austin; and the University of Liverpool. I am grateful for the generous feedback and comments I received at each of these events, which significantly contributed to the development of this book.

Amid the COVID-19 pandemic, I was fortunate to find a supportive group of people who served as guides during one of the most challenging periods our society has collectively experienced. I express my gratitude to the Puerto Rican Reading Collective and to Marie Cruz Soto, Mónica Jiménez, Pedro Lebrón, Jorell Meléndez Badillo, Sarah Molinari, Aurora Santiago Ortiz, Karrieann Soto Vega, Daniel Vazquez, and Joaquín Villanueva for their friendship and companionship.

I have been fortunate to have friends and allies who have supported and cared for me. I am grateful to Anne Alvesalo-Kuusi, Ignasi Bernat, Steven Bittle, Jesus Carreras, Pablo Ciocchini, Vickie Cooper, Luis Eslava, Gustavo García-Lopez, Daniel Jiménez, Stefanie Khoury, Marisol LeBrón, Mariely Lopéz-Santana, Christopher Power, Silvia Rodríguez Maeso, Gustavo Rojas Paez, Steve Tombs, Fernando Tormos, and Marina Zaloznaya. I consider myself fortunate to count such intellectuals among my friends. I am especially grateful to my friends and co-authors Gustavo Rojas Paez, Gustavo García-Lopez, Joaquín Villanueva, and David Whyte, who have patiently and generously collaborated with me, despite my shortcomings and numerous crises.

I am grateful for Marcela Cristina Maxfield's encouragement and guidance in writing this manuscript, as well as for the work of Austin Michael Araujo and all the staff at Stanford University Press. I am also thankful to the peer reviewers and readers who dedicated their time to read closely and provide generous feedback.

I am indebted to David Whyte, Cesar Pérez Lizasuain, Veronica Davila, and Sandra Soto, who have shown me with their friendship that when crises intensify, solidarity overflows. This book and my scholarship could not have been possible without the mentorship, friendship, and support of Dave, to whom my debt of gratitude is too *grate.*

I am forever grateful to my parents, Luz Osoria López and José Atiles Agueda, and my brother Nestor Atiles Osoria, who have supported, nourished, and accompanied me despite the multiple crises and absences throughout my adult life. I am thankful to Jim, Jodi, and Justin Gorgone for welcoming me into their family and for all their moving assistance. Finally, I am enormously indebted to Amy and Mateo Atiles, who have allowed me the time to research and write this book. If this book begins with a crisis, its trajectory and conclusion are sustained by their love.

INTRODUCTION

EMERGENCY

On September 18, 202, five years after Hurricane María devastated the archipelago, Hurricane Fiona made landfall in Puerto Rico (henceforth PR), causing forty-four deaths, a general blackout, flooding, landslides, and inflicting $6 billion in direct economic impact.[1] Immediately after Hurricane Fiona landed, the hashtag #NoLeDonenAlGobierno (Don't Donate to the Government) trended on Twitter (now X) and other social media platforms. Many posts featured pictures of abandoned bottles of water, food, and other emergency aid donated to the PR government in the aftermath of Hurricane María in 2017, which were never distributed. Puerto Ricans living in the United States and local activists campaigned for direct donations to local grassroots organizations that could effectively deliver aid to those in need. Disaster management was the actual disaster. #NoLeDonenAlGobierno conveys the general distrust in the PR government's capacity to manage and effectively address the needs of Puerto Ricans after socioenvironmental disasters. The prevailing sentiment among Puerto Ricans is that both the PR and US governments have been negligent and incapable of adequately meeting people's needs. Together with #NoLeDonesAlGobierno, a series of memes on social media read: Refuse to glorify resilience: Demand accountability.[2] After enduring a multilayered crisis for years, Puerto Ricans no longer want their suffering to be romanticized as resilient; they demand a just and equitable recovery.

Hurricane Fiona marks the latest disaster in recent Puerto Rican history, characterized by a continuity of disasters[3] and a multilayered political, financial, economic, and humanitarian crisis. PR has been a US colony or unincorporated territory since 1898, and it has been grappling with crises and disasters since 2006, when the current economic and fiscal crisis began. This economic crisis is the result of a convergence of fiscal policies developed by the US Congress, the PR government's financialization of the local economy, and the global financial crisis of 2008. After a decade of stagnation, significant out-migration, and austerity measures, the PR government defaulted on its $72 billion public debt in 2016, leading Congress to pass the Puerto Rican Oversight, Management, and Economic Stability Act (PROMESA)[4] and to impose the Financial Oversight and Management Board (FOMB) onto PR. PROMESA and the FOMB have been the US's colonial solution to address the economic crisis, secure the financial system's survival, ensure debt repayment, and reintegrate PR back into the world of finance and the stock market.

Amid this backdrop, Hurricanes Irma and María devastated the archipelago in September 2017, resulting in damages of up to $94 billion, thousands of deaths, and hundreds of displaced individuals. Subsequently, on January 7, 2020, a 6.4 magnitude earthquake struck the southern region of PR, causing the displacement of 6,400 residents, damaging over 8,300 houses, and resulting in estimated damages of $3.1 billion. When the COVID-19 global pandemic arrived in March 2020, PR was in a more precarious position than any other US state or territory, experiencing a $9.7 billion direct economic negative impact, the loss of approximately $2 billion in tax revenue, and over 6,000 lives lost due to the pandemic. It was against this backdrop that Hurricane Fiona made landfall in PR, exacerbating the already stagnant Puerto Rican economy and its legal and sociopolitical institutions.

Puerto Rican scholars and activists have demonstrated that colonialism, paired with contemporary austerity measures and governmental negligence, are critical factors contributing to the social and political conditions that foster disasters that are anything but "natural."[5] Similar to discourse about climate change and extreme weather events, it is reasonable to view colonial harms as somewhat intractable, inevitable, and thus unescapable. Yet the disasters articulated in this text are human-made, and human-perpetuated, and thus entirely contingent and changeable. There is no such thing as natural disaster.[6]

By insisting that *the disaster is political,* and *the colony is the disaster,* activists and scholars have shown that the PR and US governments are responsible for manufacturing the socioeconomic and legal conditions that enabled Hurricanes Irma, María, and Fiona and the January 2020 earthquakes to become catastrophic.[7] For instance, Yarimar Bonilla (2020a) contends that disasters are socially produced and should be understood as the outcome of long processes of structural violence; their effects are experienced differently through preexisting hierarchies of race, class, and gender—and they often sharpen those relations of inequality. Additionally, Mimi Sheller (2020) argues that the Caribbean faces extreme environmental risks and existential threat associated with climate change, which must be contextualized within the region's long history of colonial violence, slavery, plantation economy, ecological destruction, and resource extraction. Hence, the consensus among Caribbean and Puerto Rican scholars is that the crisis and disasters are manufactured by colonial structures of power, domination, and violence. *Colonialism is the catastrophe.*

Crisis by Design argues that the Puerto Rican multilayered crisis must be understood as the result of the legal, politico-economic, and racialized structure of US colonialism imposed in PR since 1898. Drawing on the works of Marx, Gramsci, Benjamin, Fraser, and Hall et al. (2013), and in conversation with a range of critical and contemporary scholars, I argue that the conditions for these crises are systemic, and intrinsically embedded in colonial capitalism, often leading to a rearticulation and redefinition of capital accumulation practices and the hegemonic position of the ruling elites.[8] As such, the Puerto Rican colonial multilayered crisis should not be view as a series of random events or a rupture with the practices of wealth extraction and capital accumulation enabled by US colonialism; instead, it represents a period of strategic accommodation and rearticulation of US imperialism, the PR state, the local elites, and transnational capital in response to a new dynamic of capital accumulation within the colony.

This book maps out the legal structure and process that manufactured the ongoing colonial multilayered crisis, to clarify and understand the sociolegal and politico-economic dynamics of wealth extraction taking place in PR. The book engages with three concerns: the role of law and emergency powers in creating, exacerbating, and/or sustaining this multilayered crisis; the role of US colonialism, the PR government, corporations, and anticorruption and pro-transparency mobilizations in the multilayered crisis; and how the Puerto

Rican case provides insight as to the role of law and emergency powers in crisis in other Global South, Caribbean, racialized communities, and in colonized societies.

To address these concerns, *Crisis by Design* unfolds a threefold conceptualization to articulate a deeper understanding of the sociolegal and juridical dynamic at play in the multilayered crisis. First, the book employs the concept of *colonial state of exception* to describe the legal structure of US colonialism in PR. US colonial policies in PR have manufactured a specific legal logic of inclusion-exclusion within the rule of law that can be better understood through anticolonial and Global South interpretations of the state of exception.[9] If the state of exception has normally been understood as the suspension of the rule of law to deal with periods of emergency or crisis, in the colonial context of PR, the state of exception has become the legal structure of US colonialism. As John Reynolds (2017) suggests, the state of emergency in the colonies is better understood as structure rather than as event. *Crisis by Design* demonstrates how the colonial state of exception is the legal structure of colonialism, rather than a US response to a crisis or an event.

Second, the book develops the concept of *colonial legality* to describe a series of legal practices, emergency powers, and criminogenic dynamics through which the PR government, with the support of the Puerto Rican elites, exercises its public authority in the context of the multilayered crisis. *Colonial legality* aims to cluster together a series of practices developed since the 1980s that collectively can be considered as a colonial governance enmeshed with neoliberal rationalities and hyper-legalistic practices. The conjunction between the colonial state of exception and colonial legality and their operation in everyday life in PR produces an assemblage of laws, regulations, norms, emergency powers, and violent policies.

Third, *Crisis by Design* proposes the concept of *legal interruptions* to signify how civil society organizations,[10] legal actors, and grassroots organizations mobilize the right to access information, anticorruption narratives, and other transparency and accountability measures to interrupt the brutal process of wealth extraction and capital accumulation enabled by colonial legality. These civil society organizations have largely engaged in legal mobilizations, litigation, and other form of activism to promoted accountability and transparency, and to resist corruption, state-corporate crime, and social harm generated by colonial legality.

Together, and often as a result of the legal interruptions, this book identifies the emergence of *colonial ruptures*: that is, a series of popular and grassroots mobilizations that have engaged in temporary and powerful ruptures with the repetitive temporality of the crisis. These popular demonstrations aim to transform the Puerto Rican state and disrupt its colonial relationship with the United States. Perhaps the most emblematic of these popular demonstrations can be found in the context of the Summer of 2019, when hundreds of thousands of demonstrators took the streets in PR to demand the resignation of former Governor Ricardo Rosselló.[11] The mobilizations began after the publication of 889 pages of a now-infamous chat popularly known as Telegramgate.[12] In addition to discussing privileged governmental information, in this chat Rosselló and his allies (including both public functionaries and private contractors) engaged in xenophobic, homophobic, misogynistic exchanges about their adversaries and degraded the memory of the most vulnerable and least privileged victims of Hurricane María. These demonstrations caused a temporary rupture and challenged the repetitive temporality of colonial legality. The mobilizations underscored a radical possibility for rendering ineffective the colonial legal structure in place in PR but are marked by the reasonable challenges in mounting effective counter-hegemonic and anticolonial movements. This book unfolds the connection between legal interruptions and colonial ruptures, and emphasizes the radical possibility to disrupt the colonial state of exception in PR.

Importantly, *Crisis by Design* does not account for every aspect of the Puerto Rican multilayered crisis, but focuses on the role of law, exceptionality, and legal mobilizations in crises that are often framed as natural, self-evident, or unavoidable.[13] This book looks at the multilayered crisis from the lenses of sociolegal and critical criminology traditions and aims to underscore the role of law as both an instrument of coercion and a contested tool for social change. In what follows, I offer a detailed account of the three concepts the book develops and the way in which they help us better understand the sociolegal underpinnings of colonialism in the multilayered crisis.

BEYOND LAW AND EMERGENCY POWERS

Conventional accounts of the state of emergency refer to the suspension of the rule of law to address periods of political violence, economic crisis, disaster, or periods in which the rule of law cannot effectively operate in its regular form, and where foundational legal frameworks and normative commitments (e.g., civil rights, liberties, due process) are suspended.[14] Hence, the suspension of the rule of law and invocation of emergency powers have been largely justified under the pretext of extraordinary circumstances that require governments to take on special powers to respond to crises by avoiding political debates and democratic participation in the decision-making. That is, the state of exception has been traditionally defined as the legitimation of using otherwise extralegal measures to manage periods of crisis.

Against this liberal definition, Carl Schmitt (2005) has argued that the implementation of the state of exception takes place when the sovereign considers the *temporary* suspension of the rule of law as necessary. "Sovereign is he who decides on the exception," famously stated the German jurist (2005: 5). The tension between the legal framing of the uses of the emergency powers and sovereign action outside the law have captivated the scholarly debates on emergency powers and exceptionality in recent years.[15] These debates have been marked by two dominant approaches: the liberal constitutional and public law scholarship[16] and the philosophical-legal scholarship that emerged in the wake of Giorgio Agamben's (1998, 2005) examinations of the state of exception.[17] *Crisis by Design* instead proposes a third approach: the anticolonial and Global South theorizations of the state of exception.

Agamben's (2005) paradigm of the state of exception as a space of anomie, or a legal vacuum between the law and the political act, have largely dominated the debates on the emergency powers in the post–9/11 era. His analysis shows that the history of the state of exception is the history of its progressive separation from periods of emergency and war, to become the administrative paradigm of contemporary democracies. To demonstrate this process, Agamben proposes a bidimensional interpretation: the politico-philosophical and ontological dimensions of the state of exception; and the analysis of the legal history or the jurisprudence of the state of exception in western democracies. In this context, the analysis of the state of exception gravitates around the codification of the state of emergency, siege, and exception in the Global North.[18]

Regarding the first tradition, Agamben (1998) considers that the ontological configuration of the state of exception is defined by the paradox of sovereignty: to be outside the law and at the same time defining the applicability of the law. The paradox of sovereignty is fundamental to understanding the political power that define the constitutive dimension of anomie or inclusive exclusion. The process of inclusive exclusion implies the superposition of sovereign power over any form of life and the constitution of spaces of anomie in which the law does not apply in its regular form. Regarding the second tradition, Agamben (2005) has shown that the state of exception has been used in various historical contexts, such as the Roman empire, the French Revolution, the Third Reich, and the post–9/11 War on Terror era.[19] Agamben (1998, 2005) suggests that from WWI onwards, the state of exception has become the norm, leaving aside its provisional and temporal character, given the crisis generated by capitalism.[20] Economic crises, political violence, and natural disasters are (in)direct products of capitalism, since it operates through the commodification of every aspect of life, with the massive exclusion of sociopolitical sectors and plunder of natural recourses.

Furthermore, Agamben (2005) suggests that the state of exception has been used as a political and legal strategy to tackle periods of economic crisis, but he fails to delve into the analysis of this dimension.[21] For example, Agamben only refers to the uses of the state of exception in economic crises dealing with the regulation of inflation in France and Germany and the uses of exceptional laws and policies in the context of the US's Great Depression, among other Global North experiences.[22] Hence, a proper theory of the uses of the state of exception as economic crises management technique or event as colonial development policy is lacking in Agamben's scholarship.[23]

Schmitt (2005) has called the uses of emergency powers in the context of economic crises an economic and financial state of emergency. This conceptualization has led to a series of examinations of the connection between the state of exception, the economy, and neoliberalism.[24] For example, David Whyte (2010) has analyzed the correlation between the state of exception and the economy in the context of the US invasion of Iraq, and has shown how the exceptionality facilitated the establishment of a capitalist economy based on foreign corporations, wealth extraction, and plunder. Reynolds (2017) argues that the development of the state of exception in the colonies cannot be understood without its direct relation to the capitalist economy. A common practice in neoliberal politics consists of using the state of exception as a strategy to promote a specific form of economic development based on wealth extraction. Reynolds (2017: 95) points out that "emergency discourses have subsequently been relevant to the operation of the Bretton Woods institutions in the Third World, where the speculative mindset of 'opportunity in crisis' came to the fore, and emergency authority served as a vehicle for the implementation of neoliberal policy."[25] The state of exception has become the governmental technology that facilitated the neoliberal legal and political transformations of the state and society.

The state of exception as a technique to manage economic and financial crises has become the norm in the Global North after the economic meltdown of 2008. This technique of governance has been implemented by governments and by international organizations, such as International Monetary Fund (IMF) and the Troika in Greece, Ireland, Portugal, Italy, Spain, and elsewhere. The arguments heralded by the crisis managers have been similar in all these countries: given the economic and financial crises, the debt, and the deficit, the governments must implement austerity measures and budget cuts to save the economy and the state. However, every time such policies are implemented under the legitimation of the state of exception, inequality increases, corruption becomes normalized, and the violence of austerity is generalized.[26] As Clara Mattei (2022) has demonstrated, the historical development and implementation of austerity measures and other fiscal adjustment policies paved the way for authoritarian politics.

Reynolds (2017) notes that there has been much work done analyzing and theorizing martial law, the state of exception, and emergency legislation as they have manifested in various context. And within this analysis come the recital of the permanent state of emergency: the amorphous wars against non-state terrorism; the cyclical crises of global capitalism; the series of "natural disasters" that become ever-more unnatural as we continue to mangle the planet's ecology; the migrant crisis; the so-called fortress that Europe has constructed for itself. Against this recital of disconnected events in which the state of exception is applied to address specific moments of rupture, this book aims to elucidate the constitutive dimension of the state of exception in the colonial context of contemporary crises in PR.

THE COLONIAL STATE OF EXCEPTION

Contrary to liberal democracies, the state of exception has always been the rule in the colonies.[27] Colonies and racialized colonial subjects are placed in a permanent space of anomie, in which their inclusion within the colonial legal system is only possible through their exclusion, just as the concept of citizenship requires the rigid policing of non-citizenship.[28] Thus, the colonial power always determines which laws and rights do and do not apply to colonial territories and subjects.[29]

Crisis by Design argues that the state of exception can be understood as the constitutive legal structure of colonial domination. The colonial state of exception is not the suspension of the rule of law, but rather the way in which empires legitimate colonial domination and enable legalized wealth extraction under the guise of law, order, and modernity. Thus, the colonial state of exception operates as both law-making violence and law-preserving violence.[30] It operates as the structure through which a colonial government defines the colonial legal and sociopolitical reality, deciding which laws apply to the colonial territory, imposing differentiate legal procedures, and creating legal subjects. Furthermore, the colonial state of exception produces colonial subjects that are not completely excluded from the sphere of law but are rather embraced and enveloped in a suffocating hold by emergency legality. This form of legality is underpinned by processes of racialization and repression.

The logic of inclusive exclusion is the constitutive dynamic of the colonial state of exception in PR, and in other colonial contexts.[31] This manifests in the legal category of unincorporated territories and the development of a dual legal fiction in the Insular Case of *Downes v. Bidwell* (1901).[32] First, the Supreme Court argued that PR "is a territory appurtenant and belonging to the US, but not a part of the US." This meant that PR was not part of the US, but rather a possession that Congress could dispense of at any moment. Second, the Supreme Court reasoned that PR is "foreign to the US in a domestic sense, because the island had not been incorporated into the US." This dual legal fiction, as Chapter 1 demonstrates, structured the logic of inclusive exclusion or the colonial and racialized accommodation of PR within the US colonial rule of law.

This book is in dialogue with a long tradition of critical and Global South scholars who have demonstrated the operativity of the state of exception in different colonial settings and oppressed populations. As Walter Benjamin reminded us in his Thesis VIII: "the tradition of the oppressed teaches us that the 'state of emergency' in which we live is not the exception but the rule" (2003: 392). For Benjamin the violence displayed against the oppressed is based on the linear-progressive perceptions of modern history. Benjamin's conceptualization of history as a constellation of catastrophic events allows us to understand how the colonial state of exception operates as the normalization of the disastrous and catastrophic structure of colonialism.

Similarly, there is a body of anticolonial scholarship that demonstrates that the state of exception is the norm in the colonies. For example, for Achille Mbembe (2003), the colony was the space of anomie that inaugurated the implementation of sovereignty as the power to decide who lives and who dies.[33] This power to decide who live and dies is what Mbembe terms "necropolitics," which aims to go beyond the debates on biopolitics and helps us understand how ideas of citizenship, residency, and human geography shape which human lives are worth protecting and at what cost. As Reynolds (2017: 13) shows, "Emergency powers were not only about detention and curfews; their socio-economic function is revealed through complicity in dispossession and (settler) colonial sovereignty: the alienation and expropriation of land that was initiated by conquest was in many instances continued and consolidated by (often banal) emergency measures." Similarly, Nasser Hussain (2003) shows how the politics of exception, and the transfer of legal-colonial knowledge created a colonial and postcolonial jurisprudence of emergency in India and Pakistan.[34] Therefore, the current uses of the state of exception, as a mechanism to deal with all types of crises and emergencies, have their roots in colonial practices. Hence, the state of exception further exemplifies the imperial boomerang effect described by Aimé Césaire (2000).[35] That is, the application of the state of exception to deal with crises in the Global North is rooted in a long history of application and normalization of exceptionality to rule colonies, criminalized anticolonial movements, and managed crises in the Global South.

Mónica Jiménez (2020, 2024), Charles Venator Santiago (2006), and Rocío Zambrana (2021) have reflected on the US's articulations of the state of exception to legally define and administer PR. Jiménez has shown the centrality of the American state of exception to racially defined the Puerto Rican reality. Emergency discourse underpins the routine violence of the law against racialized populations, feeding into processes of social ordering based on broadly construed racial markers.[36] As Reynolds suggests, "The notion of emergency as a racialized enactment of sovereignty stems from colonial contexts where their effects of a state of emergency were inherently contingent on race" (2017: 56). An understanding of racialized sovereign entanglement with colonial multilayered crisis implies that the essence of the emergency powers is of more profound historical and social consequence than binary conception of legality and extralegality.

Furthermore, the logic of inclusive exclusion deployed by the colonial state of exception has enabled the colonial legal design of PR as an offshore jurisdiction for tax, banking, finances, and other regulatory purposes. In her legal history of US imperial tax policies in PR, Diane Dick (2015) shows how the United States implemented a series of tax policies and legal reforms that favored US corporations and investors in PR. Conversely, this book argues that a central dimension of the US colonial state of exception in PR is the ontological configuration of PR and other unincorporated territories as offshore jurisdictions. This means that not only has PR enabled corporations and investors to avoid taxation, but also the archipelago has served to avoid environmental and labor regulations, banking, investment protections, and other regulations. The offshore dynamic in place in PR has mutated according to US capitalist demands and interest, and the local elites and financial institutions have used the colonial state of exception and its ontopolitical design of PR as a tax haven, to enhance their capacity to capture wealth and maintain their hegemonic position in society. The tax haven in PR has been made in the USA.

This overview of the anticolonial and Global South scholarship demonstrates that emergency powers, far from being deviant aberrations from a liberal norm, are inherent to the colonial configuration. The state of exception is the structure of US colonial domination of PR, exemplified by the legal-colonial design of PR, the criminalization of anticolonial movements, and more recently PROMESA and the FOMB. As a legal and political structure of US colonialism in PR, the colonial state of exception has created the conditions for the multilayered crisis. Alas, *a crisis by colonial design.*

COLONIAL LEGALITY

Crisis by Design proposes the concept of colonial legality as an analytical category that elucidates a set of legal practices, public policies, economic and financial prescriptions, and anticorruption narratives that have come to define the operation of the PR government since the 1980s, but particularly during the ongoing multilayered crisis that began in 2006. Scholarship on neoliberal legality[37] has developed a sophisticated critique of the structural role of law in enabling wealth extraction and capital accumulations.[38] But the concept of neoliberal legality has not received the same attention in colonial context. Thus, colonial legality aims to bring the colonial dynamics at the center of the conversations on neoliberal legality and its transnational and global manifestations.

In PR the practices of colonial legality operate within the scope of a neoliberal rationality[39] and respond to the strategic accommodation of the local elites[40] and the PR government to maintain the structure of wealth extraction within the context of the multilayered crisis. Colonial legality operates under the sovereign limitations and restrictions of the colonial state of exception described above, and it underscores how the PR government and local elites do not necessarily address the multilayered crisis itself, but rather administer the limited resources and guarantee that local elites maintain their hegemonic position in society. Thus, with colonial legality, the issue becomes how to administer and manage the crisis in ways in which capital accumulation and wealth extraction continues uninterrupted.

Colonial legality can be characterized by the following general dynamics: (1) the systemic uses of emergency powers and executive orders to enhance and expand executive powers; (2) the financialization and/or the radical transformation of PR political economy through financial policies and tax incentives; (3) the accelerated dissolution of the PR state and local government through privatization, structural adjustment, and other administrative and fiscal reforms; (4) the constitution of a regime of permission that enables wealth extraction, corruption, and other crimes of the powerful; (5) the implementation of punitive governance or punitive approaches to legislation and regulations; and (6) the criminalization of social and political movements and the deployment of repressive and militaristic policing against pro-independence and anticolonial organizations. In what follows, I discuss each of these dynamics and their contribution to the management of the multilayered crisis.

First, it entails the normalization of the uses of emergency powers, the state of emergency and ever-increasing accumulation of power by the PR executive branch and the corresponding weakening of constitutional and civil rights. Within its limited powers, the PR government has used the state of emergency to administer every aspect of public life, including the multilayered crisis. This becomes particularly salient in the wake of the enactment of PROMESA and the appointment of the FOMB in the fall of 2016, as Chapter 2 demonstrates. The state of emergency, unlike to the colonial state of exception, refers to the uses of the emergency powers by the PR government to address the multilayered crisis: that is, the state of emergency and emergency powers operated within the legal and colonial limitation and structures established by the US colonial state of exception.

The PR government has systemically used the state of emergency to administer every aspect of the multilayered crisis to the point that it has maintained a permanent state of emergency since 2006. Within this permanent state of emergency, the government has used different terminologies and an array of reasons for issuing declarations of emergency. These have included the economic and fiscal crisis; socioenvironmental disasters such as hurricanes, earthquakes, wildfires, flooding, and droughts; public health crises such as the COVID-19 pandemic, Zika virus, and flu; infrastructure and energy states of emergency; gender violence; climate crisis and coastal erosion,[41] among others. More importantly, these states of emergency have been in place simultaneously, some for an extensive period, as the case of the economic state of emergency denotes.

In all these instances executive orders have been key in the declaration, modification, and codification of the state of emergency, and the imposition of emergency measures.[42] As this book demonstrates, executive orders have come to occupy a central place in the Puerto Rican public administrations. I have identified an increasing reliance on executive orders that goes beyond the declaration of the state of emergency; rather it has become the legal technology used by the local administration to govern, administer, legislate, and address every aspect of the Puerto Rican life. Despite their centrality in the current sociolegal and political scenario, there is limited scholarship on the uses of executive orders to administer every aspect of everyday life in PR. My research contributes to the development of that scholarship and to demonstrating the methodological value of a systemic engagement with executive orders.

The normalization and overreach of emergency powers have entailed the systemic attrition of the already limited Puerto Rican internal democracy. Exceptionality and the logic of permanent state of emergency percolate and manifest in Puerto Ricans everyday experiences with the law and the state in the forms of lack of access to justice and social services, precarity and lack of resources to cover basic state functions (such education, health, social protection, environmental regulations, among other), punitive and militaristic law enforcement, and the normalization of scarcity, precarity, and vulnerability. To live in PR as a working-class, poor, racialized, and queer person is to live in a permanent state of scarcity and colonial abandonment. Under colonial legality, the state's limited resources have been allocated to guarantee the payment of the public debt, provide tax incentives for transnational corporations and local elites, foment the operation of the market economy, and maintain public safety through the increasingly militarization and privatization of law enforcement.

Second, colonial legality has entailed a profound transformation of the Puerto Rican political economy. This has materialized through the financialization[43] of the colonial economy, the development of tax-haven policies, and the uses of bond issuance and other financial instruments to cover budgetary needs causing the exponential rise of the public debt.[44] The financialization of the economy, as this book discusses in Chapters 2 and 3, entailed a rapid transformation of the Puerto Rican legal system and regulatory framework. Those transformations are not unique to PR, but rather, as the neoliberal legality scholarship has shown, they are intrinsically part of the reconfiguration of economy unfolded in the wake of the Washington consensus.[45] In PR this has manifested to an elevated tax expenditure, the promotion of the archipelago as a tax haven, and other speculative practices. Behind this transformation, local elites could maintain the structure of wealth extraction and capital accumulation, despite the systemic and profound transformation that PR is experiencing.

Third, PR has seen a reconfiguration of the state and public services. This has particularly manifested through the intensification of policies such as the reduction of administrative and regulatory structures, privatization of public services, and implementation of structural adjustment and austerity measures. Under a rubric that posits public institutions and services as corrupt, wasteful, and bureaucratically burdensome, colonial legality deploys a systemic policy of attrition and elimination of every aspect of public administration. The systemic attrition of the PR state has consisted of privatizations of public utilities, public corporations, and key infrastructures such airports and highways; disinvestment in public education, closing of schools, budgetary cuts to the University of Puerto Rico (UPR); reforms to the public service, public employee pensions and retirement; privatization of the public health system; a systemic effort to privatized common goods, such beaches, forests, and other natural reserves; and the deregulation of finances, banking and other forms of speculative and financial capitalism.[46] As Chapter 2 shows, these transformations became particularly intense after the appointment of the FOMB.

Fourth, colonial legality has constituted a *regime of permission* that enables wealth extraction, corruption,[47] and other forms of crimes of the powerful, including colonial state crimes,[48] and state-corporate crime.[49] The crimes of the powerful scholarship have developed a sophisticated understanding of the role of class to underscore the dynamic of exploitation and social harm produced by powerful actors in society (including the state, corporations, elites, and transnational organizations).[50] However, with few exceptions,[51] there has been less attention to the role of imperialism, colonialism, and race in the crimes of the powerful. My aim is to develop the colonial dimension of the crimes of the powerful and to illustrate how they ought to be understood as a central component of the crisis and as part of the structure of the colonial state of exception.

Colonial state crime refers to the criminogenic practices that the US and PR governments engage in as part of their public role in the Puerto Rican society. State-corporate crimes refer to the symbiotic relationship between the US colonial state, the PR government, the local elites, and corporations in the criminogenic practices that enable colonial theft. Examples include financial crimes, criminal negligence in the management of the disaster, regulatory failures, among others. These form of crimes of the powerful are sustained by structure of impunity or a regime of permission.[52] This is clearly portrayed in the tax incentive and regulatory policies legislated by the US and PR governments for the pharmaceutical sector in PR. As it will be shown in Chapter 5, these tax incentives and lax regulatory policies legislated for the pharmaceutical industry undermined PR fiscal and public health preparedness to address the COVID-19 pandemic.

The framework of the regime of permission serves as a useful lens to analyze the intertwined relationship among exceptionality, corruption, and state-corporate crimes enabled by colonial legality. In juxtaposition to the disaster capitalism considerations, the regime of permission framework suggests that criminogenic dynamic and corporate profiteering does not occur as result of a crisis, disaster, or *moment of ruptures*, but rather, that crimes of the powerful manufacture the sociopolitical, legal, and economic conditions for crisis. Crises are manufactured by the dynamic of wealth extraction and capital accumulation at the core of the colonial state exception. Thus, what disaster capitalism considers to be a manifestation of capital profiteering in the wake of disaster is not a new dimension of capital accumulation, but in fact another instantiation of the regime of permission.

This becomes particularly clear when we consider how PR government implemented neoliberal disaster management techniques to address the multiple disasters affecting the archipelago since 2017. Disaster response relies heavily on the uses of emergency powers and executive orders to "manage" the disasters, and it is embedded in longstanding legal practices of the colonial state of exception. These practices include the suspension of the rule of law, the militarization of the recovery efforts, the privatization of reconstruction, punitive approaches to distribution of recovery aid, criminal negligence, or state crime of omission,[53] and the normalization of social harm.

The uses of the regime of permission to frame and describe the practices of crimes of the powerful in PR should not be understood as simply a bureaucratic or technical issue that can be swiftly solved with better laws, regulations, transparency, and compliance. Instead, a key feature of this colonial regime of permission is the lack of transparency and accountability. Similarly, access to information is severely restricted despite the efforts of Puerto Rican pro-transparency civil society organizations. The structure of impunity that colonial legality has established disavows mechanisms of democratic governance or power-sharing. Thus, the framework of the regime of permission aims to shed light on specific forms of crimes of the powerful enabled by colonial legality. This symbiotic relationship has facilitated colonial plunder, wealth extraction by local elites and corporations, and structural violence based on the legal rhetoric of the rule of law and democracy.

Fifth, colonial legality has developed a punitive approach to legislation and regulation. Marisol LeBrón (2019) describes punitive governance as the ways in which the Puerto Rican state has reasserted itself in the lives of Puerto Ricans through technologies of punishment such as policing and incarceration, as well as the violence they often provoke. LeBrón argues that punitive governance also refers to the ideological work undertaken by the state to promote an understanding that punishment, justice, and safety are intrinsically linked. Punitive governance has left an indelible mark on how life and death are understood and experienced in PR and has done so in a way that reinforces societal inequalities along lines of race, class, spatial location, gender, sexuality, and citizenship status.

Punitive governance goes hand in hand with Ruth Wilson Gilmore's (2007) binomial description of state power in neoliberal times as organized abandonment and organized violence. Organized abandonment is the direct consequence of the neoliberal policies and austerity measures implemented to address periods of economic crisis. That is, while colonial legality imposes structural adjustments and engages in systemic cutbacks of welfare programs undermining the already precarious living conditions of the most vulnerable sectors of society (organized abandonment), it concurrently criminalizes and enforces stricter security measures and violent policing practices against the above-mentioned population (organized violence). These tendencies and transformations of the welfare state into a carceral state and the generalization of organized violence against poor communities is what critical scholars have named neoliberal punishment.[54] Punitive governance, thus, manifests through the normalization of authoritarian policing, state violence, and antidemocratic legislations. While the regime of permission enables the conditions for crimes of the powerful, the Puerto Rican government has deployed a series of punitive approaches to petty corruption and other manifestations of working-class and poor accommodations to the structure of inequalities created by the emergency measures implemented by the state to address the crisis.

Sixth and finally, there is the deployment of authoritarian, antidemocratic, and repressive techniques of social control targeting social movements, anticolonial, anti-austerity, and anticorruption mobilizations. Elsewhere, I have shown that the US and the Puerto Rican governments used emergency powers and the state of emergency to justify the criminalization and repression of Puerto Rican anticolonial movements and sociopolitical mobilizations.

Unlike punitive governance, which emphasizes policies targeting working and poor classes, these criminalizing policies entail the violent repression of anticolonial and sociopolitical mobilizations. The criminalization and repression of anticolonial, socioenvironmental, student, and anti-austerity movements are fundamental to understanding the dynamic of colonial legality and state criminality.

Colonial legality aims to elucidate the processes that have configured a specific rationality in the management of the crisis, but do not pretend to be all-encompassing and deterministic. By proposing this analytical category, *Crisis by Design* intends to demonstrate how the uses of law, and the constitution of a specific legality framed by exceptionality, served the local elites and the PR government to strategically accommodate the limitations imposed by the state of exception.

LEGAL INTERRUPTIONS AND TRANSPARENCY POLITICS

Legal interruptions are the resulting sociolegal effect of the civil society organizations' legal mobilizations, litigation, advocacy, and strategic uses of law to demand accountability, transparency, and access to information from the PR government, the FOMB, and the US government. These organizations, collectively named the Transparency Network,[55] emerged and developed as reactions to the multilayered crisis and have sought to demand access to information on the financial situation of PR and other information essential to challenge the structure of wealth extradition enabled by colonial legality. These organizations have constituted a strategic conceptualization of legal mobilization for transparency and access to information that go beyond the principles of neoliberal accountability, compliance, and transparency.[56] This strategic understanding is what I have called legal interruptions, referring to the resignification of transparency and access to information to interrupt the brutal process of wealth extraction PR is facing. In asymmetrical relations of power such as the colonial subordination of PR, the law, legal mobilizations, and the rights discourse became a necessary device to interrupt relations of exploitation.

The Transparency Network is composed of five organizations. The Center for Investigative Journalism (CPI) is the leading organization in investigative journalism in PR and has championed strategic litigation and legal mobilization for access to information.[57] Together with the CPI, the Law Clinic for Access to the Information of the Interamerican University Law School was established in 2008. Later, the Law Clinic would be renamed Proyecto de Acceso a la Información; it provides services to the civil society organizations, develops strategic litigation aimed at transforming PR jurisprudence, and expands access to information. CPI and Proyecto de Acceso a la Información are at the center of the legal mobilizations for the right to access information.

As law professor and co-director of the law clinic Luis José Torres pointed out in our interview, Proyecto de Acceso a la Información was established as result of a collaborative agreement between the Interamerican University Law School and the CPI in 2008. Through this arrangement, Proyecto de Acceso a la Información would provide legal assistance to the CPI, but would also provide legal assistance to researchers, organizations, and journalists working on these topics.[58] Proyecto de Acceso a la Información provides legal assistance at both the state and federal level and has brought over forty-seven cases seeking access to information and transparency in the public administration.

Espacios Abiertos initially emerged as an access to justice and civic engagement organization, and because of the economic crisis, it made transparency and the right to access information its leading cause.[59] Espacios Abiertos has mobilized the PR and federal legal systems. As lawyer and executive director Cecille Blondet explained in our interview, Espacios Abiertos predominantly engages in legal mobilizations and litigation that allows it to continue research on PR's public debt.

> We decided from the beginning that if we are going to go to court, and we have sued the government fifty-six times, we are going to use certain parameters to decide when we are going to sue. When we talk about transparency, or when we demand transparency from the government, first, we focused on the fiscal issue. It must be something that advances the research we are doing. It must be practical, that advance some public policy work, and the other thing, it must be new. That the approach that we are going to make regarding access to information breaks down a barrier, an obstacle to access to information.[60]

These principles are concomitant with the multiple transnational organizations and NGOs promoting open government and accountability reforms.[61] A "culture of opacity" in PR was a common theme in my interviewees' reasons for litigation and legal mobilizations. Another reason for the pro-transparency mobilization is the idea that openness and access to information enables participation and civil engagement. Furthermore, several interviewees argued that the local government opacity and lack of transparency and accountability create opportunity for corruption. That is, while anticorruption policies undermine the colonial state, they also uphold the neoliberal policies that caused the economic and financial crisis.

Kilómetro Cero, the fourth organization in the Transparency Network, is a law enforcement and police accountability organization. This initiative was first established as part of Espacios Abiertos, and through different grants and funding from national and international agencies and organizations, it became an independent organization in 2018. This organization has produced several reports of police brutality and violence, particularly in the context of the COVID-19 pandemic and during the anticorruption demonstrations in the Summer of 2019 or the demonstrations that ousted Governor Ricardo Rosselló.

Sembrando Sentido, the fifth organization, is a transparency, anticorruption, and accountability organization. Founded in 2020, its work revolves around public contracting, public expenditures, and accountability. Sembrando Sentido has also engaged in litigation and legal mobilization to access information concerning public contracts, the enforcement of the Anticorruption Code for the New Puerto Rico,[62] and has engaged in the drafting of bills and other advocacy activities to improve anticorruption enforcement in PR.[63]

The Transparency Network has become a social space in which knowledge, techniques, and interpretation of law, legality, and, more importantly, governance are interchanged, co-produced, and reinforced.[64] In conversation with the sociolegal scholarship on legal mobilizations,[65] cause lawyering,[66] and relational legal consciousness,[67] *Crisis by Design* underscores the efforts made by the Transparency Network to demand access to information as the co-production of a unique form of legality: an expert-led, state-centered, highly specialized form of legality—at the same time interrupting and challenging the function of colonial legality. That is, by insisting and mobilizing for compliance, accountability, and transparency, these organizations at times legitimated the state and its institutions. This is an important conundrum, and not unique to PR.[68]

This social space is not limited to these five organizations; a wide range of other civil society organizations are engaged in different types of advocacy, litigation, and democratization of knowledge and information. The list includes Ayuda Legal PR, Liga de Ciudades, ABRE Puerto Rico, just to mention a few. Similarly, there are important think tanks such as the Center for a New Economy, which has systemically produced relevant research on the Puerto Rican multilayered crisis. Additionally, US-based organizations—such as Hedge Clippers, the Action Center on Race and the Economy (ACRE), the Center for Popular Democracy, and Little Sis—have systemically documented the dynamics of wealth extraction and exploitation that PR is undergoing.

There have been limited studies on the role of pro-transparency and anti-corruption mobilizations and their impact on how we understand and come to think of and define the multilayered crisis in PR. By studying the Transparency Network, we can gather a better understanding of how knowledge about the law, crises, the economy, and governance is produced and reproduced. We can also gain access to the study of the tensions and conflict among elites. This tells us something about how liberal ideas and resources are distributed, and who has access to certain circles and fundings. By studying these organizations and experts, we can gain a deeper knowledge of the inner working of the Puerto Rican bureaucratic operations, but also how social capital, race, gender, and class relationships are reproduced and maintained. Altogether, this book provides an account of the role of law, emergency powers, corruption, and legal mobilizations in a particular dimension of the multilayered crisis.

Crisis by Design ends by describing the Puerto Rican Summer of 2019 and the mobilization for the resignation of former governor Wanda Vázquez in January 2020 (#Wandalismo). Unlike legal interruptions, the discussion of these grassroots mobilizations demonstrates the dynamic of colonial ruptures with the logic of colonial legality. In short, these ruptures point toward the emergence of sociopolitical mobilizations, in which a plurality of subjectivities, tactics, and strategies converged to demand accountability from the PR government. Faced with austerity, exceptionality, punitive governance, and the structural dimension of disaster (or colonialism as catastrophe), these grassroots mobilizations aimed to transform the PR state and its colonial relationship with the United States. These mobilizations underscored a radical possibility for a real process of decolonization—thus, going beyond legal interruptions and temporary disruptions.

METHODOLOGICAL REMARKS

This book is the result of eight years of qualitative research on the role of law, emergency powers, and the state of emergency in the Puerto Rican multilayered crisis. This research has been informed by ethnographic fieldwork with pro-transparency and accountability organizations, and participatory observation in diverse settings, including large anticorruption demonstrations, legal mobilizations, and litigations. I have conducted eighteen semi-structured interviews with directors of accountability and compliance agencies of the PR government, members of the PR legislative branch, investigative journalists, lawyers, and members of pro-transparency and accountability organizations. The interviewees were selected given their public position, their specific role in governmental office, or in pro-transparency and anticorruption organizations. Moreover, in the case of the members of the Transparency Network, I employed snowball sampling recruitment techniques. All the interviews were conducted, transcribed, and analyzed in Spanish. I have translated to English the specific quotations presented in this book.[69]

My work with the Transparency Network, investigative journalists, activists, and lawyers has demonstrated that there is a systemic lack of access to public information, which has led to a series of legal mobilizations for transparency and accountability in PR. Limitations to access public information and to data gathering are a common phenomenon in the study of crimes of the powerful,[70] playing a central role in the way in which powerful actors prevent disclosure and inquiry on their criminogenic behaviors. I tried to challenge these limitations by combining archival research at different settings, including in the PR Commission for Civil Rights Archives. To gather executive orders, laws, and other legislation, I used PR government websites such as the Department of State,[71] SUTRA,[72] and the FOMB's document website.[73] I have also systemically engaged with the work of progressive think tanks, research-oriented organizations, and investigative journalists to elucidate the politico-economic and legal processes that led to the multilayered crisis.

As sociolegal scholars, we are taught to look at the processes and practices through which people give meaning to law and legal institutions.[74] We are also encouraged to think about how people make sense and adjudicate meaning to the law. This book is the result of an examination of what it means to live in a country undergoing decades of a multilayered crisis. I began researching the Puerto Rican economic and financial crisis in 2015, when, after completing my PhD, I returned to PR to work as a visiting assistant professor at the University of Puerto Rico at Mayagüez (UPRM) (August 2014 to December 2018). During my time back in PR, I experienced firsthand the height of the debt crisis (2014–2016), the enactment of PROMESA and the imposition of the FOMB, the student strikes of 2017, Hurricanes Irma and María, and later, the protests of the Summer of 2019. Thus, this book is also a reflection of my own experiences during this period of crisis. My lived experiences cannot be disassociated from this research and from the approaches here developed.

My main contribution to critical criminology and law and society traditions is to demonstrate that the law and the emergency powers created the condition for further disaster and crisis while also enabling criminogenic practices. These policies and their consequences are not only demonstrated through document analysis and fieldwork, but also through the daily experience of living in and dealing with the crisis.

My research and this book are the ways in which I deal with the crisis and try to make sense of what it means to be a colonial subject in a country experiencing a multilayered crisis. I do so by providing a systemic and detailed study of the legal process, politico-economic interest, and criminogenic dynamic that caused the crisis. There is burgeoning scholarship coming from PR about the multilayered crisis and the Puerto Rican forms of resistance in response to Hurricane María, the debt crisis, earthquakes, COVID-19, gender violence, and climate crisis. This book aims to contribute to that emerging scholarship.

A ROADMAP TO COLONIAL RUPTURES

Crisis by Design explores the role of the colonial legality and legal interruptions in six chapters. It begins by providing an in-depth examination of the configurations of the colonial state of exception. Chapter 1 provides a historical and sociolegal overview of the Puerto Rican colonial and legal design, beginning with the Foraker Act (1900), the Insular Cases, the Jones Act (1917), and Public Law 600 (1950). Second, it analyzes the legal transformations that began in June 2016, with the US Supreme Court decisions in *Puerto Rico v. Sánchez Valle, Puerto Rico v. Franklin California,* and in 2022 *United States v. Vaello-Madero.* Third, the chapter discusses the US Congress's enactment of PROMESA and the imposition of the FOMB. Finally, the chapter engages with the analysis of the 2019 Supreme Court ruling in *FOMB v. Aurelius Investment*. Altogether, the chapter demonstrates that the colonial state of exception ought to be understood as the structure of US colonialism in PR.

Chapter 2 considers the PR government's reaction to and management of the economic and financial crisis. Engaging with the concept of colonial legality, the chapter looks at: the development of the economic and financial state of emergency; how the PR government managed the economic and debt crisis between 2005 and 2016; the impact of the austerity measures imposed by the FOMB; how the PR government has managed the crisis in the aftermath of PROMESA. In this way the chapter elucidates how the Puerto Rican government developed its form of colonial legality and its implications for the multilayered crisis.

Chapter 3 explores the implications and multiple manifestations of colonial state-corporate crimes in the Puerto Rican public debt crisis and bankruptcy process. The chapter demonstrates how the symbiotic relationship among banks, law firms, consultancy firms, and the local government, as well as the lack of federal regulation, created the conditions for criminogenic practices. It also explores the sociolegal processes that enabled the transformation of PR into a tax haven and, therefore, demonstrates the criminogenic practices emerging from this new economic structure.

From the study of the role of revolving doors, corruption, and collusion in the economic crisis, the book moves to the analysis of the role of law and emergency powers during disasters. Chapter 4 charts how the colonial state of exception and colonial legality were implemented to administer the aftermath of Hurricanes Irma and María, the January 2020 earthquakes, and Hurricane Fiona in 2022. The chapter contends that the use of emergency powers neither facilitated nor accelerated recovery efforts; instead, it created a chaotic scenario in which citizens were not provided with adequate resources. Furthermore, the chapter shows how the recovery efforts in the aftermath of the disasters were largely militarized, privatized, and externalized or contracted out. This chapter also looks at the cases of corruption that emerged from the management of the crises, at both the local and federal level, and the efforts of the civil society organizations to promote a just recovery and interrupt the trends of wealth extraction.

Chapter 5 explores the dynamic of exceptionality, crisis management, and dispossession that took place in the context of the COVID-19 pandemic. It reveals the role of the pharmaceutical industry in undermining PR's capacity to react to the pandemic by engaging in tax avoidance and excluding PR from the distribution of personal protective equipment (PPE). Furthermore, the chapter shows how amid the crisis, US politicians started to promote the idea of bringing pharmaceutical industries back to PR. This idea was based, once more, on the promotion of tax exemptions and other regulatory benefits for transnational corporations. This chapter argues that colonial legality allowed for corporate tax avoidance, corruption, and human rights violations during the COVID-19 pandemic.

Chapter 6 explores the conceptualization of and development of legal interruptions. It demonstrates how, in the context of the multilayered crisis, a series of lawyers, investigative journalists, and civil society organizations including the CPI, Espacios Abiertos, Sembrando Sentido, Kilómetro Cero, and Proyecto de Acceso a la Información began to mobilize the law to demand access to public information, transparency, and accountability from the PR government and the FOMB. To map out the conceptualization and development of legal interruptions, the chapter first discusses the legal framework defining anticorruption policies in PR. Then it engages with the Transparency Network, its legal mobilizations, and the legal history of the right to access information. Finally, it demonstrates how these legal mobilizations have constructed an understanding of transparency that allows for a systematic opposition and interruption of the brutal force of colonial legality. Thus, the chapter aims to analyze a rather unexplored dimension of legal mobilizations; namely, mobilization for transparency and accountability as a moment of interruption with the logic of colonial legality and the temporarily of state of exception.

The Epilogue reflects on the significance of the Summer of 2019 and #Wandalismo for the development of strategies, practices, and mechanisms to disrupt the logic of colonial legality. Nelson Maldonado-Torres (2019: 340) has argued that "the catastrophe of colonialism in Puerto Rico cannot be disentangled from the catastrophic effect of European colonization in the Caribbean and the US presence in the region." As PR is facing crises, disasters, and catastrophes, Puerto Ricans have been protesting and engaging in different creative demonstrations to demand a radical transformation of the colonial relationship. As it happened during the Summer of 2019, there are important experiences of resistance to these colonial dynamics. It is precisely in this context that Maldonado-Torres invites us to develop "counter-catastrophic thought and creative work . . . to reveal the various layers of catastrophe and show their entanglement. . . . Decolonial thinking requires counter catastrophic explorations of time and the formations of space, within, against, and outside the modern/colonial world" (2019: 340). The Summer of 2019 precisely attests to the emergence of a counter-catastrophic thought or a colonial rupture that confronts the dynamic of wealth extraction and exploitations enabled by US colonialism. Nevertheless, these ruptures are yet to be developed as an effective mechanism for the decolonization of PR.

Crisis by Design highlights the central role of law in colonial crises. By arguing that the colonial state of exception is the structure, this book aims to demonstrates how the colonial states utilize a series of laws, emergency powers, and public policies to administer the everyday life of the colony. However, this book demonstrates that the colonial structure is fragmented as Frantz Fanon (2004) reminds us, and that total domination is never fulfilled. Colonial legality and legal interruptions are two opposed responses to the fragmented structure of colonial domination. That is, colonial legality aims to accommodate the colonial conditions by identifying spaces for wealth extraction and preserving the local elite hegemonic position in the Puerto Rican society. Legal interruptions aim to make evident the already existing failures in the structures or to create the opportunities for new ruptures. As this book shows, the constant legislation, declaration of the state of emergency, and imposition of organic laws reveal that the colonial structure of domination is always unfinished. The task of colonial law is a never-ending project because life can never be fully captured by legality.

Law in the colonies, to be sure, is always in *action*. The colonial state of exception allows for an endless process of legal reconstitution of the structure of domination. This book demonstrates how this specific rationality has come to define, at least, one dimension of the management of the crisis and its oppositions. This book is about the entwined relationships between colonial state of exception and colonial legality, but above all it is about the failures of law to fully capture life.

ONE

DESIGNS

On January 11, 2023, the US Supreme Court heard oral arguments in the case *Financial Oversight and Management Board for Puerto Rico v. Centro de Periodismo Investigativo* (*FOMB v. CPI*),[1] considering whether the principle of sovereign immunity protects the FOMB from lawsuits in federal court.[2] The case addresses the powers and limitations that apply to the FOMB, created by the US Congress under PROMESA as a territorial entity,[3] to address the Puerto Rican economic and fiscal crisis. The dispute in question involved a provision in PR's Constitution that guarantees access to public information and obligates the government to grant access to most categories of public documents.[4] In 2017, the CPI sued the FOMB in the US District Court for the District of PR in San Juan, arguing that the FOMB's lack of disclosure and limits on access to public records violated the Puerto Rican Constitution and the constitutional right to access information.[5] The US District Court ruled in favor of the CPI in 2018, deciding that as territorial entity within PR's government, the FOMB is obliged to comply with the right of access to information under PR's Constitution. The federal judge made clear that the FOMB was not exempt from protecting key principles of democratic governance, transparency, access to public records, freedom of speech, and freedom of the press.

In an interview conducted with Carlos Ramos Hernández, one of the lawyers that brought the case to the US Supreme Court on behalf of the CPI, he explained that the FOMB attempted to overturn this decision by turning to the First Circuit Court of Appeals in Boston. There it claimed that sovereign immunity barred such a suit in federal court. The court of appeals noted that it would be an absurd result if the FOMB—established to create an open process to restore PR's fiscal health—were allowed to keep the public in the dark about its activities, which "would further erode public confidence in the FOMB and undermine its effectiveness by inviting arbitrary actions, poor administration, and corruption" (López-Santana 2022: 11). After the court of appeals denied the FOMB claims of sovereign immunity, the Supreme Court granted a review.

During the oral argument, the justices were interested in debating the juridical nature of sovereign immunity, rather than the initial claim of transparency brought by CPI. The argumentation and questioning predominantly focused on whether the unincorporated territories have sovereign immunity and, if so, what is its source.[6] At the center of this debate is whether the Eleventh Amendment to the US Constitution applies to unincorporated territories. The issue is centered on the territorial clause of the US Constitution,[7] and the continued efforts by the US Congress, the Supreme Court, and the executive branch to legitimate US colonial constitutionalism.[8]

On May 11, 2023, the Supreme Court ruled in *FOMB v. CPI* eight to one that the FOMB enjoys sovereign immunity, since nothing in PROMESA indicated that Congress intended to categorically abrogate such immunities.[9] The opinion of the court did not enter in the discussion of whether the Eleventh Amendment applies to PR;[10] rather, it narrowly focuses on Article 2126 (a) of PROMESA, and how this article does not abrogate FOMB's immunities and protections against suits.[11] When seen in this light, the question centers on the racialized and colonial legal design of PR as "appurtenant and belonging to the US, but not a part of the US," and the historic efforts since *Downes v. Bidwell* (1901) to sustain that colonial condition.

This chapter recounts the sociolegal and political genealogy of US colonial state of exception in PR. This overview aims to elucidate how the dynamic of inclusive exclusion and other sociolegal processes enabled cases of impossible logic such as *FOMB v. CPI* and constituted the legal and politico-economic reality of US colonialism in PR. My aim is to demonstrate how the colonial state of exception became the legal and political structure for US colonialism.

Simultaneously, the chapter describes how crises in this context are not events or moments of rupture with capital accumulation, liberal democracy, and the rule of law, but rather are inherent to the operativity of US colonialism.

This chapter provides an overview of the first three organic laws or exceptional laws legislated by the US Congress for PR—namely, the Foraker Act, the Jones Act, and Public Law 600. It delves into the jurisprudences established by the Insular Cases. Then, the chapter scrutinizes the legal transformations initiated in June 2016, marked by the US Supreme Court decisions in *Puerto Rico v. Sánchez Valle, and Puerto Rico v. Franklin California*, and, more recently in 2022, *United States v. Vaello-Madero*. Finally, it addresses the US Congress's enactment of PROMESA and the imposition of FOMB. This section engages in the analysis of the 2019 Supreme Court opinion in *Financial Oversight and Management Board for Puerto Rico v. Aurelius Investment*. Collectively, it demonstrates how the colonial state of exception constituted the legal framework that made crises an intrinsic part of US colonial domination of PR.

DESIGNING THE LEGAL STRUCTURE OF COLONIALISM

A substantial body of literature demonstrates how, since the early 1880s, US political and economic elites sought to expand their influence throughout the Caribbean and across the Pacific.[12] Within this expansionist context, after the economic crisis of the 1890s and energized by the colonial civilizing mission and the Monroe Doctrine, the US intervened in the Cuban war of independence against Spain, marking the beginning of the Spanish-American War.[13] The United States perceived itself as morally and racially superior to Spain and its colonial possessions, positioning itself to modernize, develop, and democratize (i.e., Americanize) Spanish colonies and other territories imagined as corrupt, lacking civilization, and without effective government. Racialized discourses of savagery, corruption, and the need for civilization are at the core of western and US imperialist expansion, justifying the domination of colonial subjects in the Global South in the name of "progress."[14]

The United States invaded PR on July 25, 1898. The Treaty of Paris ended hostilities and transferred sovereignty over PR from Spain to the United States, making it a domain of the US Congress under the territorial clause of the US Constitution.[15] Consequently, the US Congress legislated four exceptional laws between 1900 and 2016 to articulate and regulate the colonial legal, political, and economic relationship.[16] These four laws were imposed on PR without consultation or active participation of Puerto Ricans in the decision-making process. Thus, these laws not only preclude Puerto Ricans from self-determination, but also rely heavily on racialized and gendered tropes of inferiority, corruption, laziness, immorality, and inability to self-govern. Under racialized discourses of corruption and moral decadence, the United States justifies reshaping PR's economy, denies Puerto Ricans self-governance, and creates and maintains the conditions for wealth extraction and colonial plunder.

The Foraker Act of 1900 and the Legal Design of "Porto Rico"

The Foraker Act of 1900 is the first exceptional law legislated by the US Congress for PR.[17] The act concluded two years of military rule,[18] leading to the establishment of a civilian government (largely administered by the US military) and creating a classic colonial government structure in which all power emanated from the federal government. The act defined three key aspects of colonial life: the political system, economic structures, and US–PR relations.

Regarding the political system, the Foraker Act established the administrative structure that, with some changes in 1917 and 1952, remains in place to this day.[19] It created a civil government with a republican structure (executive, judiciary, and bicameral legislative system— Executive Council and House of Delegates) and imposed English as the official language of the government.[20] The US president appointed the governor, the members of the Executive Council (of which only five out of eleven could be Puerto Ricans), and the members of the Puerto Rican Supreme Court. Members of the House of Delegates were elected every two years. The Foraker Act also established the possibility for PR to send a representative to the US Congress (the resident commissioner) who would not have a voice or vote.

Among the powers conferred to the PR governor under the Foraker Act was the position of commander-in-chief of the militias. However, this law did not recognize the possibility of decreeing martial law or a state of emergency. Similarly, the act did not recognize civil rights for Puerto Ricans beyond the writ of habeas corpus. The US Congress only legislated a bill of rights for PR in 1917, with the approval of the Jones Act. In this context the US Congress avoided granting US citizenship to Puerto Ricans, paradoxically constructing them as "nationals," placing Puerto Ricans in a space of anomie sanctioned by the US Supreme Court in the Insular Case *Gonzales v. Williams* (1904).[21] Thus, in the seventeen-year period between the Foraker Act and the Jones Act, everything related to civil rights was governed by specific determinations made by Congress or by codes and laws from the Spanish colonial period.[22] The Foraker Act also provided for the establishment and redefinition of the judiciary and of the local legal system. As Sally Engle Merry (1988, 1991), Boaventura de Sousa Santos (2007, 2023), and other sociolegal scholars have shown, legal transfer and redefinition of the local legal system is a central feature of western colonialism.

The Foraker Act devotes great attention to defining the economic structures of PR and its economic relationship with the United States, including tax collection, tariffs, the definition of market economy, and the establishment of monetary policy.[23] The Foraker Act exempts PR from federal income tax and grants the application of Section 931 of the US Internal Revenue Code. Section 38 of the Foraker Act created the condition for and defined the limits of the PR government and its municipalities to issue bonds and other obligations. One reason to grant PR the capacity to issue bonds was to repay the United States for the expenses incurred in the aftermath of Hurricane San Ciriaco in 1899. One can identify how indebtedness, disaster, and emergency policies have been at the core of the US colonial state of exception since the early days.

Furthermore, the Foraker Act regulated international trade and established a free trade agreement with the United States. However, "free trade" was restricted by a series of temporary tariffs imposed on products entering the United States from PR. Thus, the act established the legal structure for exceptionality, in which PR is neither inside nor outside the union. In other words, through the implementation of tariffs and the definition of Puerto Ricans as nationals, the dynamics of "exclusive inclusion" defining the colonial state of exception were established.

In tandem with the Foraker Act, from 1898 to 1900, the United States imposed a series of economic and monetary measures that led to the devaluation of Puerto Rican currency and real estate and the impoverishment of the local *hacendados*.[24] These policies also facilitated massive land purchases by US corporations. Sugar companies' control of the land was so immense that in 1900, the US Congress passed the 500 Acres Act, which aimed to limit land concentration. The law prohibited corporate land concentration, but it did not prohibit individuals from holding more than 500 acres.[25] Along with the impoverishment of the local *hacendados*, from 1898 to 1930 the United States enforced a radical transformation of agricultural production, which consisted of changing the coffee-based and self-sustaining agriculture to a sugarcane monoculture. Consequently, PR's economic life became increasingly tied to and dependent on the decisions of US capitalists' economy. The Foraker Act entailed a radical transformation of the Puerto Rican sociolegal and politico-economic reality, with a transition of two years of military regiment and martial law, to what would become the colonial state of exception.

The Insular Cases and the Doctrine of Territorial Incorporation

Simultaneous with the politico-economic transformations of PR from 1900 to 1922, in a series of cases called the Insular Cases[26] the US Supreme Court shaped the legal design of US colonialism in PR and other territories previously claimed by Spain.[27] The juridical-political designation of PR as "belonging to, but not being part of the US" defined a specific logic of exceptionality, wherein colonial territories and subjects exist sometimes within and sometimes without the constitutional guarantees and procedures of the rule of law.

From 1900 to 1922, the Insular Cases resolved issues related to taxes and tariffs, rights applicable to the new territories (especially if the Constitution and Bill of Rights were applicable), territorial classification (Were these territories incorporated territories? Would they eventually be annexed?), nationality (Were the habitants of these territories US citizens?), migratory status (If the inhabitants of these territories were not US citizens, could they freely enter the US?), and more. The Supreme Court devised a novel distinction between incorporated territories destined for statehood and unincorporated territories, where there was no promise of eventual political equality.[28] As commonly understood, the Constitution applies in full in incorporated territories, but only in part in unincorporated territories.[29] Thus, when legislating, Congress must explicitly determine whether the legislation applies to the unincorporated territory or not.

The Insular Cases reflect the legal genealogy of US colonialism and the Supreme Court's role in legitimizing legal frameworks that are colonial in function. Critically, the Insular Cases also transformed American constitutionalism and the ability to limit the scope and scale of basic rights and civil liberties.[30] The jurisprudence established in the Insular Cases enabled the design of other spaces of exception, such as Guantánamo Bay Naval Base, where the Constitution does not apply in its full force.[31] The Insular Cases had several key impacts on PR, justifying US colonial expansion, constituting the legal and political identity of colonial subjects, creating a discursive universe for discussing every aspect of the political reality, and defining the overruling of these cases as a context of political and legal activism.

All of this shapes the colonial design of exceptionality. As Mónica Jiménez (2020) demonstrates in her analysis of *Downes v. Bidwell (1901)*, the US Supreme Court developed the racial dimension of the colonial state of exception in PR. *Downes v. Bidwell* addressed a controversy in the collection of taxes, after the enactment of the Foraker Act, which stipulated that everything related to taxes and duties to be collected in PR. As result, the case revolved around the constitutionality, relevance, and legal-political effects of the Foraker Act. The consensus regarding *Downes v. Bidwell* has been based on the opinions of Justice Brown and Justice White. Justice Brown established that the Foraker Act was constitutional since Congress, in its exercise of the plenary powers conferred by the Territorial Clause, had the power to administer the territories and to impose taxes and duties on them without anything in the Constitution preventing it. For Justice Brown, the power to acquire territories through treaties also implies the power to administer those territories and establish the terms under which the United States accepts the inhabitants thereof. This implies that PR can be treated as a foreign country for constitutional purposes, but at the same time it remains under US sovereignty in international terms. Thus, the observation that the archipelago is "foreign to the United States in a domestic sense."

Christina Duffy Burnett (2005) suggests that the justices agreed that Congress must decide if the acquisition of a territory implies its permanent incorporation and annexation or if the acquisition is temporary and eventually the United States will dispense of the territory. Additionally, Justice White insisted on the applicability of the laws approved by Congress in the territories, even though this exercise of sovereignty does not imply that Congress has opted for incorporation. This argument was then restated in *Dorr v. United States* (1903) in which the court argued that "the power to govern a territory does not require Congress to incorporate the territory or to grant a system of law."

Efrén Rivera Ramos (2007) engages in a systemic analysis of Justice Fuller's dissenting opinion regarding the doctrine of incorporation. Justice Fuller understood that the concept of incorporation is highly ambiguous, and he was opposed to the idea that when "an organized and settled province of another sovereignty is acquired by the US, Congress has the power to keep it, like a disembodied shade, in an intermediate state of ambiguous existence for an indefinite period" (quoted in Rivera Ramos 2007: 83). In fact, Charles Venator Santiago (2006: 44) considers that the best description of the zone of indistinction established by the Insular Cases is Fuller's "disembodied shade" whose "indeterminate state of ambiguous existence for an indefinite period" allows the "Sovereign to exercise a legal power that was tantamount to the 'will of Congress.'"

The doctrine of incorporation would be ratified once more in *Balzac v. Porto Rico* (1922). Jesús Balzac was the editor of a Puerto Rican newspaper who was sentenced to nine months in prison for a comment he made in his newspaper about the US governor of PR. At the time of his trial, Puerto Rican criminal law and the procedural code recognized trial by jury in felony cases but did not recognize it for misdemeanor cases. Balzac argued that he had the right to a trial by jury under the Sixth Amendment. The Supreme Court ruled that the Sixth Amendment does not apply to PR.

The court's opinion was written by Chief Justice Taft, who argued that trial by jury does not apply to unincorporated territories, since trial by jury requires citizens with the cultural background provided by the common law tradition, which Puerto Ricans lacked. In addition to judicial racism, Taft argued that according to the jurisprudence established in *Downes* and *Dorr,* neither the Philippines nor PR had been incorporated by the organic laws approved by Congress that provided them with a provisional government. Likewise, Taft held that the Jones Act of 1917 did not intend to incorporate PR, since there is no clause or declaration of purpose in the act that indicated so. Taft insisted that, if the intention of Congress had been the incorporation of PR, the Jones Act would not have included its own bill of rights and instead would have extended the US Constitution.

Four interpretations of the Insular Cases emerge from *Balzac.* First, the fundamental problem addressed by the Insular Cases was not whether the Constitution was applicable to PR, but rather, which parts were. Second, the legal-political category of unincorporated territories was defined. Prior to

Balzac, the doctrine was that granting rights to the inhabitants of the territories would be indicative of incorporation. However, after *Balzac*, the territorial status (incorporated or unincorporated) determined the constitutional protections, rights, and guarantees that its inhabitants enjoy. Third, Puerto Ricans, while living in PR, will not have access to all the protections of US citizenship. Fourth, the denial of trial by jury in the US federal court in PR ought to be understood within the legal racism and imperialistic postures assumed by the US elites concerning PR. This is demonstrated on several occasions when it was argued that the inhabitants of the newly acquired territories were culturally, racially, and politically inferior because they did not possess the Anglo-Saxon tradition, which made them incapable of jury trial.

These four interpretations condense the various critical positions that I have advanced throughout the discussion of the Insular Cases: the cases defined and established the ontopolitical principle constituting the colonial state of exception as a structure of legal administration and imperial domination. By setting in motion a pattern of inclusive exclusion, these cases enabled the ontopolitical definition of a territoriality and subjectivized it as belonging to, yet not being part of, the United States. This rather obscure legal fiction would become the constitutive dimension of the US colonial state of exception in Puerto Rico.

The Jones Act of 1917, US Citizenship, and Economic Transformation

In 1917, the second exceptional law—the Jones-Shafroth Act, commonly known as the Jones Act, came into force.[32] This law partially replaced the Foraker Act, extended a bill of rights for PR, and granted US citizenship to Puerto Ricans.[33] The citizenship conferred by the Jones Act deprived Puerto Ricans living in PR of inherent political rights and constitutional guarantees, such as representation in the US Congress, participation in presidential elections, and access to certain social and welfare services, among others. As with previous laws and policies developed by Congress, Puerto Ricans were not consulted in the legislative process. Undoubtedly, the Jones Act and the grant of US citizenship were integral components of colonial governance in PR.

Among the changes introduced by the Jones Act was the elective character of the PR Legislative Assembly—ensuring both legislative chambers were elected through general suffrage. Additionally, it acknowledged the governor's authority to declare a state of emergency or martial law, illustrating a critical aspect of the relationship between rights and state power. While certain rights are recognized, the executive branch was bestowed with additional power to control and limit the freedom of its citizens. The Jones Act did not alter policies established by the Foraker Act in areas such as immigration, trade, monetary policy, tariffs, commercial treaties, shipping, communications, the judicial system, and national security.

The Jones Act stipulated that bonds issued by PR and its authorized borrowers would be tax exempt at the municipal, state, and federal level. This triple tax exemption made PR bonds appealing to US investors, which played a crucial role in PR's indebtedness and proved to be determinative in the bankruptcy process under PROMESA.

Beyond extending the US citizenship to Puerto Ricans and a bill of rights, the Jones Act, ushered in a new phase of the colonial state of exception. This transformation coincided with a significant reconfiguration of the economic structure. For instance, in 1920, the US Congress enacted the Merchant Marine Act, commonly known in PR as the cabotage law.[34] This law regulates commerce and mandates that shipping, and trade of products imported to and exported from PR, must occur on ships made in the United States or registered there. The economic burden imposed by the cabotage law on PR persists; it was only briefly lifted after Hurricane María in 2017 and after Hurricane Fiona in 2022, and not long enough to bring any real relief. The cabotage law ensures colonial-economic domination by restricting trade, thereby intensifying PR's dependency on US markets and its economic activities.

In the 1930s, Puerto Rican institutions, political parties, and society in general underwent radical transformations due to the Great Depression. Simultaneously, the United States implemented the New Deal and emergency measures to reactivate the economy. The New Deal and the social reforms advanced by Roosevelt's administration were extended to PR through various economic measures and plans, including: the Puerto Rico Emergency Relief Administration, established in 1933 as a branch of the Federal Emergency Relief Administration; the reorganization of the US sugar industry through the Sugar Act of 1934; and in 1935, Plan Chardón, which sought to create a Puerto Rican economy that would promote sustainable development.[35] With Plan Chardón, the Puerto Rico Reconstruction Administration was created, which sought to organize economic development. These economic development policies signify a new dimension of the US colonial state of exception. As demonstrated by Agamben (2005), during the Great Depression, President Roosevelt developed the economic dimension of the state of exception by assuming plenary powers to manage the economic crisis and implementing exceptional laws as economic development policies. The extension of these exceptional laws to PR implied the development of an economic and colonial state of exception.

The US colonial policy took another turn in the 1940s with the implementation of a new series of exceptional laws that sought development through industrialization, or what was known as "industrialization by invitation."[36] Commonly referred to as Operation Bootstrap, this developmental policy legislated tax exemption for US-owned factories established in PR. The plan primarily sought to attract corporations with low wages and tax breaks in the "security of a US territory." This policy favored the US textile industry and oil refineries, limiting the development of a local industrial class.[37] In a classical colonial dynamic, capitalist development in PR aimed to benefit US corporations and create a local middle class, mainly those employed in these industries, who served as intermediaries and supporters of US colonial rule. Operation Bootstrap entailed a significant transformation in the Puerto Rican political economy, in which the legislation of economic policies moved from aiming at facilitating production or generating wealth in PR to facilitating incentives and tax exemption for US corporations. This involved a transition from extractive industries, such as big sugar and tobacco corporations, to an economic model based on tax incentives and finance.

In addition to providing generous tax exemptions and incentives, the PR government facilitated the inflow of private industrial capital by investing heavily in power, transport, water and sewer infrastructure, and human capital (mostly education and healthcare).[38] Over fifty public corporations were established, contributing to the economic development and subsequently leading to the economic downturn of PR, as the next chapter will demonstrate. Among these public corporations, key players in both economic development and the debt crisis included the Puerto Rico Electric Power Authority (PREPA, established in 1941), the State Insurance Fund Corporation (1935), the Puerto Rico Industrial Development Company (1942), the Aqueducts and Sewers Authority (1945), the Government Development Bank for PR (GDB), and the Puerto Rico Highways and Transportation Authority (1965).

The Government Development Bank (GDB) played a crucial role in creating the conditions for economic development and crisis. The GDB was established to lend money to enterprises believed to contribute to the development and industrialization goals of the PR economy.[39] As a government bank, it could not accept private deposits or hold saving accounts, but it could hold deposits of the municipal, local, and federal governments; make payments for the insular government; and handle borrowing obligations for public corporations. Borrowing in US financial markets to finance the public side of the investment program was a key feature of this economic development strategy from the beginning.

Additionally, in the 1940s, the US Congress passed the Investment Company Act, regulating the investment industry and the exchange markets.[40] PR and other unincorporated territories were exempt from the application of the act, as well as from the Security and Exchange Commission (SEC) regulations. The colonial rationale behind excluding investment firms operating in US territories from SEC's direct oversight was the travel costs associated with visiting PR. This exclusion enabled banks and investment firms to operate freely for more than seventy years. The lack of SEC regulation of financial institutions facilitated speculative and other criminogenic practices contributing to the current Puerto Rican debt crisis. To address these speculative practices, the US Territories Investor Protection Act was reintroduced in the US House of Representatives (HR 1366) in 2018, where it passed, but it is still waiting to be passed in the Senate.

Lastly, these transformations were not without opposition and conflict; rather, there is a long history of anticolonial and anti-imperialist resistance in PR.[41] Particularly, from the 1930s onward, PR witnessed the emergence of Pedro Albizu Campos and the Nationalist Party, as well as Gilberto Concepción de Gracias and the Puerto Rican Independence Party. As the next section illustrates, the socioeconomic and political changes that PR underwent during this first fifty years of US colonialism were, in many instances, responses to the anticolonial and revolutionary movements. Similarly, in the post-WWII era, PR faced anticommunist and proto-fascist repression, leading to the incarceration and death of hundreds of Puerto Rican anticolonial militants. This became evident, especially in the context of the approval of Public Law 600 and the Nationalist Revolution of October 30, 1950, and the attack on the US Capitol on March 1, 1954.

Public Law 600 of 1950 and the Commonwealth of Puerto Rico

The third exceptional law imposed on PR was Public Law 600 of July 3, 1950, or the Puerto Rico Federal Relations Act. This law allowed Puerto Ricans to draft their own constitution and established a local government with a limited degree of autonomy. The law came after the appointment of Jesús T. Piñero as the first Puerto Rican governor in 1946 by President Truman, and the enactment of Public Law 362 of 1947, that made the governor of PR an elected position.[42]

Public Law 600 was the result of a period of intense sociopolitical and anticolonial mobilizations in PR and the United States. Similar to previous exceptional laws, Public Law 600 came as reaction to the pressure that the colonial elites had been exerting for the resolution of the colonial status (especially, the Popular Democratic Party [PPD] and Luis Muñoz Marín), the international pressures for decolonization in the wake of World War II, and the intense pressure maintained by the pro-independence forces represented by the Nationalist Party, the Puerto Rican Independence Party (PIP), and various labor movements.[43]

Public Law 600 provided a very limited scope of self-determination since it did not intend to fundamentally alter the relations between the United States and PR.[44] The law only granted authority for the drafting of a constitution that would regulate the internal politics in PR. Thus, after a two-year period of constitutional convention, electoral processes, and the US Congress approval of the Puerto Rican Constitution,[45] the Commonwealth of Puerto Rico (ELA)[46] was established on July 25, 1952. The new local government recognized a limited degree of internal democracy and established a republican system of governance within the antidemocratic structures of the US colonial state of exception. This aspect, however, did not imply a substantial change in PR's political relationship with the United States; PR remained a colony, albeit with certain internal democratic guarantees.

Examples of these limitations are:

1. The federal laws that Congress did not explicitly declare inapplicable would apply in PR.

2. The federal court would continue to operate in PR.

3. Congress unilaterally excluded certain areas that would remain off-

limits to Puerto Rican voters or their elected representatives, such as citizenship, immigration, maritime commerce, trade treaties, and foreign relations, as well as all matters related to military activity, currency, and tariff policy.

4. In case of conflict between local and federal laws, the latter would prevail over the Constitution of PR.

5. Citizens living in PR would not pay federal income taxes and other US taxes, given that PR does not have representation in the US Congress, with the exception of the resident commissioner, and cannot vote for the US presidential elections. Thus, PR will be able to operate its own tax system, largely tailored to mirror the US tax code.

Significantly, the PR Constitution established that the payment of public debt would have priority over any other payment. As an example, the PR Constitution provided that when the resources available for a fiscal year are not sufficient to cover the allocations approved for that year, the payment of interest and repayment of public debt shall have priority, and only then other disbursements can be made in accordance with the order of priorities established by law.[47] All this shows the uses of the colonial state of exception for the establishment of a strict economic structure. That is, given that a great part of bondholders are US citizens living in the United States, it is no surprise that the economic policy imposed in PR aims to guarantee those US interests.

Furthermore, it has been argued that the ELA served as a strategy to legitimize US colonialism before the United Nations (UN) and the international community, as for example, when in 1953, the US government requested the UN remove PR from its list of non-self-governing territories, since PR had reached the maximum degree of self-determination. UN Resolution 748 (VIII) granted the request. Governor Luis Muñoz Marín and the PPD agreed that the status had been solved, and that the United States and PR had entered into a "compact" or agreement ending colonialism in PR. However, the anticolonial movements demonstrated the colonial nature of said compact.

Others have challenged the idea that colonial status PR was resolved in 1952. Recently, the US judiciary and the legislative and executive branches have reasserted the colonial condition of PR. Christina D. Ponsa-Kraus (2022) used the term "legal ambiguity" to describe the legal and political positions that emerged in the aftermath of the establishment of the ELA. For example, the US judiciary has reacted in different and opposing ways to the establishment of the ELA and its constitutional effects. Two positions regarding the creation of the ELA emerge from the analysis of the different legal opinions and rulings. Firstly, there are the rulings that see the ELA as the expression of local sovereignty.[48] Secondly, there is a group of cases that denies the idea that the ELA involved a transfer of sovereignty to PR, and therefore, argues that PR is still a US colony.[49] The Supreme Court resolved this dispute in *Puerto Rico v. Sánchez Valle* (2016) and *Puerto Rico v. Franklin California* (2016), in which it concluded that PR has no distinct sovereignty but continues to be an unincorporated territory or a US colony.

Similarly, the US executive branch has reiterated the colonial character of the Commonwealth of PR. For instance, in the context of *Puerto Rico v. Sánchez Valle*, US Solicitor General Donald B. Verrilli Jr. submitted an amicus brief to the Supreme Court, in which the Obama administration reaffirmed that the US government understood that PR is still a US colony and that ELA did not mean the resolution of status.[50] Lastly, on December 15, 2022, the House of Representatives approved the HR 8393 Puerto Rican Status Act, or a bill aimed at holding a plebiscite on November 5, 2023, to resolve the PR political status. The bill, which did not pass the Senate, once more demonstrates that PR continues to be a US colony.

The analysis of the opinions issued by various US courts, reports drafted by the executive branch,[51] and legislation introduced by Congress demonstrates that: the US judiciary had not developed, until 2016, a clear legal argument on the ELA; all these decisions indicate that the US government uses the law and legal opinion that best suits their interest concerning the ELA; and the US government has repeatedly argued that PR remains a colony and that the establishment of ELA does not represent the end of PR's colonial condition. Hence, the US government has affirmed that PR continues under a colonial state of exception.

RECONSIDERING PUERTO RICO'S LEGAL STATUS

This section explores what two of my interviewees referred to as the "Second Season of the Insular Cases."[52] It provides an overview of how the US Supreme Court has reacted to the economic crisis and how it has reasserted US colonial power in PR. The three cases discussed in this section—*Sánchez-Valle, Franklin California,* and *Vaello-Madero*—together tell the story of how a key legal fiction developed in the Insular Cases and in the previous three exceptional laws defined the condition for the current multilayered crisis.[53] This entails, as I have been sketching through this chapter, that the state of exception does not respond to moments of rupture or to the ticking bomb scenario, but rather the state of exception operates as the structure in colonial settings.

Puerto Rico v. Sánchez-Valle: What Type of Sovereignty Does PR Have?

Puerto Rico v. Sánchez Valle addresses the question of whether PR has a separate sovereignty from the US federal government for purposes of the double jeopardy clause.[54] The case responded to a certiorari petition brought to the US Supreme Court by the PR government, after the PR Supreme Court ruled in favor of Luis Sánchez-Valle in a double jeopardy case. The dispute revolved around the applicability of the Fifth Amendment in PR, which prohibits a defendant from being tried twice for the same exact offense.

After being indicted by a federal grand jury, pleading guilty in US District Court in PR (for selling an illegal weapon to an undercover police officer), and being sentenced to five months of house arrest and three years of supervised release, the defendant moved to have the Puerto Rican charges dropped on the grounds that he could not be prosecuted twice for the same crime. Sánchez-Valle argued that the PR legal system could not prosecute him, since PR does not have sovereignty distinct from that of the US federal government. The PR government argued that the ELA and the PR Constitution enacted in 1952 gave PR a different sovereignty that allowed it to prosecute Sánchez-Valle under its own statutes despite his guilty verdict in federal court.

The court argued that, unlike the fifty states and Native American nations, PR does not have a separate sovereignty from the federal government.[55] According to the court, PR boasts "a relationship to the US that has no parallel in our history, but it cannot benefit from the dual-sovereignty doctrine, since the 'ultimate' source of prosecutorial power remains in the US Congress." Furthermore, the majority argued that:

> Congress, in Public Law 600, authorized Puerto Rico's constitution-making process in the first instance; the people of a territory could not legally have initiated that process on their own. And Congress, in later

> legislation, both amended the draft charter and gave it the indispensable stamp of approval; popular ratification, however meaningful, could not have turned the convention's handiwork into law. Put simply, Congress conferred the authority to create the Puerto Rico Constitution, which in turn confers the authority to bring criminal charges. That makes Congress the original source of power for Puerto Rico's prosecutors—as it is for the Federal Government's. The island's Constitution, significant though it is, does not break the chain.

In this case the court—as the Puerto Rican anticolonial movements have pointed out over the last seventy years—ratified that PR continues to be a US colony. Likewise, in this opinion the court confirmed that in 1952, Puerto Ricans established an internal government under the authorization of Congress; however, this does not mean that it acquired the same legal-political status as a state of the union or a Native American nation. The sovereignty of PR, according to the court, continues to be in the hands of Congress, by virtue of the territorial clause of the US Constitution.

The opinion of the court did not simply show that the ELA did not solve US colonialism in PR, but that the United States had systematically used the law to legitimize colonialism in PR. This is evident by the opinion of the court, which pointed out that if one carried out a "test" that goes "all the way back," it would show that PR sovereignty remains in the US Congress and not in PR. What is important about "going all the way back" and the "test" to which Puerto Rican legal-political development is subjected in the opinion is that it is full of silences. The opinion confirms the colonial and imperial character of US constitutional development through continuous references to nineteenth-century jurisprudence and to the Insular Cases. Additionally, despite referencing that jurisprudence, in the attempt to go "all the way back," the court overlooks the founding violence of its colonial legal system, as well as ignoring the colonial, racial, and imperial experiences of the cases it cites as "good law."

At the same time, the dissenting opinion of Justices Breyer and Sotomayor were based on an equally colonial vision, in which they defended the compact theory. That is, compact theorists describe 1952 or the enactment of ELA as a popular act of constitution-making, in which the Puerto Rican people ratified their Constitution.[56] As has been previously established, the Constitution of PR was the result of the third exceptional law, and it was the US Congress and not the Puerto Rican people that ratified or approved the Constitution. Thus,

Justices Breyer and Sotomayor, in their attempt to defend Puerto Rican colonial sovereignty, vindicated the US colonial jurisprudence and the colonial state of exception imposed in PR throughout the 124 years of US rule in PR.

Puerto Rico v. Franklin California: Is PR a State for Purposes of Bankruptcy?

In 1984, the US Congress adopted Section 903(1) of the Bankruptcy Code[57] and introduced a new definition for state that excluded PR and its public corporations from Chapter 9 (municipal bankruptcy).[58] The exclusion of PR from the Bankruptcy Code made Puerto Rican bonds and public debt more appealing to investors, while leaving PR without any sort of protection. Subsequently, in 2014, the PR government enacted the Puerto Rico Public Corporation Debt Enforcement and Recovery Act (Recovery Act or Law 71), intending to address the exclusion of PR from Chapter 9 by creating a local bankruptcy law.

Puerto Rico v. Franklin California (2016) addresses the question of whether PR can be considered a state for the purposes of Chapter 9 of the federal bankruptcy law.[59] If PR is not a state for the purposes of the bankruptcy law, then Law 71 can remain in place. The *Franklin California* plaintiffs were managers of several mutual funds that joined this case and filed lawsuits in the US District Court for the District of PR on the same day that Law 71 (June 28, 2014) was signed into law. Franklin California Tax-Free Trust and Blue Mountain Capital Management, LLC, brought separate lawsuits against PR and various government officials. Collectively, the plaintiffs held nearly $2 billion in bonds issued by PREPA.

The majority of the court argued that the federal Bankruptcy Code preempted Law 71 and stated that the fact that PR had been excluded from federal legislation did not allow PR to legislate locally on a field occupied by Congress.[60] This decision argued that PR does not possess sovereignty since it is not a state of the union, but at the same time it is conveniently and selectively treated as a state for the purposes of federal bankruptcy laws, even if it is excluded from its applicability. Only Congress can decide to include PR into Chapter 9 or to legislate a new bankruptcy law for PR (which it did with PROMESA).

Sotomayor's dissenting opinion suggested that Congress could step in to resolve PR's crisis. But, in the interim, the government and people of PR should not have to wait for possible congressional action to avert the consequences of unreliable electricity, transportation, and safe water—consequences that members of the executive and legislative branches have described as a looming humanitarian crisis.

Puerto Rico v. Franklin California intensified the sociolegal debate on the Puerto Rican colonial condition, while it revalidated the colonial positions defended by the court in *Puerto Rico v. Sánchez-Valle*. In short, the US Supreme Court concluded in *Puerto Rico v. Sánchez-Valle* that PR has no sovereignty since it *is not* a state of the union. At the same time, *Puerto Rico v. Franklin California* concluded that PR *is* a state for the purposes of federal bankruptcy laws; hence, it is excluded from the applicability of the law. These decisions showed that, under Schmittian logic, the sovereign decides on the applicability of the law and on the exception.

United States v. Vaello-Madero: Which Policies Apply to PR under the Territorial Clause?

United States v. Vaello-Madero (2022) addresses whether the equal protection component of the due process clause of the Fifth Amendment guarantees that the federal government will not discriminate against individuals without a rational basis. While living in New York, José Luis Vaello-Madero started receiving Supplemental Security Income (SSI), a federal Social Security benefit available to any resident of the fifty states and the District of Columbia. In 2013, Vaello-Madero moved to PR, and he continued to receive payments until 2016, when he received notice that his residence in PR disqualified him from receiving the benefit of SSI. A year later, the federal government sued him in the US District Court of PR to recoup the $28,081 that it had accidentally paid him between 2013 and 2016.

The lawyer for *Vaello-Madero* argued that the powers of the territorial clause were "intended to be temporary while the territory was in pupilage," but criticized that through the Insular Cases this power became "indefinite." The US Supreme Court upheld the constitutionality of the federal legislation pursuant to the territorial clause. That is, the court ruled[61] that Congress can deny benefits to residents of PR based on the tax status of the territory.[62] The court stated that just as not every federal tax extends to residents of PR, so too not every federal benefit program extends to residents of PR. One such benefit program is SSI, which by statute applies only to residents of the fifty states and the District of Columbia.

Accordingly, Congress's decision to exempt PR's residents from most federal income tax, gift tax, and estate tax supplies a rational basis for likewise distinguishing residents of PR from residents of the states for purposes of the SSI benefits program. *Vaello-Madero*'s contrary position would usher in potentially far-reaching consequences, with serious implications for the Puerto Rican people and the economy. The court rejected the equal protection claim for Social Security benefits without considering whether there was a rational basis for discriminating against the class of would-be beneficiaries. The Constitution affords Congress substantial discretion over how to structure federal tax and benefits programs for residents of the territories, and thus, Congress may extend SSI benefits to residents of PR.

In his concurring opinion, Justice Gorsuch intriguingly addressed the issue that no one specifically brought before the court: the possibility of overturning the Insular Cases. Gorsuch asserted,

> A century ago in the Insular Cases, this Court held that the federal government could rule Puerto Rico and other Territories largely without regard to the Constitution. It is past time to acknowledge the gravity of this error and admit what we know to be true: The Insular Cases have no foundation in the Constitution and rest instead on racial stereotypes. They deserve no place in our law.[63]

Following this statement, Justice Gorsuch provided a comprehensive overview of Insular Cases jurisprudence, emphasizing that their flaws are not only fundamental but shameful. He pointed out that nothing in the Constitution refers to "incorporated" and "unincorporated" territories, and nothing in it limits certain "fundamental" constitutional guarantees solely to the latter. Additionally, he argued that the Constitution doesn't authorize judges to segregate territories and their inhabitants based on race, ethnicity, or religion. Although he criticized the Insular Cases, for Gorsuch the federal government can possess and govern territories. The problem of the Insular Cases is, erroneously and mistakenly, reduced to one about constitutional interpretation, a question of which provisions of the Constitution apply to US territories. Justice Gorsuch sought to subject colonial rule to the Constitution, to make colonialism *more* constitutional. Territorial expansion and colonialism are constitutional, if they comply with the applicable provisions of the US Constitution.

After this detailed analysis, Justice Gorsuch returned to the current case and stated, "because no party asks us to overrule the Insular Cases to resolve today's dispute, I join the Court's opinion. But the time has come to recognize that the Insular Cases rest on a rotten foundation. And I hope the day comes soon when the Court squarely overrules them." By this logic, overruling the Insular Cases operates as an effort to fix the US Constitution without addressing its colonial origin and its imperial aspirations. In the case of PR and the territories, they will still be governed by the federal government, but now under constitutional limitations. Overruling these cases, by itself, will not enable a real process of decolonization, because US constitutionalism is enmeshed in colonial exceptionality.

Lastly, Justice Sotomayor in her dissenting opinion stated that the territorial clause does not allow Congress to disregard or ignore PR forever. In response to the majority's tax-benefit ledger analysis, Justice Sotomayor emphasized that residents of PR make some contributions to the federal treasury. However, she argued that these distinctions should be immaterial because SSI recipients pay few, if any, taxes at all. This condition does not prevent Congress from extending SSI benefits to another territory,[64] and there is no other federal program operating in such a uniform, nationalized, and direct manner.[65] Equal treatment of citizens should not be left to the vagaries of the political process. Because residents of PR do not have voting representation in Congress, they cannot rely on their elected representatives to remedy the punishing disparities suffered by citizen residents of PR under Congress's unequal treatment.

At the center of the dispute is the question of taxes, analysis of which scholars have largely disregarded.[66] We must consider that the logic of exceptionality that enables the design of PR as unincorporated territory has enabled exclusionary logics such as the exclusion for basic social protection. As this chapter has been arguing, the state of exception operates as structure and not as event.

REAFFIRMING THE COLONIAL STATE OF EXCEPTION

The Puerto Rican government and its Government Development Bank (GDP) defaulted on a $442 million bond payment on May 1, 2016,[67] and a second default came on June 1, 2016, when the government could not repay a $2 billion loan.[68] PR's $72 billion in public debt falls into four categories:[69]

general obligation (GO) bonds and other debt payable through the main treasury accounts of the Commonwealth of PR; sales tax–backed debt known by its Spanish acronym COFINA and other revenue bonds; debt of public corporations such as PREPA; and debt issued by local governments (*municipios*) and other smaller entities.[70] Additionally, PR holds $49 billion in unfunded pension liability. These defaults came after at least two decades of economic recession and ten years of economic and financial crisis. Immediately, all three branches of the US government exercised their colonial power over PR.

On June 30, 2016, the US Congress passed, and President Obama signed into law, Public Law 114–118, known as PROMESA, which aimed to address the economic crisis affecting PR since 2006. Largely justified under the pretext of public corruption, lack of transparency, and the inability of the local government to run the Puerto Rican economy, PROMESA became the US government's solution for ensuring the survival of the Puerto Rican financial system, guaranteeing the payment of the public debt, and bringing PR back into the finance world and the stock markets.[71]

PROMESA does not recognize the effects of US colonialism on the Puerto Rican economy, and does not address the long history of tax, financial, and economic policies imposed by the US colonial state of exception in PR. In the US colonial imagination, the solution to the colonial-capitalist crisis is more colonialism. This is evident from the fact that PROMESA became the fourth exceptional law implemented by the US government in PR. The law does not necessarily overturn the PR Constitution and the PR government, but rather undermines their functions to the point that, even though the PR Constitution is present, in many ways, it is operatively subsumed to the powers of the FOMB.

With its enactment of broad-reaching sociolegal and political transformations, PROMESA represents a key moment in the colonial state of exception. PROMESA is comprised of seven titles. Title I and II address the establishment, organization, and responsibilities of the FOMB. Title III defines the mechanism for the adjustment of the debt and the bankruptcy procedure. Title IV provides a series of public policies, mechanisms to restructuring the debt outside the federal courts, and other provisions. Title V establishes the mechanism for the revitalization of the Puerto Rican economy. Title VI introduces creditor collective actions. Finally, Title VII establishes the US Congress pro-growth fiscal reforms.

Again, one of the key issues around the Puerto Rican debt is PR's exclusion from Chapter 9 of the US Bankruptcy Code. Instead of amending the Bankruptcy Code, the US Congress created a territorial bankruptcy regime that consists of two elements: first, the establishment of the FOMB with ample powers to impose fiscal discipline on the territory; second, a court-supervised process for the adjustment of the territory's debts and obligations. PROMESA does not include a bailout option or transfer of funds for PR. Although, as Mayra Vélez-Serrano (2018) argued, there was one certainty PROMESA provided: that Wall Street investors get their payment.

Deepak Lamba-Nieves, Sergio Marxuach, and Rosanna Torres (2021) and Mariely López-Santana (2022) have provided excellent analyses of the background and experiences that led to the configuration and development of PROMESA.[72] Lamba-Nieves et al. (2021: 3) suggest that the origins of PROMESA can be traced to "the establishment of financial control boards by state governments to manage financial crises at the city, municipal, and county level, most notably in the cases of New York City, Philadelphia, Washington, D.C., and Detroit." The authors argue that these boards usually take over the fiscal and financial policymaking functions of cities or municipalities, with the objective of making the "politically difficult decisions" necessary to get out of the crisis and that, presumably, democratically elected politicians were unwilling or unable to make. Similarly, López-Santana provides a rich analysis of the background and the legal history behind the uses of financial oversight boards to address jurisdictions in fiscal distress.[73] Furthermore, López-Santana illustrates how the Puerto Rican case, given its colonial condition and its high poverty rates, becomes a unique scenario for the study of financial oversight boards.

The FOMB consists of seven members recommended by Congress and appointed by the president to serve for three-year terms. The members are not accountable to the people of PR, even though they are considered to be officers of the Puerto Rican government. Only one member needs to be a resident of PR or to have a business in the territory, and the governor of PR is a non-voting eighth member. The members can only be removed by the president for cause. Section 104 established that neither the governor nor the legislature may exercise any oversight or control over the FOMB, nor enact any legislation, policy, or rule that may impair or defeat the purposes of PROMESA. Section 107 establishes that the expenses of the FOMB shall be funded by PR, expenses that will be determined at the "sole and exclusive discretion" of the FOMB. The FOMB can appoint an executive director to manage its day-to-day affairs.

FOMB's powers include approving budgets and fiscal plans, vetoing debt issuances, and determining which projects are funded or not. The FOMB has the power to hold hearings and to subpoena people and information it deems necessary to accomplish its mandate under PROMESA. The FOMB directs and sets schedules, by which the governor prepares and submits fiscal plans required by PROMESA, which the FOMB approves, disapproves, or certifies.[74] It can also set the budgets of the government of PR and its instrumentalities. Furthermore, it can approve contracts, including leases and contracts to a governmental entity or government-owned corporations.

The FOMB has the power to review and approve any legislation enacted in PR for compliance with the directives of the FOMB vis-à-vis the fiscal plan. Similarly, the FOMB can recommend legislation to ensure compliance with the fiscal plan or to otherwise promote the financial stability, economic growth, management responsibility, and service delivery efficiency of the territorial government, Subsection 205(a). In other words, if a law does not meet with the FOMB's approval, the legislature must amend it to be compliant with the directives of the FOMB. If the legislation as amended still does not comply, the FOMB has the power to bar its enforcement altogether.

Between 2019 and 2023, the FOMB has vetoed or asked the court to annul thirteen laws enacted by the PR government. These laws included amending the insurance code,[75] health insurance laws,[76] laws raising salaries for public employees or granting additional benefits,[77] incentives for health professionals during the COVID-19 pandemic,[78] retirement and pension legislation,[79] and labor law reform.[80] Put simply, the FOMB has the power to override the Puerto Rican legislature and the PR government.

Perhaps the most expansive power that the FOMB has is the ability to designate a territorial instrumentality as a "covered entity." A "covered entity" then falls under the purview of the FOMB, and it has authority to make decisions with respect to the finances of that entity. On September 30, 2016, the board designated the Commonwealth of PR as a covered entity, thereby taking full control over the territory's fiscal affairs. Despite this designation, as the debates on amending PROMESA in 2020 demonstrated, the FOMB neglected its responsibility to determine which services ought to be essential for the purposes of the bankruptcy.[81]

Section 209 of PROMESA states that the FOMB shall only terminate its oversight after it has certified four consecutive fiscal years with: access to short-term and long-term credit markets at reasonable interest rates; budgets in accordance with modified accrual accounting standards; and expenditures made by the territorial government during each fiscal year not exceeding revenues. PR is far from being able to fulfil these requirements, and thus FOMB could easily become a permanent feature of US colonial governance in PR.[82]

Title III of PROMESA created a unique legal framework for the restructuring of PR's debt, incorporating some provisions from Chapter 9 (municipal bankruptcies) and Chapter 11 (corporate bankruptcies) of the US Bankruptcy Code. Chief Justice Roberts appointed Judge Laura Taylor Swain, a federal district court judge, to oversee the Title III proceedings. The FOMB alone can initiate the bankruptcy process, and it alone can approve a final bankruptcy exit plan.

The FOMB initiated the bankruptcy process in May 2017, which allowed the Puerto Rican government to restructure its $122 billion public debt.[83] On January 18, 2022, almost five years later, the complete restructuring of the Commonwealth of PR public debt came to an end when Judge Taylor Swain confirmed a restructuring plan. This plan (called the plan of adjustment) included restructuring $33 billion in liabilities and reducing more than $55 billion of pension liabilities to a sustainable $7 billion. The plan of adjustment became effective on March 15, 2022, concluding the largest and most expensive public sector bankruptcy in US history.

Scholars and activists have argued that the plan of adjustment is unsustainable and that PR will find itself in a new economic crisis in the near future.[84] Public interest lawyer and expert on PROMESA Rolando Emmanuelli noted in our interview that:

> Puerto Rico can't afford the debt because there's not going to be any economic growth in Puerto Rico. And there is no country that is lacking in growth that can pay the debt. Fifty percent of countries that restructure their debt fall into a second bankruptcy in less than five years. I constantly try to explain this to people. Even the FOMB says that in 2036 expenses will cross, and we are going to enter a new structural adjustment period.

> . . . When that moment arrives, politicians would have to choose between essential services, the pensions, and bondholders again. Well, then, in that decision it may be that there is no longer room for essential services to cut down. And between pensions and the bondholders, who are they going to choose? They are going to choose the bondholders. And there you have the second crisis.

Similarly, ACRE (2021) has argued that rather than addressing Wall Street speculation, the FOMB has overseen a slow and expensive debt restructuring process using high-paid consultants and lobbyists. The restructuring process is projected to cost a total of $1.6 billion through 2026, the entirety of which is funded by Puerto Rican taxpayers. In some cases, their restructuring plans have proposed awarding hedge funds close to the full amount of their investment even though they bought bonds at steep discounts, while at the same time seeking to cut 80 percent of the payments owed to local small businesses, public sector workers, and individuals who won civil rights claims against the government.[85] The debt restructuring plans are unsustainable even based on the FOMB's own estimates and will result in deficits as early as 2036.

Title IV, entitled Miscellaneous Provisions, provides a series of public policies and clarifications, including a stay on legal action and debt repayment. At the conclusion of this period short of a year after the enactment of the PROMESA, the FOMB could initiate Title III for a court debt restructuring procedure. Additionally, Title IV contains several provisions that have more relevance to issues dealing with the status of territories than with PR's finances. For example, Section 401 provides that nothing in PROMESA is intended to limit Congress's legislative authority pursuant to the territorial clause, a redundant provision considering the nature and content of this statute.

Title V establishes the process to identify and implement high value "critical projects." These critical projects are predominantly oriented toward the development of infrastructure such as roads, bridges, and power plants. At the center of Title V, as discussed in the next chapter, are the emergency powers and the uses of the state of emergency concerning the public infrastructure.[86] Title V incorporate elements of the Puerto Rican jurisprudence of the state of emergency and the uses of the state of emergency to identify projects to be developed. Additionally, the Title V incorporates privatization and public-private partnership as key strategies to develop the projects identified as "critical projects." The inclusion of these two legal measures—emergency powers and public-private partnership—underscores how the process of reconstruction of the economy is not necessarily centered on people's necessities but rather on promoting and benefiting capital accumulation through wealth extraction.

In 2016, economic growth was one of the three central pillars of PROMESA, in conjunction with debt restructuring and balanced budgets. Yet, the FOMB has substituted the capital investment that was supposed to be generated using the Title V procedures for "structural reforms."[87] Noel Zamot, revitalization coordinator under Title V of PROMESA, left his position on March 15, 2019;[88] after the position was vacant for nearly four years, in August 2023 José R. Pérez-Riera was appointed as new revitalization coordinator. Rolando Emmanuelli provided a succinct and critical overview of Title V in our interview:

> Title V is super dangerous. It allows [them] to bypass all environmental regulations, so that polluting projects have no obstacles. But the main thing I see is that they didn't mind filling the position of director of critical projects, which is what Zamot occupied, because that is not one of FOMB's priorities. Economic growth is not their priority. Supposedly it is, they say, but their emphasis is on the fiscal plan. In fact, they are going to push for the famous structural reforms, and they are going to say that if the reforms are not made, if the "Easy [Way] of Doing Business," the "Employment at Will," the issue of regulations, permission to regulate transportation, if these structural measures are not made, they will say that the country will not grow. The country is not going to grow, and that is where they say it is the government's fault; it is not the FOMB's fault. The board said what the route was. And that is the rhetoric they must [use to] justify failure. It is that the government did not impose the structural reforms.

The emphasis on the structural adjustment, fiscal plans, and the lack of investment in public infrastructure as Emmanuelli described in our interview exacerbated the disastrous impact of Hurricane María and other disasters. Nevertheless, the FOMB has continued to emphasize the need to impose additional austerity measures.

Title VI allows for creditor collective actions, which provide definitions of bonds and other financial instruments as well as enabling the mechanism for creditors to recover their investments. Furthermore, Title VI establishes a debt restructuring process for voluntary collective action agreements, similar to procedures used in some sovereign debt negotiations.[89] The collective creditor action provisions offer an alternative approach to the debt adjustment provisions established in Title III. Title VI includes provisions allowing modifications to the terms of bond obligations through the collective action of relevant bondholders, eliminating the need for unanimous consent from all affected bondholders. Accordingly, both the bond issuer (PR or an instrumentality) and bondholders can propose modifications to bond financing.[90] The collective creditor action provisions seem designed to enable the resolution of all bond obligations of PR or an instrumentality as the bond issuer, relying on negotiated and voluntary agreements with a required percentage of bond claims across all related pools. These provisions do not seem to have a precedent in municipal bond law. Moreover, in the majority of cases the FOMB has resorted to Title III as a vehicle to address the debt restructuring.

Finally, Title VII established Congress's pro-growth fiscal reforms. This is the chapter title of PROMESA, but for Rolando Emmanuelli and other scholars, it is perhaps the most consequential in the PR-US colonial relationship. Emmanuelli argued that,

> Title VII says that the fiscal reforms that are established must be permanent reforms that facilitate the flow of capital between Puerto Rico and the United States. And that is the delicate definition of colonialism: The free flow of capital, the extraction of wealth from Puerto Rico. Because it is not guaranteeing federal funds, it is guaranteeing the free flow of capital, which is something else. It is not public money. And then, the board, due to their ideological composition and because many of them were linked and are linked to financial capital, well, they came to negotiate in favor of the bondholders. They came to determine, first, how much more could be taken from this country without creating an irreparable crisis so that they could then make the best offer to the bondholders. And that is what they disguise under the thesis of access to the markets; confidence in the markets depends on the fact that the creditors agree and have compromised, because if it is not a consensual agreement, then there will not be that confidence, etc.

In this long quote, Emmanuelli summarized a key element of PROMESA and the FOMB: the task of the law and of the FOMB is not to solve the Puerto Rican multilayered crisis, but rather to maintain the colonial structure of wealth extraction. As the fourth exceptional law imposed by the US government in PR, PROMESA aims to redefine the structure of colonial life in ways in which capital accumulation can continue or re-accommodate the new sociolegal and political scenario.

Litigating PROMESA: Legal Mobilizations Against the FOMB

Since the FOMB was established, the government of PR, the legislative branch, municipalities, and other institutions have litigated against it for what they consider overreaching on their powers. López-Santana (2022) discussed a series of cases that were aimed to challenge the power of the FOMB and define the scope of its operation. These cases included *Autonomus Municipality of San Juan v. FOMB*, which sought to clarify whether the FOMB has jurisdiction in the control of the budget and finance of the municipalities. The US district court ruled, in December 2019, that the FOMB has jurisdiction over municipalities or any other territorial entities.

Rivera Shatz v. FOMB (2018) sought to clarify whether the FOMB has jurisdiction over the legislative branch's budgetary actions and whether such intervention would entail interreference with the legislature's lawmaking power. The US district court dismissed the complaint, under the understanding that Section 303 of PROMESA empowers the FOMB to certify the budgets of the legislative branch. *Rosselló Nevares v. FOMB* (2018) and *Vázquez Garced v. FOMB* (2020) tried to limit the powers of the FOMB to control the budget of the executive branch and particularly to overwrite decisions made by the governor of PR. The First Circuit Court of Appeals established, once again, that PROMESA gave the FOMB the power to make budget decisions and consequently override the local legislature and governor.

On March 27, 2023, the US Supreme Court denied the petition for a writ certiorari filed by Governor Pedro Pierluisi in the case *Pierluisi v. FOMB*, which sought to define: (1) what standard of review governs a district court's evaluation of the FOMB's determination that Puerto Rican legislation "would impair or defeat the purposes of" PROMESA Section 108(a)[91] and its review of that legislation for consistency with the fiscal plan, Section 204(a);[92] (2) whether this standard of review requires the FOMB to reasonably and contemporaneously explain its decisions without relying on post hoc justifications; and (3) whether the court of appeals erred in affirming the Title III court and Judge Taylor Swain in holding that the FOMB's determinations regarding Puerto Rican laws were not arbitrary and capricious.

The dispute arose after the FOMB nullified four laws enacted by the PR legislature, which according to the FOMB were in violation of the fiscal plan. In 2022 the Pedro Pierluisi administration sued the FOMB in the Title III court in the US district court, for what his administration considers arbitrary and capricious derogation of Puerto Rican laws. Judge Taylor Swain stated that the actions of the FOMB were in accordance with PROMESA and that they did not constitute an arbitrary and capricious decision. Similarly, in June 2022 the US Court of Appeals for the First Circuit upheld the decision issued by the district court. Finally, the Supreme Court denied the petition of certiorari. Thus, this opinion reinforces the understanding that, given the economic and financial crisis PR is experiencing, the FOMB, as colonial emergency managers, exercise extraordinary powers that can preclude and limit the autonomy of the local government.

Simultaneously, since as early as the summer of 2016, Puerto Ricans started mobilizing against PROMESA and the FOMB. PROMESAS Are Over (Jornada se Acabaron las PROMESAS) was one of the first anti-austerity organizations to emerge in this context.[93] This organization established an encampment in front of the US district court and held countless mobilizations against the FOMB and its members. Simultaneously, the Feminist Collective in Construction has maintained a constant mobilization against PROMESA and against the burden of austerity on poor women of color. Likewise, Puerto Rican communities in the United States and University of Puerto Rico (UPR) students actively mobilized against the austerity measures imposed by the FOMB.

The 2017 student strikes are particularly relevant to show this process of resistance. Only three months after Ricardo Rosselló took office, in April 2017, students declared a strike at UPR that lasted until June 2017. The strike was in response to the reduction of UPR's budget, in opposition to the privatization of public services, and in defense of public education. The students also demanded that the Puerto Rican public debt be audited. In the context of the student strikes, professors and some staff member also played an important role, establishing a series of new organizations such as PARES, and PROTESTAmos, which would join existing professor associations such as the Puerto Rican Association of University Professors and Association of Professors of the University of Puerto Rico, Mayaguez (APRUM). PROTESTAmos and APRUM joined other unions including the UTIER[94] in the lawsuit (renamed

Aurelius) against the FOMB.[95] These legal mobilizations and activism contributed to the popular opposition to the austerity measures implemented by the FOMB and the Ricardo Rosselló administration.

Similarly, since early in the economic crisis, civil society organizations such CPI, Espacios Abiertos, Auditoria Ya, and think tanks such Center for a New Economy have been challenging the process that led to the imposition of PROMESA and the FOMB. By engaging in litigation, demanding access to public information, analyzing and making sense of fiscal and budgetary documents, these organization have disrupted and intervened with the colonial efforts to disregard Puerto Rican autonomy to address the effects of the crisis.

FOMB v. Aurelius (2020)

FOMB v. Aurelius addresses the constitutionality of the FOMB and bankruptcy proceedings initiated as part of Title III.[96] The plaintiffs challenged the mechanism for selecting the members of the FOMB on the grounds that the procedures violated the appointments clause of the Constitution.[97] Given the design of PROMESA, members of the FOMB did not undergo confirmation by Congress and thus, Aurelius Investment, LLC, claimed that they were not properly acting as officers of the United States and therefore did not have authority to begin bankruptcy proceedings or to restructure debt agreements.

Aurelius Investments, part of Aurelius Capital Group (a hedge fund), filed a lawsuit on August 7, 2017, arguing that the FOMB was an unconstitutional entity and thus did not have the authority to initiate Tittle III. Not only did Aurelius file a suit, but local unions and organizations presented a separate lawsuit challenging FOMB's austerity policies. According to Rolando Emmanuelli, who was one of the lawyers to bring the case to the Supreme Court on behalf of the UTIER,

> The purpose of the case was to annul all the actions of the FOMB—because if the appointments were invalid, all the actions of the board were annulled. Judge Taylor Swain—making use of the colonial theory of Insular Cases not directly cited but citing cases that rest on the Insular Cases—resolved that Congress has the power to establish the FOMB as part of the local government and that the local government is not subject to the appointment clause: that the appointment clause does not apply in this case, because the FOMB is a local, colonial entity. The appeal circuit revokes due to the immensity of the power that the FOMB has. Because the FOMB really came to execute supra-colonial powers and they are

> members of an entity that can be removed by a president of the United States with cause, the appeal circuit argued that the FOMB was a federal entity. The Supreme Court overturned the appeal circuit.

While both challenged the constitutionality of the FOMB, Aurelius and UTIER had different purposes. Aurelius aimed to dismiss the bankruptcy process so that the debt would not be restructured, and the bonds were paid at their full price. UTIER sued the FOMB to ensure that pensions, paychecks, and other obligations to public employees were honored. Hence, there was a tension between a hedge fund aiming at stripping PR's assets and a union seeking to put a hold to the austerity measures imposed by the FOMB.

Despite the importance of this debate, as my interviewees indicated, the oral argument on October 15, 2021, revolved around the Insular Cases, the constitutionality of the appointments, and whether the FOMB was an entity of the territorial government or a federal entity.[98] The court ruled that the appointments clause applies to "all Officers of the US, even when those officers exercise power in or related to PR"; members of the FOMB were not "Officers of the US" because they are "local officers" vested by Congress with "primarily local duties" (in contrast with "national or federal duties") under Article 4. The rationale behind this argument is that the Constitution's appointments clause applies to the appointment of US officers with powers and duties in and in relation to PR, but that the congressionally mandated process for selecting members of the FOMB does not violate the appointments clause. The court stated that given this conclusion,

> we need not consider the request by some of the parties that we overrule the much-criticized "Insular Cases" and their progeny. Those cases did not reach this issue, and whatever their continued validity we will not extend them in these cases. Neither, since we hold the appointment method valid, need we consider the application of the *de facto* officer doctrine.

Similarly, the scholarship emerging from the *Aurelius* ruling[99] and my interviewees demonstrated that there was serious consideration of the Insular Cases and their overruling. Adriel Cepeda Derieux and Neil Weare (2020) described *Aurelius*'s missed opportunity, while Rolando Emmanuelli argued that *Aurelius*, together with the cases decided in 2016, can be understood as a continuation of the Insular Cases. Emmanuelli argued that,

> *Aurelius* is the last of the Insular Cases—because *Franklin California* and *Sánchez Valle* cases are Insular Cases in disguise. You should listen to the oral argument in *Aurelius* and compare it to the oral argument in *Vaello* so that you can see the qualitative leap that the Supreme Court made from one case to another. I tell you to contrast that with *Vaello* because in *Aurelius* almost all the oral argument was about the Insular Cases.

Certainly, the most recent cases deal directly with the doctrine of incorporation, and the connections and continuities between Insular Cases and the recent rulings are evident. Additionally, Christina Ponsa-Kraus (2020) has argued that *Aurelius* also revolved around the possibility of decolonizing PR. Certainly, there is a consensus on the need to overrule the doctrine of incorporation and the Insular Cases since they have served as the legal design for colonial domination. As mentioned above, overruling the Insular Cases has become equated with decolonization and democratization of PR for some scholars and activists. While the arguments in favor of overruling the Insular Cases are compelling, that alone would not render the colonial state of exception ineffective and/or liberate the unincorporated territories. My contention is that overruling these cases would further legitimate the colonial state of exception and reassert US colonial power over PR. As this chapter has showed, the structures of imperial domination manufactured through the logic of exceptionality are enmeshed in an array of ontopolitical processes that collectively define the colonial legal reality.

The operativity of that colonial legal reality and its reaffirmation through legal reveries is attested by Justice Sotomayor's concurring opinion. Her opinion reproduced views of the colonial state of PR concomitant with those that have defended the status quo or the colonial interpretation of the legal development of PR. For instance, Sotomayor argued that, even if PR remained a territory under the territorial clause, that "does not necessarily allow Congress to repeal by mere implication its prior grant" of local self-rule. Congressional plenary power over the territories, after all, "was never intended to last indefinitely." Sotomayor reasserted the temporary character of territorial rule and argued that Congress may constitutionally relinquish its authority over local affairs. If Congress confers the full measure of local self-rule, federal tutelage of local affairs is unconstitutional. Justice Sotomayor stated that Congress "relinquished" certain powers over PR when it granted the archipelago "rule" pursuant to a "compact" between the people of PR and Congress in

1952. In this way, Justice Sotomayor has become one of the key defenders of the compact theory, as discussed above.[100]

Beyond this debate, Lopéz-Santana (2022: 16–17) summarized the impact of *Aurelius* as follows:

1. Congress has the power to dictate the terms and governance of the bankruptcy-like proceedings.
2. The FOMB is not a federal entity, even if its members are appointed by the president and Congress.
3. The FOMB is a local independent entity that is not accountable to the elected government.
4. The FOMB has budgetary powers and veto powers over fiscal decisions taken by the legislative and executive branches.

Thus, with *Aurelius*, the debates around the political and legal status of PR went all the way back to its beginning in the Insular Cases. But, more importantly, *Aurelius* demonstrates how the law and US institutions have made an extraordinary effort to guarantee the survival of the regime of permission and wealth extraction established by the colonial state of exception.

On December 22, 2023, Pedro Pierluisi filed a petition for a writ of certiorari in the US Supreme Court in the case *Pedro Pierluisi and Puerto Rico Fiscal Agency and Financial Advisory Authority v. FOMB* after the US Court of Appeals for the First Circuit sided with the FOMB, annulling Law 41, which sought to reform private labor laws. The Supreme Court granted the review. Unlike the *CPI v. FOMB* case discussed at the beginning of this chapter, the new case brought by Pierluisi demonstrates the recurring efforts of the PR government and the local administrations to maintain instances of decision-making and wealth extraction within the structure of the colonial state of exception. That is, while the CPI and other civil society organizations seek to interrupt the operations of the colonial state of exception through legal mobilization and the demand for transparency and accountability, the local government has used litigation as a mechanism to preserve its limited authority in PR. As shown in the next chapter, the efforts to retain some limited authority and spaces for wealth extraction have led to the development of colonial legality and/or a set of legal and extralegal measures destined to manage the crisis without necessarily solving it.

Amid these litigations and the lack of transparency and accountability, FOMB policies have direct consequences on the lives of millions of people living in PR. Decisions made by the FOMB on fiscal policy, austerity, structural adjustments, social programs, disinvestment in public infrastructures, school closures, and the restructuring of Puerto Rican debt have a direct impact on the livelihoods of millions of Puerto Ricans. These decisions are too important to be made without public knowledge. Lack of transparency in this context can be detrimental to the livelihood and survival of Puerto Ricans, with potentially devastating consequences in the context of austerity politics and disasters.

In this context, this chapter has argued that the concept of the colonial state of exception provides a deeper understanding of the historical dynamic and recommendations of colonial domination in PR. My understanding of the state of exception is different from Agamben's conceptualization of this paradigm as a space of anomie, or a legal vacuum between the law and the political act. I argue that the state of exception ought to be understood as the constitutive legal structure of colonial domination. The colonial state of exception is not the suspension of the rule of law, but rather the way in which the US empire has legitimated its colonial domination of PR. The colonial state of exception is the structure through which the colonial government defines the sociopolitical reality, deciding which laws apply to the colonial territory, imposing different legal systems, and creating legal subjects.

The Puerto Rican sociolegal condition is defined, as this chapter has shown, by a suffocating hold by legality, law, and emergency powers. Law is everywhere, all the time, sometimes in duplicitous ways, and other times in contradictory ways, but always violently threatening the possibility of capturing and transforming a political life into a legal dispute. The hyper-presence of law in PR and its ubiquitous violence materialized a colonial regime reliant on the uses of exceptionality for its self-preservation from its multiple and recurrent crisis.

TWO

CRISIS

Introduced in the Puerto Rican legislature on February 9, 2021, the bill titled Law for the Supervision and Accountability in Times of Emergency aimed to establish terms and controls on the governmental declaration of a state of emergency.[1] Following its approval by the PR legislature on December 1, 2021, it faced a setback when Puerto Rican governor Pedro Pierluisi vetoed it on January 6, 2022. The bill aimed to curtail the emergency powers wielded by the executive branch, impose limitations on the duration of a state of emergency, regulate the processes of hiring and procuring services during a state of emergency, and address corruption amid emergencies. In essence, the bill sought to forge a legal framework for overseeing the utilization of emergency powers, providing clear policies on their deployment during periods of crisis.[2]

In my interviews with the co-sponsors of the bill, Representatives Denis Márquez (PIP)[3] and José Márquez (MVC),[4] they highlighted that the bill was introduced after years of executive orders and declarations of states of emergency, attempting to address every aspect of Puerto Rican life. Notably, they emphasized that the bill aimed to rectify the misuse of emergency powers, which have enabled corruption. José Márquez explained:

> The biggest problem is when emergencies are declared by a single person through executive order, doing many things, such as restricting mobility, civil and constitutional rights. This is precisely what the bill sought

to limit. Because this distorts all the procedures that exist to protect the public interest and then it facilitates cronyism and corruption—pure and hardcore corruption.

In a similar vein, Denis Márquez stated that

> The issue is that they use the executive orders to avoid the legislature, to order by decree, but also to benefit the big interests, contractors, and builders, streamlining spending processes. And it seems to me that, to the extent that the governor vetoed the measure, which was a good measure, he didn't want to relinquish some of his powers, but at some point, you must be accountable to the legislature.

Both interviewees were concerned with how the use of the state of emergency has created the conditions for corruption and also undermined legislative authority. However, Governor Pierluisi justified his veto by arguing that the Puerto Rican Constitution, the Political Code of PR, Law 20 of April 10, 2017,[5] and US jurisprudence already provided a sufficient legal framework for declaring a state of emergency. Therefore, the bill was rendered unnecessary. Pierluisi stated that "this bill leads us to ask if it is possible to legislate an emergency, and if the very powers that the Puerto Rican Constitution defines as necessary to deal with emergencies, can be subordinated to the political-partisan forces that control the Legislature."[6] Furthermore, Pierluisi argued that "the bill is detrimental to the needs of the people in times of emergency," and "in times when the bureaucracy should not interfere in the mitigation, recovery, and reconstruction efforts that emergencies require. We cannot predict the future, and not all emergencies are the same, so the need to be able to respond quickly is essential."[7]

Contrary to Pierluisi's assertions, Luis José Torres, law professor and co-director of the Proyecto de Acceso a la Información, argued in our interview that "the emergency phenomenon has become institutionalized and is the modus operandi for enacting law and governing administrative agencies in PR." Likewise, law professor and former director of the UPR Resiliency Law Center Adi Martínez-Roman emphasized in our interview that

> what I see is that legally and sociologically in PR, there is an elite that governs based on a colonialist legal scheme, which are concern with how they could manage the funds of the empire. That elite, that has been the ruling class in PR, basically makes decisions, perhaps some based on public interest, but what I have seen after the economic crisis is that the

> decisions are made on individualistic interest with a privatizing neoliberal ideology, excluding the needs or voices of the communities. We do not have a functioning legislature, and on top of it the government has been governing and legislating through the emergency mechanism and state of emergency. And, that happens all the time.

The bill and the debates on the normalization of the state of emergency narrate the history of the role of law and emergency powers in a colonial setting during times of crisis. More significantly, they unveil the sociolegal history behind a *crisis by design*. This chapter underscores how, given its limited powers, the PR government has used the state of emergency to administer every aspect of public life, including the fiscal and economic crisis and the public debt. Moving beyond US colonial policies, this analysis explores how the Puerto Rican government and elites have accommodated to the US colonial state of exception and its policies. The argument presented here is that in recent years, Puerto Rico has witnessed the development of a colonial legality in which the permanent state of emergency plays a central role.

As a response by the local government to manage the economic and fiscal crisis, colonial legality consistently accommodates and negotiates its place within the US colonial rule. This chapter contends that colonial legality does not necessarily aim to *address and solve* the crisis, but rather *administers* the limited resources while ensuring that local elites maintain their hegemonic position in society. With colonial legality, the issue becomes how to administer and manage the crisis in ways that capital accumulation and wealth extraction continues uninterrupted. Hence as the bill illustrates, the debate revolves around administration, legislation, accountability, and good governance.

The chapter delves into the analysis of central elements of the economic and fiscal crisis, including the development of colonial legality and the historical process that led to the crisis. It examines how the local administration managed the economic and debt crisis between 2005 and 2016, as well as in the aftermath of the enactment of PROMESA. It also considers the structural adjustments and austerity measures implemented by the FOMB and discusses how the PR government has intensified its tax haven policies as an alternative to maintaining the structures of wealth extraction and capital accumulation.

CRIOLLO FINANCIALIZATION AND THE EMERGENCE OF COLONIAL LEGALITY

The development of colonial legality has occurred since the mid-1980s, involving systematic attrition of the Puerto Rican welfare and public institutions. This was the result of the confluence between a new global economic scenario and colonial policies imposed by the United States. These new juridical-political and economic scenarios resulted in the stagnation of the Puerto Rican economy and an increase in public debt, as well as a greater socialization of economic losses produced by speculative finances.

As discussed in the Introduction to this book, colonial legality can be characterized by: (1) the normalization of the uses of the state of emergency and ever-increasing concentration of power by the executive branch, resulting in the corresponding weakening of constitutional and civil rights; (2) the financialization of the colonial economy,[8] the development of tax haven policies, and the reliance on issuing public debt to cover budgetary needs, causing the exponential rise of the public debt; (3) the transformation of the administrative and regulatory policies and the imposition of neoliberal measures such as the privatization of public services, structural adjustment, and austerity measures; (4) the constitution of a regime of permission that legalizes corruption and other forms of crimes of the powerful; (5) the development of a punitive approach to legislation and regulations; and (6) the deployment of authoritarian, antidemocratic, and repressive techniques of social control targeting social movements, anticolonial, anti-austerity, and anticorruption mobilizations. These six characteristics aim to articulate the process that has configured a specific rationality at play in the management of the crisis, but do not pretend to be all-encompassing and deterministic. To be sure, the concept of colonial legality is an analytical tool for the examination of the rapid and modular articulation of the law in periods of crisis.

PR's financial, economic, and public policies have been largely determined by US congressional legislation. From World War II to the present, the Puerto Rican economy has relied heavily on tax incentives for US corporations.[9] However, these incentives were established for a term of years, and when the term expired, industries would often move their operations to other jurisdictions. A key moment in the transformation of US economic policies toward PR took place after the oil crisis of 1973, when the economic model of industrialization by invitation entered a recession.[10] Following the crisis of 1973, unemployment rose to 18.1 percent in 1975 and maintained an upward trend until 1985 when unemployment increased to a 21.8 percent.[11]

The US government eventually responded to the recession and the unemployment in PR by increasing federal transfer payments to PR, including programs such as US food stamps and Medicare, and enacting Section 936 of the Internal Revenue Code (1976),[12] which sought to encourage US corporations to establish themselves in the archipelago by providing tax exemptions that would permit repatriation of profits as soon as they were realized. These tax exemptions were particularly directed at capital and knowledge intensive operations, including banking and financial services, pharmaceutical and medical devices, and electronics industries.[13]

It was in this context of economic turmoil that Rafael Hernández Colón of the Popular Democratic Party (PPD)[14] became governor, from 1985 to 1992. Hernández Colón was one of the first governors to incorporate neoliberal discourses as part of his political program, and his administration introduced policies that contributed to the marketization and financialization of the PR economy. For instance, Hernández Colón's administration incorporated policies such as decentralization of the public administration, privatization of public-owned corporations, and government downsizing. Hernández Colón also started changing the discourse around the role of the local government in the Puerto Rican society, paying more emphasis to the socialization of economic losses and the privatization of profits under the capitalist assumption that the economy must have priority over social and public interest. That is, Hernández Colón's administration set the tone in which colonial legality became the form of government in contemporary PR.

Although initiated by Hernández Colón's administration, Pedro Rosselló's administration from 1993 to 2000—the New Progressive Party (PNP)[15]—continued the implementation of neoliberal policies. The eight years of Rosselló's administration (Pedro's son Ricardo would be elected governor in 2016) were characterized by four dynamics. First, Rosselló's administration radicalized the processes of privatization and outsourcing of public services. His administration privatized, among other services: prison administration, training programs for new public employees, shipping companies, public transportation, the public health system, water distribution, and the telephone company. In the case of public healthcare services, Rosselló's administration established a universal healthcare plan (called *la reforma*) for all indigent Puerto Ricans that consisted of contracting services from private insurers for people who, traditionally, had used public healthcare. Given the structural disparity in access to Medicaid, earned income tax credit, child tax credit, and other federal programs, the privatized healthcare services introduced by the Rosselló administration contributed to the rapid increase in its public debt.[16]

Rosselló also developed a strong anti-worker policy that included legislation limiting unions in the public sector, banning strikes and collective action, and promoting US-based unions in PR.[17] Further, Rosselló's administration developed large infrastructure projects that led to a massive increase of the public debt and were also characterized by high levels of corruption. These projects included the Tren Urbano, the Superaqueduct, the Coliseum of PR, the Convention Center, and numerous roads and bridges. These major infrastructure projects required substantial financing through public borrowing. Governor Rosselló borrowed $10.5 billion during his first term and $13.7 billion during his second.[18] This infrastructure development through massive indebtedness gave the false impression of economic growth and stability, while increasing the public debt and contributing to a real estate bubble that paved the way to PR's current crisis.

At the same time, Rosselló's administration enhanced Puerto Rican activism for statehood. As part of its pro-statehood mobilizations, Rosselló's administration played a key role in the elimination of Section 936. In 1995, at the height of Section 936, manufacturing accounted for 42 percent of GDP, created more than 30 percent of deposits in the archipelago's banking system, and directly generated 17 percent of total employments.[19] The economic model of PR depended on policies not controlled by local government. Meanwhile, the excessive local tax incentives contributed to the reduction in government revenues. Critics of Section 936 in the United States complained of excessive tax-base erosion in the country due to the territory's tax system, and they eventually succeeded in bringing the system to an end.[20] The elimination of the tax incentives was also the result of the negotiations to enact the North American Free Trade Agreement (NAFTA).[21]

The elimination of Section 936 enhanced the conditions for public indebtedness. Pedro Rosselló used infrastructure development to partially mitigate the elimination of Section 936, but these policies increased public indebtedness faster than they induced economic growth.[22] Given that PR did not have access to the limited revenues generated through Section 936, the PR government resorted to issuing bonds as a mechanism to cover public expenditures. The lack of economic growth "accentuated by the international oil and financial shock in the mid- and late 2000s has led to a public debt crisis and a massive wave of outmigration to the US. Puerto Rico now faces a triple challenge in debt, demography, and economic growth" (Caraballo-Cueto and Lara 2017: 3). In line with these financial policies, the PR government resorted to issuing debt as a mechanism to cover budgetary deficit, instead of developing a tax policy that addressed the lack of appropriation.[23]

Simultaneously, Rosselló's administration manufactured the legal framework for the development of the permanent state of emergency by legislating Law 76 of May 5, 2000, which established the procedures to administer an emergency.[24] The law defines emergency in overly broad terms, including hurricane, fire, flooding, threat to public safety, bombardment, and serious problems of deterioration in the physical infrastructure that put life, public health, or safety of a sensitive ecosystem at risk. Law 76 defined the jurisprudence of emergency for the first part of the economic crisis,[25] and it was largely used to allow for the construction of highly controversial infrastructure projects. As mentioned in Chapter 1, the jurisprudence created by this law would be used as a framework for Title V of PROMESA.

Rosselló's administration would not be the last to expand the public debt and use emergency powers to deal with every aspect of Puerto Rican life. Subsequent governors Sila Calderón (2001–2004), and Aníbal Acevedo Vilá (2005–2008) increased the total debt by $17.9 billion and $22.7 billion, respectively.[26] Governor Calderón's administration was largely marked by three important public policies. First, Calderón deployed an anticorruption and pro-transparency discourse that materialized through several public corruption investigations into the Rosselló administration. Known as the Blue Ribbon Committee and led by pro-independence representative David Noriega, the committee found that fraud, graft, bribery, and embezzlement were systemic in the Rosselló administration. As former legislator and legal scholar Victor Garcia San Inocencio highlighted in our interview, the widespread and systemic dimension of public corruption within the Rosselló administration became evident through the arrest and prosecution of over thirty of its members. Garcia San Inocencio also highlighted the significance of the Blue Ribbon Committee, which was one of the first nonlegislative investigations into public corruption in PR. Before this, legislative inquiries in PR were primarily focused on cases of state terrorism.[27] According to Garcia San Inocencio, the committee significantly transformed how accountability is understood in PR, paving the way for the emergence of a series of anticorruption and pro-transparency civil society organizations.

Second, the Calderón administration legislated the Puerto Rico Special Communities Integral Development Act of March 1, 2001. The law was aimed at developing a public policy to address inequality in underserved communities.[28] In many ways, the impact of this public policy was limited by the economic and financial crisis.

Finally, despite the rapid decrease in governmental appropriation and the accelerated increase in public indebtedness, Calderón's administration did not implement significant policies to change the disjunction between tax expenditure and appropriations. In 2004, two years before the economic crisis began, there were approximately forty tax exemption laws for the private sector. As the crisis gained momentum, more tax incentives were enacted, and by 2008 there were around sixty. In 2020, after more than a decade of economic depression and a profound fiscal crisis, there were more than ninety tax exemption laws limiting a substantial flow of income to the government.[29] These laws had not been revised, and along with other types of subsidies, the numbers of incentives keep increasing.

COLONIAL LEGALITY AS CRISIS MANAGEMENT

The Puerto Rican case is consistent with the Global North's experience with financialization, structural adjustment, and uses of the state of emergency to manage periods of crisis. As Nancy Fraser (2019, 2022) has consistently shown, crises in a financialized capitalist economy are structural and multidimensional. Many economists and the FOMB agree that the economic crisis in PR is not cyclical but structural; however, they disagree about how to address the crisis. Some emphasize the role of supply-side reforms such as privatization, austerity, and labor market reforms, without demonstrating observable positive impact on economic growth or on social equality; others propose legal reforms that addresses the tax system, wasteful expending, and corruption and a more just restructuring of the public debt.[30] Certainly, debt and financialization are at the center of the Puerto Rican experience.

The following section discusses how the PR government reacted to the economic crisis between 2005 and 2016. The section also shows how the state of emergency evolved into the legal measures developed by colonial legality to administer and manage the economic and financial crisis. This does not imply that the process of administering the multilayered crisis have been free of conflict and resistance. On the contrary, there has been systemic resistance to the US and PR economic policies coming from anticolonial movements, grassroots movements, and environmental and anti-austerity organizations. There is also resistance coming from civil society organizations, think tanks, and other advocacy and pro-transparency organizations that have consistently opposed the local government emergency and financialization policies.

Extra-Constitutional Debts: Acevedo Vilá's Administration (2005–2008)

Governor Aníbal Acevedo Vilá's (PPD) administration was key in the transformation of colonial legality into the form of government for economic and financial crisis management. By 2005, the PR government acknowledged the existence of a structural deficit approaching 2 percent of the GDP, and credit rating agencies (CRAs) began to press for "corrective actions,"[31] threatening to downgrade the government's bonds.[32]

In May 2006, the Puerto Rican legislature and Governor Acevedo Vilá came to an impasse on a budget and how to address the looming fiscal challenges. Acevedo Vilá issued executive order OE-2006–10, which partially shut down the government, given that it had no money for employee payroll. After the shutdown ended, Acevedo Vilá's[33] administration implemented a series of austerity measures that were particularly felt at the University of Puerto Rico (UPR) and other public services.[34] By the beginning of 2008, the Great Recession reached PR and exacerbated the economic situation. Simultaneously, President Barack Obama's stimulus policies had only a limited impact on the Puerto Rican economic crisis. For example, there was a package of $7 billion (spent from 2009 to 2013) to inject capital into the local economy through the American Recovery and Reinvestment Act of 2009. These funds were disbursed primarily to cover operating expenses, and a relatively small portion went to cover infrastructure investments that would have had a more direct impact on job creation.[35]

One of the most important contributions of Acevedo Vilá's administration to the PR crisis was the establishment of the Puerto Rican Sales Tax Financing Corporation (COFINA).[36] Established as Special Purpose Entity or a public corporation controlled by the Government Development Bank (GDB),[37] COFINA was key in the rapid public indebtedness of PR, generating over $17.58 billion in debt. The history of COFINA exemplifies the logics of colonial legality and the efforts to administer the crisis rather than address it. That is, after the CRAs downgraded PR's general obligation (GO) bonds nearly to junk status in 2006,[38] local officials and financial advisors came to view bonds backed by sales tax revenues as one way to manage the budgetary crisis and their lack of access to bond markets. The new sales and use tax, which replaced an excise tax, served to pay off old debts without a clear means of repayment. Approximately, $7.6 billion was used to pay for preexisting debt, and $1.175 billion was used to pay underwriters and cover issuance fees and insurances expenses.[39]

The tax-backed bonds were able to obtain a high credit rating and thus could be issued with a lower yield, reducing debt service costs to the PR government. Originally the sale tax was 7 percent, with one-and-a-half percent going to municipalities and the rest equally divided between the central government and COFINA. With the deepening of the fiscal crisis, on July 1, 2015, PR raised its sales tax from 7 percent to 11.5 percent, one of the highest sales tax in the United States. As regressive tax policy,[40] this sale tax aggravated already existing inequalities and poor and working-class communities' vulnerabilities. Furthermore, the sales—tax together with structural adjustment and austerity measures—reproduces class biases and a narrative that insists on blaming poor and working-class communities for the economic and financial crisis.[41]

COFINA provided funds to the government and helped service its debts, but its proceeds were not tied to infrastructure projects or any real investments. Instead, funds covered past debts and continuing operating budget deficits—a process termed "scoop and toss." As the Great Recession of 2008–2009 strained PR's economy and public finances, more COFINA bonds were issued under questionable circumstances. Those bonds were viewed as a more favorable financing option because they carried better credit ratings than GO bonds. COFINA was established as a public corporation with one intention: to generate new debt above the limits established by the PR Constitution, according to which the annual debt payment shall not exceed the 15 percent of annual revenues.[42]

As Andrew Austin (2022) explains, PR treats public corporations as legally separate from local government, although in practice governors largely control them indirectly via appointments to those corporations' boards. Debts of most public corporations are also considered separate from debts of the central government. In his systemic study of the Puerto Rican debt, Austin (2022: 14) identified five key constitutional provisions that should play an important role in the enactment of fiscal policy: a balanced budget requirement that appropriations not exceed available resources (Article 6, Section 8); a priority for payment of interest and principal for securities backed by the "full faith and credit" of the PR government in the case of a budgetary shortfall (Article 6, Section 8); a "clawback" provision, mandating the reapplication of revenues to debt service of full faith and credit pledges (Article 6, Section 2); a prohibition on issuance of new GO debt if average debt service costs over the two preceding fiscal years equaled or exceeded 15 percent of the average of total revenues for those two years (Article 6, Section 2); and a thirty-year limit on GO bond maturities, except for housing bonds, which were permitted maturities of up to forty years (Article 6, Section 2).[43]

Furthermore, Austin showed that the 15 percent limit and the thirty-year maturity limit were considered to apply only to GO debt, not to so-called extraconstitutional debt of public corporations and COFINA. The GDB, by serving as a conduit for transferring resources between the government and public entities, weakened the effective distinction between constitutional and extra-constitutional debt. Moreover, others have contested whether some post-2012 debt issues conformed to the 15 percent limit, as well as the reach of the clawback measures used to bolster resources for payment of GO debt. Interpretations of those constitutional limits have shaped much of PR's public finance policy as well as PROMESA's Title III litigation.[44]

Thus, COFINA was the strategy of the PR government and the local elite to evade the constitutional limitation to public indebtedness and maintain the structure of wealth extraction. In the legislation of COFINA, the Acevedo Vilá administration relied on emergency powers and the logic of the state of emergency to define the internal structure of the corporation and its relationship with the rule of law. Emergency powers enable the design of an extra-constitutional institution that could continue capital accumulation, while simultaneously circumventing constitutional limitations.[45]

The dispute on the legality of the bonds issued by COFINA and the financial techniques implemented by Wall Street and the local government to issue debt illustrates a key aspect of the argument presented herein: colonial legality enables a regime of permission that legitimizes corruption and fraud. In the wake of these disastrous policies, the next administration deployed a radical campaign of austerity measures and financialization that exponentially increased the public debt, while also expanding the repression of social movements. That is, the Fortuño administration became the main architect of this neoliberal colonial regime.

Emergency Powers and Tax Haven Policies: Fortuño's Administration (2009–2012)

Luis Fortuño's administration is perhaps the most consequential in the radical transformation of the Puerto Rican economy, politics, and legal institutions. The legal, tax, financial, labor, and pension reforms, as well as the regulations and fiscal policies introduced by his administration, were key in the acceleration of the Puerto Rican economic crisis. The effects of those policies reverberate to this day. Often dismissed by Puerto Ricans commentators for his limited time in office and for his neoconservative, free market, and right-wing Republican stands, Fortuño's harmful legacy has been largely disregarded or overlooked.[46] But to really understand how colonial legality became the form of government in PR, we must look closely at Fortuño's legal, social, and economic policies.

Fortuño's management of the crisis is characterized by the following elements. First, he legally framed, systematized, and normalized the use of the state of emergency and emergency powers to administer every aspect of Puerto Rican public life. This radical articulation of the state of emergency as a technique of government constituted a new epistemic regime in which emergency powers were rapidly deployed to address any and every sociopolitical issue. Fortuño managed to make the state of emergency a hyper-modular technique of governance capable of being adapted to any scenario. Second, he systematized aggressive structural adjustments and austerity measures, particularly targeting public employees, public education, and the social welfare. His administration assumed that to maintain a good credit rating, the state and society had to move to the rhythm of transnational investment and credit rating agencies (CRAs), such as Moody's, Standard & Poor's, and Fitch Ratings.[47] Third, he changed the local tax policies that established a highly deregulated tax landscape that contributed to the establishment of speculative finances, tax haven polices, and money laundering activities in PR. Fourth, he deregulated corporate activities on the archipelago and designed a series of incentives for transnational corporations. For instance, the Fortuño administration granted tax incentives to biomedical and biotechnology sectors; to agrotechnological and seed industries; to natural gas and coal industries; and to security, technology and other sectors serving the US military. Fifth, the Fortuño administration privatized public infrastructure and established public-private partnership (P3) initiatives.[48] Sixth, the administration criminalized social protest. And finally, Fortuño's administration normalized revolving doors, financial crimes, and other manifestations of crimes of the powerful that contributed to the debt crisis.[49]

Fortuño's administration developed a permanent state of emergency through a series of executive orders in which he declared a state of fiscal emergency.[50] Later, this declaration was enacted into law through the Special Act to Declare a State of Fiscal Emergency and to Establish a Comprehensive Financial Stabilization Plan to Salvage the Credit of Puerto Rico (Law 7 of March 9, 2009). The main arguments for enacting the state of fiscal emergency were that PR was facing a serious economic and fiscal crisis that required austerity measures, budgetary cuts, and reduction in governmental expenditure and the workforce. That is, the declaration of the state of fiscal emergency relied on the assumption that the rule of law could not effectively address the economic crisis. On February 3, 2010, the Puerto Rican Supreme Court ratified the constitutionality of Law 7 and of the declaration of the state of fiscal emergency in the case *Olga Domínguez Castro, et al. v. Puerto Rico, et al.* The ruling argued that, given the crisis, Law 7 and the state of fiscal emergency constituted reasonable actions to save the solvency of the Puerto Rican treasury.[51]

The austerity measures implemented by the Fortuño administration had the following effects: the dismissal of over 30,000 public employees;[52] the modest reduction of government expenditures by slightly over $100 million, from $1,365.3 million in 2009 to $1,259.7 million in 2012; the reduction of the budget of UPR, which led to the 2010–2011 student strikes and a series of anti-austerity mobilizations;[53] and the privatization of public services. Despite austerity measures imposed by Governor Fortuño during his first two years in office and the approval of tax reforms, PR's public debt kept mounting. The total public debt increased by $18.5 billion between 2009 and 2012, while the central government's debt increased by $3.1 billion during the same period.

The fact that the Fortuño administration still had access to bond markets, and that PR received recovery funds from the American Recovery and Reinvestment Act of 2009 (ARRA),[54] gave the impression that in 2010 the country was moving away from the crisis. For example, there were some investments in infrastructure and some limited improvements in the unemployment rates. However, towards the end of 2010, it became evident that PR's economic crisis was deepening as the ARRA funds were coming to an end, issuing debt was becoming more expensive, and the housing market was not improving.

At this time, pro-transparency organizations began engaging in legal mobilizations to challenge the legality of Law 7 of 2009 and other emergency management policies. For example, as Carlos Ramos Hernández (2016) highlighted, in *Center for Investigative Journalism v. ELA* (2011), the CPI sent a letter to then-president of the Government Development Bank (GDB) and the Fiscal and Economic Restructuring Board, Carlos García, requesting access to all contracts, invoices, and reports concerning Law 7, in particular, those referring to the layoff process. When the letter was not answered, the CPI filed a lawsuit alleging that to adequately exercise its journalistic function of informing the people and investigating how public administration is handled, it was essential for it to have access to the requested public documents. The Court of First Instance ruled that all documents not covered by any statute of confidentiality must be delivered to the CPI. Then, the PR Court of Appeals denied the petition of certiorari requested by the PR government, thus confirming the decision of the primary forum. Together with this case, the CPI, the Proyecto de Acceso a la Información, and other organizations fielded seven cases between 2011 and 2015 demanding access to public information, transparency, and accountability from the PR government. These cases often served as legal interruptions to the rapid unfolding of austerity measures deployed by the Fortuño and García Padilla administrations.

Furthermore, contrary to general understanding, Law 7 of 2009 is mainly a tax reform bill and is focused on developing new tax incentives for transnational corporations and investors. Law 7 did more than just provide the legal framework for Fortuño's austerity measures; it also cut back regulations that protected taxpayers against predatory financial practices. As Saqib Bhatti and Carrie Sloan (2016: 4) have shown:

> Prior to the passage of Law 7, the PR laws prohibited the uses of refunding bonds to create new debt. The Commonwealth could only use refunding bonds to refinance the outstanding principal, premium, interest, issuance fees, and other related payments for existing debt, and it was only permitted to do so if it would save money. Furthermore, PR law limited issuance fees or refunding bonds to 2% of bond principal. Public law 7 did away with these provisions.

Hence, with Law 7, refunding bonds were no longer required to provide savings, allowing the government to issue refunding bonds to make interest payments on other bonds without paying down the principal.

Fortuño also reformed the tax structure in significant ways. The first part of the reform was the enactment of Law 154 of 2010, which imposed, for the first time in PR's history, an excise tax of 4 percent on multinational corporations. However, corporations can deduct this 4 percent tax on their federal tax returns, *de facto* becoming a federal tax business expense deduction for US corporations operating in PR. By 2017, tax revenues from Law 154 were estimated to be $1,924 million or 21.3 percent of the total general fund revenues of $9,045 million.[55] Nevertheless, the enactment of the Tax Cuts and Jobs Act on December of 2018 by the Trump administration threatened this policy, and even the US Treasury Department demanded the elimination of Law 154. One of the key reasons is that this law has facilitated corporate tax evasion. The second aspect of the tax reforms consists of the enactment of Acts 20, 22, and 273 of 2012, which have become the backbone of the swift move from industrial tax exemptions to individual tax exemptions and a tax haven economy. The impact of these laws will be discussed later in this chapter.

Finally, the Fortuño administration issued several declarations of state of emergency regarding infrastructure and energy.[56] The state of emergency on energy demarcated a new sphere of legal-political action under the state of emergency; it was now applied to energy and infrastructural purposes, problems that did not directly threaten the colonial administrative structure.[57] Thus, the state of emergency opened the door for the privatization of the generation of energy in PR, which will be key in the later privatization of PR Electric Power Authority (PREPA).

Fortuño's administration radically transformed the legal and political landscape in PR and created the conditions for colonial legality to become the form of government. Simultaneously, his administration significantly enhanced the public debt and set in motion a series of policies that exacerbated the precarity and vulnerability of poor and working communities. Consequently, his administration was highly unpopular, which led to Fortuño's defeat in the 2012 elections and opened the path to a new PPD administration under the leadership of Alejandro García Padilla.

Unpayable Debts: García Padilla's Administration (2013–2016)

García Padilla's PPD administration began during an intense economic crisis, for which it did not have adequate economic and fiscal policies. Hence, his administration implemented neoliberal and emergency measures that were developed over the last decade. For instance, on January 3, 2013, just two days after taking office, García Padilla issued an executive order establishing a fiscal policy to control and reduce administrative expenditure.[58] Subsequently, García Padilla's administration issued an executive order allowing PR's Office of Management and Budget to impose a series of measures and fiscal adjustments to control expenditures and to ensure that the public administration did not run out of funds.[59] This executive order stated that the administration was committed to promoting the fiscal and economic health of the government through the control of expenses, and the implementation of rightsizing measures while ensuring the rights of public employees to work.

Shortly after García Padilla took office, in 2014, PR's debt reached $67.3 billion and obligations to pension funds added another $50 billion.[60] However, García Padilla's administration did not increase debt significantly. This was because municipal markets were closed to Puerto Rico, and only high-risk investors such as hedge funds were an option for loans. In total, PR borrowed $3.7 billion during the García Padilla administration, with most of this debt issued as GO bonds.[61] As PR's fiscal and economic crisis intensified in 2014, the credit agencies (Moody's, Fitch Ratings, and Standard & Poor's; henceforth "CRAs") downgraded the ratings of PR's government and its public corporations to the lowest possible level. The CRAs played an important role in the rapid indebtedness and economic downturn of PR. In 2014 alone, the CRAs downgraded the credit of the GDB, COFINA, and other instrumentalities of the Puerto Rican government.[62] By the end of García Padilla's tenure in 2016,

PR bonds were downgraded to non-investment grade by all the credit rating agencies. This reduction brought about an intensification in the regressive and attritional fiscal policies previously developed by the Fortuño administration.

On July 17, 2014, the García Padilla administration enacted the Special Law of Fiscal and Operational Sustainability of the Government of the Commonwealth of PR (Law 66 of 2014), which declared a new state of fiscal emergency. The preamble of Law 66 argued that the declaration of the state of fiscal emergency was made to guarantee the fiscal and economic recovery after the degradation of PR's credit and the decrease of tax collection that affected the government's liquidity. Representative Denis Márquez suggested in our interview that one of the consequences of Law 66 is that it froze all new hiring of public employees:

> And then the retirement windows came, and people began to leave. Because of that, during the Ricardo Rosselló and Wanda Vázquez administrations, there were almost no employees in the government. Coupled with that, the FOMB did not approve the budget to hire new employees. Consequently, services are not provided because there are no people; there are no natural resource guards; no nurses; no teachers for special education; and that is corruption too. Because to the extent that the rights of citizens are violated by the state, this violation of rights becomes corruption.

The austerity measures imposed through the state of emergency created conditions for abandonment and criminogenic practices. Systemic and consistent austerity measures, including those imposed by the Fortuño administration, depleted the resources available for the basic operation of the state to the point that several areas of the public administration became inoperable. This systemic attrition, leading to rendering public utilities and offices inoperable, facilitated the conditions for privatization. Furthermore, the lack of personnel in governmental offices meant that the government had to externalize basic functions of its operations to the private sector. This created the condition for the emergence of a new market, in which law firms, consultancy and accounting firms, technology services, research and policy think tanks, and even cleaning service companies started contracting with the PR government to provide all kinds of services. This transformation of the function of the state in society—from provider of services to contractor—constituted just another instance in which austerity measures and colonial legality enabled the local,

US, and transnational elite to capitalize on the management of the multilayered crisis.

Subsequently, the Puerto Rico Public Corporation Debt Enforcement and Recovery Act (Law 71 of 2014) was passed. Law 71 was intended to address the exclusion of PR and its corporations from Chapter 9 of the US Bankruptcy Code. As discussed in Chapter 1, *Puerto Rico v. Franklin California* and the enactment of PROMESA were in reaction to the legislation of Law 71. In addition to the enactment of the "local bankruptcy law," García Padilla's administration enacted laws that reformed public employee retirement, imposed two special taxes on oil, cut the budget for all public agencies, increased the sales taxes described above, and privatized public infrastructure and corporations through public-private alliances.

Alongside these laws, the PR government invested significant resources in reports on the economic and financial status of PR. Ramos Hernández (2016) pointed out that in February 2015 the digital newspaper *Sin Comillas* and the PR Association of Journalists sued the government to request the publication of a report conducted by the consultancy firm KPMG on a possible tax reform to be implemented by the García Padilla administration.[63] The court granted access to the document, enabling a public discussion of the impact of the new taxes the administration was intending to put in place.

Furthermore, in 2015, the PR government hired Anne O. Krueger (former director of the IMF) to conduct an analysis of the Puerto Rican economic and fiscal crisis. The resulting report (the Krueger Report[64]) had two important effects: it supported the neoliberal policies taken by García Padilla's administration and asserted that PR's public debt was unsustainable and unpayable. The report's recommendation was to restructure and renegotiate the debt. Additionally, the report emphasized that solutions to the crisis could not only focus on structural adjustments, but on the implementation of new economic development policies and institutional credibility. The policies that Krueger proposed coincide with traditional structural adjustment packages promoted by international financial organizations, such as reducing the minimum wage, labor reform, and tax reform. Later, Krueger (2017) published a short paper reiterating her analysis and the need for the imposition of additional neoliberal policies.

García Padilla, responding to the recommendations of the Krueger Report, issued an executive order[65] and established the Working Group for Fiscal and

Economic Recovery of Puerto Rico.[66] The primary objective of this working group was to formulate a comprehensive fiscal and economic adjustment plan, offering a set of recommendations to address the prevailing economic and fiscal crisis. The plan was officially released on September 9, 2015, reaffirming the neoliberal colonial policies implemented by the administration. The numerous reports and executive orders attest to an epistemic feedback loop, wherein a recurring set of shortsighted solutions, legal measures, and fiscal policies are continually reproduced and rebranded. This process is a fundamental characteristic of neoliberal rationality and underscores the operativity of colonial legality in PR. Through this epistemic feedback, colonial legality establishes an interpretative framework, wherein solutions, crisis management strategies, and even envisioning a post-crisis future are subsumed to a limited set of alternatives, all encapsulated within the specific hegemonic rationality.

This rationality is further evidenced in the public rhetoric implemented by the García Padilla administration. For instance, on June 29, 2015, García Padilla delivered a livestream statement in which he called PR's $72 billion public debts "unpayable." At the beginning of August 2015, three small public bond issues were in default. At the end of November 2015, Governor García Padilla issued an executive order authorizing a clawback of balances and revenues from transportation and infrastructure entities.[67] Continuing with the emergency policies, on April 6, 2016, the Puerto Rican legislature enacted the Puerto Rico Emergency Moratorium and Financial Rehabilitation Act (Law 21 of 2016). With Law 21, the legislature gave the governor the power to declare the non-payment of the public debt. Additionally, this law created the Financial Advisory Authority and Fiscal Agency of PR, which was structured as a public corporation of PR's government and had the mandate to articulate the exceptional policies issued by the executive branch to address the debt crisis.

The approval of Law 21 paved the way for the issuance of seven executive orders in 2016.[68] On June 29, 2016—two days before a $780 million GO debt service payment was due—García Padilla signed executive order OE-2016–30, which suspended payments on GO and commonwealth-guaranteed bonds, leading to the first defaults on commonwealth debt. This is fundamental for understanding the argument hitherto presented since these executive orders declared the state of fiscal emergency. Thus, it can be argued that all government public policies regarding the economic and fiscal crisis were based on the deployment of the permanent state of emergency.

In short, with García Padilla's administration, we can identify how the emergency policies implemented by every administration since 2005 were not adequate to solve the economic and fiscal crisis. Colonial legality provided the mechanism for the local administration to manage and administer the crisis without solving it, radically transforming PR's political-economic and socio-legal structures. PR experienced an accelerated process of economic financialization and a reconfiguration of public and administrative law that granted extraordinary powers to the executive branch, resulting in the systemic deterioration and privatization of public infrastructure, schools, the university, and utilities; the recodification of tax policies that transformed the archipelago into a tax haven; and finally, an extraordinary high level of out-migration, which weakened the social and political structures. Nevertheless, all the "sacrifice" and the social harm produced by these fiscal policies that were intended to solve the crisis instead maintained the existing power structure and the logic of colonial wealth extraction.

This radical transformation of the colonial state was possible using colonial legality as PR's governmental form. It required a set of legal measures and emergency powers that systemically undermined and eroded the legal institutions and juridical-political structures without necessarily attracting the public attention. These emergency measures were always characterized as necessary, time sensitive, and inevitable. They compressed the perception of time and space to the point that immediacy was the only solution to the crisis. However, underneath the immediacy and the sometimes confusing, often contradictory emergency management policies, a more systemic legal and political economic process was taking place: the ongoing and profound transformation of Puerto Rican life. When the moment of rupture occurs, such as the default, it does so in the context of a long-unfolding engineered process of transformation.

FOMB AS EMERGENCY MANAGER

The enactment of PROMESA and the appointment of FOMB's members brought a new dimension to the administration and management of the economic crisis. As mentioned in the previous chapter, members of the FOMB are appointed for a three-year period, which means that, to date, there have been two different compositions of the FOMB.[69] The operation of the

FOMB has taken place within three different local administrations of the same political party (Ricardo Rosselló, Wanda Vázquez, and Pedro Pierluisi), and the FOMB austerity measures have been imposed under the backdrop of Hurricanes Irma and María (2017), earthquakes (2020), COVID-19 (2020–2023), and Hurricane Fiona (2022). According to Espacios Abiertos (2023), the FOMB annual operational budget, which is paid by Puerto Rican taxpayers, is on average $60 million, of which a large percentage is expended on legal and consulting services. Table 2.1 provides a detailed distribution of the FOMB budget and its expenses from 2017 to 2023. As result of the limited funds available, local elites will reaccommodate and renegotiate their position and their capacity to extract wealth from the state. Colonial legality does not attempt to solve the crisis; instead, it manages it, maintaining structures of wealth extraction.

As crisis managers, the FOMB has emphasized two approaches to the economic crisis.[70] First, it has made its central policy the restructuring of the debt through Title III of PROMESA. Second, it has imposed several structural adjustment, cuts, and austerity measures designed to "rightsize" the local government and public corporations.[71] Particularly important in the austerity measure has been the development of fiscal plans and certified budgets.[72] Every fiscal plan developed by the FOMB since 2018 has been approved by the PR government without changes.[73]

The structural adjustment policies developed by the FOMB are concomitant to those developed by the International Monetary Fund (IMF) and the World Bank (WB) in the Global South and by the Troika in Europe. These include, first, merging, closure, or complete privatization of certain parts of the PR government and privatizing public corporations; imposing rate hikes; and decreasing the number of employees by public corporations. This became evident with the privatization process of PREPA, which fully materialized in 2023. The corporation was divided between generation, transmission, and distribution, and it was marked by serious conflict of interest.

The FOMB's policies resulted in weakening labor protections and reducing the minimum wage for workers under twenty-five. This also included cutting bonuses, scholarships, and other services provided to public employees. Ricardo Rosselló's administration supported some of these policies and even pushed for further labor reforms. As well, the FOMB enacted massive cuts in education funding including school closures and tuition increases at UPR.

TABLE 2.1. **FOMB Budget, 2017–2023**

Total income and spending for the seven-year period.

	2017	2018	2019	2020	2021	2022	2023
Total income	$31,012,064	$60,009,000	$64,762,000	$57,852,043	$57,625,000	$59,585,000	$59,527,000
Total spending	$31,012,000	$59,828,000	$64,750,000	$57,625,000	$57,625,000	$59,585,000	$59,527,000
Spending on consulting services (legal and professional services)	$30,179,000	$55,522,000	$53,345,690	$42,812,977	$39,472,000	$37,333,088	$39,109,300
Spending on consulting services as percentage of total spending (legal and professional services)	**97.31%**	**92.80%**	**82.39%**	**74.30%**	**68.50%**	**62.66%**	**65.70%**

Source: Espacios Abiertos, "Their Advisors, Your Money: Lack of Access to the Data That Have Informed the Restructuring Process in Puerto Rico," August 2023, p. 8: https://drive.google.com/file/d/11Nw8yAtzLN74suGatdcMMyeLLNhOcGm9/view

These policies led to the student strikes in the spring semester of 2017, which aimed to resist the almost $153 million in cuts to the public university (discussed in Chapter 1).

The FOMB proposed a $2.226 billion reduction of the operational budget of the Department of Education from fiscal year 2019 to fiscal year 2024.[74] As a result of this austerity policy, since 2016, 450 public schools have been closed. Some of these schools were privatized, others were sold to investors, and many others were abandoned.[75]

The FOMB also cut pensions for current and future retirees. It proposed an 8.5 percent cut to the pension of retirees with benefits of more than $1,500 per month. The negotiations around the restructuring of the retirement systems were marked by conflict of interests and a revolving door, which threw doubt on the validity of the agreements.[76] Nevertheless, on January 19, 2022, Judge Taylor Swain approved the amended plan of adjustment, making official the dramatic cuts to the pensions of thousands of public employees.

In addition, the FOMB forced cuts to healthcare, even amid the COVID-19 pandemic. This also included other welfare services, such as narrowing eligibility for the nutritional assistance program. There were also cuts to the funding of municipal government and municipal corporations, despite municipalities consistently showing to be more effective in addressing people's needs in times of disasters. The FOMB has systemically undermined municipal autonomy and imposed a $130 million cut on their budgets under the pretext that municipal governance is plagued with corruption, nepotism, and patrimonialism. Anticorruption policies have become an all-encompassing argument to justify all kinds of austerity measures and privatizing neoliberal policies, disregarding the particularities of the case or the veracity of the accusations. Simultaneously, all of my interviewees occupying leadership positions in the accountability offices of the PR government pointed out the prevalence of corruption in the municipal government and reiterated their support for the FOMB anticorruption efforts.

These structural adjustments ignore tax incentives while prioritizing a significant fiscal surplus. This last point speaks to one of the central arguments this chapter aims to develop: that is, the management of the economic crisis has transformed PR into a tax haven. The FOMB and the PR government have consistently cut essential services while ignoring the sizable impact of tax incentives, which comprise two-thirds (67.7 percent) of PR's general funds spending. For example, tax expenditure in PR for the fiscal year 2022 amounted to $23 billion, which doubles the annual budget.[77] However, the FOMB has not addressed this tax expenditure and has instead focused on producing fiscal surplus and disinvesting in public services. This phenomenon is not exclusive of PR, but rather is part of a global trend of tax incentives and the regulatory policy. However, with 20.53 percent of tax expenditure, PR is the jurisdiction that spends the most among ninety-two countries[78] and among US jurisdiction.[79]

There is a consensus among scholars and activists that the above-described austerity measures, and the debt restructuring process initiated by the FOMB, have undermined PR's capacity to deal with the multilayered crisis.[80] These policies have impoverished PR, exacerbated an already high migratory process, and set PR on a path toward a new or prolonged crisis. Despite these policies, it is interesting to note how the PR government has reacted to the FOMB and to the austerity measures. Concomitant with the development of colonial legality, the PR government and its elites have used the presence of the FOMB in PR to justify a series of legal reforms that have enhanced their capacity to extract wealth from the management of the economic crisis.

COLONIAL LEGALITY IN TIMES OF PROMESA

The enactment of PROMESA and the imposition of the FOMB entailed a new sociolegal and political-economic scenario in which the PR government and the local elites had to renegotiate their position within the colonial governance. Thus, the PNP administrations of Ricardo Rosselló, Wanda Vázquez, and Pedro Pierluisi articulated the logic and practices of colonial legality to manage the crisis within the exceptional and antidemocratic framework of PROMESA.

Ricardo Rosselló took office on January 2, 2017, only months after the enactment of PROMESA. In his first days in office, Rosselló issued six executive orders aimed at tackling the economic and fiscal crisis.[81] In this way, Rosselló became part of the emergency managers and of the tradition of administrating PR's economy through the state of emergency. However, unlike previous governors, Rosselló had to accommodate and negotiate with the FOMB, which meant a radicalization of the logic of colonial legality. In what follows, I chart the process that led to recodification of the permanent state of emergency within the limited political and legal autonomy granted by the FOMB.

Executive order OE-2017–01 of January 2, 2017, declared a state of fiscal emergency and introduced a new set of austerity measures. At the same time, the legislative branch approved the Law to Address the Economic, Fiscal and Budgetary Crisis to Guarantee the Functioning of the Government of PR (Law 3 of 2017), and the PR Financial Emergency and Fiscal Responsibility Act (Law 5 of 2017). While Law 3 created the legal condition for imposing the austerity measures required by the FOMB, Law 5 made a legislative declaration of the state of fiscal emergency. That is, while Law 3 provided the legal instruments for austerity politics, Law 5 legalized the permanent state of emergency as the technique of government.

Furthermore, on April 10, 2017, Law 20 of 2017 was enacted with the intention of creating the PR Department of Public Safety (a consolidation of all different public safety and law enforcement agencies). Law 20 of 2017 is important because of what it stated in its Article 5.10 about the extraordinary power of the governor in case of an emergency. Aside from reaffirming the power of the governor to declare the state of emergency (which has already been established by the Constitution of PR and by Law 221 of 1999), the law established in Article 5.10, Section B that the governor can amend and revoke regulations and amend and rescind orders deemed convenient to govern during the state of emergency. The regulations or orders issued during a state of emergency or disaster will have force of law while the state of emergency or disaster lasts. Furthermore, Sections E and F establish that the governor may acquire properties needed during the crisis by purchase, expropriation, or forced removal following the governor's best judgment. This law confers power to the governor to acquire properties without the required due process in times of crisis, which was exactly what happened during the crisis generated by Hurricane María, when Rosselló's administration overreached on the executive powers, generating several corruption cases.

Law 5 of 2017 and Law 20 of 2017 are perhaps the most important emergency legislation enacted by Rosselló's administration and would transform the landscape of emergency powers in PR. While Law 5 enables the declaration of the fiscal state of emergency, Law 20 allows for the declaration of the state of emergency to address disasters and pandemic. For example, all the executive orders concerning the management of hurricanes, earthquakes, and the COVID-19 pandemic relied on Law 20 of 2017. Similarly, every declaration of the state of fiscal emergency after 2017 would be based on Law 5 of 2017. Hence, these two laws became the legal framework for the permanent state of emergency in the aftermath of PROMESA.

Rosselló issued five executive orders[82] that extended the state of fiscal emergency for six-month increments each until December 2019.[83] Similarly, both Governor Wanda Vázquez and Pedro Pierluisi also extended the state of fiscal emergency in several instances. That is, using this legal framework, PR has been in an uninterrupted state of fiscal emergency since January 2, 2017, to this day.

The Rosselló administration used the executive powers and the state of emergency to create new departments and transform existing ones to serve economic and financial interests. This is the case for the Fiscal Agency and Financial Advisory Authority (FAFAA).[84] This agency oversees developing and implementing the fiscal plan and the austerity measures that would guarantee payment of the public debt. Also, FAFAA operates as an intermediary between the government and the FOMB, and it took over the role of the GDB for financial advising and fiscal agency. This new agency relies heavily on contracting with law firms and consultancy firms, which in many ways contributes to the cost of the debt restructuring. But also, it raises issues of conflicts of interest and other criminogenic practices.

Together with the FAFAA and the imposition of a series of structural adjustments, Rosselló's administration created the Center for Federal Opportunities,[85] with the intention of centralizing and facilitating applications for federal funds and grants. The creation of this office, under the guise of the economic emergency and the need for funds, shows once again the uses of the executive power to legislate and to create new instrumentalities. Additionally, throughout January 2017, a series of executive orders were enacted that dealt with the creation and definition of new agencies, positions, and governmental instrumentalities.[86] These executive orders show the processes of transformation of PR's government, and how, more and more often, the governor used executive powers to create new agencies, without consulting the legislative branch. Colonial legality has radically transformed public and administrative law, as well as reshaped the structure of the state to enable the administration and management of the crisis. This transformation illustrates not only the operation of a colonized state subordinated to the colonial state of exception, but also the effective reshaping of legal and political institutions to preserve capital accumulation and wealth extraction, without regard to the well-being of its citizens.

Additional examples of the government transformation are the different laws passed in 2017 to modify or eliminate existing rights including labor law reforms;[87] to promote economic development and growth;[88] two different laws to encourage private investors to move to PR;[89] and two laws to encourage private capital funds to move to the archipelago.[90] All of these laws referenced PROMESA, the FOMB, and the economic and financial crisis as their justification. That is, the Rosselló administration implemented a series of techniques of neutralization to deflect responsibility from its imposition of austerity measures and pointed exclusively at the United States, the FOMB, and previous administrations as those to blame for the suffering of Puerto Ricans.

Rosselló's administration issued executive order OE-2017–03 on January 2, 2017, to declare a state of emergency regarding the infrastructure, and created an office that would facilitate the development of infrastructure projects.[91] Through this executive order and through Law 1 of January 11, 2017, Rosselló's administration opened the doors for public-private partnerships (P3s)[92] to "rebuild the damaged infrastructure of PR." This executive order is like the one issued by Governor Fortuño in 2010 to declare a state of emergency on energy.[93] Thus, under the guise of an emergency, local administrations use executive orders to assign contracts without abiding to the legal framework and the rule of law. This further supports my contention that the permanent state of emergency serves to legitimate corruption and normalize fraud.[94]

On January 10, 2017, Rosselló issued OE-2017–10, which established a public policy regarding transparency and accessibility to information for the executive branch. Rosselló ignored that—given the antidemocratic nature of executive order, he was trying to introduce "transparency" through the same techniques that constituted the legal framework for corruption and state criminality. Furthermore, the Rosselló administration implemented a series of anticorruption and transparency reforms that will be discussed in Chapter 6.

At the same time Rosselló was promoting transparency, he eliminated the Puerto Rico Commission for Comprehensive Audit of Public Credit,[95] previously created by García Padilla's administration. The commission then became Auditoria Ya*:* an advocacy group demanding transparency and accountability in the debt restructuring process.[96] Auditoria Ya called for a thorough nongovernmental audit of the public debt, canceling those parts of the debt that were contracted illegally and that were result of predatory dealings with Wall Street. Eva Prados Rodríguez (2019: 251) suggested that a comprehensive citizen debt audit would evaluate: how much is really owed in principal and interest; the legality and legitimacy of each bond issuance; the conduct of every involved actor and financial institution; how the money was spent; and how political and economic elements, such as colonialism and financial capitalism, played a crucial role in the accumulation of PR's public debt. Such an audit would also become a powerful tool for fostering citizen involvement, participation, and mobilization in the decision-making processes related to PR public debt and policy measures advanced by the government and the FOMB to address the fiscal and economic crisis. With the elimination of the commission, Rosselló's administration showed his connivance regarding financial, economic, and political interests, which led PR to its current crisis.

On October 17, 2017, less than a month after Hurricanes Irma and María struck Puerto Rico, Rosselló sent a bill to the Legislative Assembly entitled Bill to Create the New Government of Puerto Rico.[97] This bill aimed to allow the governor to restructure the executive branch without consulting the legislative branch. Thus, the bill was intended as an emergency measure that would allow the governor to exercise executive law-making authority to deal with the economic and financial crisis, as well as with the aftermath of the hurricanes. Additionally, this delegation of power would last ten years, and it would be implemented not just to restructure the executive branch, but also to further externalize and privatize services traditionally provided by the government. In December 2017, after several amendments and a bitter debate between the executive and legislative branch, the bill became Law 122 of 2017.

In the next chapters I will be engaging with the legislation and policies implemented by the Rosselló administration to deal with Hurricane María and the anticorruption and pro-transparency mobilizations. For now, it is important to note how Ricardo Rosselló's administration, under the guise of the economic and financial crisis, eliminated the social and political protections, as well as the economic regulations, that had served Puerto Rico for years. Thus, the crisis has been used as a period for radically transforming the colonial state, a process wherein the permanent state of emergency—and thus the suspension of democratic practices—has been a key dispositive.

STRATEGIC ACCOMMODATIONS: WANDA VÁZQUEZ AND PEDRO PIERLUISI ADMINISTRATIONS (2019–2024)

Wanda Vázquez, former secretary of justice, became governor on August 2, 2019, following Ricardo Rosselló's resignation. As previous governors had done before her, on December 31, 2019, Vázquez renewed the declaration of a state of fiscal emergency to deal with the economic crisis.[98] Similarly, amid the COVID-19 pandemic, Vázquez's administration issued two executive orders, which extended the state of fiscal emergency until June 20, 2021.[99] These executive orders symbolized the continuation of colonial legality developed since 2006 to deal with the economic crisis. Vázquez's administration was marked by the negligent management of a series of earthquakes and the COVID-19 pandemic, which was largely dependent on emergency declaration and executive orders. Similarly, Vázquez had to negotiate with the FOMB and administer the austerity measures imposed by the fiscal plans. Nevertheless, her administration was marked by a series of corruption cases and federal and international interventions with the local government. All this paved the way for Pedro Pierluisi's administration (PNP).[100]

Pedro Pierluisi became governor in January 2021 amid the COVID-19 pandemic and in the context of the debt restructuring process. As Vázquez did before him, Pierluisi extended the state of fiscal emergency in seven instances.[101] Pierluisi's political trajectory has been entwined with the economic and financial crisis, including his role as a lawyer in the O'Neill & Borges law firm (2017–2020) in which Pierluisi worked as consultant for the FOMB.[102] While Pierluisi has a long history of revolving doors and conflicts of interest,[103] he also uses executive powers to implement anticorruption and transparency measures (see Chapter 6).

Pierluisi used emergency powers to create the position of chief financial officer (CFO), which is held by the secretary of the treasury and operates with the advice and support of FAFAA and the Office of Management and Budget.[104] The CFO position was intended to centralize governmental financial management, strengthen internal controls and accountability, and ensure the proper implementation of the provisions of PROMESA in coordination with FAFAA. This included the implementation of the certified fiscal plan, investment policies developed by FAFAA, and other financial plans. Perhaps one of the most important functions of this position is to generate audited financial statements, which has been a point of controversy in the management of the debt and the fiscal plan, as the government of PR has not issued or has delayed the issuance of these plans. The creation of this position through an executive order demonstrates the continuity with the logic of exceptionality discussed above, but it also denotes how anticorruption intervention often operates by centralizing, financializing, and implementing corporate-like governmentality.

In addition to the negligent management of Hurricane Fiona in September 2022, the Pierluisi administration was marked by the end of the bankruptcy process and the privatization of PREPA.[105] Pierluisi enacted Law 53 of 2021 to end the bankruptcy of PR, establishing the plan of adjustment to pay the debt associated with the GO bonds. Similarly, in November 2022, FAFAA stated that PR was on its way toward completing the bankruptcy process.[106] In January 2023, FAFAA argued that the 2024 fiscal plan could be the first one in a decade without austerity measures.[107] The celebratory tone continued in February 2023, when members of the Pierluisi administration led by FAFAA met in New York with Standard & Poor's, Moody's, and Fitch Ratings to get their ratings on Puerto Rican credit, which would allow the government to go back to the financial markets and issue bonds.[108] On May 18 and 19, 2023, FAFAA and the Pierluisi administration organized the PR NOW event in New York City, which was intended to bring PR back to the financial markets. A promotion of the event, which emphasized the idea of restoring growth through fiscal responsibility, states:

> Puerto Rico's historic turnaround has grown that much stronger, bringing in a new period of economic expansion, financial stability, and numerous chances. Don't miss the most recent installment of this inspiring tale of resiliency and recovery, in which an A-list group of financial experts, policymakers, and business leaders offer insightful commentary on PR's ongoing evolution.[109]

The Puerto Rican evolution, as the promotion of PRNOW evidenced, has entailed a radical transformation of the economic and legal systems, as well as society in general.

Notwithstanding the celebratory tone, early in 2024, a series of reports confirmed precisely what Rolando Emmanuelli predicted in our interview would happen with the Puerto Rican economy after the bankruptcy was completed. According to the 2022 financial statement of the PR government, the first year after the end of the bankruptcy process, the PR government had a $51,100 million deficit.[110] Largely the result of payments to bondholders and other fiscal policies put in place by the Pierluisi administration, the deficit meant that the PR government and the FOMB would be imposing additional austerity measures. Simultaneously, on April 9, 2024, Pierluisi issued executive order OE-2024–04, which aimed to promote fiscal stability, established the Governor's Economic Council, and created the Working Committee for the Recovery of the Credit Rating of the PR government and its public corporations. This new working committee is composed of the executive director of FAFAA, the CFO, and the director of PR's Office of Management and Budget. It will function as an advisory body to evaluate the factors considered by the credit rating agencies with the objective of guaranteeing PR's access to the capital markets under favorable conditions. The working committee "will make recommendations to FAFAA to incorporate the parameters considered by the CRAs in public policy and will coordinate its efforts with the FOMB." Interestingly, the executive order maintains the celebratory tone discussed above and declares that the Puerto Rican economy is "robust" and that all economic indexes indicate strong economic activity in PR.

This positive outlook was put in question on April 16, 2024, when the IMF reported at its spring meeting that the Puerto Rican economy decreased by 0.7 percent in 2023 and will again decrease by 0.2 percent in 2024. Even in 2025, the IMF forecasts zero percent growth.[111] Puerto Ricans have endured austerity and a multilayered crisis for almost two decades, only to find that the local elites and the PR government have taken PR back to the financial markets and to Wall Street—to the same institutions and rationales that caused the economic and financial crisis in the first place.

RESTORING GROWTH BY MANUFACTURING A COLONIAL TAX HAVEN

One of the most important consequences of colonial legality as crisis management is the manufacturing of a colonial tax haven in Puerto Rico. Both the US government and the PR government contributed to the development and implementation of tax policies in PR. For example, the IRS exempts taxpayers from paying taxes on income earned within PR if they have lived on the archipelago for an entire taxable year. Similarly, the PR government legislates its own tax incentives and policies, as long as they follow federal rules. The PR government has used this colonial condition to implement tax policies that, while enabling corporations and individuals to avoid taxation, increase the possibilities for the local elite to accumulate capital. Given that the economic crisis has limited capital-generating possibilities, local elites have resorted to various methods to capture capital when entering PR to maintain their class status. This is particularly clear when one studies the emergence of a service sector, such as real estate, law firms, insurance companies, and banking, which are designed to serve the beneficiaries of tax exemptions and tax dodgers living in PR.

Luis Fortuño's administration enacted Acts 20 and 22 of 2012, which have become the backbone of the swift move from industrial tax exemptions to the financialization of the economy. Act 20 contributed to the transformation of Puerto Rico into a tax haven by granting corporations and individuals: 4 percent maximum income tax on companies that export their goods or services outside of PR; 100 percent exemption on income tax on dividend distributions; 60 percent exemption of municipal license taxes; 90 percent exemption of real and property taxes; and a twenty-year tax decree, renewable for an additional ten-year period. Those that may qualify for these benefits include, among others, economic, technological, scientific, computing, and auditing consulting services; investment banking; electronic data processing centers; and computer program development. The promoter services clause of Act 20 created a sector of intermediaries, law firms, and nonprofit organizations seeking to encourage migration to PR. Qualified promoters receive 10 percent of the corporation's income tax for fifteen years.[112]

Act 22 frees individuals, particularly investors, who move to PR from paying taxes on dividends and capital gains. Act 22 contains 100 percent tax exemption on passive income, interest, and dividends. It also contains capital gains exemptions, including that all capital gains accrued after becoming a new resident will be 100 percent exempt from PR taxes. The United States will not tax any prior unrealized gains if recognized after ten years of PR residency.

Ricardo Rosselló followed the lead of his predecessors and enhanced the uses of Acts 20 and 22. However, Rosselló did so in the aftermath of Hurricane María and largely expanded the uses of Act 20 and 22 to entice investors in cryptocurrency and tax dodgers to relocate to the archipelago. While these two acts originally carried certain restrictions requiring direct capital investment and job creation, these rules were lifted under Rosselló's administration.[113] Now, any individual who spends three months in Puerto Rico can receive exemptions from federal and local taxes, capital gains taxes, and taxes on passive income until the year 2035. Similarly, Rosselló tried harder than previous administrations to attract billionaires to relocate to and purchase properties in PR, thereby accelerating the process of displacement of poor communities.[114]

One of Rosselló's last official acts before being ousted as a result of the Summer of 2019 was to solidify Acts 20 and 22 and include them in a broader incentives bill known as Act 60 of 2019.[115] Act 60 has eleven chapters including an array of tax incentives for individuals, exporters, financial servicers, the creative economy, and entrepreneurs. This law captures most of PR's tax incentives under one code and establishes an "efficient" process for granting tax exemptions to investors and corporations. The act provides a 4 percent flat income tax rate, zero percent distribution of dividends rate, 75 percent property tax exemption, 75 percent exemption on construction taxes, 50 percent exemption on other municipal taxes, and a 50 percent municipal patent exemption. This law also introduces a "charitable donation of at least $10,000" requirement to nonprofit companies operating in PR.[116] This requirement is important, since the resources and taxes that the state does not collect can now go directly to private organizations that frequently perform the role of the state. Moreover, Hedge Clippers (2024) has shown how beneficiaries of Act 22/60 appear to be creating tax loopholes and founding their own tax-exempt charities to meet the charitable giving requirement on paper. In their investigation, Hedge Clippers documented how several foundations further enhanced the impact of the tax haven policies and demonstrated how the PR government has not regulated these activities.

Act 60 has been heavily promoted among US investors and international venture capitalists by the PR government and nonprofit organizations. Oftentimes, the nonprofit organizations promoting these tax incentives are the same that receive charitable donations by the beneficiaries of Act 60. One of these nongovernmental organizations is the 20/22 Act Society, which allocates resources to promote and educate investors on the benefits of Act 60.[117] Additionally, social media influencers—mainly wealthy white men—have promoted the benefits of Act 60 among other US citizens, mainly targeting other wealthy white men.

While the PR government is promoting the archipelago as a tax haven, Alexis Santos-Lozada (2021) found that Acts 20 and 22 had limited or no job creation potential.[118] These tax incentives have largely failed in providing any real economic development.[119] As investigative journalist Carla Minet pointed out in our interview,

> Acts 20 and 22 are part of the efforts to bring a type of economic development focused on attracting foreign capital, millionaire individuals, and that type of capital to PR. I think time has passed since these laws were enacted, and that there are clear data that lead us to conclude that these acts did not have the result that has been promised. They don't even come close to that. In terms of job creation, in terms of the idea of trickling down, that by bringing in large private capital, that will somehow trickle down to the most vulnerable or disadvantaged groups. Or that it will bring investment in terms of infrastructure. We can see that there was practically not a single major project that came out of those acts.

A rough estimation by the Department of Economic Development and Commerce (DDEC) has placed the cost of these tax policies at around $20 billion, which is more than double the operational budget allocated to the government for the 2017 fiscal year,[120] in a country with a bankrupt government where 43 percent of the population lives below the federal poverty level. The numerous scandals surrounding these laws, alongside a rapid decrease in governmental appropriations, led to an intervention by the IRS on November 7, 2020, after it detected cases of fraud and tax evasion taking place under Act 60. Similarly, there has been an intense campaign by social movements, anticolonial organizations, and civil society organizations to eliminate Act 60.[121] Despite this, both the Wanda Vázquez and Pedro Pierluisi administrations have maintained these laws. As Abner Dennis (2020b) has shown, Pedro Pierluisi and others in the PNP received important campaign contributions by hedge funds and investors as a result of Act 60. This illustrates how the local elites use tax legislation to extract capital and preserve their status without necessarily addressing the crisis or people's needs. It is, in other words, a colonial tax haven.

Colonial legality cements the effective conjunction between the permanent state of emergency, financialization, and the use of the law to legitimize the antidemocratic actions implemented by the PR government to manage the crisis. Since the 2000s, PR's government imposed various exceptional legislations that sought to manage the economic and financial crisis. These policies have radically transformed the PR legal and political structure and have enabled the continuity of the crisis for over two decades.

At the center of this chapter lays the key issue of how to understand and define what constitutes a crisis in a colonial setting. Against the limited understanding of the crisis as a moment of rupture, the case of PR demonstrates that the structure of wealth extraction, exploitation, and inequality that often are associated with crisis are embedded in legality or in the everyday legal experiences of Puerto Ricans. Colonialism is an ongoing catastrophe. Thus, while the task of the local elites and the US administration has consisted in prolonging and extracting wealth from the catastrophe, the dynamic of legal interruptions and intervention had entailed a disruption with the logic that made possible the crisis in the first place. The next chapter precisely demonstrates how the local elites, financial institutions, and governmental actors engaged in a series of criminogenic dynamics that caused and then prolonged the crisis.

THREE

BANKRUPTCY

In January 2023, a year after the enactment of the Puerto Rico Recovery Accuracy in Disclosure Act (PRRADA) by the US Congress,[1] both local and US-based newspapers featured opinion pieces and news stories highlighting the law's effectiveness in addressing the issue of undisclosed conflicts of interest among consultancy and law firms providing expert services to the FOMB and the PR government in the debt restructuring process. Introduced by Representative Nydia Velazquez (D-NY) and Senator Bob Menendez (D-NJ) in 2021, PRRADA amended PROMESA by specifying disclosure requirements for professionals involved in the bankruptcy process.[2] PRRADA was a response to several instances of conflict of interest, collusion, and fraudulent dealing involving global management consulting firm McKinsey & Company and the Puerto Rican law firm O'Neill & Borges, along with other firms and experts profiting from the bankruptcy process.

In June 2020, after Puerto Rican civil society organizations and members of US Congress called for investigations of hedge funds and their alleged insider trading on nonpublic information obtained in confidential debt negotiations, Judge Laura Taylor Swain required all the parties involved in the bankruptcy process to disclose their holdings. The systematic lack of disclosure in the restructuring process has been critiqued by organizations such as Espacios Abiertos, Center for Investigative Journalism (CPI), and progressive think tanks such as Hedge Clippers, ACRE, and Little Sis; all have decried the intimate ties between hedge funds, banks, local politicians, and legal actors. Furthermore, these organizations have shown that several of the FOMB's members have significant conflicts of interest, raising questions about whether the FOMB is truly acting in the best interests of PR.[3] For example, Espacios Abiertos found that despite having a website devoted to financial disclosure, the information provided for some of FOMB's employees is limited, incomplete, or altogether absent.[4] Similarly, *Espacio Abiertos* found that a substantial portion of the FOMB budget is spent in contracting services such as law firms, consultancy firms, and other professional services.

Colonial emergency management is never accountable, as the *FOMB v. CPI* (2023) case made patently clear, but the $1.5 billion projected cost of the debt restructuring process attested to its predatory dynamics.[5] The projected overall fees that Puerto Rican taxpayers would pay are more than five times what Detroit spent on its $20 billion bankruptcy in 2013, previously the largest local-government default in US history, and higher even than the Lehman Brothers $613 billion corporate liquidation.[6] Morever, lack of transparency and accountability are not limited to the bankruptcy process; rather they are embedded in the structure of colonial capitalism that manufactured the conditions for the economic and fiscal crisis.

The Puerto Rican debt crisis is the result of a series of legal and extralegal processes enabled by US colonial state of exception and by the collusion between the PR government, banks, hedge funds, and law firms—which condition and normalize regulatory frameworks of extraction. Scholarship on crimes of the powerful[7] and state-corporate crimes[8] inform my discussion of the processes that led to the debt crisis. Engaging with these scholarships provides a systematic analysis of the legal and extralegal practices that generated the public debt, going beyond an ontological discussion of the debt and its epiphenomenal *landing* in PR.[9] This chapter contends that public debt, as a legal and politico-economic relation of power, can be systemically studied, dissected, and deconstructed to the point that the predatory practices that produced it become transparent.

This chapter presents a detailed and systematic discussion of the primary resources, data, documents, and research produced by progressive think tanks and organizations that sought to uncover, understand, and explain the economic and financial practices that led to the crisis. Among these organizations are Espacios Abiertos, Center for a New Economy (CNE), CPI, ReFund America Project, Action Center on Race & the Economy (ACRE), Hedge Clippers, Eyes on the Ties, and the Public Accountability Initiative. Centering these organizations and their research is crucial for my analysis for several reasons. These organizations have conducted a sophisticated, well-documented analysis of the Puerto Rican debt and economic crisis, systemically contributing to building a clearer understanding of the structural, political, and economic precursors to the debt; toxic financial deals; and the legal and extralegal processes that brought PR to its current financial crisis. Moreover, these organizations are instrumental in legal mobilizations for transparency, democratic and civic engagement, and fiscal accountability. Ultimately, my aim is to enhance the theoretical analysis conducted by these organizations by introducing the concept of colonial legality.

The chapter is structured in five sections. Initially, it delves into the role that banks, law firms, and local officials played in manufacturing the public debt and economic crisis. Subsequently, it explores the impact of hedge funds and asset management firms in creating the conditions for the bankruptcy and pushing for austerity measures. The third section scrutinizes the conflict of interests surrounding the FOMB, its employees, and its contractors. Following that, it examines the criminogenic practices taking place during the debt restructuring process, or what I call "bankruptcy crimes." Finally, the chapter explores the sociolegal processes that enabled the transformation of PR into a tax haven and therefore demonstrate the criminogenic practices emerging from this new economic structure. By looking at the role of revolving doors, corruption, and collusion in the production of the economic crisis, this chapter illustrates how colonial legality constituted the conditions for the crimes of the powerful in PR.

MANUFACTURING THE COLONIAL DEBT

This section focuses on five debt instruments, or techniques of wealth extraction and dispossession, implemented by banks and the local elites: capital appreciation bonds; scoop and toss deals; variable-rate debt; toxic swaps; and auction rate securities. These techniques reveal how the law and emergency powers enable a colonial regime of permission that led to the massive public debt. It looks at what Katharina Pistor (2019) has described as minting debt, and/or the legal process through which financial instruments and debt instruments become embedded in the legal system. Furthermore, this section closely follows the research conducted by organizations such ACRE, Hedge Clippers, and ReFund America Project that have systematically analyzed the toxic deals that led to PR's indebtment.

The discussion of the toxic financial deals that led PR to its current economic and fiscal crisis means avoiding the misleading interpretations that insist on blaming only Puerto Ricans for the current debt. PR did not come to take on record levels of debt on its own. With every bond PR issued, there were credit rating agencies (CRAs) evaluating PR credit, banks willing to underwrite the bond, and investors willing to buy it, knowing full well PR's financial situation. As the previous chapters showed, the imposition of the colonial state of exception in PR created the conditions, and even normalized, the financial crimes and state-corporate crimes here discussed.

Legalizing Plunder: Capital Appreciation Bonds (CABs) and COFINA

Scholarship on the Puerto Rican debt crisis has remained silent when it comes to an analysis of *how* PR ended up with a $72 billion public debt and $49 billion in pension obligations. Saqib Bhatti and Carrie Sloan (2016a) have noted that $33.5 billion out of $72 billion in debt is not actual debt, but rather the accumulation of interest on $4.3 billion worth of capital appreciation bonds (CABs). That is, nearly half of the debt owed by PR is not actually money that the government and its public corporations borrowed, but interest, at a 785 percent rate, owed to investors on bonds underwritten by Wall Street firms, demonstrating how Puerto Rican debt is the result of toxic financial deals with Wall Street. As an example, Wells Fargo underwrote seven different issuances of CABs for PR. These CABs have an outstanding debt of $21.5 billion, the principal of which is $2.6 billion and the remaining $18.9 billion is attributed to interest, an effective rate of 734 percent.[10] Goldman Sachs underwrote six issuances of CABs, amounting to $2.5 billion for which PR will pay $18.8 billion in interest, an effective interest rate of 746 percent.[11]

Capital appreciation bonds are the municipal version of a payday loan.[12] CABs are long-term bonds with compounding interest in which the borrower does not make any principal or interest payments for the first several years, and, in some cases, until the final maturity of the bond.[13] CABs are like a negative amortization mortgage, in which the outstanding principal grows over time because the unpaid interests get tacked onto the amount owed. Because of this structure, borrowers often end up paying extraordinarily high interest rates.

PR has $37.8 billion in outstanding CABs. However, the underlying principal of these CABs is just $4.3 billion. That is, PR only borrowed and used $4.3 billion. However, given the way these deals were structured, most of the debt is in interest that has not even accrued yet, which means that an important part of the $33.5 billion is constituted by future interest on payday loans.[14] These usurious practices exemplify how state-corporate crimes operate in the PR colonial context. Given that its exclusion from the regulation of the SEC in the early 1940s, that PR bonds are triple tax exempted, and that PR was not allowed to go into a bankruptcy before PROMESA was enacted, the US government paved the legal way for toxic financial practices that would not be allowed in any other jurisdiction of the United States. At the core of the extractive and usurious deals with Wall Street lies the exceptional colonial legal structure imposed by the United States in PR. Therefore, these techniques of dispossession are embedded in the colonial capitalist system and should be understood as a financial manifestation of a long history of colonial plunder.[15]

An important contributor to PR's debt is the constitutionally and legally dubious COFINA. As discussed in Chapter 2, COFINA was established in 2006 by PR's local government to refinance its extraconstitutional debt and tackle the lack of access to bond markets. Instead, it worsened the crisis by issuing high levels of CABs at usurious interest rates. COFINA generated $36.9 billion of PR's debt, of which $23.9 billion are CABs. However, the underlying principal on COFINA bonds is only $3.3 billion. The remaining $20.6 billion is accrued interest at the effective rate of 614 percent. Furthermore, on COFINA's CABs alone, banks charged PR $221 million in issuance fees.[16] This was possible given the exclusion of PR from the SEC regulations and given that local elites sought resources in financial markets instead of taxing corporations doing business in the archipelago.

Refunding Debt Through Fictitious Capital

Refunding bonds is the municipal version of refinancing, and it is used to refinance older debt, while scoop and toss financing is the practice of issuing new bonds to refinance older ones in order to push current debt payments into the future.[17] These debt instruments rely on the legal articulation of temporality to enable wealth extraction. While the temporal logic of the crisis exploits the necessity of "immediacy" to implement drastic austerity measures, these debt instruments rely on futurity as a mechanism to create artificial contractual relations through which banks and local elites can extract wealth. Though these practices are not by definition illegal, given PR exclusion from SEC's regulations, their use created the conditions that perpetuate colonial extraction and subjugation.

Two criminogenic instances emerge from refunding and scooping and tossing practices: excessive issuance fees and capitalized interest. Both phenomena produced extraordinary profits for Wall Street, while increasing the levels of indebtedness. Because Puerto Rican bonds are triple tax exempted and the PR Constitution guarantees repayment of debt, every financial transaction attracts a high demand from investors.

> Many of the Commonwealth's bonds were oversubscribed over the years, which meant that investors wanted to buy more bonds than were available. In order to close more deals and collect more fees, Wall Street banks began pitching scoop and toss deals so that they could make money off the same underlying debt multiple times. (Bhatti and Sloan 2016b: 3)

As a result, the PR government kept refunding its bonds to pay off the old bonds, generating long-term indebtedness. Nearly half of the $134 billion in debt that the Commonwealth of PR and its public corporations have issued since 2000 has been refunding debt.[18]

Predatory lending is an important part of PR's scoop and toss deals. These deals "were structured in a way that simply pushed payments into the future and, in some cases, actually increased overall indebtedness as issuance fees and capitalized interest got tacked onto the outstanding principal" (Bhatti and Sloan 2017d: 6). Every time the government refunds its debt, it must pay new issuance fees, which in turn ends up raising the level of indebtedness. Thus, the interest of the older bonds become part of the debt as money borrowed (capitalized interest), and the new issuance fees also end up accounting for part of the debt.

These deals raise some legal issues given that PR's Constitution does not allow the issuance of loans for more than thirty years, and it does not allow filling of budget gaps with debt. In many cases, PR, contrary to what is the norm, used scoop and toss to extend the maturity of the bonds passing the thirty-year mark, and the practice of filling budget gaps with debt was common. ReFund America estimates that UBS, Citi, Goldman Sachs, and Barclays have made $1.6 billion in fees on PR's scoop and toss deals since 2000—an amount that is now part of PR's outstanding debt.[19]

Even though the normal percent paid by borrowers in issuance fees is 1.02 percent, since 2000, PR has paid a 2.86 percent on average in its refunding bond issuance fees. In a particular case in 2011, PR paid 9.02 percent in issuance fees. These predatory practices have forced the PR government to pay $1.6 billion in total issuance fees for their $61.5 billion in refunding debt since 2000.[20] Furthermore, some banks, when underwriting these deals, charged PR with issuance fees in five instances. A telling example is the case of the UBS branch in PR. UBS served as an advisor to the Commonwealth's Employees Retirement System, led the underwriting of a $2.9 billion bond issuance for the pension agency in 2008, and then stuffed half of those bonds into a family of closed-end mutual funds, selling exclusively to customers on the archipelago.[21]

All of this was possible thanks to the elimination of the prohibition of paying more than the 2 percent on issuance fees under the Fortuño administration and the emergency legislation Law 7 of 2009. Likewise with Law 7, refunding bonds were no longer required to provide savings for PR and allowed the government to issue refunding bonds to make interest payments on other bonds without paying down the principal. This is a telling example of state-corporate crimes given that without the shift in regulation of bond issuance by Law 7, these fees would not have been possible.

Furthermore, a significant number of PR's refunding bonds were issued to make interest payments on older debt. This practice, known as capitalizing interest, turns the interest on older debt into principal and forces taxpayers to pay interest on interest. Since 2009, PR has paid $1.6 billion on capitalized interests.[22] This is to say that PR did not borrow to build infrastructure or provide services for residents, but rather borrowed money to pay out profits to investors and backed that with the full faith and credit of the PR government.

Banks applied the same practices that led to the 2008 global financial crisis to PR by profiting from deal volume, while being unconcerned with PR's ability to repay. Wall Street banks pushed much of refunding debt onto PR to safeguard their own profits. Investors and banks knew that PR's debt load was unsustainable, but they convinced public officials to borrow even more money to enable them to pay interest and fees. In the end, of PR's $72 billion debt, $36.7 billion is illegitimate. Unsurprisingly, the US regulatory agencies failed at preventing these criminogenic practices or to even hold accountable those who profited from these colonial state-corporate crimes.

Extra-Legal Techniques of Dispossession

Wall Street used three additional techniques to extract wealth from PR: variable-rate debt, toxic swaps, and auction rate securities. An important aspect of these techniques of dispossession is that Wall Street implemented them when the financial situation in PR had already worsened. These techniques were sold as alternatives in moments during which access to markets was limited and money was highly needed. In this way, banks targeted PR with complex debt deals, generating millions in profits for investors. History has shown that these techniques were, in fact, predatory lending structured in a way that would protect the banks even if PR was unable to pay the bondholders.

Beginning in 2000, banks convinced the PR government to refinance its debt into new variable-rate structures to take advantage of historically low interest rates.[23] These new variable rates were similar to adjustable-rate mortgages (ARMs), the same kind of toxic financial products that generated the 2008 foreclosure crisis in the United States and Europe. With ARMs, banks promise lower interest rates at the beginning of the mortgage. This comes with risk, however, because changes in the market can lead to significantly higher interest rates and balloon payments in the future. Wall Street promoted this variable-rate debt to get better deals and save money, and because of this, more than half of the refunding bonds that PR issued from 2002 to 2008 had variable interest rates.

Moreover, variable-rate debt products were not as good for borrowers as they were for underwriters. This is by design. Wall Street banks aggressively pushed the PR government toward riskier variable-rate debts so that they could sell expensive add-ons and collect millions more in fees. These fraudulent practices meant that the money that borrowers saved in interest from lower variable rates was offset by higher fees they paid for add-on products like toxic interest rate swaps and letters of credit.[24] In short, the same banks that created the risky products also developed and sold insurance protecting borrowers from the effects of their own risky products.

These add-ons also have their own risks, which have been called "toxic swaps" or "interest rate swaps." This is the second technique of dispossession implemented by Wall Street in PR. Perhaps the biggest risk of this kind of complex financial product are the outrageous termination clauses. PR was forced to pay at least $780 million in termination penalties to get out of these costly toxic swap deals. PR issued new bonds to pay many of these penalties, and, in several cases, the banks that underwrote these new bonds were the very same banks to which PR had to pay swap penalties.[25] The $780 million that PR paid is not money that the banks lent, but money that represents the future profits of the banks. This means that those banks collected swap penalties and underwriter fees from the same transaction.

The final technique of dispossession is auction rate securities (ARS). ARS are variable-rate bonds in which the interest rates are set at auctions. If no investors submit a bid at an auction, then the municipal borrower that issued the debt could be forced to pay a double-digit penalty interest rate to the bondholders that are unable to sell. That was exactly what happened to PR in 2008, when the ARS market froze. As a result, PR had to pay $630 million in outstanding ARS debt. It did so by either converting or refinancing its ARS into different debt structures that required even more add-on products like standby purchase agreements and letters of credit. Puerto Rico paid millions in additional fees to various financial actors for services like underwriting and remarketing bonds and providing credit enhancements.[26]

A key problem with the ARS is that Wall Street banks misrepresented the risks that this product represented. The fact that PR had to pay $631 million is not the result of bad luck, but rather the result of colonial state-corporate crimes.

> The underwriters that misrepresented how risky these deals were likely broke federal security law. Many municipal borrowers have successfully taken legal actions and recovered their losses stemming from ARS deals. The lead underwriters on PR ARS included banks like Goldman Sachs, Morgan Stanley, UBS, and Lehman Brothers. These are the Wall Street firms that targeted PR with these predatory loans. (Bhatti and Sloan 2017a: 6)

Neither bankers nor members of the PR government have been held accountable for their involvement in these predatory deals. While residents of PR have been enduring austerity measures, and consistently told that the financial crisis is the result of social expenditure, this section demonstrates that the debt is the result of collusion and toxic deals with financial institutions. The colonial state of exception imposed onto PR normalized colonial state-corporate crimes and guaranteed impunity.

TOXICS DEALINGS: FROM BANKS TO HEDGE FUNDS

While banks were manufacturing the public debt through the above-described techniques of dispossession, a group of hedge funds started buying Puerto Rican bonds. Originally the debt was bought by mutual funds such as Oppenheimer Fund, Franklin Adviser, Popular Securities, UBS, and Santander Asset Management,[27] but, as the crisis progressed, more and more bonds were bought by hedge funds. Up to 2016, PR's bonds were traded in Wall Street's secondary market at 5 cents on the dollar, which means that hedge funds who bought these bonds were expecting to make a 95-cent profit for every 5 cents they invested or a 1,900 percent return on investment.[28] Hedge funds were expecting that the debt would not be paid, and in that way, they would be able to engage in aggressive litigation and negotiations that would allow them to extract additional wealth from these financial instruments and toxic deals.

Critical sociolegal and criminological scholarship on hedge funds in US and US-centric markets is limited,[29] and in PR it is inexistent. However, as is true of many of the sociolegal and criminogenic issues discussed in this chapter, investigative journalists and progressive think tanks have systemically studied the role of hedge funds in PR. For example, Hedge Clippers (2021b) found that, like in Argentina, Greece, and Detroit, hedge funds have used a well-established playbook in PR, which includes: buying sovereign debt at a steep discount; holding out during debt negotiations to block any restructuring deals; initiating lawsuits to drain countries of resources and further stymie efforts to restructure debt; taking advantage of austerity measures and any debt relief initiatives; and maximizing payouts at the expense of local communities. Let's consider how hedge and vulture funds applied this playbook in PR.

Given its colonial status, PR's debt does not fall within the sovereign debt category, but rather it is traded in municipal bonds markets. PR bonds are very attractive to hedge funds and other investors since, as discussed above, they are triple tax exempt, have the constitutional guarantee that the government will repay, and could not (until the enactment of PROMESA) declare bankruptcy. Thus, when Moody's, Standard & Poor's and Fitch downgraded PR credit to high risk or junk status in 2014, over sixty hedge funds held $16 billion or 22 percent of PR debt.[30] Hedge funds became the sole investors willing to lend to PR, making up nearly all the participants in the 2014 sale of $3.5 billion general obligation (GO) bonds.[31] Approximately 275 investment firms tried to buy into PR junk debt, ordering more than $16 billion combined of the $3.5 billion initially offered.[32] PR government's top-three creditors between 2013 and 2016— Oppenheimer, Franklin, and UBS—started buying PR bonds in 2015, the same year that García Padilla declared the debt unpayable.[33]

Furthermore, hedge funds bought massive amounts of PR's bonds in the year following Hurricane María.[34] For example, Golden Tree Assets Management owned $587 million worth of PR's bonds before María, and a year after it owned $1.5 billion. Tilden Park Capital Management, another COFINA creditor, increased the value of its holdings by $370 million over the same period. General obligation bondholders Aurelius Capital Management and Monarch Alternative Capital increased their holdings from $39 million before María to $488 million.[35] These hedge funds saw Hurricane María as an opportunity to capitalize on PR's devastation, not as a humanitarian catastrophe.

Hedge funds hold out during debt negotiations to delay or block any restructuring deal. By not negotiating, hedge funds obstruct the debt restructuring process making it more volatile and expensive; drain the money and resources that can be allocated for financial recovery; and ensure that taxes designed for debt relief are reallocated to them. Similarly, vulture funds cash in while creditors who are participating in the restructuring get less.[36] For example, Blue Mountain Capital Management, Franklin California, and Aurelius brought lawsuits against the government's effort to enact a local bankruptcy law and lobbied in the US Congress to enact PROMESA.[37]

The influence of hedge funds in Congress is particularly evident when considering the role that Antonio Weiss, Treasury Department official and former employee of the investment bank Lazard Freres, played in the enactment of PROMESA.[38] Lazard was fundamental in PR indebtedness by marketing Puerto Rican bonds to hedge funds and even funding some hedge funds investments.[39] Lazard had significant investments in PR, and therefore, Hedge Clippers (2015c) suggested that Antonio Weiss should had recused himself from participating in the drafting of PROMESA. Instead, Weiss was a key player in the design, legislation, and implementation of PROMESA.

Since early 2016, bondholders and hedge funds were suing the local government at the state and federal level, demanding the repayment of the debt, as a strategy to drain PR's resources.[40] Aurelius Capital, which had just 0.5 percent of PR's debt at the time, challenged key aspects of PROMESA, going all the way to the US Supreme Court. *Aurelius Investment v. Puerto Rico*, as Rolando Emmanuelli recalled in our interview, was aimed at challenging the legitimacy of FOMB appointments with the intention of rendering any agreement or debt restructuring process null and void and thus providing an opportunity for Aurelius to further capitalize on PR debt. Hence, these hedge funds not only obstructed the negotiations, but also intervened in cases initially created to challenge the power of the FOMB in favor of unions and workers.

Several hedge funds were able to co-opt the bankruptcy proceeding to their benefit, thus, preventing unsecure creditors from receiving equal access to the bankruptcy procedures.[41] These investment firms and hedge funds formed groups according to the type of bonds they held, hired law firms, acted as an alliance during the debt restructuring process, and systemically excluded unions and pensioners from participating of that process.[42] The Mutual Funds Group claimed the largest amount of debt with $7.2 billion in various types of bonds.[43] This group also holds $478 million in GO (general obligation) bonds, COFINA, and Highways and Transportation Authority bonds. Other groups represented in the Title III process are the COFINA Senior Bondholder Coalition, the Ad Hoc Group of General Obligation Bonds, the ERS Secured Creditors, the QTCB Noteholders Group, and the Puerto Rico Electric Power Authority's group of bondholders.[44] The insurers National Public Finance, Insured Guaranty, Ambac Insurance, Syncora, and Financial Guaranty are also part of the litigation but are not in a group.

Similarly, elite global law firms played a key role in every step of the PR debt and bankruptcy process. In 2017 there were over fifty-five US law firms representing hedge funds, mutual funds, and banks in the Title III process.[45] These law firms were involved in the design of the specific financial instruments that generated the debt, in its underwriting, in crafting the contracts that made possible its allocation, in the litigation and negotiation processes, and even in the implementation of the austerity measures.

Hedge funds have pressed the PR government to implement budgetary cuts, privatization, and rate increases for public services even after PR has faced several disasters. Some of these hedge funds have requested substantial transformations of labor laws, salary freezes, pension cuts, reduction of governmental employees, and benefits cuts. Another example of how these hedge funds take advantage of debt relief initiatives can be found in the aftermath of Hurricane María. A day after María struck the archipelago, Oppenheimer Mutual Fund was promoting an optimistic narrative of PR capacity to repay its debt, and even suggesting that the government could use the municipal bond market to retrofit or replace critical infrastructure or embark on a master plan to rebuild areas that were largely destroyed. Similarly, several hedge funds started pushing for the privatization of public utilities and for lax regulations of finances and tech industries.[46] Perhaps two of the most troubling strategies implemented by hedge funds were, first, to keep pressuring the local government and the FOMB to prioritize debt repayment and impose additional austerity measures, disregarding the serious needs Puerto Ricans were enduring in the aftermath of María.[47] Second, these funds pressured local government to use aid relief and recovery funds to repay the debt.[48]

In the aftermath of Hurricane María, private equity firms, hedge funds, and Wall Street investors also started buying residential loan mortgages and foreclosing them, which deepened the archipelago's foreclosure crisis.[49] Hedge fund billionaire John Paulson and the private equity firms Blackstone Group and TPG Capital and its affiliate Rushmore Loan Management have been aggressively foreclosing on Puerto Rican mortgages, as well as buying properties on the archipelago. As it will be discussed in the next chapter, this became a key issue in the recovery efforts in the aftermath of the earthquakes of 2020.[50]

In 2015, hedge funds were meeting with the local officials and pushing for the complete repayment of the public debt at the expense of local communities. Hedge funds made over $1 billion in the restructuring of COFINA and over $7 billion in the Commonwealth or GO restructuring. As mentioned above, PROMESA does not provided a specific framework for addressing possible financial fraud or criminogenic practices. Similarly, there is not a binding international sovereign debt restructuring framework that could apply to PR given its colonial status. In the absence of such a framework, activists and organizations started mobilizing the law and the legal system of the state of New York. Given that most of sovereign debt contracts are governed by either New York State or English law, according to Hedge Clippers (2021b), New York State is uniquely positioned to address the criminogenic, fraudulent, and predatory practices implemented by vulture funds. One of these possible frameworks is the application of the Champerty law, enacted in 2004 by the New York State Legislature, which forbade invoking the "Champerty defense."[51] Notwithstanding these alternatives, the FOMB and the PR government moved ahead with the debt restructuring, which illustrates how the Puerto Rican crisis is the result of the crime of the powerful and impunity.

While hedge funds pressured the PR government to repay its debts, hedge fund managers have been using the archipelago as a tax haven to avoid paying taxes in the United States.[52] As discussed in Chapter 2, Act 22 of 2012 allows investors who move to PR to pay only 4 percent in taxes on dividends, interest, and capital gains. Similarly, Act 20 of 2012 provides tax exemption for companies, including hedge funds, that export their services outside of PR.[53] All of this, combined with the transformation of PR into a 98 percent opportunity zone, meant that more than 200 hedge funds have moved to PR, including John Paulson, Stone Lion Capital, Fortress Investment Group, and several other hedge funds involved in the Puerto Rican debt crisis.[54] Furthermore, several of the hedge fund beneficiaries of Act 22 contributed to the political campaign of Governor Pedro Pierluisi—yet another dimension of how law and legal decision-making enable predatory and criminogenic dynamics that manufacture a crisis by design.[55]

CAPITALIZING ON THE BANKRUPTCY PROCESS

The appointments of FOMB's members have been surrounded by allegations of patrimonialism, conflict of interest, and revolving doors. This section addresses some of the conflicts of interest in the two different compositions of the FOMB.[56] For example, after suing the FOMB in 2018, CPI obtained over 5,600 documents, letters, and emails that reveal how the US government, members of Congress, and lobbyists were in constant conversation about the next steps to be taken by the FOMB.[57] From which creditors and controversies to address first, to petition of information as to why members of the FOMB had not met major creditor groups including Oppenheimer, Franklin, Goldman Sachs, and Ambac, the emails demonstrate the constant colonial pressure.[58] Conflicts of interest are not limited to undue intercommunication with members of the FOMB by Congress; they extend from antidemocratic/ authoritarian ideology to active participation in the manufacturing in the public debt.

For example, David Skeel's background and academic career on bankruptcy can reveal substantial information on the ideological configuration of the FOMB. Skeel has worked closely and co-authored with Clayton Gillette,[59] author of "Dictatorships for Democracy: Takeovers of Financially Failed Cities" (2014), in which Gillette argues that takeover boards with near-dictatorial powers, including those that coerce or displace the authority of elected local officials, may be the most effective means of addressing the shortfalls and consequences of normal politics. Gillette and Skeel (2016a) expanded this thesis in "Governance Reform and the Judicial Role in the Municipal Bankruptcy," in which they argue that municipal bankruptcy proceedings should not be limited to debt restructuring, but should also reform the governance structure, given that, in their view, fiscal distress is usually a product of governance dysfunction.[60] Later, these advocates of authoritarian governance in the name of fiscal prudence published a white paper entitled "A Two-Step Plan for Puerto Rico," which outlined the main elements of what eventually became PROMESA.[61] Skeel (2019) has also published on the developments and implementation of PROMESA, and on his Christian conservative views of the bankruptcy process.

In terms of active participation in the manufacturing on the public debt, the conflict of interest surrounding José Carrión III, Carlos García, and José González are illustrative. Former chairman José Carrión is a Republican insurer with family ties to Banco Popular and brother-in-law of PR's Governor Pedro Pierluisi.[62] Hedge Clippers (2018b) published a systemic analysis of the alleged conflicts of interest surrounding Carrión and his family. For example, Carrión's wife, Gloria Benitez, as a director of the Health Insurance Administration (ASES), approved a series of contracts that benefited Medical Card System (MCS);[63] the principal shareholder is Advent Morro Equity Partners, for which Carrión served on the board of advisors. Two employees (Agnes Suárez and Eduardo Emanuelli) of Carrión's insurance brokerage firm Carrión, Laffitte & Casellas were appointed by Governor Luis Fortuño to the board of directors of the GDB and were in charge of overseeing several bond issuances. As well, the Carrión family business, Banco Popular, was not included in FOMB's lawsuits against a long list of underwriters in over $6 billion of bonds potentially issued illegally.[64] These connections between Carrión, the GDB, and other public corporations generated significant conflict of interest, particularly when considering that the FOMB authorized debt restructuring deals that granted immunity to current or former employees of Carrión's firm.[65]

The two bankers—Carlos García and José González—spent the last two decades working at Santander Securities and the GDB, playing a key role in the configuration of PR's $72 billion public debt. José González served as president of the GDB between 1986 and 1989, and later established and served as the CEO of Santander Securities (1996–2001). He also established a series of mutual funds known as First Puerto Rico, managed by the subsidiary Santander Asset Management, which as discussed above, mainly invested in PR's bonds.[66] In 2002, González became CEO of BanCorp, Santander's holding company in PR, where he served until 2008, even as he continued to serve as chairman of Santander Security. Carlos García became Santander Securities CEO during that time and was central in transforming Santander into a key player in PR public finances.

From 2009 through 2011, former FOMB member Carlos García held senior positions in GDB, including serving as its president.[67] Carlos García also presided over the Fiscal Restructuring and Stabilization Board, a board created by Law 7 of 2009, which managed the firing of thousands of public sector workers.[68] Carlos García assembled a team of former Santander executives to run the GDB,[69] and after leaving the GDB he returned to Santander where he became executive vice president of the US Bank holding company (US Bancorp).[70]

Santander participated in toxic financial deals that included CABs, capitalized interest, and interest-rate swaps that manufactured PR's debt crisis.[71] Santander helped underwrite a bonds issuance in 2011 to raise money to pay a $400 million interest-rate swap termination. Santander played an underwriting role of $61.2 billion—almost as much as the figure currently used as an estimate of the commonwealth's total outstanding debt load of more than $70 billion.[72] More than $1 billion was diverted from these bond deals as issuance fees for Santander and other banks underwriters. During his time at GDB, García authorized the issuance of approximately $19.7 billion in public debt. This translated into $236 million in commissions paid for the underwriters, including Santander.[73] To summarize, Carlos García and Santander were fundamental in creating and manufacturing the public debt crisis.

After serving over four years in the FOMB, José Carrión, Carlos García, and José González resigned from their positions in August 2020. President Trump then appointed Justin M. Peterson, Antonio Medina, Betty Rosa, and John Nixon as new members to the FOMB. David Skeel became the chairman, and Arthur González and Andrew Biggs remined in their position for another term.

Peterson, a managing partner of DCI Group, actively lobbied to oppose comprehensive bankruptcy protections and advised hedge funds pressuring for exorbitant debt payments.[74] DCI carried out a major media campaign to discredit the PR government and its debt restructuring proposal in 2014, on behalf of Doral Bank, which was seeking $229 million from the PR government.[75] The appointment of Peterson further demonstrates how hedge funds captured the FOMB and the bankruptcy process.

Medina was a former executive of Merck and executive director of the PR Industrial Development Company (PRIDCO) during the García Padilla administration (2013–2016).[76] Medina seems to have had an interest in Title V of PROMESA or the provision related to economic development and construction of critical projects. Accountant John Nixon helped Michigan Governor Richard Snyder develop and implement a series of austerity measures, pro-corporate tax framework, and cuts that paved the way to the Flint water crisis. That is, Nixon's public record as an emergency manager demonstrates a clear emphasis on preserving and enhancing capital accumulation to the detriment of poor and racialized communities' health and safety.

The conflict of interest and revolving doors are not limited to the members of the FOMB, but also extends to its employees. For instance, the executive director of the FOMB has a base salary of $650,000— amid the fiscal crisis. The role was first occupied by Natalie Jaresko, and it is currently held by Robert Mujica. Natalie Jaresko's alleged conflicts of interests have been systemically denounced by activist and pro-transparency organizations. After resigning, Jaresko became executive director at Ernst & Young, one of the consultancy firms involved in PR's debt restructuring. The revitalization coordinator has a base salary of $325,000 and was first occupied by Noel Zamot, who resigned in 2019 after denouncing several cases of corruption in the PR government. After being vacant for close to four years, in August 2023 José R. Pérez-Riera was appointed as revitalization coordinator. Pérez-Riera has a long history in investment banking—including UBS, Lehman Brothers, and Barclays—

and positions in the PR government. For example, before being appointed to this position, he served as secretary of economic development and commerce (2009–2013) where

> he personally negotiated the terms of tax decrees and other economic development incentives, including efforts as part of the team that oversaw the drafting and implementation of Act 154–2010, the Export Services Incentives Act (Act 20–2012) and the Individual Investors Incentives Act (Act 22–2012). More recently, he was a key figure in the drafting of the Incentives Code of Puerto Rico (Act 60–2019) as a consultant to DEDC.[77]

Finally, the in-house counsel, Jaime El Koury, has a base salary of $225,000. To these salaries we must add the payroll of over twenty-nine employees and millions spent on consultants and law firms. The FOMB and its appointments raise ethical and accountability concerns and illustrate the revolving doors between private and public services. This constitutes a clear example of how the colonial state of exception has enabled a regimen of permission in which the crimes of the powerful are normalized to the point that they become embedded in the policies implemented to management the crisis.

Specialized Knowledge as a Technique of Wealth Extraction

Around 1,000 lawyers, law clerks, and financial consultants, employed across more than forty firms, work directly on PR's bankruptcy; their fees are paid by Puerto Rican taxpayers. Hundreds more advise, and invoice, from the sidelines, without being required to go through the evaluation of the court.[78] Each side, the PR government and the FOMB, has its own law firms, financial consulting firms, and advisors, and their duplicitous work has cost taxpayers at least $1.5 billion between 2017 and 2023.[79] Table 3.1 provides a distribution of consulting expenses.

These lawyers, consultants, and advisors operate behind the scenes; some design and implement the fiscal plans and their structural reforms, other litigate in court or sit at the negotiation table. Some analyze the numbers and come up with the projections. A few design the solutions to the archipelago's fiscal and economic crisis. None of them, however, consider people's voices or what the Puerto Rican communities would believe is a just restructuring process. This is a multimillion-dollar operation in which, beyond the coffee or the

TABLE 3.1. FOMB Distribution of Consulting Expenses, 2017–2023
Distribution of expenses in consulting firms for the seven-year period.

Expenses for consultants, Financial Oversight and Management Board	$297,774,055
Expenses for consultants, Title III process	$1,192,798,602
Expenses for fee examiner	$9,780,502
Total consulting expenses	$1,500,353,160

Source: Espacios Abiertos, "Their Advisors, Your Money: Lack of Access to the Data That Have Informed the Restructuring Process in Puerto Rico," August 2023, p. 7: https://drive.google.com/file/d/11Nw8yAtzLN74suGatdcMMyeLLNhOcGm9/view

taxi paid while visiting PR (both covered by the government as reimbursable expenses), 98 percent of the expenses go to US firms.[80]

Luis Valentín (2018a) has also shown how the FOMB established a parallel government with hundreds of lawyers, consultants, and advisors. Among them, Proskauer Rose and another twelve law firms have been billing millions in the bankruptcy process. O'Neill & Borges, with Pedro Pierluisi, have also been key players in the negotiations and served as legal consultant for the FOMB. In addition to Proskauer, consulting firms McKinsey, Ernst & Young, and Citi Global Markets, along with another ten consultancy firms, directly influence the FOMB decision-making.[81] They advise on everything, from solutions to the fiscal crisis, macroeconomic projections, cash management, infrastructure projects, budgets, and fiscal plan.

In the fiscal year 2018, the government spent $90 million, some $25 million more than the FOMB, in contractor and consultancy fees and legal fees.[82] For instance, in one year, government contractors invoiced more than $1.7 million only in transportation and hotel expenses, over $220,000 in meals and about $260,000 in photocopies, printing, and electronic research. In the case of FOMB they billed less in transportation and hotels (roughly $260,000), almost the same in meals (some $200,000), and three times as much as the government in photocopies, printing, and research (over $850,000).

Espacios Abiertos (2023) analyzed the cost of the six most important bankruptcy cases brought under PROMESA between 2017 and June 2023 and found that the FOMB and the PR government paid $1.2 billion in consultancy and legal fees. As Table 3.2 indicates, the restructuring of the Commonwealth of Puerto Rico was the most expensive.

Together with these expenses, Espacios Abiertos (2023) identified all the consultancy and law firms providing services to the FOMB and the PR government, which includes thirty-four law firms (thirteen of which are local) and several consulting and advising firms. According to that investigation, the 44.2 percent of the $1.5 billion, or $527 million, has been paid to law firms and attorneys. They are followed by financial advisors and consultants, in what can only be understood as an extraordinary process of wealth extraction. Table 3.3 illustrates the top-earning twenty-five consultancy and law firms capitalizing on the bankruptcy process. Emergency management and debt restructuring in colonial settings, as the book has demonstrated, are not designed to address, and solve the crisis but rather to maintain and create news structures of wealth extraction. Certainly, legal knowledge plays a key role in that process.

TABLE 3.2. Estimated Cost per Restructuring Case

Distribution of expenses for restructuring the debt for each debt-issuing institution.

Case	Payments	Percentage
Commonwealth of Puerto Rico	$870,449,697	72.98%
Puerto Rico Electric Power Authority	$181,100,752	15.18%
Puerto Rico Sales Tax Financing Corporation	$62,816,102	5.27%
Highways and Transportation Authority	$41,004,842	3.44%
Employee Retirement System	$36,658,795	3.07%
Public Buildings Authority	$768,412	0.06%
Total	$1,192,798,603	100%

Source: Espacios Abiertos, "Their Advisors, Your Money: Lack of Access to the Data That Have Informed the Restructuring Process in Puerto Rico," August 2023, p. 11: https://drive.google.com/file/d/11Nw8yAtzLN74suGatdcMMyeLLNhOcGm9/view

TABLE 3.3. Top-Earning Consultancy and Law Firms During PR's Bankruptcy Process

Consultants and Law Firms	Payments
McKinsey & Company	$277,343,455
Proskauer Rose LLP	$224,501,233
Ernst & Young LLP	$133,822,886
O'Melveny & Myers	$93,106,672
Citi Group Global Markets Inc.	$80,065,662
Paul Hastings LLP	$74,465,049
PJT Partners LP	$57,500,000
Deloitte	$55,497,713
Ankura Consulting Group LLC	$43,353,310
Alvarez & Marsal North America, LLC	$35,689,438
Willkie Farr & Gallagher LLP	$30,104,642
Filsinger Energy Partners	$27,431,364
Jenner & Block LLP	$23,957,441
Zolfo Cooper LLC	$21,562,845
Greenberg Traurig	$15,952,155
FTI Consulting Inc.	$15,642,814
Rothschild & Co US Inc.	$15,243,782
Diaz & Vazquez Law Firm P.S.C.	$13,620,287
Brown Rudnick LLP	$10,740,427
DiCicco, Gulman & Company LLP	$9,316,429
O'Neill & Borges LLC	$8,748,714
Brattle Group Inc.	$7,656,017
Conway MacKenzie	$7,500,000
Kobre & Kim LLP	$6,721,929
DLA Piper	$6,340,489

Source: Espacios Abiertos, "Their Advisors, Your Money: Lack of Access to the Data That Have Informed the Restructuring Process in Puerto Rico," August 2023, p. 13: https://drive.google.com/file/d/11Nw8yAtzLN74suGatdcMMyeLLNhOcGm9/view

McKinsey: Conflict of Interest and Insider Trading

McKinsey has been central in the development and implementation of austerity measures, budgetary cuts, and other structural adjustments that have undermined PR's capacity to address the crisis. As shown in Table 3.3, McKinsey was the top earner among consultancy firms in the bankruptcy process, receiving $277 million in payment. One cannot understand the devastating impact of Hurricane María in 2017 without looking at the policies developed by McKinsey and their implementation by the FOMB and the PR government.[83]

The tasks of McKinsey included reviewing economic and financial projections, developing and executing fiscal plans, managing liquidity before and after Hurricane María, advancing in the bankruptcy cases, coordinating FOMB public hearings, compliance with fiscal measures, communicating with creditors and federal agencies such as the US Treasury, and evaluating the government's tax proposals.[84] McKinsey was contracted as the FOMB's "strategic consultant," signing a three-page vendor conflict of interest disclosure certification, in which it stated that McKinsey is not separately working with any people on the FOMB or any branch of the PR government. However, the statement said nothing about McKinsey's own investments or other potential conflicts of interest. As mentioned at the outset of this chapter, Congress exempted FOMB contractors and subcontractors from disclosure requirements under US bankruptcy law, allowing McKinsey to receive compensation for consulting on debt restructuring cases, such COFINA, in which its subsidiaries owned bonds.[85] These conflicts of interest ultimately led to the enactment of PRRADA in 2021.

Documents filed by McKinsey under PRRADA, however, indicate that conflicts of interest involve more than just repayments to bondholders. The firm has also reviewed public-private contracts and participated in the restructuring of government agencies. Mary Walsh (2018) explained that the investments in COFINA bonds were made through a subsidiary of the consulting firm, MIO Partners.[86] MIO manages roughly $25 billion for McKinsey's thousands of employees, alumni, and retirees. MIO, in turn, runs three hedge funds that have reported owning the sales-tax bonds and are seeking $20 million in repayments, according to regulatory filings and bankruptcy claims.[87] The firm also has millions of dollars invested in Whitebox Advisors, a hedge fund that through various investment funds holds more than $170 million in COFINA bonds.[88]

The FOMB commissioned an audit to Luskin, Stern & Eisler, and the report, made public on February 2, 2019, asserts that McKinsey's investments posed no conflict, although they "could create the appearance of a potential conflict." The following day, McKinsey paid $15 million to settle claims that it failed to disclose conflicts of interest in fourteen other bankruptcy cases. In November 2021, the SEC levied a $19 million fine on MIO Partners, a subsidiary of McKinsey.[89] McKinsey was just another vulture fund.[90] It was part of a predatory circle in which global financial institutions invented exotic new debt instruments; sophisticated investors bought them, even as they plunged into default; and then the high-priced consultants came along to ensure that PR paid the bill.

BANKRUPTCY CRIMES AND THE RESTRUCTURING OF PUBLIC DEBT

Puerto Rico has four primary types of public debt: general obligation (GO) bonds, sales tax-backed debt (COFINA), debt from PR public corporations (PREPA, PRASA, among others), and debt issued by localities.[91] This section focuses on the conflict of interest surrounding the debt restructuring process. ACRE (2021: 38) has shown that the FOMB has been complicit with predatory and criminogenic practices in the context of the bankruptcy by: proceeding with a debt restructuring process without a debt audit, which could have helped invalidate bonds held by hedge funds; engaging in extensive negotiations with hedge funds without offering local creditors a seat at the table; backing away from a legal challenge to bonds held by hedge funds; largely turning a blind eye to allegations of insider trading; and suing the government of PR when it tried to push back against unsustainable deals that would hurt its most vulnerable communities. Let's consider some of these criminogenic dynamics.

Legalizing Theft: Government Development Bank (GDB) and Title IV of PROMESA

The first debt to be restructured was the $4 billion debt of the GDB in early 2017, and it is paradigmatic of the revolving door and the questionable practices implemented by the FOMB.[92] Unlike bankruptcy processes under Title III, the GDB debt restructuring was conducted through Title IV of

PROMESA, an out-of-court process with limited sharing of information and transparency.[93]

The Government Development Bank Debt Restructuring Act (Law 109 of 2017) allowed for the restructuring of the $4 billion debt. Law 109 also created the GDB Debt Recovery Authority, an obscure statutory public trust and governmental instrumentality designed for the purpose of issuing bonds and acting as the manager of the deposits of GDB. This law limited the legal accountability of any of those involved in the debt creation, and its Article 702 established the biding effects of the restructuring transaction. This procedure precluded legal accountability of the individuals and corporations involved in the manufacturing of the public debt.[94]

Additionally, this deal normalized the revolving doors and conflicts of interest, as the case of Santander and Gerardo Portela illustrate. Gerardo Portela oversaw $5 billion in public financing deals during his time as a Santander Security executive, and then, as FAFAA executive director, represented the PR government in the GDB negotiating.[95] Together with Portela, Paul Hopgood, a former Santander executive, Portela was advising two credit union coalitions during the negotiations. Furthermore, as discussed above, Carlos García and José Gonzalez, at that time members of the FOMB, were former executives of Santander Securities and of the GDB, and José Carrión had former and current employees working with the GDB.[96]

In tandem with Santander and FOMB's conflict of interest, Jorge Irizarry Herrans—a former UBS executive, former president of the GDB and COFINA, and president of the board of trustees of the Employees Retirement System (ERS)—was advising the Bonistas del Patio coalition. During his time as president of the GDB and the ERS, Irizarry Herrans authorized three transactions, totaling $3 billion. These transactions were led by UBS, which fulfilled three roles: advisor, underwriter, and seller of the bonds. Despite referral to the SEC and an investigation conducted by the PR House of Representatives, Irizarry Herrans was able to avoid legal actions.

Nevertheless, lack of transparency in the GDB is not limited to conflicts of interest and negotiations behind closed doors. The PR government and the GDB have systemically denied access to information and blocked disclosing the bondholders.[97] The CPI sued the GDB and the government in 2015 to challenge the GDB's claim that creditor information is confidential and private.[98] All of this illustrates the revolving door between Santander, UBS, the GDB, and the FOMB and demonstrates how the colonial state-corporate crimes operated in the context of the negotiations, committing what can only be considered bankruptcy crimes.

COFINA and Title III of PROMESA

Only a year after Hurricane María devastated the archipelago, the PR legislature enacted the Puerto Rico Sales Tax Financing Corporation Act, which allowed the restructuring of the COFINA debt, making evident the techniques of dispossession implemented by hedge funds, the FOMB, and the PR government.[99] The public debt was never audited, and the above-described CABs deals were not addressed in this restructuring process.[100] Moreover, the FOMB significantly resisted motions for independent investigations of the public debt. In response to these demands, the FOMB decided to contract with disputes resolution and investigations firm Kobre & Kim to review how PR's debt was created. Kobre & Kim produced a 600-page general report summarizing key events that were crucial to the creation of the debt, without identifying officials and actors responsible for the toxic financial deals. The report does not constitute an audit but rather a survey of possible legal conflicts related to some bond issuances, the context in which they were made, and how PR's municipal bond issuers piled up debts.[101]

On February 4, 2019, Judge Taylor Swain approved the COFINA settlement and confirmed its restructuring plan, making it one of the largest municipal bond restructurings in US history. Thus, on February 12, 2019, old COFINA debt with a value of $17.6 billion was exchanged for $12.02 billion[102] in new COFINA bonds, which were divided into several current-interest-bearing bonds and capital accumulation bonds (CABs), for which balloon payments would be due in future decades, the last ones ending in 2058.[103] The COFINA plan of adjustment will result in payments of $32.3 billion in forty years.[104] That is, the COFINA agreement turned to the exact same financial instruments—CABs—that generated the crisis in first place. It is estimated that this plan resulted in over $1 billion in profits for the hedge funds that brokered the debt restructuring deal and will extend for forty years the life of the largest sales and use tax in the United States.

The biggest beneficiaries of this agreement were the hedge funds that purchased the debt when bond prices fell significantly between 2014 and 2016.[105] One of the hedge funds involved in COFINA debt restructuring was Whitebox Investment Funds, a subsidiary of McKinsey, which together with Compass Fund and McKinsey posed conflicts of interest that were not properly disclosed. The plan to restructure COFINA bonds benefited Wall Street, harmed most local Puerto Rican creditors, sent the Puerto Rican economy into an even steeper decline, and significantly increased the chances that PR's debt would again become unpayable within just a few years.

Challenging the Legality of the Debt Without Addressing Impunity

In 2019 the FOMB initiated a series of lawsuits intended to deal with extra-constitutional debt and other toxic financial deals. First, on January 14, 2019, the FOMB challenged the validity of $6 billion of general obligation (GO) bonds issued between 2011 and 2014. Three issuances were challenged in this initial lawsuit: a $415 million issuance in March 2012, a $2.3 billion issuance in April 2012, and a $3.5 billion issuance in March 2014.[106] The FOMB argued that these three debt issuances exceeded the constitutional debt limit and should be declared null and void.[107]

Abner Dennis (2019a) and ACRE (2021) have provided a detailed account of FOMB's rationale for challenging this $6 billion. Banks such Barclays, Santander, UBS, Morgan Stanley, and Popular made $294 million by underwriting these bonds, while Morgan Stanley, UBS, and Bank of America benefited twice on these deals by securing both underwriting fees and swap termination fees. Barclays was also a double beneficiary, acting as underwriter on a deal that was used to repay $342 million in short-term notes wherein Barclays had been the sole original purchaser. Banco Popular initially advised PR Government Development Bank to not pursue the 2014 bond offering, but then went on to underwrite the bond. In total, $36.8 million in underwriting fees were divided among the banks underwriting this 2014 offering.[108]

Banks are not the only entities that benefited from these transactions—law firms also received substantial fees. For example, Greenberg Traurig acted as bond counsel on all three deals, signing off on the legal validity of the debt. The law firm also acted as counsel on twelve bond issuances worth $9 billion. O'Neill & Borges, which has been the local legal advisor of the FOMB since 2016, also worked on each deal as counsel to the underwriters. On January 19, 2023, the FOMB filed a motion to request Judge Taylor Swain disqualify O'Neill & Borges for conflict of interest incurred in violation of PRRADA.[109]

In May 2019, the FOMB sued dozens of banks and financial firms over their role in the issuance of $9 billion of debt illegally.[110] The challenges included over 250 lawsuits against banks, bondholders, and companies that may have violated federal and Puerto Rican laws. The lawsuit included transactions related to four public entities: the Commonwealth of PR, the Public Building Authority (PBA), the Employee's Retirement System (ERS), and the Highways and Transportation Authority (HTA).[111] The 250 lawsuits could be divided in three groups: (1) government vendors that provided services to the commonwealth, ERS, and HTA in the last four years; (2) underwriters that participated in the bond issuances; and (3) bondholders with more than $2.5 million in holdings of the challenged GO and pension bonds.

In total, the bonds challenged by the FOMB totaled about $12.1 billion. This represents around 58 percent of the bonds included in the debt adjustment plan. Dennis (2019b) suggested that if we add the interest that the PR government will have to pay on these bonds in the next forty years, the challenged debt could increase up to $29 billion.

Despite these challenges to the legality of the debt, the FOMB attempted to negotiate a deal with hedge funds in 2019. Later, on July 24, 2019, amid the Puerto Rican demonstrations that ousted Ricardo Rosselló, Judge Taylor Swain paused the litigation challenging the validity of the bonds and ordered mediation.[112] The process lasted until November 30, 2019, which meant that for a significant part of the mediation the PR government and the FAFAA had limited representation, given that the executive branch was undergoing a series of changes after the resignation of Rosselló. Following the court-mandated mediation, in early 2020 the parties announced a new agreement that would rescind the legal challenges to the bonds and give the bondholders of the challenged bonds a much higher return. That is, despite millions of dollars spent in litigating to demonstrate that parts of the public debt were contracted illegally, no one was held accountable. Furthermore, the FOMB reached an agreement in which even those who participated in the illegal bond issuances would be paid. This is a telling example of what I have termed "bankruptcy crime."

But the story of illegality does not end there. In February 2020 several organizations raised suspicions that some of the hedge funds involved in the court-mandated mediation traded on nonpublic information learned through the confidential mediations.[113] A disclosure, filed on July 2020, revealed that some hedge funds increased their bond holdings by almost 400 percent, from

$16.96 million on August 30, 2019, to $83.945 million in January 2020. Similarly, some hedge funds sold off a substantial portion of the challenged bond just as its price soared considerably as result of the new agreement.

On August 5, 2020, four members of US Congress sent a letter to NY Attorney General Letitia James voicing concern about an insider trading allegation and calling on her to launch an investigation (ACRE 2021). Hedge Clippers (2020), for example, asked Attorney General James to use the powers of the Martin Act of 1921 to investigate and prosecute these hedge funds that profited from insider trading.[114] Nevertheless, James did not initiate an investigation.

On October 5, 2020, the National Public Finance Guarantee Corporation, a bond insurance company, filed a motion asking Judge Taylor Swain to order an investigation into whether hedge funds violated mediation confidentiality and engaged in insider trading. Similarly, Congressman Raul Grijalva, chair of the House Committee on Natural Resources, along with six other members of Congress, sent a letter to the FOMB requesting an independent investigation and asking for a halt to the negotiations with bondholders until the investigation was completed.[115] On October 8, 2020, Judge Taylor Swain denied the request to investigate these allegations, and the negotiation continued.

On January 18, 2022, Judge Taylor Swain confirmed the plan of adjustment for the Commonwealth of PR to restructure the $33 billion of liabilities against the Commonwealth of PR, PBA, and ERS and the more than $55 billion of pension liabilities—to $7 billion.[116] The plan of adjustment became effective on March 15, 2022. The Public Accountability Initiative estimated that, in the restructuring, hedge funds made $1.1 billion in profit.[117] The plan of adjustment includes cash payments of $7 billion for hedge funds,[118] which came from the savings generated by the austerity measures imposed by the FOMB in previous years. That is, each budget cut generated savings that is now being used to pay bondholders. Alas, the violence of austerity.

The plan also contains pension cuts of 8.5 percent to all retirees whose monthly pension exceeds $1,500. However, if the pension cuts and the elimination of benefits enjoyed by both pensioners and active employees are added, the adjustment plan would imply total cuts of 19.3 percent.[119] On June 9 of 2021, Pedro Pierluisi signed into law the Dignified Retirement Act (Law 7 of 2021), which sought to protect the pensions and benefits acquired by governmental retirees. Nevertheless, after the FOMB sued the PR government and the Pierluisi administration in federal court for understating that Law 7 of 2021 violated the fiscal plans, Judge Taylor Swain nullified the law.

BACK TO THE BANKS: OFFSHORE FINANCIAL INSTITUTIONS AND MONEY LAUNDERING

While the process of wealth extraction through the restructuring of the Puerto Rican public debt was unfolding, the US and the PR governments implemented additional tax policies that redefined and enhanced the role of Puerto Rico as a tax haven. In 2017, after the enactment of the Tax Cut and Jobs Act, as well as the implementation of tax-incentive policies known as "opportunity zones," 98 percent of PR became an opportunity zone. The law allows investors to reduce taxes on capital gains that they have earned elsewhere by shifting them to an opportunity zone. Investments held in these zones for at least a decade are not subject to any capital gains tax. This legislation has been key in bringing venture capitalists to PR and contributing to the establishment of international banks and financial services in PR.

It is precisely under this regulatory scenario that the PR government created the International Financial Center and promoted the establishment of offshore banks under the International Financial Center Regulatory Act (Law 273 of 2012). This law, now under Chapter 4 of Act 60 of 2019, grants tax incentives for new banking and financial activity in PR that provides services to non-Puerto Rican clients. The law created the financial and regulatory framework for at least eighty international banks or international financial entities (IFEs) to take advantage of the colonial tax haven.[120] According to the Office of the Commissioner of Financial Institutions (OCFI), offshore banks employed over 11,000 individuals in 2019. Act 60 established the legal framework to create a banking system for the tax haven.

An entire sector of intermediaries—including law firms, accounting firms, and governmental offices such as Invest Puerto Rico[121] and Discover Puerto Rico—have been promoting the archipelago as a tax paradise for wealthy US individuals.[122] Moreover, the Tax Justice Network (2021) noted that PR is the thirteenth largest contributor to tax evasion in the world. Similarly, other international entities, such as the European Commission, have consistently blacklisted PR, claiming that it is a money laundering jurisdiction. On April 18, 2019, the New York Federal Reserve (NYFR) intervened with PR's $50 billion offshore banking industry after it identified violations to US sanctions on Venezuela by offshore banks based in PR.[123] Violations included money laundering, conspiracy to launder funds embezzled from Venezuela, and tax evasion. Furthermore, Reuters reported that sixteen of PR's eighty offshore banking and financial service firms are owned by Venezuelan individuals or companies.

On August 4, 2022, the former Puerto Rican governor Wanda Vázquez was arrested by the FBI after a federal grand jury indicted her, the Venezuelan banker Julio M. Herrera Velutini (owner of Bancredito), and the former FBI agent Mark T. Rossie for alleged cases of conspiracy, corruption, bribery, and wire fraud. These arrests took place at time in which several federal and international law enforcement agencies have been intervening with PR and the banking activities established in the archipelago. For example, on July 3, 2019, the FBI raided the offices of South Bank International LLC in PR for alleged money laundering and wire fraud. Similarly, the Pandora Papers revealed that Blue Ocean International Holdings, a boutique bank based in PR, was one of the key players in the transnational networks of money laundering and tax evasion.[124] On October 19, 2020, the *New York Times* reported that a team of international investigators from the United States, Australia, the UK, Canada, and the Netherlands were investigating Euro Pacific Bank—another boutique financial firm based in PR—for money laundering.[125] The investigation portrayed how wealthy US citizens used PR's tax incentives and regulations to engage in money laundering, tax evasion, and fraud. Finally, on June 1, 2022, the IRS placed PR in its Dirty Dozen tax-scam list for 2022.

These instances of US and PR legislation and regulations demonstrate a particular pattern in the development of tax policies in PR. First, the historical shift in the regulation of financial and banking activities in PR created a particularly favorable regulatory environment that enabled offshore banks to be established in PR without adequate accountability. Second, the PR government sought to encourage investors to move to PR by providing tax exemptions and weak enforcement of regulations. Finally, the US government enabled wealthy individuals to relocate and evade taxes in PR through the creation of opportunity zones.

In April 2023, after almost completing the restructuring of the PR public debt, the FOMB published its certified fiscal plan, warning of potential budget deficits on the archipelago in 2027 or 2028.[126] After years of structural adjustments, the social harm produced by the austerity measures, and expending close to $1.5 billion in restructuring of the debt, Puerto Rico has been unable to address the structural conditions causing the crisis. This further attests to the central argument of this text: emergency management in a colonial setting is designed to manage the crisis and maintain the existing structure of wealth extraction, and not necessarily to address the crisis. Furthermore, the colonial state of exception imposed by the United States onto PR created a tax haven economy that enhanced the current crisis.

In contrast to the logic of colonial legality, solving the PR crisis requires a departure from purportedly technical strategies that end up legitimizing the exceptional measures and laws that generated the crisis. For instance, rather than holding accountable the financial actors and the political class responsible for the crisis, or addressing the exceptional tax haven structure, the US government has chosen to enhance the harmful impact of the crisis by imposing widespread austerity measures. Furthermore, it retains the very individuals who generated the crisis as crisis managers, without holding corporations, banks, law firms, and hedge funds accountable, exposing a troubling structure of impunity.

PROMESA does not provide mechanisms for holding accountable those who engaged in criminogenic practices. This structure of impunity is based on a legal design, and in the way in which bankers, emergency managers, and local elites designed the restructuring process. It is in this context that it can be identified how exceptionality, colonialism, and state-corporate crimes interact and define the colonial economy and how every sector profits, except for the people.

FOUR

DISASTERS

Hurricane María struck the archipelago as a Category 4 hurricane, with reported wind speeds up to 155 miles per hour on September 20, 2017, just two weeks after Hurricane Irma. María's landfall devastated the already fragile infrastructure and made Puerto Ricans even more vulnerable to numerous forms of harm and state violence.[1] As critical disaster and environmental justice scholarship remind us, Hurricane María was destructive, but what happened in its aftermath is what really became catastrophic.[2] For instance, on October 30, 2017, the UN high commissioner on human rights concluded that PR remained in an alarming situation, without an effective emergency response more than a month after the hurricane.[3] The commissioner emphasized that María had aggravated the archipelago's existing dire poverty and human rights situation caused by the public debt and neoliberal policies. Years after Hurricanes Irma and María, the earthquakes in January 2020, and the aftermath of Hurricane Fiona in 2022, the situation in Puerto Rico has only worsened.

After years of an ongoing economic and fiscal crisis, austerity measures, and systemic erosion of PR's public institutions, the Puerto Rican government was unprepared to confront any disaster, let alone four major socioenvironmental events in the span of five years. The repercussions of the disasters constitute a particular case of what I call colonial state crimes, and/or the criminogenic practices that the governments of the United States and Puerto Rico and their representatives incur and engage in as part of their public role in Puerto Rican society. This critical engagement with disasters involves thinking about how structures of power, legal configurations, and criminogenic dynamics can transform a geophysical or atmospheric phenomenon into a catastrophe.

This chapter describes how colonial legality addresses the period before, during, and after the disasters. To illustrate this dynamic, the chapter is structured into four sections. First, it demonstrates how colonial legality constituted a regime of permission that normalized colonial state crimes as part of neoliberal disaster management. Second, it discusses the uses of law and emergency powers to address the Hurricanes Irma and María. This section illustrates how the use of emergency powers did not facilitate or accelerate the recovery efforts, but rather created a chaotic scenario in which citizens were not provided with adequate aid relief, information, and recovery aid. In my engagement and discussion of Hurricane María, I also relay my own experiences and observations as a resident of the archipelago involved in grassroots relief and recovery efforts. Certainly, writing about Hurricane María, even years later, involves memorializing the abandonment, rage, and disorientation experienced by many Puerto Ricans in the wake of the hurricane. Thus, analyzing María from sociolegal and criminological perspectives aims to enhance our understanding of the impact of law and emergency powers in crisis management, and to make sense of the colonial abandonment experienced in the aftermath of the hurricane.

Third, the chapter discusses the management of the earthquakes and covers the cases of corruption that emerged from that management; as a result of the earthquakes, civil society organizations arose to promote a just recovery and to interrupt the trends of wealth extraction. Finally, the chapter describes the neoliberal colonial management of Hurricane Fiona.

Altogether, this chapter demonstrates how the austerity measures and the criminogenic dynamic discussed in the previous chapters created the conditions for these disasters to become catastrophic. Austerity measures systematically undermined social protection and weakened state capacity to react to crisis, which in turn exponentially increased the likelihood that poor, working class, and racialized communities would be harmed by the emergency management.[4] Thus, this chapter tells the story of the failures of emergency powers and argues that the mismanagement of these disasters must be understood as an additional episode in a long history of colonial state crimes.

NEOLIBERAL DISASTER MANAGEMENT AND COLONIAL STATE CRIMES

Studying disasters through a sociolegal and criminological lens demands a critical approach beyond a depoliticized view of socioenvironmental crises. It involves scrutinizing governmental attempts to depoliticize the state's role and elites' influence in shaping disaster conditions. These depoliticizing efforts often overlook the structural roots of crises, focusing solely on relief and recovery. Following Penny Green and Tony Ward's (2004) framework, vulnerability to disasters hinges on poverty, political authoritarianism, and corruption. PR exemplifies these factors, with colonialism playing a pivotal role.

Law and exceptionality are at the center of contemporary disaster management policies.[5] For instance, exceptionality is clearly present in the uses of the state of emergency, executive orders, militaristic rhetoric, and reliance on the private sector and corporations to handle the crisis. [6] In the United States and PR, disaster recovery is legally framed by the Robert T. Stafford Disaster Relief and Emergency Assistance Act (Stafford Act) of 1988.[7] This law set the statutory authority for federal disaster response activities, including the Federal Emergency Management Agency (FEMA). Generally, after a disaster occurs, the governor of a state or territory may request a presidential disaster declaration that activates an array of federal programs to assist state and local officials in the response and recovery effort. Additionally, the US Department of Homeland Security created the National Disaster Recovery Framework (2016) (NDRF), aimed at more effectively addressing disasters. In total there are over seventeen federal agencies that provide disaster assistance and aid, all of which require the declaration of a state of emergency to mobilize or to begin helping communities affected by disasters.

The aftermath of a disaster puts to a test the law's power to mitigate human suffering in the short term and to institute the kinds of social change that would prevent or at least mitigate future devastation. That is, legal processes delimit disaster, not only in statutes but in the process of defining, preventing, and allocating responsibility for disaster in courts and administrative agencies. Adi Martínez-Roman, the former director of the UPR Resiliency Law Center, pointed out in our interview that legality and the law are constantly being put to the test in PR. She argued that,

> a very particular problem of law in PR is how the federal regulations do not adjust to the reality of a highly impoverished locality like PR with a different civil law culture, which is not the same as the US. And not to mention the patent discrimination against us due to the lack of political participation and our blackness.

Martínez-Roman showed that it is not just that US laws and regulations do not adjust to PR's reality, but also that US emergency management policies and FEMA do not address PR's sociolegal reality. She pointed out that "the logic of governing in a state of emergency has evolved. There are theories that the emergency can no longer be quick, that it must be inclusive. But FEMA remains stagnant in the past." The negligent role of FEMA in post-disaster management in PR and its lack of preparedness became a salient exemplification of colonial state crimes.[8] Law and legal process are at the center of the neoliberal disaster management.

However, the limitations of the legal management of the disaster and overreach in the use of emergency powers is not simply due to the US colonial state of exception, but it is also palpable in the PR government's use of emergency powers. For instance, while discussing disaster management and the state of emergency, pro-statehood lawmaker José Márquez (Movimiento Victoria Ciudadana) argued that,

> I do not question the use the state of emergency. I think it is justified if you have a hurricane, if you have some earthquakes, you have a pandemic because you have to move, you have to move quickly to attend to those issues due to the immediate pain of many communities that are experiencing and people that are passing away. The government is not agile enough. The problem is the abuse, how far can that go in a government that aspires to be democratic. It seems to me that these powers must have substantive limits, which is what can be done in an emergency, and they also must have temporary limits.

Likewise, pro-independence lawmaker Denis Márquez (Partido Independentista Puertorriqueño) pointed out that Hurricane María and the earthquakes became the perfect justification for the governor to bypass the legislative process:

> As a mechanism, I say, there were moments in Hurricane María that I think issuing executive orders were necessary. Because we in the legislature came to meet after two or three weeks. Therefore, obviously there must be an executive order, but the executive order cannot be a substitute for the legislative process. Because, even theoretically, we represent, well, theoretically and politically, we represent the country, and we are the reflection and here it is that public policy is generated.

Both Denis Márquez and José Márquez argued that the uses of executive orders constitute an overreach in governmental powers and affirm the need to limit uses of the state of emergency. However, their conceptualizations of the state of emergency during a disaster reproduces the understanding that crises are moments of rupture within the normal functioning of democratic regimes.

The utilization of states of emergency in disaster management epitomizes the colonial legality, creating a temporal and spatial realm where regulations are disregarded. This approach, rooted in neoliberal rationality, posits that disasters necessitate extralegal and technocratic responses to ensure uninterrupted capital accumulation. Governmental declarations of emergency, ostensibly aimed at the preservation of public safety in the public eye, actually serve to depoliticize the disaster by emphasizing an immediate reaction to the emergency while ignoring the structural conditions that generated the devastation; maintain existing practices of capitalist accumulation; and serve the purpose of legitimating state crimes, such as systemic corruption, clientelism, post-disaster cover-ups, and concealing evidence.[9]

The concept of colonial state crime elucidates the dynamics of neoliberal disaster management and the relentless efforts of the colonized state to secure capital accumulation and wealth extraction even amidst socioenvironmental disasters. The uses of the state of emergency to manage the aftermath of disasters have not only created the opportunity for corruption and state-corporate crimes—an argument defended by disaster capitalist literature—but have also manufactured further crises and disasters. This conceptualization aims to shed light on specific forms of colonial plunder, wealth extraction by local elites and corporations, and structural violence based on the legal rhetoric of the rule of law and democracy.

There is prolific scholarship about political corruption in the aftermath of disasters.[10] This literature has critically engaged with issues surrounding

NGOs and neocolonialism, aid relief and disaster capitalism, and colonial and racist definitions of corruption in the Global South. Despite their important contributions, these analyses approach corruption and state crime from a moments of rupture framework. Oftentimes these analyses ignore the structural dynamics that enable corruption and state crimes, focusing only on the specific criminogenic behavior taking place in the aftermath of the disaster. They ignore that crises are often the result of legal designs. By following the concept of colonial state crimes, this chapter shows that corruption is not the result of a moment of rupture, but rather is essential to the function of capitalism in colonial settings.[11] Furthermore, given the economic crisis, I argue that corruption operates as a central element of disaster management since it allows local elites to continue with the process of capital accumulation, despite the limitations in capital reproduction interposed by the emergency.

In short, neoliberal disaster management has consisted of militarization; deregulation; outsourcing the management of the disaster and the recovery efforts; privatization of common goods and services; delays, lack of preparedness, and criminal negligence in the management of the crisis; transformation and redesign of public and administrative law; and the reconfiguration of the state. The systematic use of executive orders, deregulation, and militarization of crisis management has not provided relief and recovery for the people, but rather, has enabled corruption and chaotic management of the crisis.

HURRICANES IRMA AND MARÍA: EXCEPTIONALITY AND COLONIAL LEGALITY

After years of economic crisis, colonial legality and dismantling of the social welfare state, PR was unprepared to confront the damage done by Hurricanes Irma and María. This lack of preparedness included weaknesses in the power grid, the water and sewer infrastructure, and the telecommunications system depleted by years of disinvestment and mismanagement; inadequate communications and emergency preparedness among hospitals, health professionals, and the Department of Health; lack of clear emergency plans that citizens, public employees, and the private sector could implement;[12] weak social protection in areas such as housing and other basic services; a lack of food sovereignty and/or inability to locally supply basic needs; and a predominantly punitive approach to managing public safety.[13]

Hurricane Irma showcases how PR's colonial status—manifested through decades of disinvestment in the country's infrastructure, the overreliance on imported goods, and state neglect of social needs—increased PR's vulnerability to natural hazards.[14] Hurricane Irma served to contextualize the particular conditions of the archipelago, providing a sociopolitical referendum as to what María would entail.[15] The lack of preparedness and the mismanagement of the response to Hurricane María constituted a clear example of the systemic violence that colonial legality entails. Scholars and activists have shown that the local government collapsed and failed to offer an adequate response to the needs of the people, who were left without electricity, drinking water, telecommunications, fuel, hospitals, food, housing, and roads. This collapse also entailed a lack of communication from the government, which did not share any official data, statistics, or information for the first weeks following Hurricane María.[16]

Hurricane María has reshaped Puerto Rican sociopolitical legal structures and society, and as result, there has been significant examination and scholarship on the issue. This scholarship—together with the work of civil society organizations and advocacy groups—has shed light on issues ranging from political, environmental, and health concerns to racialized and gendered dynamics in the recovery efforts, to humanitarian and grassroots organizing and community empowerment. Building off that scholarship, this section demonstrates how colonial legality exacerbated the sociopolitical, economic, and humanitarian consequences of the hurricane. This section discusses three key issues: the uses of emergency powers in the management of Hurricane María; the cases of state-corporate crimes and corruption; and the undermining impact of the management of the hurricane on PR's capacity to address the economic crisis and future socioenvironmental disasters.

Hurricane María and Colonial Legality

Ricardo Rosselló's administration confronted Hurricanes Irma and María by invoking a state of emergency and imposing restrictive measures, such as a curfew, to manage the crisis. On September 17, 2017, Rosselló declared a state of emergency due to the imminent impact of Hurricane María. On the same day, the Trump administration approved a major disaster declaration for PR. Under Title V of the Stafford Act, FEMA was authorized to provide aid with any necessary emergency measures. Later, on September 27, 2017, President

Trump authorized a 100 percent federal cost share for debris removal and emergency protective measures. This included direct federal assistance for 180 days from the initial declaration.

Governor Rosselló issued thirty-one executive orders to address every aspect of Hurricanes Irma and María.[17] First, Rosselló issued two executive orders before each hurricane made landfall enacting the state of emergency and activating the Puerto Rican National Guard (PRNG) to assist in the preparation and recovery.[18] Similarly, on September 20, 2017, the Rosselló administration imposed a curfew from 6 pm to 6 am and mandated the PR police department and the PRNG to "take all necessary measures to enforce it."[19] The curfew was extended on September 23 and lasted for twenty-nine days.[20] According to Kilómetro Cero (2018a), the PR police intervened with over 125 individuals and arrested at least 67 for violating the curfew.[21] Mari Mari Narváez, executive director of Kilómetro Cero, noted in our interview that, despite legal challenges to the uses of the curfew and concerns over human rights violations, the PR government dramatically increased its uses of curfew to manage every subsequent crisis, as the fourteen months of consecutive curfew during the COVID-19 pandemic illustrates.[22]

Simultaneously, PR saw an increase in US military, policing, and private security contractors. In addition to mobilizing the PRNG and the US Army Reserve, the Rosselló administration created the Peace Officer Corps,[23] which authorized local or federal employees to arrest people in violation of the curfew or in violation of any law. Wanda Vázquez's administration expanded this punitive logic by enacting Law 144 of 2020,[24] which established that during an emergency or disaster, any public employee under the jurisdiction of the government of PR—whose duties include preventing, detecting, investigating, and making arrests of persons suspected of having committed a crime—should be considered a member of the Peace Officer Corps.[25] This expansion of public order agents entails a further extension of executive powers and exceptionality during periods of emergency, and it is concomitant with what the sociological and criminological scholarship on disaster has described as militarization of disaster management.

Rosselló's administration also allowed the secretary of public safety to accelerate the procedure to issue licenses to carry guns to private security officers.[26] Furthermore, in October 2017, employees of Academi (formerly known as Blackwater) were providing security services in affluent areas of San Juan,[27] and multiple US-based police departments also sent police officers to assist in the management of public safety. Many of these police officers did not speak or understand Spanish, had never previously visited PR, and lacked basic geographic, cultural, or sociopolitical understanding of the archipelago. This militarization and privatization of public safety in the aftermath of María entailed an intense emphasis on security and the unfolding of punitive approaches to the management of the emergency. Investments on reinforcing security created a general sense of military occupation, in which heavily armed individuals—mainly white American men—patrolling the streets contributed to the idea of state presence through the hyperbolic threat of violence, with vulnerable populations cast in the role of a threat to public safety.

The military occupation and its representation of force was aimed at securing the continuation of wealth extraction. These militaristic performances instituted a visual narrative of statehood in which the threat of violence became the primary interaction between the PR government and its citizens. Citizens affected by the hurricane became, through this rationale, the enemy of the colonial state; they needed to be surveilled, controlled, and excluded from public spaces. Thus, militarization did not contribute to the effective management of the shortages of fuel and water or the lack of electricity and telecommunications, which in turn undermined people's capacity to effectively address the emergency. Militarization of public safety became the only expression of "disaster recovery" that many citizens experienced in the aftermath of María.

Together with the militarization and privatization of public safety, PR saw an accelerated process of deregulation. On September 27, 2017, while Puerto Ricans found themselves without power and access to telecommunications, Governor Rosselló suspended all collective bargaining in the public sector for thirty days.[28] Likewise, on September 28, Rosselló suspended rules and laws regulating the process of hiring, contracting services, and public procurement by governmental agencies.[29] This executive order opened the doors to contracting and hiring without the need to follow regulations and anticorruption measures developed by the PR Comptroller's Office and the PR Office of Government Ethics.[30] Civil society organizations, and members of the PR accountability agencies have consistently characterized public procurement in the context of disasters as prone to malfeasance and corruption.

Similarly, Rosselló issued a series of executive orders delegating additional powers to the secretary of the treasury. First, Rosselló authorized the secretary to take all necessary fiscal measures, such as the suspension of VAT (value added tax) to address the emergency.[31] Second, on October 8, Rosselló established a body of auditors to oversee the distribution of aid relief, assess the damages caused by Hurricane María in each of the seventy-eight municipalities, guarantee that the procedures and transactions made by the executive branch follow the law, serve as auditor of any department, and fulfill any other function that the secretary of the treasury delegated to them.[32] This new body of auditors was independent of the Comptroller's Office, which could be read as an effort to weaken and limit the capacity of the comptroller to fulfills its constitutional duties. Third, the secretary of the treasury was empowered to exempt small businesses from paying VAT,[33] to exempt those who participate in the reconstruction of the electric grid from paying income tax,[34] and other measures that further enhanced the powers of the Department of Treasury. Rosselló's administration accelerated this process of deregulation and reshaping of the executive branch in the months after María.

The distribution of emergency aid sits at the intersection of militarization and privatization of public safety and the deregulation of the management of the emergency. For instance, on October 9, 2017, Rosselló issued an executive order allowing the municipal governments to distribute aid relief, emergency supplies, gas, and other necessities to address the aftermath of the hurricane.[35] With this executive order the Rosselló administration aimed at decentralizing the distribution of relief, since, up to this point, the distribution of aid had been largely administered by FEMA, the PRNG, and the PR government. However, this decentralization came too late, and the distribution of emergency relief in the aftermath of María constituted a clear example of criminal negligence or state crimes.[36]

FEMA was tremendously slow and inefficient in distributing aid provisions.[37] There were corruption cases involving the distribution and installment of provisional tarps or roofs, in which companies such as Tribute Contracting LLC did not fulfill its contracts. Two million meals went undistributed by companies hired by FEMA.[38] As Adi Martínez-Roman pointed out, almost all of corruption cases in the post-disaster management were associated with FEMA employees and US corporations.

Naomi Klein (2018) and others have described these practices as manifestations of disaster capitalism. These commentators argue that disaster capitalism implies the use of *shock* or moments of rupture to sweeping capital accumulation, disregard of legal structure, and the long-term dynamics of colonial legality. Against the logic of rupture, this book illustrates that the dynamic of exploitation, wealth extraction, and profiteering from crises ought to be understood as part of a long-lasting colonial entanglement of violence and domination.[39] Post-disaster predatory extraction constituted an acceleration of capital accumulation *already taking place* within the colonial legal structure of US imperialism and of colonial legality. The modularity of this framework, constituted through exceptionally, permits a rapid repositioning of the capitalist interest to extract wealth from this singular instance. Thus, the logic of ruptures defended by disaster capitalism only accounts for specific instantiations of the dynamics of colonial wealth extraction.

These dynamics were accompanied by negligence, cruelty, and incompetence. For instance, the Rosselló administration ordered that aid supplies—such as bottles of water and other emergency relief—should be stored and not distributed. While PR was enduring a leptospirosis[40] outbreak and some Puerto Ricans were drinking contaminated water from a Superfund site in Dorado,[41] the local government argued that they should not distribute the aid water and other supplies because they did not want to harm local businesses selling water. As a result, 16.5 million bottles of water were left abandoned in Dorado, and 20,000 pallets with bottles of water were left at the Roosevelt Road airport.[42] At least ten trailers full of food, water, and baby supplies donated for victims of Hurricane María were left to rot in the parking lot of the PR Election Commission Office in San Juan.[43] The trailers belonged to United for Puerto Rico, a group founded by PR's first lady, Beatriz Rosselló, to serve as an umbrella for donations. United for Puerto Rico was highly ineffective in distributing emergency aid relief and donations, and as several investigative journalists have shown, Beatriz Rosselló and other politicians allegedly deviated funds collected by this organization for their private use. Hundreds of thousands of dollars in donations remained unaccounted for, and no one has been held responsible for the mismanagement of the distribution of the emergency aid.[44]

The lack of distribution of aid relief was exacerbated by the limitation imposed by the colonial state of exception, and particularly by the Jones Act of 1920 or the cabotage laws. As discussed in Chapter 1, the cabotage laws were only lifted for a week in October 2017, and after Hurricane Fiona in 2022,[45] and not long enough to bring any real relief. PR imports about 85 percent of all the food it consumes, which meant that Hurricane María and the limitations imposed by the cabotage laws generated a food shortage. In addition to the restricted access to fresh food, the limited meals distributed by FEMA and other federal agencies were high in salt, sugar, and generally unhealthy, which in many cases enhanced the impact of María on the population's well-being.[46]

The Department of Health was unprepared to manage the public health crisis caused by María.[47] Days after the hurricane, the Rosselló administration resorted to executive orders as a mechanism to address the public health crisis. For example, OE-2017–57 and OE-2017–58 of October 6, 2017, allowed physicians and health professionals from other US jurisdictions to practice in Puerto Rico and be protected from any liability.

Omaya Sosa Pascual and Jeniffer Wiscovitch Padilla (2020a) have shown that the PR government established a Center for Emergency Operations in the Convention Center in San Juan between September 20 and October 31 of 2017. The center—which had electricity, water, internet, and telecommunications services—was intended to be a hub for all government offices to provide services and to coordinate emergency recovery efforts. However, it quickly became a space for "doing business": seeking contracts with the government and lobbying. In this context, the Department of Health granted millions of dollars in contracts to corporations linked to the PNP.[48] As Carla Minet, the executive director of the Center for Investigative Journalism (CPI), noted in our interview, the work of the CPI in the context of Hurricane María consisted largely of documenting and providing evidence for the lack of accountability and corruption:

> All the work we have done on public health, which since Hurricane María has been a permanent topic on our agenda, is completely tainted by corruption. Either because the contracts that are made in the Department of Health do not follow the parameters, or the contracts are for political favors, or because the officials do not have the credentials, they do not have the expertise, that is, they do not comply with what they are supposed to comply. Because public policy developed by officials is not informed by the data. They are all variants of the same theme. . . . They are different angles of issues that always lead to the issue of corruption, misuse of public funds, partisanship, involved in contracting—all these types of dynamics that ultimately result in the issue of corruption.

Hundreds of Puerto Ricans died as result of the lack of effective distribution of aid relief, the lack of preparation of the Department of Health, and the negligent management of the emergency by the PR and the US governments. Mismanagement of the emergency also meant that there was a lack of accurate reporting on the death toll resulting from María. Originally, the PR government reported sixteen deaths for several days. After the infamous visit of President Donald Trump on October 3, 2017, the local government changed the death toll to sixty-four casualties. As civil society and investigative journalists pressured the administration for more information,[49] the Rosselló administration created, on January 3, 2018, a task force to investigate the death toll resulting from the aftermath of María.[50]

It is important to consider the legal mobilizations to access the information on the hurricane's death toll. Carla Minet (2019) explains that very early in the emergency, the CPI started a database with information on all the cases of people who died amid or in the aftermath of María. CPI systemically gathered information and investigated the lack of legal documentation, including many people who were buried without an official death certificate or without any legal acknowledgment. CPI, together with Proyecto de Acceso a la Información, sued the PR government and the executive director of Demographic Registry Wanda Llovet-Díaz on February 7, 2018, requesting that all the information regarding the death toll resulting from Hurricane María be made public. The co-director of Proyecto de Acceso a la Información, Luis José Torres, recalls a demonstration that took place on July 1, 2018, in which thousands of shoes were placed at the PR Capitol building by families and individuals whose loved ones died as result of Hurricane María:[51]

> We always talk about the case of the deaths of María, but I think that the case cannot be discussed without talking about the shoes in the Capitol in 2018. The demonstration of the shoes in the Capitol, happened two weeks before the court's sentence came out, acknowledging that the information is public and should be released. So, there is a symbiotic relationship between mobilizing on the street and handling these claims, in which mobilization and collective indignation nourishes all the legal cases that we bring. But also, the cases we bring to the court seek to generate even more mobilization or more discussion.

In this clear example of cause lawyering and strategic litigation, Torres demonstrated how the legal mobilization for access to information or to know how many people died as result of the negligent management of the aftermath of Hurricane María constituted yet another instance of legal interruptions.

Moreover, the powerful display of mourning was key in the memorialization of the victims of the hurricane and set the path of the Summer of 2019.

A report by Nishant Kishore et al. (2018) found that over 4,645 people died in the aftermath of María, while the George Washington University Milken Institute School of Public Health published a report identifying 2,975 excess deaths between September 2017 and February 2018. While these organizations were trying to clarify the death toll, the Trump and Rosselló administrations tried to discredit these institutions. Rosselló and Trump took issue with these different reported numbers and argued that they were attempts to discredit their administrations and the recovery efforts. That is, the pain, suffering, and death of racialized bodies only count insofar as it helps manufacture a moral narrative of effective leadership.

The Rosselló administration deployed a series of classist, racialized, and colonial discourses around those who died in the aftermath of María, which caused rage and indignation among Puerto Ricans.[52] The demonstration of "the Shoes in the Capitol" and Rosselló's callous mockery in the Telegram chat led to the Summer of 2019 and the popular demonstrations that would oust him. The widely used number 4,645, the death toll of Hurricane María, during the Summer of 2019 demonstration became a reminder of those who died as a result of the negligent management of the aftermath of María.[53] This number served as a symbol of mourning, but also reflected the general understanding that Rosselló's administration, by not providing basic recovery in the wake of María, was responsible for the fatalities.

While the CPI and the pro-transparency organizations mobilized to access public information, the Rosselló administration systemically redefined the structure of the executive branch. In December 2017, the Law to Create the New Government of PR (Law 122 of 2017) was enacted, allowing the governor to restructure the executive branch without consulting the legislative branch. The law was intended as an emergency measure to allow the governor to exercise his or her executive law-making authority to deal with the aftermath of Hurricanes Irma and María. Simultaneously, Rosselló issued two executive orders with the intention of creating the Central Recovery and Reconstruction Office of PR (henceforth COR3).[54] This new office was created under the guise of the state of emergency declared to manage Hurricane María and was placed under the umbrella of the recently created Public-Private Partnership Agency (P3).[55] Two of the main arguments to create this new office were to organize the recovery and reconstruction efforts under one agency and to guarantee transparency on the spending of federal funds, especially after the numerous cases of corruption or mismanagement of public funds in the aftermath of Hurricane María (see as an example the $300 million contract to Whitefish and Cobra[56] energy corporations[57]). COR3 oversees and administers emergency funds for recovery efforts and developed a transparency campaign targeting petty corruption. The enactment of Law 122 and the creation of COR3 sheds light on the neoliberal rationality behind the use of the state of emergency as a dispositive to administer disasters.

Together with the creation of the COR3, the Rosselló administration declared the state of emergency regarding infrastructure aiming at accelerating the development of projects in energy, transportation, water, and other emergency projects.[58] The deregulations for the processing, evaluation, and designation of strategic projects were also created through executive orders.[59] Later, on March 20, 2018, Governor Rosselló issued another executive order to appoint the director of the COR3 as the representative of the government of PR before FEMA.[60] This appointment would be rather insignificant if we were not developing a sociolegal history of how the colonial legality and emergency powers became the key dispositive of government and, thus, of PR's public and political life.

The reconstruction of the power grid was largely conducted through executive orders and other emergency legislations. For example, on November 8, 2017, Rosselló delegated to the Fiscal Agency and Financial Authority (FAFAA) the executive powers to procure and acquire supplies for PREPA.[61] FAFAA was conceived as a semi-autonomous agency with the capacity to hire consultancy firms and seek external advice in an array of emergency and fiscal policies, thus enabling it to be more efficient at imposing austerity measures and other policies needed to administer the multilayered crisis. Similarly, the Rosselló administration suspended all environmental regulations limiting the uses of backup electric generators.[62] This deregulation contributed to an increase of air and noise pollution, which particularly affected people experiencing pulmonary and other respiratory health issues.

In their efforts to underscore the limitations and lack of information in the management of the disaster, Annette Martinez Orabona et al. (2022) have demonstrated the structural problems in PREPA and in its management of the aftermath of María. In addition to the $9 billion debt and the structural problems created by the austerity measures imposed by the FOMB and the PR governments, PREPA's emergency plans were inadequate, lacked information of the status of the power grid, and did not coordinate with the PR government. Likewise, PREPA did not have the necessary materials for repairing the electric grid, such as poles and cables. Additionally, the utility company failed to provide sufficient information to the public, leading to confusion regarding the estimated time for energy restoration.

Furthermore, as Fernando Tormos-Aponte, Gustavo García-Lopez, and Mary Painter (2021) have shown, the power restoration was largely uneven and marked by clientelism and patrimonialism. The authors noticed that those communities that traditionally voted for the PNP or the ruling party received their power back faster than those communities traditionally identifying with other parties or communities with a large migrant populations. Similarly, Tormos-Aponte et al. (2022) have shown how clientelism in the form of pork barrel spending and disaster resource allocation contributed to the unequal recovery. This became particularly clear in the context of power restoration and the distribution of aid relief.

It was in this context that the Rosselló administration, with the support of the FOMB and the Trump administration, initiated the privatization of PREPA. As Hedge Clippers (2018b) has shown, central in this process of privatization were banks such as Citi and JPMorgan Chase, which sought to capitalize from Hurricane María. Citi and JPMorgan Chase actively participated in underwriting bonds issued by PREPA in the 2010s. Citi served as an advisor to the FOMB in the privatization process.[63] Likewise, corporations capitalized on the post-disaster recovery by benefiting from FEMA's and the PR government's emergency policies on no-bid contracts. For example, Hedge Clippers (2018b) pointed out that FEMA awarded $17 million to Verizon, $6 million to AT&T, $7.9 million to IBM, and $8 million to a subsidiary of insurance giant Marsh McLennan. AECOM and its subsidiary Disaster Solutions Alliance were awarded a $122 million no-bid contract to provide food to hurricane survivors.[64] Moreover, Adjusters International, an insurance company based in Utica, New York, was awarded a $133 million contract in December 2017 to oversee 75,000 potential home repairs.

In the aftermath of Hurricane María, the Puerto Rican government was promoting the archipelago among US-based investors as being *open for business*. Brock Pierce, one of the key advocates of crypto economics in PR, was working with the PR government and local investors to transform the archipelago into a crypto paradise named Puertopia.[65] The idea was to use the devastation as an opportunity to rebuild the archipelago anew. Using the official slogan "Paradise Performs" and Acts 20 and 22, the PR government attempted to entice crypto investors to relocate to PR. Similarly, in March 2018, the PR government hosted the Blockchain Unbound conference in San Juan, seeking to attract "digital nomads."[66] Cryptocurrency became an intrinsic part of governmental efforts to recast the Hurricane María devastation and the economic and financial crisis as an opportunity: that is, the archipelago was promoted as a blank canvas, as an open and safe tax haven in which rich US individuals could evade taxes while keeping their American passport.

The crisis generated by Hurricane María proves the utter inefficacy of the state of exception as a policy to deal with crises. This undemocratic model proved incapable of meeting people's real needs, while simultaneously allowing the local elites, corporations, and transnational investors to use the hurricane to accelerate the process of wealth extraction and colonial dispossession.

US Colonial Interventions in the Wake of Hurricane María

Former President Donald Trump and his administration engaged in a colonial pattern of denial of basic aid and disaster relief while simultaneously engaging in performative acts of caring for Puerto Ricans. The well-known image of the former president throwing paper towels to people gathered in a church in the affluent town of Guaynabo attests to the Trump administration's response to Hurricane María, which was marked by disdain, colonial and racist tropes, and blatant disregard for the lives of Puerto Ricans.[67] The denial of basic aid and relief constituted a particular example of the logic of disaster aid evaluation and the ways distribution can exclude, discipline, and discriminate against marginalized populations. Based on anticorruption narratives, these interventions and denials of aid and relief became key features in neoliberal disaster management. That is, the corruption narrative and anticorruption intervention by the Trump administration became the disaster management policy.

First, FEMA insisted on imposing preconditions, such as the creation of accountability structures and transparency measures that guaranteed the proper use of funds. In response to this pressure, the Rosselló administration created the COR3. The agency administered over $38 billion under the Stafford Act and FEMA Emergency Assistance and Disaster Relief Act. It was precisely in this context that COR3 hired the transnational consulting firm CGI Technology Solutions to create a transparency portal to account for all the funds that were distributed in PR.[68] The first contract to CGI, issued on June 7, 2018, totaled $88.5 million. Since then, P3 has issued eighteen additional contracts to CGI, totaling over $194 million.

Espacios Abiertos has highlighted the lack of transparency behind the CGI contracts. For example, on October 27, 2018, Espacios Abiertos published a report calling for more information on the rationale for issuing these contracts.[69] Similarly, Espacios Abiertos noted that the COR3 transparency portal did not adhere to federal policies on open data and that the provided information was incomplete. On February 14, 2019, Espacios Abiertos issued a second report questioning the work of CGI in the transparency portal.[70] While CGI and COR3 were developing this platform, the US government did not transfer any recovery and reconstruction funds to PR. The distribution and allocation of recovery funds were slowed down by the lack of a proper mechanism to account for the uses of the funds.

Rafael Díaz Torres (2019) noted that to address citizen complaints regarding the management of the recovery funds, the transparency portal provided telephone number for Ethics Global.[71] However, when choosing the Spanish option, the system redirects users to a call center in Mexico, in which the personnel lacked sufficient knowledge of the ongoing situation in PR. Likewise, the portal lacked information on the status of complaints made by citizens, and the section of the website called "Report Information" was empty. Between 2018 and 2019, the transparency portal provided limited information on public procurement, contracts, and other details.

Moreover, COR3 did not conduct background checks on the companies it contracted in the early days, leadings to conflicts of interest and revolving doors.[72] This is the case of FEMA's former federal coordinator for disaster recovery for PR, Michael F. Byrne, who was senior vice president of ICF Incorporated between 2006 and 2010. ICF had twenty contracts with COR3 between 2018 and 2023, totaling $470 million. This makes ICF the largest contractor so far with COR3. In April 2019, Byrne transferred from FEMA to Deloitte Touche, one of the companies favored for contracts by the PR government.[73] Between 2018 and 2023, P3 issued twelve contracts to Deloitte totaling over $92 million. These contracts are intended to provide administrative consulting in all matters related to the management of disaster funds, including allocation and utilization. They also involve formulating budgets for general recovery efforts, training COR3 employees in fraud detection and prevention, and ensuring compliance with legal requirements related to disaster and recovery issues. The establishment of COR3 illustrates the dynamics of wealth extraction and that the profits from anticorruption measures are the result of a legal design, rather than moments of rupture or a period of emergency, which in turn exemplifies the operativity of the colonial regimen of permission in PR.

The Rosselló administration enacted the Anticorruption Code for the New Puerto Rico (Law 2 of 2018).[74] The law aimed at unifying the different existing anticorruption laws, and it was designed to address the administrative limitations imposed by the federal government in the aftermath of the hurricanes. Although it is true that the administrations of Rosselló and Wanda Vázquez were under investigation for possible mismanagement of public funds, behind these restrictions and requirements lay racialized and colonial understandings of corruption.[75] This is exemplified by the fact that these restrictions and preconditions were not required of the government of Texas in the aftermath of Hurricane Harvey.[76]

The denial of funds came from more than just the executive branch and FEMA, but also from other federal agencies. For example, the Department of Housing and Urban Development (HUD) was initially supposed to distribute $9.7 billion in aid to PR in September 2019 to help address the devastation caused by Hurricane María, which it never did.[77] After the 2020 earthquakes, on January 12, 2020, HUD released only about $1.5 billion of those funds. HUD cited corruption and financial mismanagement as the reason for refusing to distribute the aid fund. Later that week, after numerous Puerto Rican diasporic groups and congressional members pressured the Republican administration to release the funds, President Trump approved a major disaster declaration for PR of an additional $8.2 billion in disaster mitigation. Nevertheless, the release of aid relief came with a new layer of federal supervision and anticorruption measures.[78] For instance, FEMA appointed Alexis Amparo as the coordinating officer for federal recovery operations in the affected areas, and HUD appointed Robert M. Couch as the financial monitor to oversee the administration and disbursement process of disaster recovery funds. These anticorruption measures, and the imposition of federal supervision, have undermined PR's preparedness to address other potential future disasters.

The PR government and the pro-transparency civil society organizations reacted in different ways to the requirements and limitations put in place by the US government. For example, when I asked PR's Comptroller Yesmín Valdivieso, the Director of the Office of Governmental Ethics Luis Pérez Vargas, and the PR Inspector General Ivelisse Torres to discuss the cases of corruption in the wake of Hurricane María, they all pointed out two phenomena: that the US federal government put in place better and more effective anticorruption and anti-fraud measures and that the cases of corruption were limited to petty corruption. Pérez Vargas noted that "corruption has found fertile ground in two instances: in necessity and in abundance. In the face of the crisis, the unscrupulous person seeks to look for benefits to survive. In the face of abundance, like what we have seen after María with the recovery funds, the unscrupulous person seeks to benefit." This last point is further expanded on by Valdivieso who noted that

> After María, there was so much money here, and there was a lot of investment from the US Inspectors General Office to come and make sure that it was being used well. Because it was a huge risk. That the former president, you know, considered us all corrupt. But the reality is that right after María, and because of the amount of money, there was a lot of involvement from the *federales,* and they came and met with me, and I always said the same thing. I am here to help you and if we find something in any audit, we will refer it to you as we have always done. If they audited something, I would get out of the way because we don't have enough resources. Because we have two entities and more when we are talking about federal funds, they had the greatest burden of responsibility. So, we saw a lot of movement and involvement from the inspectors general, thank goodness, and thanks to the US comptroller general. The truth is that he helped. Otherwise, I don't know how we could have been able . . . because right now I don't even have the resources.

Here, Valdivieso offered important insights into the role of the federal government in overseeing the distribution of recovery funds and in the prevention of corruption. Valdivieso argued that the PR comptroller offices do not have the resources to audit and supervise the uses of the recovery funds, and that the federal government was central in preventing fraud and corruption in the management of the funds.

However, none of these interviewees identified problematic or questionable federal interventions with the PR government and the lack of distribution of recovery funds. This is particularly important when it comes to HUD's Community Development Block Grant-Disaster Recovery Program (CDBG-DR).[79] These funds, which have not been fully distributed since Hurricane María, show that anticorruption measures exacerbated populations' vulnerability and manufactured new conditions for disasters. Lack of transparency, accountability, and accessibility have marked the management of the CDBG-DR funds. Several of my interviewees noted the issues with these recovery funds and their distribution. For instance, Cecille Blondet noted that Espacios Abiertos had to sue the PR government and the FAFAA to make accessible the action plan and to provide additional time for its evaluation. She stated:

> After the money for María's recovery came, the FAFAA had to draft a plan and submit it to Congress. PR had 180 days or something like that, which was a requirement that none of the other jurisdictions had; there were very special requirements for PR. The plan had to be consulted with citizens before submitting it to Congress, and FAFAA presented it for public consideration for two weeks. It was 400 pages and a very technical thing, and they presented it in English. On the fourth page of the document it said that 78 percent of the population of PR does not speak English. The language became another barrier to access to information; the document is available, but it was not understandable for the people. So, we went to court. We went for two things: one to get it translated into Spanish, and two to get it to extend the public comment period. And that was another injunction that we also won.

This legal mobilization initiated by Espacios Abiertos generated a broader discussion about accountability and transparency in the uses of the recovery funds. It also enabled other civil society organizations to investigate how the PR government allocated the funds. For example, Sembrando Sentido (2021) carried out an evaluation of the uses of CDBG-DR funds and analyzed 127 contracts, 101 tenders, and over 700 relevant documents to assess the transparency of government contracting process, the efficacy of procurement, and the equity of the contracts awarded. Sembrando Sentido (2021) found that, in terms of transparency and access to the information, the PR Department of Housing (PRDoH) created a web page for CDBG-DR funds, which lacked basic information for tenders, contained unreadable or hard to read documents, and failed to disclose key information such as the contracting process, payments, and other assessments. Sembrando Sentido also found that the web page does not publish information on the subrecipients (including municipalities, private entities, NGOs, and governmental agencies). The subrecipients have been awarded $838 million in funds that do not necessarily appear on the portal in real time. Similarly, the report found that the great majority of contractors and subcontractors are US corporations or its subsidiaries. This has been an ongoing issue, and as reported by the Center for a New Economy,[80] a disproportionate number of contracts were awarded to US companies.[81]

Sembrando Sentido (2021) pointed out that the Tu Hogar Renace (Your Home Reborn) program operated under highly questionable contracting practices. For example, PRHoD made payments to contractors for purchase orders that exceeded $5 million, and that included work that was deficient or not carried out at all. Sarah Molinari (2019) has provided a detailed analysis of Tu Hogar Renace and has demonstrated the systemic problems with this recovery initiative.

Finally, restriction in the uses of recovery funds to repair the electric grid has entailed constant power outages and lack of reliable electric system.[82] Limitations in the uses of funds to rebuild public housing and affordable housing have exacerbated the housing crisis. Furthermore, the lack of recovery and unpreparedness to deal with disasters was exemplified by the devastating effect that Hurricane Fiona had in the southern region of the island, or the region that was affected the most by the earthquakes.[83]

The restrictions and oversight imposed by the Trump administration have limited or slowed the recovery and reconstruction efforts in the aftermath of Hurricane María. Fraud prevention and the anticorruption narrative uphold neoliberal disaster governance, inform state incredulity around ownership claims, and discipline state-survivor interactions. The importance of this cannot be overstated since disaster fraud prevention is a significant concern of the federal government. Nevertheless, what the Puerto Rican experience shows is that these disaster fraud preventions and anticorruption policies, which often operate along racialized, class, and gendered lines, became yet another manifestation of colonial state crime.

Federal Investigation on the US Management of Hurricane María

Three federal reports on the US government's management of Hurricane María were published in September 2022: the GAO (2022); the US Commission on Civil Rights (USCCR 2022); and the Office of the Inspector General of Homeland Security (September 29).[84] Both the GAO and the Office of the Inspector General audits concluded that FEMA did not manage the PR Disaster Case Management Program (PR-DCMP) in accordance with federal regulations. The US Office of the Inspector General noted that FEMA had no assurance that $17.1 million paid to eight providers was necessary to perform DCMP activities. Additionally, FEMA could not ensure the remaining $47.9 million in costs was adequately supported, thereby increasing the risk of fraud, waste, and abuse of funds.

In its examination of the federal response to Hurricane María, the USCCR (2022) found systemic violations to Puerto Ricans' civil rights. USCCR pointed out that disparities in aid funding between Harvey and María continued over time. For example, Harvey survivors received $1.28 billion within the first two months after landfall compared to $1 billion María survivors received in aid four months after landfall. The report recommends greater focus on the needs of most the vulnerable populations, including people of color, low-income households, immigrants, people with disabilities, and LGBTQ communities. Similarly, the report noted the importance of increasing the number of staff fluent in languages other than English. The lack of fluency or inability of FEMA staffers to speak a language other than English represented a significant limitation in addressing survivors of Hurricanes María and Harvey.[85] Furthermore, basic information regarding emergency shelter recovery support and emergency funds appear only in English.

Deepak Lamba-Nieves and Raúl Santiago-Bartolomei (2023) have noted that given the high poverty levels in PR, only 10 percent of the affected households were eligible for the Small Business Administration's (SBA) disaster loan program. Similarly, only 5 percent of households living on floodplains were insured by the National Flood Insurance Program. Largely, FEMA's Individual Assistance (IA) Program has been the most important source of housing aid and assistance in the initial years of Puerto Rico's post-disaster reconstruction process. However, it is rife with inconsistencies regarding approval of applications and denial of support.[86] Lamba-Nieves and Santiago-Bartolomei (2023) have shown that under the IA program, FEMA provides several housing assistant subprograms, including transitional sheltering assistance and rental assistance. FEMA under-used these programs, or the resources were not adequately distributed in the aftermath of María.

For instance, FEMA received over 1.1 million applications for individual housing assistance in PR and denied nearly 60 percent of those applications. According to the USCCR (2022), these denials were the result of "lack of proof of homeownership." In PR it is estimated that as many as 55 percent of homeowners did not hold a title at the time of Hurricane María, and at least 77,000 applicants were denied FEMA assistance due to title documentation issues. These denials were based on FEMA's interpretation of a Stafford Act requirement that assistance be limited to owner-occupied residences; however, nothing in PR's laws or regulations requires homeowners to register their properties.

Adi Martínez-Roman pointed out that in this context she and other lawyers, with the support of US-based funders, created the Emergency Legal Fund that was intended to provide legal help to people experiencing problems due to administrative issues such as the lack of proof of ownership. Martínez-Roman state that the organization, law students, and lawyers effectively managed to help people in need and engaged in advocacy to change these FEMA limitations. Thus, legal mobilizations initiated by the Emergency Legal Fund and civil society organizations, such Ayuda Legal and the Law Clinic of the UPR Law School, enabled modifications of these requirements in the post-disaster context.[87] In September 2021, FEMA adopted a new policy to make it easier for disaster survivors to prove ownership and occupancy of damaged primary residences. On December 23, 2022, the PR government enacted Law 118, aimed at accelerating the process to grant property titles to people lacking proof of homeownership.

According to FEMA's data, the agency approved 464,621 applications for the individual and household assistance program, which covers repair costs to primary residence, personal property, and household structural damage in designated essential living areas.[88] But this number fails to account for those who were approved but underfunded and for the more than 300,000 applicants who were denied. Furthemore, FEMA denied or did not respond to 79 percent of the appeal claims.[89]

Colonial legality has undermined PR's capacity to effectively address and manage disasters, exacerbating multiple forms of harm and violence in the aftermath of Hurricane María. Under these precarious conditions, Puerto Ricans have been asked to be resilient, to withstand disasters, and to be responsible for themselves, their communities, and the local economy. Once again, we can see how colonialism, and its never-ending legal entanglement with colonial life, is the catastrophe.

EARTHQUAKES, NEOLIBERAL DISASTER MANAGEMENT, AND NEGLIGENCE

On January 7, 2020, a 6.4 magnitude earthquake struck the southern region of PR. The earthquake and its aftershocks caused the death of an elderly person; the displacement of 6,400 residents who then took refuge in makeshift outdoor shelters;[90] over 8,300 damaged houses,[91] 2,500 of which were declared uninhabitable; and an estimated $3.1 billion in damages.[92] The tremors came while PR was still recovering from the devastation of Hurricanes Irma and María, including limited access to recovery funds and the austerity measures imposed by the PR government and FOMB to manage the economic and financial crisis. The ongoing multilayered crisis and austerity measures worsened the impact and devastation of the earthquakes and exacerbated PR's precariousness and population's vulnerability.

Former Governor Wanda Vázquez declared a state of emergency[93] and issued nineteen executive orders between January 7 and March 12, 2020, to address the aftermath of the earthquakes. Altogether, the executive orders follow neoliberal disaster management techniques delineated by the Rosselló administration during Hurricane María. The executive orders included: the mobilization of the PRNG to assist in the recovery and relief efforts,[94] as well as the creation of "peace officers" to support and maintain security and order;[95] authorizing physicians and engineers from other jurisdictions to work in the recovery efforts;[96] distributing recovery funds among affected municipalities and "freeing" governmental resources to help in the recovery efforts;[97] deregulating the process of contracting out private corporations during the emergency;[98] protecting animal welfare during the emergency;[99] and establishing some transparency measures and delegation of powers.[100]

The normalization of the uses of the emergency powers and executive orders has not only eroded PR's limited democracy but has also enabled a framework for corruption and human rights violations. The US and PR governments' handling of the multilayered crisis has manufactured a threefold criminogenic scenario in the wake of the earthquakes.

First, the Trump administration's reaction to the hurricanes and earthquakes and the lack of aid relief enhanced the devastation. As happened during Hurricane María, the Trump administration cited concerns with corruption and mismanagement as the main reason for denying the transfer of federal funds. A week after the earthquakes struck the island, President Trump issued a declaration of major disaster in PR, under the legal framework of Stafford Act, which allows FEMA and other federal agencies to assist in the recovery efforts. This declaration came after several public controversies and the imposition of new conditions on the archipelago's government to access $8.3 billion in delayed recovery funds for Hurricanes Irma and María in 2017. Furthermore, President Trump was reticent to sign the Puerto Rico Earthquake Supplemental legislation (Bill H.R. 5687), which provides $4.7 billion in funds for a broad range of disaster recovery and reconstruction activities, as well as providing additional tax exemptions.[101] President Trump's veto threat was based on the misleading argument that there is enough money in PR's disaster pipeline. This is deceptive for two reasons: in the context of Trump's veto, the federal government had not released the bulk of the recovery and reconstruction funds almost four years after Hurricane María; and the $45 billion is authorized to be spent on hurricane-related activities, not the earthquakes.

Second, a housing crisis manufactured by local banks, Act 60 (formerly Act 22) beneficiaries, and US investors undermined PR's capacity to house families affected by the earthquakes. Third, irregularities concerning the government warehouses and the investigation on former Governor Vázquez (i.e., negligence, post-disaster cover-ups, and concealing evidence) enhanced people's distrust in Vázquez's administration and led to popular demonstrations demanding her resignation. In what follows I discuss these criminogenic scenarios.

Banks, Housing Crisis, and State-Corporate Crimes

PR has seen the unfolding of a housing crisis since 2006, when the economic and financial crisis began. Jennifer Hinojosa and Edwin Meléndez (2018) have described two important aspects of this crisis: the number of vacant houses in PR has steadily increased since 2006; and the number of foreclosed houses has steadily increased since 2006 (with a short decline in the aftermath of Hurricane María). That is, while the stock of vacant houses has been increasing in PR, Puerto Ricans lack access to housing.

At the center of this crisis are local financial institutions, short-term rentals, and US investors. Between January 2008 and November 2019, financial institutions foreclosed on 44,788 houses in PR.[102] Banco Popular has executed a total of 19,066 mortgages or 42.5 percent of all foreclosures during these same years. In September 2019, financial institutions owned 2,952 residential properties of which Banco Popular owned 824 homes. Banco Popular is the leading retail bank in PR, and its board of directors is composed of family members of José Carrión III, the former FOMB chairman, and Governor Pedro Pierluisi.[103] These connections between the PR government, the FOMB, and Banco Popular demonstrate how state-corporate power creates the structural and economic conditions that exacerbate the impact of disasters.

As part of the austerity measures imposed by the FOMB, the PR government has managed to save $8.7 billion—in other words, it has created an artificial budget surplus by disinvesting in social welfare.[104] In 2020 the cash reserve had $8.7 billion—money that is destined to pay bondholders, hedge funds, and Wall Street banks that invested in the public debt. This cash reserve has been held in Banco Popular, and to make matters worse, the PR government lost over $49 million from not charging interest to Banco Popular and other custodians.[105] This exemplifies how the local elites use the PR government to guarantee their control over public funds. In the absence of federal recovery and relief funds, these missed funds were resources that could have been used to address the devastation generated by Hurricane María and the earthquakes.

The earthquakes exacerbated the housing crisis in the following manner: FEMA reported over 33,000 damaged homes across 33 municipalities; 36,523 individuals applied for FEMA assistance; a total of 18,980 occupants were 65 years old or older.[106] While this was happening, the local government did not take direct actions to allow the earthquake survivors to move into vacant houses owned by banks or the same financial institutions that have systematically profited from the economic crisis, the housing crisis, and corporate welfare.

In tandem with the disaster, short-term rentals or Airbnb have contributed to the housing crisis. Similarly, Act 60 and other tax exemptions have also contributed to the steady increase in short-term rentals (Airbnbs, vacation rentals, etc.) and to the housing crisis.[107] Hence, the housing crisis manufactured by banks, crypto investors, US-based investors, short-term rentals, and lack of regulation exemplify how neoliberal disaster management techniques enable corporations to profit from disaster.

Abandoned Warehouses

While Puerto Ricans endured the scarcity of basic disaster relief materials, on January 18, 2020, a group of citizens discovered a government warehouse in the southern city of Ponce with thousands of unused disaster relief materials waiting to be distributed since Hurricane María.[108] This discovery led to public outcry and a series of anticorruption mobilizations.[109] On January 23, thousands of protestors gathered to demand the resignation of Governor Wanda Vázquez for hoarding and stalling distribution of disaster supplies. On Twitter, the hashtags #WandaRenuncia and #Wandalismo trended on January 25 and 26. #Wandalismo, a Spanish play on words, combines the first name of Wanda Vázquez with vandalism, aiming to convey that Vázquez's administration, by not helping the affected communities, was engaging in vandalism against the people. These imaginative responses to colonial state crimes constitute an example of what I term *colonial ruptures*.

The warehouse in Ponce, as well as others around the archipelago, belong to the Puerto Rican Agency for Emergency and Disaster Management (henceforth Disaster Management Agency).[110] The warehouses were established in the aftermath of Hurricane María, in collaboration with FEMA, and were administrated by the PRNG. However, in May 2018, the PRNG transferred the administration of the warehouses and the emergency supplies to the Disaster Management Agency, which in turn did not distribute the supplies and ultimately abandoned the warehouses.

The discovery of the warehouse led to three investigations of the Vázquez administration's management of the earthquakes. The first investigation was conducted by the Bureau of Special Investigation in the forty-eight hours following the discovery of the warehouse, as instructed by Governor Vázquez.[111] The investigation focused mainly on official documents, some undisclosed interviews, and the analysis of the structural status of the warehouse. The investigation showed that the warehouse lacked electricity, water, and maintenance. The investigation did not shed light on the reasons as to why the supplies were not distributed, and it did not assign responsibilities. However, the investigation referred its findings to the Division of Public Integrity of the Department of Justice for further investigations.

Héctor López Sánchez, the author of the report by the Bureau of Special Investigation, who at that time was the commissioner of the bureau, was appointed as state judge on September 28, 2020. The appointment of López Sánchez as judge took place after the House of Representatives recommended further investigations against him for perjury, lying under oath, and concealing evidence.[112] In fact, the former secretary of justice, Dennise Longo, who was dismissed after recommending a special prosecutor investigate former Governor Vázquez's involvement in the case of the warehouse, referred López Sánchez to the PR Office of Special Independent Prosecutor's Panel (OPFEI).[113] The OPFEI would not investigate either Wanda Vázquez or López Sánchez.

As a result of the questionable investigation conducted by López Sánchez, the House of Representatives conducted its own investigation of the warehouse. The final report, RC 1696, focused on three aspects: the government's response to the discovery of the warehouse; López Sánchez's and the Bureau of Special Investigation's questionable investigation of the warehouse; and the lack of cooperation with the legislative investigation and possible perjury of Elmer González Román (secretary of state) and Dennise Longo (secretary of justice). The RC 1696 found that the state emergency management plan was inadequate and outdated; the Department of Public Safety lacked coordination and preparedness to address and mitigate the earthquakes; there was a lack of proper information and monitoring of the emergency supplies the government has available to address an emergency; the emergency supplies were improperly distributed; the Bureau of Special Investigation committed cover-ups and concealed evidence; and members of the executive branch refused to cooperate in the legislative investigation.

The RC 1696 made several recommendations including: the establishment of a special independent prosecutor to further investigate the preliminary findings of the RC 1696 and to prosecute any violation to the PR Code of Ethics and administrative and penal laws; the Office of Governmental Ethics investigate any violation to the PR Code of Ethics; a special independent prosecutor and the Department of Justice investigate and prosecute former Secretary of Justice Dennise Longo and Secretary of State Elmer González Román and Bureau of Special Investigation Commissioner López Sánchez for perjury, lying under oath, and concealing evidence; and refer the findings to the Office of the Comptroller for further investigation of any illegal uses of public funds.

The legislative investigation did not refer former Governor Vázquez for further investigation. Nevertheless, the Department of Justice recommended a special independent prosecutor for Vázquez and six members of her cabinet. Despite these referrals, on December 10, 2020, Wanda Vázquez, former Secretary of Justice Longo, Secretary of State González Román, and former commissioner of the Bureau Special Investigation López Sánchez were exonerated by the OPFEI.

The three investigations focused on legalistic and purely administrative aspects, such as lying under oath, whether the state emergency plan was updated, and the warehouse was up to code. Meanwhile, the negligence and criminogenic practices that led to thousands of emergency supplies being wasted when people needed them the most were relegated to secondary concerns. Thus, the use of the state of emergency propagated a colonial regime of permission that normalized impunity and negligence. This is particularly clear in the case of the investigation conducted by López Sánchez against the Disaster Management Agency. Furthermore, the emphasis of the anticorruption measures targeted petty corruption or low-level public servants, while ignoring the criminogenic behavior of those in positions of power. Most significantly, Governor Vázquez was never investigated, despite multiple referrals, and after a clear obstruction of justice for dismissing Longo for investigating the governor's involvement in the corruption case.[114]

Finally, none of the investigations mentioned the role of austerity measures and banks in undermining people's capabilities and the government's response to the earthquakes. The role of Banco Popular in the housing crisis, and the role of the FOMB in limiting the amount of funds available for the reconstruction, are largely ignored. This is the result of neoliberal disaster management techniques and its depoliticized understandings of the role of the state in socioenvironmental disasters, which mainly emphasize aid and disaster relief in the aftermath of the earthquakes and ignore the structural dynamics that propitiated an additional episode in a long history of colonial state crimes. Hence, by looking at disasters as moments of rupture, and not as part of neoliberal disaster management embedded in colonial legality, these investigations legitimated criminal negligence, abandonment, and impunity.

HURRICANE FIONA, VULNERABILITY, AND LEGALIZED NEGLIGENCE

On September 18, 2022, Hurricane Fiona made landfall in PR, leaving behind forty-four deaths, a general blackout, catastrophic flooding, and $6 billion in direct economic impact. The devastation generated by Hurricane Fiona further illustrates how colonial legality and neoliberal disaster management have exacerbated the impact of disasters, while further creating the sociopolitical, economic, and environmental conditions for new disasters.[115] It also demonstrates how human-induced climate change is increasing the frequency and intensity of extreme weather events for which PR is particularly vulnerable because of its inability to finance disaster preparedness and climate change adaptation projects.[116] Moreover, when Hurricane Fiona struck, the archipelago was in the midst of the COVID-19 pandemic and still recovering from the 2020 earthquakes. Thus, the financial crisis, the lack of investment in the reconstruction of the infrastructure after Hurricane María and the earthquakes,[117] bureaucratic limitations in the uses of recovery funds,[118] and anticorruption interventions created the conditions for the disaster to become a catastrophe.

Federal limits on access to funds have consistently hindered Puerto Rican recovery efforts. The US government explicitly earmarked $65.7 billion in aid for the 2017 disasters but has paid out just $19.3 billion, as of September 2022. Many of the fixes involve temporary haphazard construction.[119] This became clear in the aftermath of Hurricane Fiona, when scholars, and investigative journalists denounced the lack of reconstruction and investment in preparedness that left PR vulnerable to the impact of Hurricane Fiona.[120]

Governor Pedro Pierluisi's administration followed the disaster management techniques developed by the Rosselló and the Vázquez administrations to manage the aftermath of Fiona. Pierluisi issued seven executive orders to address the emergency. First, executive order OE-2022–45 of September 17, 2022, declared the state of emergency to address the impact of Hurricane Fiona. Unlike previous declarations of emergency, this executive order included a series of sections defining key economic and fiscal policies. For example, Section 3 provided for the activation of the emergency procurement procedures to acquire supplies and services. Sections 4 and 5 provide for development and implementation of an emergency budget. In this case, the FAFAA must authorize the implementation of such an emergency budget. That is, this executive order emphasized the economic and administrative measures to be taken in the management of the emergency.

On September 21, 2022, President Biden declared a major disaster under the Stafford Act, authorizing federal assistance for PR, local municipal government, nonprofits, and individuals through FEMA.[121] This enabled the transfer of $865 million in federal emergency funds to PR. These funds are divided between individual assistant programs; SBA approval of disaster loans; FEMA public assistant funding to assist communities by reimbursing costs for emergency works; the National Flood Insurance Program, among other assistance. Certainly, the distribution and management of emergency funds under the Biden administration has been more effective. Adi Martínez-Roman noted:

> Fiona's declaration of emergency included all municipalities in the North except Loiza, and all the municipalities in the South that were affected by the earthquakes except Cabo Rojo. That didn't make sense, and I asked the administration what the requirements are for us as an organization to be able to help municipalities to meet these requirements. You know, if you tell me what the requirements are, then I can help. Well, then the governor said one thing and FEMA said another, and then who do you believe. After our mobilizations and the mobilizations of the people, the White House fixed it.

Thus, legal mobilizations led by activists and civil society organizations forced a change in the declaration of emergency to include the predominantly Black and historically discriminated against town of Loiza.

Pierluisi's administration mobilized the PRNG[122] to assist in the management and recovery efforts, prohibited the sale of alcohol while the state of emergency lasted,[123] granted immunity to physicians and other health professional assisting the government during the emergency,[124] and established the Peace Officer Corps.[125] These executive orders follow the framework of militarization, privatization, and deregulation of emergency management.

Governor Pierluisi extended in several instances the state of emergency concerning infrastructure.[126] This executive order addressed Hurricane Fiona and included the recovery and reconstruction of the infrastructure damaged by the earthquakes and Hurricane María. The declaration of the state of emergency concerning infrastructure has been key in deregulating and accelerating the procedures to contract corporations and services, which as Sembrando Sentido (2021) has shown, has led to mismanagement of public funds and conflict of interest. According to Sembrando Sentido (2022), PR loses up to $3 billion a year due to corruption and flaws in public contracting processes, which result in low-quality, unreliable, and unnecessarily expensive essential services. These flaws—specifically surrounding efficiency, transparency, and equity—become evident in PR's inability to build back better. As Issel Masses (2022), executive director of Sembrando Sentido, put it:

> The sad reality is that corruption in PR is growing, not shrinking. States of emergency, such as during and in the aftermath of a hurricane, exacerbate the misuse of funds. That's when procurement controls are thrown out the window, allowing the government to use the "urgency" excuse to address foreseeable needs without rigorous planning, competition, or transparency. No doubt that spending fast is critical in an emergency. But it needs to be transparent to ensure it is accountable.

As Masses stated, urgency and/or emergency have been consistently used to deregulate the process of procurement, which simultaneously entails the rapid privatization of transfer of public good to private hands. As this chapter has demonstrated, with every disaster, a new process of privatization or public-private partnership initiative takes place. However, the emphasis on anticorruption and fraud prevention remains focused on cases of petty corruption, while these cases of wealth transfer and colonial plunder remain unaddressed.

On November 22, OE-2022–53 established special economic measures and tax incentives to promote the recovery in the aftermath of Hurricane Fiona. This introduced a new dimension of emergency management policies; the executive order authorizes the Department of Economic Development and Commerce to issue new tax and economic incentives by deregulating the process. For instance, the executive orders allow for expediting the process of issuing contracts, incentives, and other tax exemptions to corporations, investors, and contractors working in PR and provides for issuing no-bid contracts.[127]

As the Pierluisi administration was deploying neoliberal disaster management techniques, a series of scholars and activists started demanding transparency and accountability in the management of the crisis. In an effort to interrupt the logics of extraction, the CPI published a series of investigations evidencing that PR was unprepared to handle the hurricane. A considerable amount of the discussion revolved around the power grid and the fact that after five years, billions invested in the restoration of the power grid, and the privatization of PREPA, PR found itself under a general blackout lasting several weeks. The recovery of the power grid after Hurricane María was marked by patronage and clientelism, which in turn left PR ill-prepared for the earthquakes and Fiona.[128] Likewise, the privatization of PREPA and the bankruptcy process further undermined what was left of the power utility. When Fiona hit PR, only $40 million of the $9 billion in federal funds allocated to rebuild the power grid since María had been spent.[129] Similarly, LUMA's (PR's energy company) lack of planning during the transition as the archipelago grid operator resulted in daily blackouts, interruptions of critical electricity services to hospitals, damage to public and commercial equipment, and even fires. Despite these inefficiencies LUMA has been granted control of over $9.5 billion in recovery funds, without clear contractual obligations to comply with existing local and federal renewable energy goals.[130]

Similarly, FEMA has failed to create mechanisms for evaluating, responding to, or addressing the agency's recovery objectives. When Hurricane Fiona struck the archipelago, PR was already living under disaster-like conditions.[131] For example, LUMA did not follow its own emergency plan and did not provided information to governmental offices such as the Disaster Management Agency.[132] The lack of access to information on the recovery efforts has been a key pattern identified in the management of the disaster in PR, which is now exacerbated by the fact that LUMA is a private corporation. Lack of transparency and accountability became one of the key issues in the aftermath of Fiona.

In addition to the lack of reconstruction and preparedness of the power grid, the PR government and local suppliers or wholesalers of fuel and diesel were not prepared to address the emergency.[133] The Department of Economic Development and Commerce (henceforth DDEC) did not have a plan to address the emergency. According to the Energy Transformation and Relief Act (Law 57 of 2014), the DDEC's Public Energy Policy Program must be prepared and revised every year, before hurricane season begins. This energy assurance plan is meant to address the supply and distribution of fuel during an emergency, but despite the allocation of emergency funds to develop and implement such plans, the DDEC did not follow through.[134] Thus, immediately after Fiona made landfall, PR started experiencing a shortage of diesel, which affected hospitals in the southern region of the island in particular. This replicates the limitations and challenges faced by hospitals during Hurricane María. The lack of an emergency plan further exacerbates populations' vulnerabilities and undermines governmental, community, and individual capacities to address the general blackout caused by Hurricane Fiona.

An additional example of lack of preparedness as a result of the bureaucratic burdens and anticorruption measures imposed by FEMA and the Trump administration is the case of the Aqueduct and Sewer Authority (PRASA). After Hurricane María, FEMA and HUD allocated $5.6 billion in funds to ensure access to safe drinking water, to rebuild the public water utility and its damaged infrastructure, and to implement mitigation measures to face another storm.[135] However, five years after María, less than 1 percent of emergency funds had been used to buy emergency generation for water punts. Water distribution in rural parts of PR rely on electric punts and other electric equipment, which means that there is also a lack of drinkable water. The lack of investment and long-term planning have meant that in the wake of Hurricane Fiona, hundreds of thousands of Puerto Rican households were once again without potable water.

When Hurricane Fiona made landfall in PR, government-certified hurricane shelters were lacking water tanks, showers, emergency power generators, food, medical services, and other basic services for the people taking refuge there.[136] This is despite the enactment of the Service Provision Guarantee Act (Law 88 of 2018), which requires that the Department of Public Safety guarantee that all certified hurricane shelters have alternate sources for water and electricity services.[137] Law 88 of 2018 also sets the emergency guidelines to be followed by healthcare facilities, dialysis centers, nursing homes, gas stations, airports, and facilities that are used by the Departments of Education and Housing as shelters and other establishments in the event of an emergency caused by a disaster. The law was legislated in the aftermath of Hurricane María to address the serious deficiencies that caused the lives of thousands of Puerto Ricans. However, the law was never implemented given the austerity measures imposed by PR and the FOMB. The great majority of the shelters suffered severe damage after the earthquakes of 2020 and were never repaired, while those that were not affected by the earthquakes were never equipped with the basic services required by Law 88 of 2018.[138]

In addition to this law, the Disaster Management Agency failed to comply with the Essential Communication Act (Law 39 of 2019).[139] The law was enacted with the intention of guaranteeing that local press—including radio, television, newspapers, and digital media—had access to emergency supplies and equipment so that they can communicate with the public. The law came into effect as result of the general loss of communications during Hurricane María and in its aftermath. One of the key issues with telecommunication in the aftermath of Hurricane María was that cell towers, radio stations, and other essential services did not have emergency power generators or did not have access to fuel. The law aimed at facilitating access to fuel during the disaster, but the Disaster Management Agency and the COR3 did not have a plan to guarantee such access.

The aftermath of Fiona attests to the incapacity of colonial legality to effectively address people's needs amid disasters. The lack of compliance with the multiple laws and regulations legislated in the aftermath of Hurricane María demonstrates the inability of colonial legality to effectively address disasters and crises through legal interventions. At its core, this legal dynamic is more of an effort to manage the crisis than to provide citizens with the necessary instruments to endure disasters. It was precisely in this context that grassroots organizations and communities developed effectives strategies to address and face the disasters.

This chapter has demonstrated how the PR government developed a series of neoliberal disaster management techniques to address the multiple disasters affecting the archipelago since 2017. Neoliberal disaster management relies heavily on the uses of emergency powers and executive orders to manage the disasters, and it is embedded in longstanding legal practices of colonial legality. These practices include the suspension of the rule of law, human rights infringements, and multiple forms of state violence—generating or systematizing what I have called colonial state crimes.

Neoliberal disaster management shows how the colonial structure and multilayered crisis created an ideal scenario for state-corporate crimes, and criminal negligence. That is, banks, US-based corporations, hedge funds, and other disaster managers would not be able to profit without the tax incentives and corporate welfare provided by the US and PR governments. Similarly, banks and the FOMB were central in manufacturing the housing crisis and in undermining PR preparedness for disasters through the systemic imposition of austerity measures. Negligence and corruption in the management of disaster are a fundamental part of the structure of colonial state crimes in PR.

Simultaneously, the Trump administration, by embracing colonial anti-corruption policies and denying the transfer of aid relief funds, exacerbated the economic and social impact of the disasters here discussed. The Trump administration manufactured a public rhetoric of corruption and the imposition of colonial technologies that legitimized the corruption of the powerful. Meanwhile, the civil society organizations, legal actors, and grassroots organizations systemically demanded accountability, access to information, and transparency. These mobilizations in many instances created the conditions for interrupting the accelerated process of wealth extraction and capital accumulation.

Several scholars and activists have shown how the emergence of grassroots organizations, community efforts, and mutual support initiatives in the aftermath of Hurricanes María and Fiona and after the earthquakes played a central role in the recovery efforts.[140] From mutual support centers or CAMs, to feminist organizations, to collectives of independent farmers, the recovery after disasters was largely made possible by grassroots organizations disentangling from the local government and the state. For example, Jacqueline Villarubia-Mendoza and Roberto Vélez-Vélez (2020) have shown how the CAMs were the result of a long process of activism that led to these organizations being better situated to address the emergency. As Vélez-Vélez and Villarubia-Mendoza (2021) point out, the counter-narrative of mutual aid and solidarity that was articulated and put into motion by these organizations sought to undermine the other narratives generated by the government's disaster management by sharing, cultivating, and nurturing practices of implicative participation, reciprocal commitment, and collectivist resource management, all towards a new sociability. In addressing recovery and development from a bottom-up approach that empowers communities and intervenes in the structural conditions that manufacture peoples' vulnerability, the CAM projects reproduced solidarity as practice and principle, structure and agency, key elements in a proposal of social transformation. These principles entailed a significant rupture with the logic of disaster management in PR and set the foundations for the Summer of 2019.

FIVE

PROMISES

The management of the COVID-19 pandemic by the PR government constituted a further instance of how colonial legality rapidly reaccommodates to administer a crisis while maintaining existing forms of capital accumulation and creating new spaces for wealth extraction. Puerto Rico implemented legal measures and emergency powers to address the public health crisis caused by the COVID-19 pandemic.[1] Some of these interventions included stay-at-home orders, lockdowns, quarantines, mask and vaccination mandates, travel restrictions, rules for business operations, restrictions on alcohol sales, and curfews. The continuous use of emergency powers to contain the impact of the COVID-19 pandemic and the lack of a well-defined emergency policy further eroded Puerto Rican internal democracy and exacerbated previously existing forms of social harm, inequality, and vulnerabilities generated by the multilayered crisis.

It is precisely in this context that the state of emergency, executive orders, and the emphasis on individual responsibility had become key emergency measures for dealing with any crisis. For example, overreach in the uses of emergency powers is particularly evident in how the administrations of Wanda Vázquez (August 2019 to December 2020) and Pedro Pierluisi (January 2021 to this writing) managed the COVID-19 pandemic. Between March 12 and December 30, 2020, former Governor Vázquez issued forty-eight executive orders to address the pandemic, while Governor Pierluisi issued forty-six executive orders to this same end after taking office on January 2, 2021. These executive orders and emergency declarations were often contradictory, unclear, and ineffective in addressing the pandemic.

PR has been experiencing a public health crisis driven by limited resources allocated for preventive healthcare, austerity measures, and primary care privatization since the early 2000s.[2] The economic crisis, PROMESA, and the FOMB were at the center of the lack of resources to address the pandemic and the further weakening of public health in PR.[3] The effects of austerity on public health are palpable for residents of PR—especially for people with mental and physical disabilities, municipality island residents, rural residents, sexual and gender minorities, and migrants—who struggle with a lack of dignified healthcare access. Under these precarious conditions, Puerto Ricans were again asked to be resilient, to withstand disasters (without the protection of the US and PR governments), and to be responsible for themselves and their communities.

This chapter interrogates the role of law and emergency powers in the pandemic. To begin, it describes how multiple declarations of a state of emergency, along with frequent renewals, resulted in a contradictory and often chaotic public policy. Next, the chapter delves into the role of pharmaceutical companies in undermining PR's capacity to react to the COVID-19 pandemic. This discussion follows debates in the United States and in PR that explored the possibility of bringing back or onshoring the pharmaceutical industry. The dynamic of tax evasion and profiteering deployed by the pharmaceutical and biotechnology industries in PR clearly exemplifies how the colonial state of exception enables wealth extraction. Simultaneously, it highlights how the new tax exemptions and policies created under Trump's administration for the pharmaceutical and biotech industries in PR reproduced a moral economy of fraud based on the same colonial and exceptional practices that brought PR to the current multilayered crisis. Then, the chapter explores the cases of fraud and corruption surrounding the procurement of COVID-19 test kits and medical equipment, and the distribution of Paycheck Protection Program (PPP) loans.

Finally, the chapter looks at the punitive policies implemented by the PR and US governments during the pandemic. Particularly, the section looks at the impact of Law 35 of 2020, which imposes severe penalties on those who disobey an executive order. Under this law, hundreds of Puerto Ricans were arrested, fined, and even sent to prison for violations of executive orders. This section of the chapter also examines how, under the guise of anticorruption and fraud prevention, the PR government implemented anticorruption policies that limited access to Pandemic Unemployment Assistance (PUA) to those who needed it the most (mainly poor and racialized individuals, immigrants, and working women). Thus, the chapter argues that colonial legality created the conditions for corporate tax avoidance, corruption, and human rights abuses, while exacerbating the impact of the COVID-19 pandemic.

COVID-19 PANDEMIC, EMERGENCY POWERS, AND COLONIAL LEGALITY

Public health and law scholarship has consistently underscored the limits, failures, and contradictions in the legal response to the pandemic.[4] For instance, Andrew Rudalevige and Victoria Yu (2020) introduced an important discussion of the powers and limits of the US statutory framework, including the National Emergency Powers Act,[5] the Stafford Act,[6] the Defense Production Act,[7] the Public Health Service Act,[8] and several other statutes that enable the use of emergency powers in the United States. This overview is important for analyzing the pandemic emergency powers since the US and PR public health policies mainly operated under the protection of these statutes and administrative law. However, in the case of PR, we can identify a colonial dimension of this operation, given that in every instance, the US Congress must decide the extent and scope of the applicability of these statutes and other emergency laws to PR.

Despite the centrality of law in pandemic management, it has not been free of debate and contention, especially in Global North liberal democracies where misinformation and polarization defined the societal reaction to COVID-19.[9] On one hand, several scholars have argued that the management of the COVID-19 global pandemic has been heavily based on the uses of the state of exception, executive orders, militaristic rhetoric, the private sector, and corporations.[10] On the other hand, David Pozen and Kim Lane Scheppele (2020) have demonstrated how the Trump administration systemically underreached or did not apply its presidential powers to address the pandemic. The authors convincingly demonstrate that the overreach or expansion of emergency powers and executive orders does not have to be the norm. Instead, neoliberal and authoritarian governments can choose not to use their emergency powers. These debates neglected the relationship among colonialism, the state of emergency, and corruption.

The logic of neoliberal disaster management was key in the colonial management of the COVID-19 pandemic in PR. Right from the beginning of the pandemic, Vázquez's administration declared a state of emergency,[11] and between March 12 and December 31, 2020, this declaration was extended and modified twenty-two times.[12] In total, Governor Vázquez issued forty-eight executive orders to address different aspects of the pandemic. Similarly, Pedro Pierluisi's administration has issued forty-six executive orders since January 2, 2021, and has extended or modified the state of emergency in twenty-four instances.[13] Furthermore, as Mari Mari Narváez, the executive director of Kilómetro Cero, pointed out in our interview, PR was under lockdown and some form of curfew for fourteen consecutive months (March 15, 2020, to May 23, 2021), during which twenty-four executive orders were issued by both the Vázquez and Pierluisi administrations.[14]

During the first days of his administration, Pierluisi issued a series of contradictory and sometimes opposed executive orders, many of which amended previous executive orders or derogated the public health measures implemented by Vázquez's administration. These executive orders had the opposite effect of their intended outcomes, increasing COVID-19 cases, misleading people, and creating the conditions for public corruption. These executive orders used Law 20 of April 2017 to declare a state of emergency.[15] As previously discussed, Law 20 of 2017 confers extraordinary power to the governor in case of an emergency, including the capacity of amend or revoke regulations, and to acquire properties without the required due process, among other powers. Vasquez's administration used these powers to acquire personal protective equipment (PPE) and test kits, generating several corruption cases.

As the PR government issued emergency measures, Puerto Ricans faced exponential increases in unemployment rates; lack of access to testing and proper monitoring of people infected by COVID-19, and during the early stages of the vaccine rollout, limited access to the vaccine;[16] a dramatic escalation in families facing food insecurity;[17] and unequal federal emergency relief.[18] For example, a considerable portion of Puerto Ricans did not receive the economic support provided by the CARES Act or any other federal aid relief.[19] The different measures taken by these two administrations in dealing with COVID-19 entailed the systemic erosion of an already degraded internal democracy and the reconfiguration of colonial legality to management of a pandemic. A short overview of some of the executive orders issued by these two administrations can shed light on the uses of state of emergency as the central dispositive to administer the pandemic.

Repurposing Neoliberal Disaster Management

During the pandemic, the PR government repurposed neoliberal disaster management techniques to respond to the emergency. The Vázquez administration issued a series of executive orders to activate the PR National Guard (PRNG), allowed the Department of Health to use medical resources from the PRNG, and further militarized public safety.[20] Vázquez's administration also deregulated procurement processes and the procurement of essential materials, such as test kits and PPE,[21] and began the process of hiring experts to manage the crisis.[22] That is, the administration followed the framework of militarization and deregulation and opened the gates for "external experts" to operate in PR developed in the context of the hurricanes and earthquakes.

On March 15, 2020, the Vázquez administration established a lockdown for fourteen days and a curfew from 9 pm to 5 am.[23] Executive order OE-2020–29 of March 30, 2020, expanded the lockdown for another fourteen days, modified the curfew from 7 pm to 5 am, and imposed additional restrictions on outdoor activities, including limiting the circulation of cars on designated days based on their license plate. More restrictions came with executive order OE-2020–32, which enforced the mandatory closure of essential services for the weekend of April 10 to 12, 2020. These measures generated a chaotic situation in local grocery stores and put Puerto Ricans in a dire humanitarian crisis, to the point that Vázquez's administration had to retract the emergency measures. The curfew was amended in several instances until May 2021, when both curfew and lockdown were finally derogated, after a period of fourteen months.[24]

As Mari Mari Narváez stated in our interview, the permanent lockdown and curfew was accompanied by several arrests and highly visible cases of police brutality.[25] These punitive emergency measures were intensely contested by Puerto Rican human rights and civil society organizations.[26] In *American Civil Liberties Union (ACLU) v. Wanda Vázquez Garced* (2020), the ACLU sought to overrule executive order OE-2020–29 and to halt the emergency measures imposed by the Vázquez administration. However, the court dismissed the case, claiming that the ACLU did not have legal standing to sue the administration. In *Auto-Cine Santana v. Wanda Vázquez Garced* (2020), a drive-in theater company sought to challenge the constitutionality of executive order OE-2020–41 and the lockdown. The PR Supreme Court upheld the constitutionality of the executive order, as it has done in every declaration of state of emergency since the multilayered crisis began in 2006.

While the administration developed contradictory and chaotic policies, on April 16, 2020, the PR legislature enacted Law 43, which provided that COVID-19–related medical treatments would be free of charge while the state of emergency lasts. This measure is similar to the public health measures implemented by the Trump administration, and while important, it does not address the key limitations of a public health system that has been completely privatized. Furthermore, Vázquez's administration decided to grant immunity from civil cases to "medical facilities and professionals" providing services to COVID-19 patients.[27] This provision generated discomfort among Puerto Ricans since it does not guarantee access to PPE or hazard pay for healthcare workers but instead focused on guaranteeing immunity to corporations that administer the hospitals.[28]

Similarly, OE-2020–40 of May 15, 2020, delineated the process of distributing the $2 billion in relief funds received under the CARES Act. The strategic plan not only set up an unequal distribution of the funds, giving more funds to private entities, including hospitals, than to public corporations, but also created the new Committee for the Oversight of Disbursements.[29] The committee, made up of members from Vázquez's administration, would need to establish new accountability and oversight processes, ignoring previously existing emergency relief agencies, such as COR3, which further delayed the distribution of funds. Pierluisi's administration further empowered this committee by granting it additional authority to administer, allocate, and distribute relief funds.[30]

Ignoring the recommendations of its own medical task force and pressured by the private sector,[31] Vázquez issued executive orders to begin the process "to reopen the economy" in early May 2020.[32] Executive order OE-2020–41 of May 21, 2020, provided more guidelines for reopening the economy while maintaining a curfew. OE-2020–44 of June 12 amended the curfew from 10 pm to 5 am and led the way to an almost complete reopening of the economy. The reopening came alongside PR's lack of implementation of expansive testing and contact-tracing mechanisms, just as the local government had not provided the transparent and necessary information on reported cases.[33] PR lacked the urgent and robust public health capacity to care for patients and frontline workers. Thus, it backfired in July, when the government had to walk back on reopening, given the acceleration of COVID-19 infections and new cases.[34] Nevertheless, the government decided on September 11, 2020, to completely reopen the economy and the country while maintaining the curfew from 10 pm to 5 pm.[35] Later, new restrictions had to be put in place. In the following months, the curfew was amended in several instances.[36]

From a public health perspective, the Puerto Rican government response to the first months of the pandemic is overwhelming, chaotic, and contradictory. But the key operativity and rationality of colonial legality does not consist of effectively addressing a crisis. Instead, its objective is to administer the crisis in a way that wealth extraction and capital accumulation can continue. The executive orders, the state of emergency, and the law enable these processes, and from the colonial legality perspective, the government response was doing exactly what it intended.

On January 2, 2021, Pedro Pierluisi took office and picked up the disaster management techniques developed by the Rosselló and Vázquez administrations. On January 2, Pierluisi mandated the secretary of health to develop all the necessary mechanisms to administer COVID-19 tests.[37] Similarly, on July 1, Pierluisi delegated more authority to the secretary of health to implement additional prevention policies.[38] An important difference between the Vázquez and Pierluisi administrations, identified in the analysis of the executive orders and the uses of emergency powers, is that Pierluisi has delegated the power to manage the pandemic to executive branch members. The delegation of power was particularly clear in the policies implemented to require travelers to show proof of vaccination or negative COVID-19 tests.[39] Given its colonial condition, PR could not limit or control the air traffic or impose limitations on who enters PR since this is part of the federal domain.

Like in the United States, in PR the rollout of vaccines was conducted mainly by private corporations and legally framed through executive orders. For example, Pierluisi issued executive orders[40] to establish the vaccine mandated for the executive branch employees and contractors, and for employees or workers in the service sector (such as barbers and waitresses).[41] Similarly, the Pierluisi administration ordered that the abovementioned workers, students, essential workers, and other members of the service industry should receive the third dose of the vaccine or the booster shots.[42] On February 22, 2022, his administration established further guidelines for the vaccination of students ages five and older.[43] Moreover, the vaccine rollout was marked by a lack of transparency and little sharing of information with the public. This led to CPI and Proyecto de Acceso a la Información suing the Department of Health to demand that the information concerning the distribution of vaccines be shared with the public.[44]

In December 2021 and January 2022, PR saw an increase in COVID-19 cases due to the Omicron variant. The Pierluisi administration issued a new set of executive orders and emergency declarations. During this period, the administration did not impose a curfew, but there was restriction on mass events,[45] an additional request for travelers,[46] booster shot mandates,[47] and orders to close bars, restaurants, and other businesses.[48] On March 25, 2022, Pierluisi imposed additional controls for emergency contracts issued during the pandemic and declared a state of emergency in PR's public schools; this executive order allowed for contracting services for the improvement and rehabilitation of the school's infrastructure to facilitate the process of reopening.[49]

The use of the state of emergency and executive orders by Vázquez and Pierluisi's administrations shed light on how the law and emergency powers have been at the center of managing the public health crisis. The continued use of emergency powers is embedded in disaster management strategies. This has contributed to further sociolegal transformations of Puerto Rican institutions. Particularly, the overreach in the use of emergency powers demonstrates how the local administrations have enhanced their administrative control and undermined the powers of the other branches of government. Conversely, the uses of emergency power, the normalization of the state of emergency, and the systematic use of executive orders have not provided relief or recovery for the people. Instead, they have facilitated disinformation, chaotic management of the crisis, and several corruption and fraud cases.

THE PHARMACEUTICAL INDUSTRY IN PR: TAX AVOIDANCE AND SOCIAL HARM

During the pandemic, the Trump administration, newspapers, and scholars started to promote the idea of bringing back or onshoring the pharmaceutical industry from China and India to the United States. Largely justified under national security discourses and the logic of emergency, commentators argued in favor of onshoring active pharmaceutical ingredients (APIs), medical devices, and pharmaceutical products back to PR. For instance, in a series of statements, former President Trump suggested that his administration would be bringing back the pharmaceutical industry. He stated, "We will make our medical supplies right here in the United States. And you've probably heard me today, you know, it used to be—Puerto Rico did tremendous dollars in medical supplies and then what happened? They made a lot. They did a good job and Obama-Biden destroyed it. They took away the incentive, all of the taxes, and they took away the incentive and Puerto Rico went down a long way."[50]

Together with this and similar statements, the Trump administration implemented a limited set of policies to encourage onshoring of the pharmaceutical industry. For example, on August 6, 2020, Trump signed executive order 13944 aimed at boosting US production of medicines and medical equipment, lowering drug prices, and protecting the United States against shortfalls in a future pandemic.[51] The order aimed to strengthen the supply chains of essential medicines, medical countermeasures, and critical input by increasing production in the United States. Many commentators saw this executive order as an opportunity and argued that PR would be the ideal place to encourage this industry. According to these commentators, the archipelago has the conditions for supporting the pharmaceutical industry and for becoming once again a key player in the global supply chain.[52]

Similarly, the FOMB hired Boston Consulting Group (BCG)[53] to assess how PR could best position itself to attract more biopharmaceutical and medical device manufacturing companies to the archipelago. The report was delivered on August 4, 2020, only days before Trump signed the abovementioned executive order. One of the key ideas promoted by BCG was the use of economically distressed zones (EDZ) and opportunity zones as vehicles to promote PR as an ideal context to bring back the pharmaceutical industry.[54]

Thus, the central idea was to implement additional tax incentives for an industrial sector that already enjoys extraordinary tax, regulatory, and economic benefits in PR.

In tandem with the work of BCG, Lynne Garcia and Michael Beverley (2021) have examined and developed a strategic plan for the possibility of reinvigorating the pharmaceutical industry in PR. Their proposal encompassed several legal and tax reforms, including the proposal of redeveloping some version of Section 936, which allowed existing pharmaceutical manufacturers in PR to expand their operations and lower their tax rates. Another idea was to provide a "most-favored nation" type of status to the Puerto Rican tax rate for pharmaceutical intellectual property, which will make PR competitive again.

The implementation of tax exemptions and deregulatory frameworks to attract transnational corporations to the archipelago is one of those zombie legal policies haunting PR policymaking.[55] Despite numerous studies, the current multilayered crisis, and the international interventions with PR's lax tax regulation, legal scholars and policymakers keep favoring the implementation of such policies. The following section examines the legal policy of onshoring the pharmaceutical industry through the implementation of additional tax exemptions. Two key aspects of the pharmaceutical industry in PR are explored. First, the section discusses how tax and deregulatory policies have allowed the pharmaceutical industry to harm communities, the environment, and its employees. Second, it addresses how the pharmaceutical industry undermined PR's capacity to address the pandemic. Ultimately, the section investigates what actually happened when it was said (such as by Donald Trump) that the pharmaceutical industry left PR, and then it challenges the desirability of promoting more of that industry in the archipelago.

Tax Engineering and the Colonial State of Exception

There are fifty Food and Drug Administration (FDA) approved pharmaceutical plants and several other biomedical and medical equipment plants operating in PR. In fact, PR produces more than half of the world's top-selling prescription drugs, which are used to treat patients with arthritis, strokes, and cancer.[56] On average, the pharmaceutical industry generates $47 billion annually, or 74 percent of the total exports of PR. In 2018, 36 percent of the value of all manufactured products came from pharmaceuticals and medical equipment.[57] Pharmaceutical corporations started moving to PR in the 1970s after the federal Internal Revenue Code introduced Section 936, which allowed these companies to avoid paying corporate income tax on profits made in PR. These breaks resulted in a heavy focus on attracting large multinationals headquartered in the United States, at the expense of investing in activities that would support local Puerto Rican businesses and economies. This dynamic put an unfair burden on Puerto Rican taxpayers and allowed large multinationals to dominate the archipelago's economy. Section 936 ultimately cost taxpayers $24.7 billion in unpaid tax.[58]

After the elimination of Section 936, the PR government developed a series of very generous tax exemptions for the pharmaceutical industry. These companies enjoy the benefits of Law 135 of 1998 and Law 73 of 2008, which reduce the company's maximum income tax rate to 4 percent and grant tax credits for job creation and the purchase of manufactured products in PR. These pharmaceutical corporations are also subject to Law 154 of 2010, which imposes a 4 percent tax on foreign corporations; however, the federal treasury reimburses them with a tax credit.[59] The pharmaceutical industry also receives approximately $14.5 billion annually in tax breaks from PR.

These tax breaks are larger than the total operating budget of the PR government. In total, the government granted $100.5 billion in tax benefits between 2017 and 2023.[60] These tax breaks fail to create large numbers of jobs for the archipelago's 3.3 million people. An estimate for the fiscal year 2020 found that tax breaks only generated 7,000 direct and indirect jobs, or 0.6 percent of the total workforce.[61] The pharmaceutical industry operating in PR has managed to avoid paying taxes on $140 billion. Tax engineering is a key tactic through which the pharmaceutical industry has used PR as a tax haven. For instance, the pharmaceutical industry has engaged in transfer pricing, transfer of their intellectual property, and shifting profit to gain additional tax breaks.

At the core of these corporate welfare policies are the FOMB and its members, including Antonio Medina, who is a former executive of Merck and former director of PRIDCO.[62] Additionally, McKinsey, which has been advising the FOMB on bringing back the pharmaceutical industry, has a serious conflict of interest. In May 2022, new disclosures revealed that McKinsey is on the payroll of pharma corporations like AbbVie, while simultaneously advising the FOMB to keep pharma's corporate taxes low.

Additionally, the PR government has met these corporations with a very lax regulatory environment. For example, safety and health regulations and environmental protections have been systemically weakened to enable these corporations to do business in PR. The pharmaceutical industry enjoys access to underground water, a specialized and well-prepared workforce, lax waste management policies, and low wages. All these benefits, which are often considered externalities, ought to be placed at the center of the subsidies that these corporations received as part of the governmental efforts to maintain these companies in the archipelago.[63]

Deregulation of labor protection is another example of the benefits that these corporations enjoy. The pharmaceutical sector in PR employs over 10,000 workers, many of whom earn $8.50 an hour, or $23,000 per year. Furthermore, the pharmaceutical industry largely subcontracts many of its cleaning, security, and groundskeeping jobs to third parties.[64] Many of the workers hired by subcontracting companies earn the federal minimum wage. Similarly, Hedge Clippers (2022a) found that an overwhelming majority of workers received no benefits, including healthcare, pensions, or job training.

Additionally, in the last ten years there have been systemic health and safety issues,[65] including over eighty complaints, accidents, and reports to the Occupational Safety and Health Administration (OSHA). Some safety crimes involved chemical exposures, scalding, and amputations.[66] For instance, after seventy pharmaceutical workers in Manatí were exposed to hazardous chemicals, the company Warner Chilcott was only fined $2,275 by the PR government.[67] On top of this, pharmaceutical workers are not represented by unions in PR.

Pharmaceutical corporations have also contributed to environmental degradations, fueling climate change. Johnson & Johnson, Abbott, Merck, Pfizer, and others have created fifteen toxic waste sites or EPA-designated Superfund sites.[68] Abbott and Bristol Myers Squibb have consistently depleted and polluted PR's groundwater supplies in places like Barceloneta and Manatí. Similarly, for years the pharmaceutical industry has emptied hundreds of thousands of metric tons of toxic waste along the northern coast of PR.[69] These corporations have systematically violated the Clean Air Act and critical environmental regulations.[70] Communities living near the operations of the pharmaceutical industry, mainly in the northern part of the island, have experienced chronic health issues such as asthma and respiratory illnesses and high rates of cancer, as well as toxic chemical exposures and unsafe drinking water.[71]

The environmental degradation and the social inequities caused by the pharmaceutical industry became particularly clear in the aftermath of Hurricanes María in 2017 and Fiona in 2022.[72] In the wake of Hurricane María, while PR was enduring the largest blackout in US history, the pharmaceutical industry operations continued thanks to independently powered generators. These corporations ran diesel generators 24/7 during the entire blackout, in some cases for a period of 120 days.[73] In the aftermath of Hurricane Fiona, all major pharmaceutical corporations in PR had already established their private microgrids capable of maintaining the production without the need to stop.[74] That is, the legal structure of the colonial state of exception, and the strategic accommodation of the local elites through the logic of colonial legality, have enabled these corporations to continue their processes of capital accumulation and wealth extraction uninterrupted.

Structures of Irresponsibility

The presence of the pharmaceutical industry in PR is also relevant since two of the major COVID-19 test kit producers—Abbott and Roche—and the producers of the vaccine—Pfizer, Johnson & Johnson, and AstraZeneca—have been operating in the archipelago under the numerous tax exemptions described above.[75] Despite the PR government having created the corporate conditions for the pharmaceuticals to thrive, even amid the multilayered crisis, these companies did not provide PR with the necessary equipment to tackle the pandemic, and even placed the archipelago at the bottom of the distribution list.[76]

For instance, Abbott and Roche profited from COVID-19 without exercising any sort of social responsibility. While PR lacked testing, PPE, and medical equipment to address the pandemic, these corporations were producing massive amounts of test kits and medical equipment. As early as March 12, 2020, Roche received authorization from the FDA to distribute its molecular tests. Four days later, Roche announced the start of its distribution in the United States with the shipment of 400,000 test kits. Similarly, on March 18, 2020, Abbott announced that it received authorization from the FDA to distribute its molecular test.[77] Later, Abbott announced that it had sent over a million molecular tests to all fifty states; however, none of these tests reached PR. Additionally, in the case of the distribution of the reagents necessary to analyze the tests, Abner Dennis (2020d) informed us of the scarcity and slowness with which Roche sent its products to PR:

> the fact that PR projects to have low levels of contagion, due to the small number of tests carried out, has implied that Roche has the island at the end of the reagent distribution list. In this way Roche contributed to a vicious circle, where there are not enough tests to know the real level of contagion, and since not enough tests have been done, then the necessary reagents are not sent to process the tests because the supposed level of contagion is low.[78]

The lack of social responsibility of these corporations in PR is striking, especially when both corporations have been profiting from PR's tax exemption and permissive environmental regulation. Dennis (2020d) showed that a significant part of the $3.6 billion net profits reported by Abbott in 2019 were earnings produced in PR. Similarly, Roche reported having generated profits of up to $14.5 billion in 2019. Thus, while the COVID-19 pandemic generated debates about using PR as a strategic place for US pharma to operate, this discussion ignored the pharmaceutical industry's absence in the Puerto Rican efforts to manage the pandemic.

Despite the role of the pharmaceutical industry in harming communities, the environment, and the state's capacity to address disaster and crisis, some scholars and politicians still advocate that PR encourage more pharmaceutical industry in the archipelago. Garcia and Beverley (2021) emphasized the issues that the PR government must address if it wishes to continue to attract the pharmaceutical industry, including public corruption, political instability, infrastructure concern, transportation, and shipping. In their work, Garcia and Beverley ignored the issues discussed here, disregarding Puerto Rican self-determination and the catastrophic impact of the tax haven economy.

CORRUPTION AND FRAUD AMID THE COVID-19 PANDEMIC

While the debates about onshoring the pharmaceutical industry were taking place, the local elites were engaging in different strategies to capitalize and profit from the management of the pandemic. Since the state of emergency was declared on March 12, 2020, the purchase of test kits, medical equipment, and PPE to manage the emergency was plagued by irregularities involving members of the executive branch, the medical task force, the PRNG, and the private sector. Over $45 million in public funds were spent during the emergency under irregular circumstances.[79] Much of the spending took place under the legal framework of OE-2020–24 of March 16, 2020, which deregulated the procurement and compliance processes in the purchase of medical equipment to address the pandemic.

The irregularities were first denounced by former interim Secretary of Health Concepción Quiñones de Longo, after resigning on March 26, 2020. Later, the Puerto Rican House of Representatives (PRHR) investigated the allegations made by Quiñones in a series of public hearings and published a report on June 29, 2020.[80] The PRHR identified a pattern of irregularities and negligence in the management of the pandemic, including irregular and fraudulent procurement of medical equipment, involvement of governmental employees in the purchase of medical equipment, and fraudulent transactions in PR's preparedness for the pandemic. The report disregarded the fact that many of those involved in these transactions were former governmental employees with close ties to the ruling party (PNP).[81] Similarly, the emphasis of this report ignored the colonial regime of permission that normalized corruption and state-corporate crimes as part of colonial legality. In reference to the cases of corruption in the procurement of the COVID-19 test, Denis Márquez, member of the House of Representatives for the PIP and part of the PRHR investigation, noted in our interview:

> This entire process was made possible by executive orders and administrative orders, and it was clearly a case of corruption. It was a political scheme, because clientelism is in all of that. I do not have the slightest doubt that the Health Commission directed this process . . . the Health Commission was in absolute control. The procurement procedure disappears, given the state of emergency, and new parameters were established for the purchase of tests, without auditing. In the public hearings it was shown that there was no type of control. And I maintain that it was a scheme.

Denis Márquez and the PIP challenged the final report, given the lack of accountability and the limited engagement with corruption cases. As result, Márquez (2020a, 2020b) published two minority reports aimed at addressing the serious limitations in the official report published by the PRHR. Lack of transparency in governmental procurement has been, according to Márquez, one of the key causes of corruption in PR.

There were three major purchases of COVID-19 antibody screening tests and medical equipment. These transactions aimed to acquire more than 1.1 million rapid tests from local suppliers: Castro Business,[82] Apex General Contractors,[83] and 313 LLC.[84] None of the transactions was completed in the time frame agreed upon, and only one was canceled. In the end, just over 10,000 test kits of the 1.1 million purchased finally arrived at health centers and hospitals. All these purchases followed the same scheme: rather than going directly to the manufacturer, the PR government went through various layers of intermediaries or corporations, some local and linked to the PNP, and others foreign (mostly US-based) with businesses on the archipelago and beneficiaries of tax incentives such as Act 60. Through this supply chain, participants at all levels earned money: the business front, the partners, the intermediaries, and the manufacturer.[85]

The PRHR also shows the involvement of public employees in these alleged fraudulent and corrupt transactions. An example is the establishment of a purchasing team led by the medical task force.[86] This team was created in tandem with the Purchasing Office of the Department of Health, and it was composed of public employees with ties to the PNP. The members of the task force were key in the irregular procurement of test kits. As the report mentions, one of the key issues with this purchasing team was that it did not have the preparation, experience, or ability to handle specialized and sensitive purchases, such as test kits, PPE, and ventilators.

Denis Márquez (2020a) has characterized the procurement of PPE, test kits, and other medical equipment as a corruption scheme. In our interview, Márquez emphasized the structural dynamic of corruption and clientelism. Similarly, he stressed that the management of the crisis by the Department of Health was negligent and in violation of the most basic emergency rules and procedures. Furthermore, in his second report, Márquez (2020b) demonstrated how the corrupt scheme surrounding the procurement of the COVID-19 test kits during the state of emergency was enabled by the symbiotic relation among the government, the PNP, and the private sector.

The handling of the pandemic exacerbated PR's vulnerability and left hospitals unprepared to treat COVID-19 patients.[87] Similarly, despite the public funds spent and the fact that two of the major producers of COVID-19 equipment were based in PR, the archipelago lacked test kits, ventilators, and PPE for first responders. As the next section shows, these fraud cases do not take place in a vacuum. The governmental management of the multilayered crisis affecting PR since 2006 has manufactured a colonial regime of permission that normalized corruption as administrative ethos.

THE PAYCHECK PROTECTION PROGRAM AND THE COLONIAL TAX HAVEN

The Paycheck Protection Program (PPP)[88] was one of several emergency programs included in the $2.2 trillion economic stimulus package known as the Coronavirus Aid, Relief, and Economic Security Act (CARES Act).[89] The PPP, an $813.7 billion program, offered low-interest loans to small businesses, self-employed workers, sole proprietors, nonprofit organizations, and tribal businesses, with the promise of loan forgiveness as long as the funds were used for qualifying expenses such as payroll, paying mortgage interest, rent, and utilities. Between April 2020 and May 2021, private lenders, backed by the Small Business Administration (SBA), issued a total of 11.46 million loans, amounting to $793 billion in three successive rounds.[90] The program operated as a public-private partnership, with private lenders responsible for processing and underwriting PPP loans. The SBA backed 100 percent of the loans to encourage lending, thereby removing concerns about borrower default. The program's design minimized underwriting requirements, reducing lenders' incentives to exercise caution or put in place anti-fraud measures.

PPP funds played a paradigmatic role in keeping the Puerto Rican colonial tax haven operating amid the pandemic. According to the Pandemic Oversight website, the archipelago received $2.8 billion in PPP funds that were distributed through 70,200 loans, of which 68,400 were forgiven.[91] I have found that 2,066 beneficiaries of tax incentives under Act 60 received PPP loans. The legal and regulatory framework of the PPP intensified existing criminogenic dynamics given the symbiotic relationship and institutionalized revolving doors among the banking sector, financial institutions, law firms, corporations, and the state.

For instance, PR banks played a significant role in processing and underwriting PPP loans. Notably, Banco Popular underwrote $1.8 billion in PPP loans. As shown in Chapter 3, Banco Popular is deeply integrated into every facet of the PR government, acting as a key economic institution, holding the PR treasury accounts, advising, underwriting, processing bonds, lending to the government, and more. Banco Popular has managed to capitalize on every aspect of the PR economy, including the informal sectors. For example, on January 23, 2023, it was reported that Popular Bank, a subsidiary of Banco

Popular Inc., had to pay $2.3 million over alleged PPP fraud after the Federal Reserve fined it for processing six loans totaling $1.1 million in August 2020.[92]

FirstBank,[93] the second-largest retail bank in PR, underwrote $745 million in PPP loans, of which $26 million in PPP loans went to the PR financial sector. Oriental Bank underwrote $437.6 million in PPP loans of which $8 million went to financial and insurance companies. On May 18, 2023, it was reported that the US attorney for the District of PR had indicted individuals for their participation in a $1.2 million fraudulent scheme involving the PPP and the Economic Injury Disaster Loan (EIDL) program.[94] According to the indictment, Oriental Bank did not effectively exercise its due diligence in preventing fraud and in fact capitalized on processing fees from these fraudulent loans. Banesco US, the smallest commercial bank in PR, underwrote $35.2 million in PPP loans. José Carrión III, former chairman of the FOMB, sits on Banesco's board of directors, making it part of the revolving door between the state and the PR financial sector. Collectively, these four lenders (Banco Popular, FirstBank, Oriental Bank, and Banesco) underscore the symbiotic relationship between the state and the financial sector, shedding light on how local elites leverage their privileged position to capture resources and capital within the archipelago.

Like lenders, borrowers directly benefited from the tax policies implemented by the PR government. International Financial Entities (IFEs), including seven international banks, received over $600,000 in PPP loans.[95] IFEs accessing PPP funding illustrate the colonial regimen of permission enabling the presence of a broad sector of financial institutions in PR. This is particularly clear in the way wealth management and investment firms operate in the archipelago, taking advantage of the tax incentives provided by Act 20 or the Export Services Act. Twenty-three wealth management and investment firms, all beneficiaries of Act 20, received over $2.3 million in PPP loans. This sector played a significant role in the tax haven's operation, since IFEs are by law designed to conduct business outside PR with clients that are not based locally.

Law firms constitute the last category of institutions that received PPP loans, receiving $66.8 million in PPP funds. Thirteen law firms specializing in corporate and tax law and providing crucial services to the operation of the tax haven, as well as being beneficiaries of Act 20 and other tax incentives, received $14 million in loans. McConnell Valdés, Pietrantoni Mendez & Alvarez, Ferraiuoli LLC, and AMG exemplify this, focusing on tax-related services. The legal management of the tax haven emerges as a lucrative enterprise, generating substantial profits for law firms and other service sectors. Revolving doors and collusion between the PR government, private corporations, and law firms are evident. For instance, O'Neill & Borges, McConnell Valdés, and others have contracted with the PR government, its instrumentalities, and the FOMB for legal advice and representation on an array of issues. Pirillo Law, which received $248,000 in PPP loans and is the former law firm of the current director of OCFI (Office of the Commissioner of Financial Institutions), has become a specialist on tax incentives, enabling cryptocurrency and blockchain proponents to relocate to PR.

The intricate relationship among lenders, borrowers, and intermediaries within the colonial tax haven did not generate significant anti-fraud interventions. Instead, the PPP program, initially designed to alleviate economic challenges caused by the pandemic, served to sustain and perpetuate the colonial tax structure. The contradiction between the dynamics of wealth extraction described in this section, and the punitive policies implemented by both the US and PR governments become explicit in the next section.

ANTICORRUPTION AND PUNITIVE GOVERNANCE

Under the guise of public safety and anticorruption, the US and Puerto Rican governments implemented regressive policies that directly targeted poor and working communities. These public safety and anticorruption measures were disproportionately focused on small offenses and petty corruption, when corruption of the powerful was overlooked. Additionally, by imposing additional hurdles or bureaucratic burdens that limit access to state services, these anticorruption measures undermined PR's capacity to handle the pandemic, exacerbated the pandemic's impact, and created an unequal recovery scenario. These policies included, first, Law 35 of April 5, 2020, which imposed severe penalties on those who disobey an executive order; second, anticorruption policies that limited access to Pandemic Unemployment Assistance (PUA) to those who needed it the most (mainly poor and racialized individuals, immigrants, and working women). These measures reproduced punitive notions of neoliberal disaster management that are inextricably tied to race, class, gender, and colonial relations of power.

Punitive Emergency Management

As the executive branch issued executive orders, the local legislature approved Law 35 of 2020,[96] which criminalized the spreading of "misinformation during periods of crisis" and any breach of an executive order that enacts a curfew, lockdown, and/or state of emergency. The sanctions or penalties for breaching an executive order included up to six months in prison or a $5,000 fine, while for spreading misinformation the law imposed a fine of $10,000.[97] As part of its legal mobilization for transparency and accountability, Kilómetro Cero sued the PR Police Department to make public the documentation on arrests and fines issued during the fourteen months that the lockdown and curfew lasted. They found that, in total, 1,205 individuals were arrested for violations of executive orders, and 3,889 received citations or fines.[98] Kilómetro Cero (2023) also found that during this period, 2,246 calls were made to 911 reporting cases of gender violence. Despite these numbers, the management of the pandemic lacked a gender perspective or even an emergency protocol to address these cases of violence.

Furthermore, the official numbers do not reveal that hundreds of individuals arrested, fined, and even sent to prison for curfew violations were working poor, Afro-descendant, immigrants, and other minoritized populations.[99] Arrests were often conducted while these individuals were driving or walking to and from their places of work or running errands such as grocery shopping. All of this took place as citizens were enduring the effects of lockdown without the necessary information, economic resources, and access to essential services. The arrests under this law are an exemplary case of colonial legality: that is, the use of law and pandemic emergency powers to control, discipline, and punish the most vulnerable populations, rather than using these powers to prevent the contagion and guarantee the well-being of the PR population.

On March 31, 2023, the US District Court for the District of PR ordered the PR government to not enforce Law 35 and parts of Law 66.[100] In *Sandra Rodriguez Cotto et al. v. Pedro R. Pierluisi-Urrutia et al.*, the court found that these laws and the penalties imposed for the "disseminating of misinformation" violated the First Amendment of the US Constitution. The case was brought by the ACLU and journalists Sandra Rodriguez Cotto and Rafelli González on May 20, 2020. The derogation of Article 5.14a is important since it constitutes another instance of a legal interruption with the systemic expansion on the emergency powers of the local government. An additional dimension of punitive approaches to the pandemic can be found in the implementation of anticorruption laws and policies aimed at preventing fraud in the distribution of PUA.

Pandemic Unemployment Assistance (PUA)

In the context of the COVID-19 pandemic and stay-at-home mandates, the Pandemic Unemployment Assistance (PUA) program, created by the CARES Act, provided direct assistance to workers by temporarily expanding the unemployment insurance program eligibility to self-employed workers, freelancers, independent contractors, and part-time workers impacted by the pandemic. PUA provided a minimum of $66 to a maximum of $190 per week for a period of thirty-nine weeks for workers who were not eligible for traditional unemployment insurance.[101] PUA beneficiaries could receive the Federal Pandemic Unemployment Compensation (FPUC) equivalent of $600 per week, between April 4, 2020, and July 30, 2020. These federal programs were distributed through states' unemployment insurance programs, which in PR was carried out by the Department of Labor and Human Resources (henceforth DLHR).

As part of these programs, states were required by the US federal government to put in place legal measures that would prevent fraud and malfeasance. On March 1, 2022, President Joseph Biden set in motion a series of initiatives to address COVID-19–related fraud, including the establishment of the interagency COVID-19 Fraud Enforcement Task Force and the design and implementation of an oversight website in which all information concerning COVID-19 relief spending could be found.[102] At this writing, these websites contain limited information on fraud-related prosecutions or the impact that anti-fraud policies had in the management of the COVID-19 emergency in PR. Despite the lack of information, one can identify how under the guise of fraud and corruption, the US and PR governments implemented regressive and punitive anticorruption and anti-fraud measures that made it more difficult for those most in need of PUA and other economic assistant programs—mainly poor and racialized individuals, as well as immigrants and working women—to access these programs. The key rationale was to prevent corruption and fraud by limiting access to economic assistance programs or imposing burdensome administrative hurdles that would discourage individuals from seeking governmental assistance.

These punitive approaches put in place by the PR and US governments caused three general issues: (1) the development and implementation of a new platform for the application to PUA, which had embedded anti-identity theft and anti-fraud protection, failed or malfunctioned repeatedly, preventing people from accessing the economic assistant programs; (2) lack of transparency on the allocation of PUA, coupled with systemic denial of this benefit for applicants, and lack of information concerning why such a denial occurred; and (3) systemic deployment of punitive anti-fraud measures, which resulted in arrests of mainly racialized and impoverished individuals. These three instances are just a few examples of how punitive governance, anticorruption interventions, and the chaotic management of the pandemic systemically harmed communities and individuals in need. I discuss these three instances in detail in the following.

Technological Failures in the Management of PUA

The DLHR put in place a series of technological measures aimed at preventing identity theft and fraud. These included a website named SABEN, through which individuals applied for unemployment insurance, the PUA, and other pandemic assistance programs. This website was not designed to manage the high volume of visits and applications, and, on the first day that the benefits were available (April 28, 2020),[103] the website collapsed leaving thousands of applicants unable to receive any unemployment benefits or economic assistance.[104]

The PR government then moved to the development of a new platform named Fast PUA. Under the guise of efficiency, the DLHR outsourced the development of this platform, a call center, and the technology to process applications to EVERTEC,[105] a local corporation subsidiary of Banco Popular.[106] The establishment of the new platform further limited access to PUA in several ways. For example, it did not consider the individuals who did not have physical access to computers, smartphones, or the internet, or who did not possess the knowhow to operate these devices. That is, claims needed to be conducted online (except for the call center, see below), despite the digital divide and lack of access to reliable internet and electric service in post–Hurricane María PR. Furthermore, family members who could have helped with the application process were discouraged from doing so given anti-identity theft and anti-fraud measures embedded in the platform.[107]

The systemic issues with the platform, and the lack of other means to access, apply, or follow up with the application to PUA, meant that numerous applicants lacked access to information on the status of their applications. As a result, some applicants resorted to informal or casualized jobs to substitute for the lack of income. Oftentimes this meant that individuals risked being in violation of PUA's anti-fraud measures, since one could consider that they were working while at the same time having stated that they were unable to work because their places of work were closed. Additionally, these individuals were also putting themselves in situations in which they could be found in violation of the curfew, or even putting themselves and their family at risk of infection. In absence of clear information or faced with colonial abandonment, people put themselves in risk-prone situations that enhanced their vulnerability and the likelihood that they would face some form of state intervention and punishment.

Similarly, the call center established by EVERTEC did not have the necessary personnel to respond to the substantial number of calls received daily. As a result, people spent hours on the phone waiting for someone to answer their calls.[108] This left numerous unemployed individuals without assistance to make their initial claim. Ayuda Legal (2021) reported that between June 2020 and October 2021, they helped 1,448 applicants with the request for PUA and unemployment insurance, many of whom had been unable to receive any governmental help with their applications. Faulty technology, compounded with the digital divide and lack of personalized services, enhanced people's vulnerability, adding to the socioeconomic impact of the pandemic.

The systemic problems on the platform and the lack of personnel at the DLHR and the call center, led to an official inquiry by the PRHR on May 11, 2020.[109] The inquiry found a negligent implementation of the website and lack of oversight by the DLHR and recommended that the PR Department of Justice (PRDJ) conduct further investigations. One of the issues that the inquiry addressed is that the platform automatically raised "errors" with the application that prevented individuals from receiving any type of assistance. The anti-fraud measures put in place were technologically designed to raise "controversial points."[110] These controversial points meant that the applicants could not receive the economic help provided by PUA until they solved or eliminated those issues with their applications in one of the offices of the DLHR, or they were resolved at the call center. A key problem was that given the stay-at-home orders, the DLHR offices reminded closed, and applicants to PUA where unable to address the issues with their applications. Ayuda Legal (2021) found that over 50,000 controversial points were raised during the period that the PUA lasted. That is, there were some 50,000 applicants who were unable to receive any economic assistance because of such errors.

Between July 24 and October 25, 2020, the PR Office of the Inspector General of PR (OIG) issued three reports on the management of the PUA by the DLHR. In the first report, the OIG noticed that DLHR's employees accepted bribes and payments to accelerate or to facilitate the process of the PUA and unemployment applications.[111] Similarly, the three reports revealed that corruption, fraud, and bribery were enabled by the technological inefficacy and failures embedded in the platform created by EVERTEC and by the lack of oversight.[112]

The technological failures illustrate a dual dimension of the administrative structures of colonial legality. First, it shows how colonial emergency powers are implemented to deregulate governmental procurement of services without adequate oversight or compliance. Second, it shows how colonial abandonment and bureaucratic management of the pandemic contributed to curtail the access to necessary economic resources for those who needed it the most. Thus, individuals were caught in between emergency powers, anti-fraud policies, corporate harm and profiteering, and the constant thread of punishment.

Lack of Information and Anti-Fraud Interventions

In addition to the technological issue, there was inadequate information about how many individuals received unemployment assistance during the pandemic. While there is information on initial claims, the DLHR did not make public how many people received these benefits. According to the PRHR inquiry mentioned above on May 11, 2020, there were 238,934 applications to the state unemployment insurance and over 90,000 applications to PUA. Similarly, according to the information gathered by the Federal Reserve Bank of Saint Louis during the height of the pandemic, on May 23, 2020, there were 67,611 initial claims;[113] nevertheless, there is no information on how many of those claims were adequately processed or even granted.

The DLHR provided limited information on these numbers, even after my request for information, and after Ayuda Legal initiated a series of legal actions, including a lawsuit,[114] requesting that the DLHR publish the information on how many people had received the economic assistance. The PR government and the DLHR argued that this information was not protected under PR's transparency jurisprudence,[115] and its publication could threaten the privacy of the recipients of this benefit or facilitate fraud and identity theft. Finally, the DLHR shared partial information with Ayudal Legal on November 3, 2021; however, it was in a format that was difficult to read and contained contradictory data. Furthermore, in my personal communication with the lawyer who brought the lawsuit for Ayuda Legal, she noted that the DLHR did not even have the information; rather, the corporations running the platform—EVERTEC and Fast Enterprises LLC—were the ones holding the information. Accordingly, the DLHR had to request this information from these corporations, and they were the ones that put together the data for the DLHR to share with Ayuda Legal.

The lack of access to this basic information raises important questions about whether the DLHR and the local government had a clear idea of how many people received economic assistance. This shows how the lack of information operated at multiple levels, including: general information that could be shared with governmental institutions as part of the regular process of accountability and transparency; data/information that could be effectively shared with the public (including researchers and pro-transparency organizations); and relevant information that could be shared with applicants or people seeking economic assistance. Another problem arose from the unclear and contradictory information available, which further hindered applicants' access to economic assistance.

This last point is particularly clear when considering the contradictory information that immigrant communities were given. Many immigrants, especially Dominican women living in PR, were left out of economic assistant programs due to their migratory status. José Encarnación (2020) pointed out that undocumented immigrants were excluded from the CARES Act, but several US jurisdictions took steps to fill that gap. However, PR was not one of them, and the DLHR did not share this information widely. Thus, some immigrants applied for the benefits of PUA, under the understanding that in other US jurisdictions they were entitled to this economic assistance, which in turn put them at risk of being arrested for fraud.

A further example of the convergence between lack of information, punitive approaches, and colonial abandonment can be identified in the assistance program for the payment of rent and utilities known as COVID Renta. This program was created to help underserved communities with basic rent payments; however, as Ayuda Legal noticed, the PR government and the PR Department of Housing did not inform people that they might be eligible for these programs. As a result, on June 30, 2022, the PR government returned $85.2 million in unused funds to the federal government.[116] Moreover, while the PR government did not distribute these funds that could have alleviated the economic burden faced by undeserved and racialized communities, Ayuda Legal reported that PR did not enforce the eviction moratorium put in place by the US HUD. That is, poor and working-class communities were left to fend for themselves, despite the availability of economic and regulatory mechanisms to protect them in the context of the pandemic. Hence, colonial abandonment.

The Violence of Anticorruption

Finally, the ways in which the local and federal administrations have been prosecuting cases of petty corruption constitute an example of punitive governance and demonstrate the violent effect of anticorruption. At the local level, there have been several reports of fraud to PUA; however, PRDJ and the Federal Bureau of Investigation (FBI) have not provided an official account of these cases. Valeria Collazo and Adriana De Jesús (2021) pointed out that, in February 2021, 61 cases of fraud were under investigation; 93 cases were already charged and brought to court; and another 368 cases were under preliminary investigation. On June 26, 2023, the PRDJ responded to my request for access to information and shared that the Office of the Chief Prosecutor had on the record, as of May 31, 2023, forty cases that had been filed in court and sixty-eight additional cases under investigation.[117] However, the PRDJ did not provide additional information on the status of previous arrests and prosecutions.

Although the arrests and prosecutions of fraud cases might have been accurate, what struck many commentators was that the people charged with fraud were mainly racialized and minoritized individuals, while affluent individuals received different prosecutions. For example, Victoria Leandra (2020) has shown how high school students at an elite private school defrauded the

PUA program while thousands waited to receive benefits. Collazo and De Jesús (2021) found that while many of the privileged students involved in the fraud against PUA were not charged or prosecuted, PRDJ was working on several other cases of fraud against PUA. Anticorruption policies and prosecutions in PR reproduce racialized and class relations of power.[118]

The PR anticorruption and anti-fraud interventions were coupled with the US federal government's anti-fraud policies. Based on the analysis of the press releases issued by the US Department of Justice in PR between April 21, 2021, and May 23, 2023, thirty-four individuals were arrested for fraud to the PUA program by the federal authorities. According to the same press release, these thirty-four individuals defrauded over $2 million in PUA assistance.[119]

Another case that demonstrates the uses of anti-fraud and anticorruption interventions as punitive governance is the collections letters sent to individuals who received PUA benefits. Particularly salient here are the hundreds of women heads of household who received collection letters for PUA payments. These women, many of whom could not work because they did not have access to childcare, could have applied for unemployment insurance but instead applied to the PUA program given the information provided by the DLHR.[120] Ayuda Legal (2021) found that there were approximately 23,824 cases of collection actions. The organization found that the DLHR misled the applicants and then sent them collection letters because they were ineligible for the benefits of the PUA. Furthermore, the DLHR outsourced the issuing of collection letters to EVERTEC and Fast Enterprises LLC and paid these companies to update the Fast PUA platform to include a section for individuals who had received a collections letter to pay their debt.[121] This further exemplifies how these two corporations have profited from the mismanagement of the pandemic and their own technological failures.

By September 4, 2021, when PUA was finally discontinued, thousands of individuals had never received the help and economic support offered by the economic assistance program. Altogether, this is an example of how anticorruption interventions often end up targeting minoritized populations, by limiting access to necessary governmental services to the underserved communities. Anticorruption interventions were used to control, discipline, and punish the most vulnerable populations, rather than using these powers to prevent the contagion and guarantee the well-being of the population. Punitive governance transforms the state's emphasis from providing essential services to policing the access to those services.

On May 11, 2023, Governor Pedro Pierluisi issued OE-2023–12, terminating the COVID-19 pandemic state of emergency, three years after its enactment. This termination coincided with the expiration of the federal declaration of emergency by the Biden administration. However, it did not mark the end of the detrimental impact of colonial legality in PR. Rather, it signified another shift in the dynamics of colonial legality, accommodating local elites to sustain wealth extraction and capital accumulation structures.

This chapter elucidated the role of law in three important aspects of the pandemic. First, the uses of the state of emergency and executive orders to manage the COVID-19 pandemic and its social, public health, and economic consequences are embedded in longstanding legal and crisis management practices of colonial legality. And from within this context, these crisis management techniques are exponentially amplified or expanded in every instance. A telling instance is that Governors Vázquez and Pierluisi have overreached in their uses of executive orders and imposed draconian emergency measures, such as the approval of Law 35 of 2020: that is, legal and administrative efforts to address periods of crisis enhanced and exacerbated the impact of the crisis on underserved and vulnerable populations. COVID-19, as with many other crises, drastically impacted poor communities, people of color, precarious workers, the elderly, migrants, queer communities, and the unhoused.

Second, the chapter discussed the role of the pharmaceutical industry in PR and demonstrated how these corporations have systematically undermined PR's capacity to address the multilayered crisis. These corporations have engaged in a dynamic of wealth extraction without effectively contributing to the Puerto Rican society. That is, in Puerto Rico the uses of the colonial state of exception creates a colonial regime of permission that enables lack of accountability. It is precisely in this context that this chapter aimed to interrogate the promises of economic development through tax exemption and deregulation. Promoting or onshoring the pharmaceutical industry ignores the systemic harm of the economic development policies implemented by the US and PR governments that had attracted these corporations to PR.

Third, the use of anticorruption and anti-fraud policies exacerbated the impact of the pandemic among poor and working-class communities. Anticorruption policies focused on petty corruption and limited the access of minoritized populations to basic state or governmental services. At the same time, these policies disregarded the large-scale and pervasive forms of fraud in which local elites and government officials engage in wealth extraction and capital accumulation. Similarly, there was no attention paid to the large frauds perpetrated on the PPP loans. Grand corruption in the management of the COVID-19 pandemic, as in previous crises, is a fundamental part of the structure of colonial legality. Therefore, the structural dynamics of grand corruption in recovery and relief efforts drastically exacerbate the impact of crisis and manufacture further crises and disasters.

Emergency powers, punitive anticorruption measures, and emergency legislation (instead of enabling an effective and humane response to the pandemic) undermined PR's capacity to deal with the crisis. The next chapter looks at the sociolegal mobilizations for the access to information and their efforts to interrupt the dynamic of wealth extraction.

SIX

TRANSPARENCY

Transparency and anticorruption interventions are often discussed as key legal and public policy measures to address and manage the Puerto Rican multilayered crisis.[1] There is a general understanding in Puerto Rico and the United States that the multilayered crisis is the result of corruption, patrimonialism, misuse of public funds (including pork barrel spending), and lack of transparency in public administration. Corruption narratives became particularly salient in 2016, when the US Congress was debating the bill that would become PROMESA.[2] Politicians, commentators, and public policy practitioners argued that PROMESA would help PR in its fight against corruption and therefore help the archipelago restructure its failing economy. In many ways, PROMESA and the FOMB were constructed as an anticorruption intervention that—by imposing austerity measures, privatizing public services, and reducing the number of public employees, among other prescriptions—could alleviate PR inefficiencies and the poor governance that led the archipelago to the financial and economic crisis. In this corruption narrative, the crisis was highly moralized and was defined as the result of Puerto Ricans' lack of fiscal discipline and unscrupulous spending.[3] Thus, the solution to the crisis consisted of curtailing corruption by denying Puerto Rican self-governance and overriding PR's limited internal democratic processes. Paradoxically, in this corruption narrative, colonialism and colonial legality are often absent.

As the history of the 2008 Great Recession demonstrates, economic and financial crisis are often moralized and blamed on citizens, and not on the legal and economic structures that manufactured the conditions of the crisis.[4] In this context, the PR government and the local elites effectively articulated and accommodated their positions to manage US colonial anticorruption interventions. As a result, the PR government started implementing limited transparency and anticorruption policies aimed at curtailing corruption in the public administration. Largely embedded in the anticorruption and transparency global trends that emerged in the post–Cold War era, several government officials, politicians, and commentators made the anticorruption fight their own crusade.[5] These people focused on cases of petty corruption or corruption in the public sector, while disregarding the corruption of the powerful. Thus, anticorruption has become an integral part of the logic and practice of colonial legality, and of the ways in which the local elites re-accommodate to maintain their strategic position in the colonial structures of wealth extraction and capital accumulation.

Despite the PR government's articulation of anticorruption as part of colonial legality, the civil society organizations studied in this book, have consistently challenged state-imposed anticorruption policies. These organizations, which emerged in the context of the economic crisis and in the wake of the Hurricane María, have systemically used legal mobilizations, litigation, and advocacy to strategically demand the right to access information and to challenge the structure of wealth extradition enabled by colonial legality. Although these organizations might reproduce principles of neoliberal accountability, compliance, and transparency, I have found that they also provide a strategic conceptualization of legal mobilizations for transparency and access to information that challenges those neoliberal understandings. This is what I have called legal interruptions, or the resignification of transparency and access to information to interrupt the brutal process of wealth extraction enabled by colonial legality. In asymmetrical relations of power such as the colonial subordination of PR, legal mobilization and the discourse of rights become an effective device to resist and interrupt the exploitation.

Furthermore, the legal mobilizations of organizations such as Center of Investigative Journalism (CPI) and Proyecto de Acceso a la Información have ignited sociopolitical demonstrations. Their mobilizations have responded to, for example, the death toll caused by the criminogenic mismanagement of Hurricane María (discussed in Chapter 4), FOMB's austerity measures and lack of accountability (discussed in Chapters 1 and 3), and the role of the CPI in publishing the leak of a now-infamous chat popularly known as Telegramgate, which led to the Puerto Rican Summer of 2019.[6] These demonstrations prompted the resignation of Ricardo Rosselló as governor of PR on the evening of July 24, 2019, after more than two weeks of demonstrations, in which hundreds of thousands of Puerto Ricans protested, marched, and rallied (in PR, the United States, and worldwide), demanding his resignation, transparency, and accountability.[7] The Summer of 2019, as shown in the Epilogue, can be understood as an anticorruption mobilization; in a broader sense, it symbolizes a period of rupture with Puerto Rican legal and political practices. This time period suspended the repetitive temporality of colonial legality and represented an opportunity for enactment of *a real state of exception.*[8]

This chapter shows how anticorruption and pro-transparency policies have shaped significant segments of the Puerto Rican resistance to US and PR crisis management, and to the dynamic of wealth extraction put in place by US colonialism. Legal interruptions are examples of the opposition to the symbiotic relationship among corruption, law, and colonialism in PR.[9] First, the chapter discusses the legal framework defining anticorruption policies in PR. This section focuses on the definitions and understandings of corruption deployed by the PR government in the face of the multilayered crisis. Second, it engages with the Transparency Network, its legal mobilizations, and the legal history of the right to access information. Finally, it demonstrates how these legal mobilizations have constructed an understanding of transparency that allows for a systemic opposition and interruption of the brutal force of colonial legality.

FRAMING ANTICORRUPTION INTERVENTIONS

In previous chapters, I have shown how US interventions with the PR government in the wake of Hurricane María, the 2020 earthquakes, and the COVID-19 pandemic undermined PR's capacity to address these disasters and the multilayered crisis. At every stage of the multilayered crisis, corruption and anticorruption narratives have been instrumentalized by the US government to deny Puerto Rican self-determination in deciding how to better address the emergency. Corruption narratives have also limited access to disaster relief funds and imposed additional oversights and legal limitations on PR's self-governance. These anticorruption interventions served to blame Puerto Ricans for their own suffering, rather than addressing the colonial practices that render Puerto Ricans as less deserving of federal government support. That is, US colonial anticorruption interventions in PR operate as additional instances in the structure of domination and subordination constituted by the colonial state of exception. Therefore, these colonial anticorruption interventions operate along the lines of race, gender, class, and colonial forms of power and have systemically harmed communities in PR.

Elsewhere, I have engaged with a systemic analysis and discussion of the sociolegal, criminological, and Puerto Rican scholarship on corruption and anticorruption, in which I have demonstrated how Puerto Rican anticorruption laws contribute to the multilayered crisis.[10] Hence, this section only provides a short discussion of how anticorruption became central in the operation of colonial legality. In this sense, it is helpful to incorporate the framework of coloniality to underscore the operativity of US colonial anticorruption interventions in PR.[11] That is, corruption narratives serve as colonial differences, in which the colonized other is categorized as inherently corrupt. It is under such racialized understandings that colonies and colonized people are constructed as corrupt.

Colonial anticorruption interventions have blended with global capitalist dynamics and economic policies, becoming part of the hegemonic global economic system, institutionalized by the history of colonization and sustained by the structural forces of capitalism. Corruption has been key to the historical transformation of global capitalism, from colonialism to the neoliberal globalization. This shows that the dialectic of corruption and anticorruption is in constant movement, as each anticorruption effort transforms the logic of corrupt practices, and each corrupt practice calls forth new kind of anticorruption measures. Similarly, ideas of corruption and economic backwardness have consistently featured in imperialist and racialized historical narratives that invoke the primitiveness of less developed states to justify colonial interventions. Thus, corruption narratives were, and continue to be, key technologies for justifying colonialism of non-western societies.

In this colonial narrative of the corrupt "other," western rule of law and "democratization" are bestowed as anticorruption technologies for the colonies.[12] In the colonial anticorruption narratives, places lacking bureaucratic liberal institutions, rule of law, a market economy, and a strong private sector are almost always equated with corruption. Colonial anticorruption interventions in colonial contexts can be understood as a form of power-mongering: a means of maintaining economic and political dominance of a particular elite group.

The US colonial anticorruption interventions in PR constituted a paradigmatic example of how corruption narratives are inextricably tied to race, class, gender, and colonial relations of power. For example, in the wake of Hurricane María, PR was systemically portrayed by the Trump administration and in the US media as one of the most corrupt jurisdictions in the United States. The Trump administration paved the way for dehumanizing policies, in which colonial, racialized, poor, and gendered subjects are not worthy of full legal and moral consideration. These colonial and racialized anticorruption interventions have systemically harmed PR—either through specific actions, interventions, or omissions that precluded the PR government from developing adequate emergency preparedness or through anticorruption policies put in place by the colonial state of exception. This becomes particularly clear when the PR government and local elites' accommodation to the US government anticorruption interventions are considered.

Anticorruption and transparency have become central in the operation of colonial legality after PROMESA was enacted.[13] Between 2017 and 2019, Ricardo Rosselló's administration legislated a series of policies intended to transform the PR government. These laws followed internationally led anticorruption practices, such as good governance policies, administrative and civil service reforms advancing meritocratic hiring, wage incentive programs, electronic government platforms, and publicly accessible databases of official incomes and public procurement. As a result, Rosselló's administration and local elites manufactured an understanding of corruption associated only with specific violations of law.

This focus produced a hyper-emphasis on individual cases of fraud, bribery, kickbacks, and pay-for-play incurred by public employees. This ignores the structural dynamics of corruption and how it manifests through cronyism, patrimonialism, and the legislation of laws and economic policies that favor corporations and the local elites to the detriment of the public good. As the co-founder of CPI, investigative journalist and lawyer Oscar Serrano commented in our interview,

> PR has seen a process of legalization of corruption in every instance. You see people using government power for their own benefit, and that is corruption. The concept of "private benefit" is open-ended. It is not only for officials, but it can extend to friends, relatives, acquaintances. And whether it is encoded is something else. Because one thing that I can tell you, what I have seen, is an increasing effort to legalize these processes—to legalize these forms of corruption.

The process of legalizing corruption described by Serrano can be identified in Rosselló's anticorruption measures that ignore the dynamic of wealth extraction described earlier. For example, Rosselló's administration implemented the following anticorruption laws and policies: an executive order to establish the public policy on transparency and accessibility to data in the executive branch;[14] the Government of Puerto Rico Administration and Transformation Act;[15] a law to create the Office of the Inspector General of the Government of PR;[16] the Anticorruption Code for the New Puerto Rico;[17] an executive order to create a public registry of lobbyists;[18] the Puerto Rico Open Data Act;[19] and the Transparency and Expedited Procedure for Access to Public Information Act.[20]

These laws and executive orders attest to the Rosselló administration's legalistic view of transparency and anticorruption policies. But they also illustrate a pattern of implementing anticorruption legal reforms that do not represent a real commitment to addressing corruption; rather, they are a legal façade that allows governmental figures to claim that they have implemented the necessary measures to fight corruption. This is part of the logic of colonial legality, which consists of not actually addressing the issue at hand but rather managing it in a way that wealth extraction can continue. Serrano's reflection on the intertwined connection among law, state of emergency, and corruption is perhaps the best description of this phenomenon:

> The emergency orders themselves, for example, that is a state of exception. Take for example the so-called request for proposal: the use of request for proposals to manage government purchases instead of an auction. The law says that you must hold an auction, but the emergency allows you not to do that or not to do it exactly as it should be done. And then why do we have the constant extension of the state of exception to the point of it becoming the norm? That is a stretch to legalize what is not legal. It is not legal. They only become legal by exception and are supposed to be

> justified—justified at the highest level that exists, which is an emergency that affects the entire country. But that, instead of being the exception, becomes the norm. And it becomes the norm governor after governor, without the legislature questioning, without saying anything.

Serrano elucidated how corruption becomes embedded in colonial legality. He further demonstrated that the legalization of corrupt practices happened as part of the management of the crisis. Thus, demonstrating the legislation of anticorruption measures within the colonial legality is intended to normalize practices of wealth extraction, as we saw in the aftermath of Hurricane María, by giving the appearance of addressing corruption, without in fact doing so.

This logic of anticorruption is particularly clear in the enactment and implementation of the Anticorruption Code for the New Puerto Rico (Law 2). Law 2 was aimed at unifying the different existing anticorruption laws, therefore, "strengthening the tools to fight corruption and broaden the protections available to individuals who report acts of corruption."[21] The law was approved to some extent as a prerequisite for obtaining federal recovery funds and was designed to address the administrative limitations imposed by the federal government in the aftermath of Hurricane María. As part of my participatory observation in the drafting of a series of amendments to Law 2, I identified a consensus among the civil society organizations on the limits of this law in targeting corruption. That is, Law 2 ignores the systemic and structural dynamics of corruption in PR.

For instance, the law defined corruption as the "abuse of a public authority to obtain undue advantage, generally secretly and privately." It goes on to argue that other forms of corruption in PR are the "improper use of privileged information, patronage, bribery, influence peddling, extortion, fraud, embezzlement, malfeasance in office, *quid pro quo*, cronyism, co-optation, nepotism, impunity, and despotism." This definition largely equates corruption to bribery and focuses on agent-based or individualistic acts of misappropriation. This definition of corruption disregards the structural dynamic and historical processes and organizational instances that enable corruption. These are definitions that often see corruption as a problem of the public sector, bureaucracy, individuals with personal interests, and as a result of the unnecessary concentration of economic decision-making in the hands of governments. This narrow definition of corruption has produced similarly restrictive anticorruption policies, such as privatization of public agencies and corporations, deregulation, and opening to the free market. These public policies do not close the door to corruption, but rather normalize corruption of the powerful and increase inequality and wealth extraction.

Even when Law 2 acknowledges that the most common manifestations of corruption in PR are the result of the strong ties between public officials and the private sector, and the normalization of bribery, the anticorruption measures developed by the law are merely targeting the public sector. Several of my interviewees agreed that public procurement and the government's contracts of services are the main cause of corruption. Yesmín Valdivieso, the PR comptroller, stated in our interview that "today, most of the problems are always in contracting, and corruption is related to a contract." Similarly, Luis Pérez Vargas, director of the Office of Governmental Ethics, noted in our interview "that corruption in public procurement, in contracting services and nepotism at the municipal level are the most frequent manifestations of corruption in PR."

Despite the consensus on the prevalence of corruption in the symbiotic relations between the private and the public sectors, and malfeasance steaming from the outsourcing and privatization of governmental services, Law 2 pushes further on the artificial distinction between the public and the private sector. For instance, Title III introduces the Code of Ethics for Contractors, Suppliers and Applicants for Economic Incentives of the Executive Agencies. Law 2 established the way the public and private sectors should interact, and most importantly, how the private sector ought to interact with public employees or what type of behavior is allowed.

In tandem with this, Law 2 promotes a punitive approach to anticorruption.[22] To advance this approach, it expands the list of offenses that are excluded from the benefits of the "suspended sentence." Additionally, the law expands the mandatory training on sound administration; facilitates access to public information and transparency; and broadens the rights of whistleblowers (see Section 4.2).[23] Training and capacity building are described by Yesmín Valdivieso, Luis Pérez Vargas, and Ivelisse Torres Rivera (the inspector general of PR) as one of the most important measures introduced by the law. For them, the best mechanisms to curtailing corruption in PR is promoting a better understanding of the norms and laws and creating the mechanism for denouncing cases of corruption. Once again, the emphasis is on the public sector rather than examining the structural dynamics of corruption in colonial legality.

Section 6 of Law 2 constitutes a further example of the punitive approach, establishing that the PR Department of Justice (PRDJ) must create a public registry of persons convicted of corruption and related offenses.[24] Section 6.5. establishes the secretary of the PRDJ as the custodian of the information entered in the registry with the responsibility of keeping and updating the information in the registry.[25] Moreover, the department shall ensure that the information of the registry is available electronically for examination by government agencies and the public. The PRDJ and the secretary of justice did not make the registry public, obstructed access to the information, and did not invest in its maintenance.

This is particularly clear when considering the litigation initiated by Sembrando Sentido and Proyecto de Acceso a la Información to gain access to this registry. On March 7, 2021, Sembrando Sentido successfully sued the PRDJ to make public the registry (Serrano 2021). This happened after several requests made by Sembrando Sentido and Proyecto de Acceso a la Información. On March 21, 2021, the PRDJ sent the list of names or a preliminary registry with only nineteen individuals to Sembrando Sentido (Serrano 2021). After additional efforts made by Sembrando Sentido, the PRDJ created the website and made the information public. The registry constitutes an archive of the ways in which the Puerto Rican government has manufactured a concrete idea of corruption associated with poor and racialized individuals. That is, the registry reflects that petty corruption is inextricably tied to race, class, gender, and colonial relations of power.

Law 2 also created an Anticorruption Interagency Group (Section 7), with the participation of members of the federal and local governments, involving the following functions: guaranteeing proper interagency communication and cooperation in all anticorruption efforts; collaborating with the Office of Government Ethics in any effort geared towards preventing and eradicating corruption; improving the ability of the government to receive information on potential acts of corruption; and improving procedures so as to avoid impunity (Section 7.2). Luis Pérez Vargas, the director of the Office of Government Ethics and coordinator of the group, noted in our interview:

> When I got to my first meeting, I decided to create a scaffolding so that regardless of who is the head of the agency, the group could work. And we began to identify where it was that we were crashing. And I made sure that the administrative investigation yields to the criminal investigations. One of the issues that was happening was that investigations were being carried out, perhaps at the federal level, the administrative level, and the state criminal level at the same time.

Pérez Vargas further argued that one of the most important measures taken by him and his team was to implement a system of communication that allowed all the members to better articulate the investigations. All my interviewees occupying governmental positions emphasized the need for developing better and more effective criminal investigations. Criminal law and punishment occupy a particular prominent place in colonial legal responses to sociopolitical and economic issues.

Despite these laws and anticorruption reforms put in place by the PR government, recent cases of corruption have been brought by the US Department of Justice. Unlike other US jurisdictions, PR is not allowed to bring state charges against individuals who have been already convicted in the federal justice system. This is a result of *Puerto Rico v. Sánchez-Valle (2016)* discussed in Chapter 1, in which the US Supreme Court ruled that prosecution by PR state courts cases that have already been prosecuted in federal courts violates the double jeopardy clause of the Fifth Amendment. As result of the colonial state of exception, the PRDJ is unable to prosecute individuals convicted of corruption at the federal level. Thus, the PRDJ has mainly used Law 2 to address cases of petty corruption, which are not normally prosecuted in the federal system.

One year after the enactment of Law 2, the Rosselló administration found itself facing numerous corruption cases, including the leak of the Telegram chat. Even when the Summer of 2019 had begun, Rosselló's statements emphasized describing the case as a technical problem that a law or executive order could solve. And so, it was under this understanding that Rosselló's administration created a list of lobbyists who in theory would bring transparency.[26] The executive order follows the same rationale as Law 2—that is, it focuses on petty corruption and on the separation between the public and private sectors.[27] In this context, the Rosselló administration also enacted[28] the Puerto Rico Open Data Act (Law 122) and the Transparency and Expedited Procedure for Access to Public Information Act (Law 141). Several members of the Transparency Network noted that Law 122 made it even harder the access statistical data and other important information, exacerbating the lack of transparency in the PR government.

Oscar Serrano, reflecting on the multiple cases of corruption, noted in our interview that, "if the public, if the governed accept corruption, there is no stopping it. There is simply no stopping it." And he continued by noting that the CPI and the Transparency Network are constantly seeking to demonstrate that

> corruption is not only illegal and the work that we do is not only to point out illegalities. It is also to point out immorality. Things that should not happen. The job is not that of the prosecutors who simply must see if the conduct is going to find a code that is already written. And the public discussion should not be that. The public discussion should not be if the law allows it. If the law allows it, there is a problem with the fact that the law allows it. And I see more and more as the public conversation turns more and more about what is legal and what is not legal.

Despite the constant pressure exercised by the Transparency Network and civil society organizations, the PR government continued implementing punitive legislation to target corruption in the public sector. This legalistic and punitive approach is exemplified by the Pedro Pierluisi administration, which issued a series of anticorruption and transparency executive orders declaring a "war against corruption"; the administration established a public policy of systemic collaboration with the local and federal law enforcement agencies[29] and established guidelines for promoting transparency and accountability in the contracting of professional services.[30] This happened while multiples cases of environmental crime and green corruption were emerging and after the FBI arrested several local politicians, including former Governor Wanda Vázquez. Thus, anticorruption legislation has largely been ineffective in curtailing corruption.

LEGAL INTERRUPTIONS: THE LEGAL MOBILIZATIONS FOR THE RIGHT TO ACCESS INFORMATION

Throughout this book I have shown how a series of civil society organizations have engaged in legal mobilizations, litigation, advocacy, and strategic uses of the law to demand accountability, transparency, and access to information from the PR government, the FOMB, and the US government. The Transparency Network has mobilized the PR and federal legal systems and has even brought cases to the US Supreme Court in an effort to curtail the brutal force of colonial legality. Most litigation for the right to access information has come from the collaborative and strategic efforts of the CPI, Proyecto de Acceso a la Información, Espacios Abiertos, and Sembrando Sentido. Think tanks and research organizations have joined with these organizations to systemically produce and democratize the information about different aspect of the multilayered crisis.

Carlos Ramos Hernández, one of the lawyers who argued *FOMB v. CPI* in the Supreme Court, described in our interview the legal mobilizations for the right to access information as part of three objectives: impact litigation, civic education, and legislative advocacy. When asked if he considered his work as a form of cause lawyering, Ramos Hernández stated,

> It is more than that. It is more high impact litigation. That I file a lawsuit, almost like a test case, like a test case thinking about the result, we don't know where it's going, but if it goes well, we're going to change the state of things. I see it a bit like that. *Yes, cause lawyering. Rebel Lawyering 100 percent.* That's what I was thinking we do.

Rebel Lawyering paints a powerful image of interruption and resistance to the state's lack of accountability. The ideas of impact litigation and rebel lawyering are embedded in a long line of Puerto Rican lawyers and activists who mobilized the law to create the conditions for social change. From anticolonial mobilizations, labor rights, and environmental protection to the defense of the most vulnerable communities, there is a long tradition of strategic litigation in PR. Thus, legal interruptions and their sociolegal impact must be understood as part of that tradition.[31]

Similarly, Luis José Torres, the co-director of Proyecto de Acceso a la Información, provided important descriptions of the role of lawyers and cause lawyering in the mobilizations for the access to information. Torres pointed out that the work of Proyecto de Acceso a la Información could be considered as part of the strategic litigations or the cause lawyering tradition.

> We think of ourselves as activists and operators of the law, but activists within the law. The truth is that I never saw myself as a traditional lawyer, or as a lawyer . . . and when I say a traditional lawyer, [I mean one] whose

> practice was so oriented towards litigation. On the contrary, during my first years in the profession, I believe that my interest in community advocacy and advocacy prevailed more, precisely because it seeks to demystify and deconstruct the judicial process. As [I] look precisely to convey this idea that law is as political as anything else, and that law is just another sphere where these power struggles take place.

Law is as political as anything else, and thus the mobilizations against colonial legality must also take place in this sphere. The politicization of the legal process, as Torres pointed out, is important for the organizations that have systemically engaged in litigation as a strategy of interruption. As Torres noted "the access to information cases could be a vehicle to propitiate things outside of court":

> We bring claims in which we first understand that we are addressing a gap in the public discussion. To say, there are issues that are not being discussed and that we precisely understand that they are not being discussed because there is a lack of transparency and a lack of access to information. And that perhaps the conditions are in place to make visible whatever can be achieved and then it will be smoothed out, that can promote changes in public policy or generate a sense of collective indignation that brings people into the streets.
>
> So, we try to choose cases with those elements in mind, and we have been fortunate to have found this kind of niche where we do very well. Either for reasons of pure luck, that we are at a juncture where the court hears these cases, some judges have arrived with sensitivities, or because it is not politically viable for the government to handle these cases in a way that is too antagonistic to the country. And I think that this has been important.

The importance of the legal mobilization for transparency and access information in PR is evidenced by the long list of cases brought by Proyecto de Acceso a la Información, Espacios Abiertos, Sembrando Sentido, among other organizations. Legal mobilizations were strategically implemented to interrupt the policies put in place by the colonial state of exception and the local elites to maintain the structure of wealth extraction. For example, CPI has brought several cases against the FOMB, demanding that the courts clarify whether the FOMB violated key principles of democracy, transparency, and accountability. This demand for public information became the US Supreme Court case *FOMB v. CPI* discussed in Chapter 1. That is, a dispute for the access to information promptly became a legal dispute about the colonial status of PR and the nature of the colonial sovereignty.

In what follows, I describe the emergence of the constitutional right to access information in PR and shows how the Transparency Network has used this jurisprudence to demand information and accountability from the PR government. This discussion evidences the centrality that the right to access information and transparency plays in legal interruptions.

The Right to Access Information and Colonial State Crimes

Oscar Serrano, Luis José Torres, and Carlos Ramos Hernández all mentioned the importance of the constitutional right to access information for the legal mobilizations for transparency in PR. Each noted that the right to access information has allowed civil society organizations to develop a litigation strategy aimed at holding the PR government accountable. For example, the Bill of Rights of the Puerto Rican Constitution recognizes the right to access information as derived from the right to free speech.[32] Ramos Hernández (2016) argued that during the Constitutional Convention in 1950, some delegates proposed including an article that expressly acknowledges the right to access of information—without the need to be subordinated to the right to free speech—but they were unsuccessful. Furthermore, the Code of Civil Procedure establishes that every citizen has a right to inspect and take a copy of any public document.[33] It is important to note that the Puerto Rican jurisprudence was largely developed before the enactment of the Freedom of Information Act (FOIA) of 1967.

Similarly, Luis José Torres and Carlos Ramos Hernández noted that the constitutional right to access information is entwined with the US and PR governments' historical repression of Puerto Rican pro-independence and anticolonial movements. That is, the right to access information cannot be understood without the long and brutal history of colonial state crimes in PR. The right to access information was recognized as a fundamental constitutional right following the PR Supreme Court's (PRSC) ruling in *Soto v. Secretary of Justice* (1982). In this case, documents from the Department of Justice regarding the political assassination of the anticolonial activists Carlos Soto Arriví and Arnaldo Darío Rosado were requested by Pedro Juan Soto and Ángeles Rivera Castillo, Soto Arriví's father and Rosado's widow, respectively. Soto Arriví and Rosado were murdered by PR police officers in *Cerro*

Maravilla (July 25, 1978). The PR Department of Justice denied the request for information due to a legal provision that decreed that documents generated during a police investigation had to be kept confidential. However, the PRSC ordered the delivery of the documents. By recognizing the constitutionality of the right to access information, the PRSC followed the federal jurisprudence of FOIA and established a standard of judicial review of strict scrutiny where all legislation must be interpreted in favor of the right of the people to be informed.

Carlos Ramos Hernández stated in our interview that "it is important to remember that this case [*Soto v. Secretary of Justice*] was not brought by the press, but by private citizens wanting to know what happened to their loved ones. In other words, the right of access to public information in Puerto Rico arises from citizens seeking to hold the government accountable." Ramos Hernández emphasized the role that citizens play in developing the constitutional right to access information, highlighting that this right should be understood as a collective right rather than an individual one. As the history of its development in the next decades has shown, legal mobilizations for this right have emphasized the collective right to access information, rather than individual use of the information.

Numerous other cases further developed the constitutional right to access information. *Noriega v. Hernández Colón* (1988) addressed the *carpetas* or files on "subversive activists,"[34] which were based on information collected illegally against members of the PR independence movement. In this case, the PRSC ordered the PR government to end this practice and make public the information that was illegally gathered. *Ortiz Rivera v. Bauermeister (2000)* clarified the requirements for those requesting access to documents. In *Bauermeister*, some citizens requested permission to examine files, reports, and determinations in criminal cases. Like most decisions after *Soto, Bauermeister* allowed the disclosure of the information requested. That is, the PRSC has consistently reaffirmed the constitutional nature of the right to access information.

Ramos Hernández (2016) has also shown that in cases such as *Nieves Falcón v. Junta de Libertad Bajo Palabra* (2003), the PRSC has limited the access to certain information. In this case the renowned anticolonial activist, scholar, and lawyer Luis Nieves Falcón sought access to the archives and documents related to pardons issued by former Governor Carlos Romero Barcelo between 1976–1984. Romero Barcelo is considered, by anticolonial activists, to have ordered the political assassination of Soto Arriví and Rosado in Cerro Maravilla. The request for access to pardons and other documents was conducted with the understanding that those documents could provide evidence of Romero Barcelo's role in the political assassination. Unlike previous cases, the PRSC ruled that the information was confidential, given that the information was not connected with the administration of justice in a criminal case and because the information could infringe on the rights of third parties. Despite this precedent, the PRSC has maintained as a general rule citizens' rights to access information.

Civil society organizations have also resorted to the right to access information when seeking information regarding acts of state violence and police brutality. Oscar Serrano points out that one of the first cases that the CPI investigated, together with Proyecto de Acceso a la Información, was against the PR Police Department in 2010.[35] In this case the CPI requested information about the rules and guidelines that police follow to record or videotape people participating in political demonstrations. The police admitted that they did not have any guidelines or rules in place and were ordered by the court to develop such policies. Additionally, in 2016, Proyecto de Acceso a la Información brought a case requesting access to the videos recorded by the police during the 2010 and 2011 UPR student strikes.[36] On October 3, 2016, the police delivered forty-eight DVDs; however, these DVDs did not contain the information requested.[37] The police argued that they did not have additional materials.

Similarly, Mari Mari Narváez, the executive director of Kilómetro Cero, noted in our interview that her organization has used the jurisprudence of the right to access information to request information about cases of police brutality and other instances of state violence.[38] Mari Narváez noted that

> We now have thousands of documents on police use of force. Every time a police officer uses force, it must be documented. We sued the police for access to information because we were asking for data on deaths and use of force. The deaths and the wounded and the mutilated by the use of force. We went to the [PR] Supreme Court, we had a victory in the Supreme Court, we coordinated the deliveries with the police, because they began to complain that they couldn't deliver so much at once. Later we negotiated a delivery schedule with the police, they knew this since April 2021. We coordinated a delivery schedule and we have already filed a motion saying they did not deliver the dead for the year 2021.

Mari Narváez mentioned a common problem identified in my interviews: that is, that the PR government consistently fails to deliver the requested information. Cecille Blondet also noted that sometime the PR government does not deliver the information.[39] In other instances, however, Oscar Serrano, Carla Minet and Cecille Blondet observed that the PR government has poor record keeping, which enhances the difficulties of holding the state accountable. The lack of recordkeeping and disorganized state of the Puerto Rican archives have been exacerbated by the multilayered crisis, austerity measures, and the disinvestment in preserving public documents.[40]

The Right to Access Information and the Economic and Financial Crisis

During the economic crisis, a notable transformation took place in legal mobilizations and litigations advocating for the right to access information. CPI, Espacios Abiertos, and Proyecto de Acceso a la Información began to utilize the constitutional right to access information to request financial, economic, budgetary, and public policy information from the Puerto Rican government and the FOMB. Between 2009 and 2019, Proyecto de Acceso a la Información brought seventeen cases to court—seven of them requested financial and economic information from the PR government and two requested information from the FOMB. This entailed a broadening of the scope of the right to access information, beyond the cases of state violence. That is, as a result of the multilayered crisis, these organizations began requesting highly specialized documents and information that would otherwise have remained concealed from the public. This change in focus became central to the research on how the public debt was manufactured and who participated in the process of indebtedness.

Organizations such as CPI, Espacios Abiertos, and Sembrando Sentido have made a significant effort to democratize the data gathered as a result of the legal mobilizations and have worked with scholars, progressive think tanks, and newspapers to contextualize, explain, and disseminate the information. For instance, the investigative journalist Carla Minet pointed out how members of the CPI, including herself, are part of the International Consortium of Investigative Journalists, and how they worked on the investigations leading to well-known cases such as the Pandora Papers, the Panama Papers, and the Paradise Papers.[41] Minet argued that,

> It is a job with a lot of impact, in terms of international politics, and it is also a training opportunity for us. Also establishing support networks, contact networks, is very valuable to us. And there are two stories that stood out, one that is about different people from Puerto Rico, headed by Chayanne[42] and Daddy Yankee,[43] who had properties and offshore accounts. But above all the most important story, the investigation that took us the longest, was the one on the international banks that have arrived in Puerto Rico in the last decade.[44] Many of which have offshore accounts as well.

Again, the transformation of PR into a colonial tax haven has been taking place as part of the emergency measures put in place to address the multilayered crisis. My interviewees noted that one of the most conspicuous issues consists of having access to the information on the tax expenditures and tax incentives that the PR government grants to corporations and investors. Particularly, Cecille Blondet, executive director of Espacios Abiertos, mentioned the legal mobilizations for the access to information regarding who received the tax incentives provided by Act 60. Similarly, Blondet noted that this tax policy constitutes an example of corruption and lack of transparency in the public administration:

> In Espacios Abiertos we believe in open government. Why do we believe in open government? Let us create an open, transparent, participatory government that is accountable and will also be a fairer and more equitable one. To the extent that we can all participate, not only those who have access to power, but everyone, we will be able to have a fairer and more equitable country. . . . The lack of transparency costs us. And we don't want to accept that. It costs us in many ways, the worst is corruption. The lack of transparency, opacity, is the seedbed of corruption.

Many of my interviewees noted that their efforts to increase intelligibility were done as part of initiatives to create civic engagement and empowerment and to counter corruption. Fighting corruption and compliance with the law, quickly became one of the main reasons to mobilize the right to access information. This is particularly clear in the legal mobilizations of the CPI and Proyecto de Acceso a la Información demanding transparency from the FOMB. As Efrén Rivera Ramos (2023) noted, in the wake of the Supreme Court ruling in *FOMB v. CPI*,

> The Supreme Court ends up endorsing the FOMB's burning desire to continue operating in the shadows. Without giving us good and solid reasons, the Court has constitutionally blessed the secrecy with which the FOMB tries to govern us. The majority of the Court is totally indifferent to the undemocratic effects of their decision. It is easy to conclude that, perhaps except for the period of the military regime in force between 1898 and 1900, we have never been so close to suffering a dictatorial government as at present. Because, how else to characterize the imposition of an unelected governmental body that invalidates the decisions of the elected representatives of the people and that now, to top it off, has just been authorized by the highest US judicial forum to govern without being accountable to the governed?

In the same vein, Carlos Ramos Hernández noted that "from the outset, the implications of the decision are disastrous for PR and the effective supervision of the decisions made by the FOMB." Ramos Hernández continued:

> This decision only applies to the FOMB and not to the government of PR or any of its dependencies, which continue to be subject to the constitutional right of access to information recognized by the PR Supreme Court more than forty years ago. In other words, this constitutional and fundamental right is still in force in our country. Only, for the moment, the FOMB appears to be exempt from it.

Thus, legal mobilizations for the right to access information have become, once again, a form of anticolonial opposition. In this way, mobilizing for access to information has become embedded in the struggle against the FOMB. Simultaneously, the civil society organizations have also tried to underscore the criminogenic dynamic at play in the management of the multilayered crisis.

TRANSPARENCY LAW AND LEGAL MOBILIZATIONS

On August 1, 2019, just a day before Rosselló's resignation became effective, his administration enacted the Transparency and Expedited Procedure for Access to Public Information Act (Law 141). Law 141 was described by the PR government as a mechanism to frame the constitutional right to access information and to provide a clear administrative process to access public information. The enactment of Law 141 of 2019 raised legal concerns among the Transparency Network, since it introduced new limitations to accessing governmental information and data.[45]

The law follows the transnational patterns of access to information laws enacted in other jurisdictions.[46] These laws allow governments to make credible promises of greater transparency and anticorruption efforts, while preserving their position of power.[47] Neoliberal implementation of transparency policies also could imply that the state would become less transparent, forcing citizens and activists to become proficient in bureaucratic literacy in order to audit and petition the state.[48] The idea of transparency as a bureaucratic virtue is not entirely new, but in the 1990s it became prominent as the central idea in global governance and economic development reforms.[49] During this period, information became the grease of both the market economy and democracy. Hence, failures of democracy and markets in the Global South were attributed to a lack of transparent information available to the citizenry. Law 141 is certainly one of the ways in which the PR government intended to legitimize an approach to transparency that allows it to maintain the structures of impunity or a colonial regime of permission.

Oscar Serrano, Carla Minet, Cecille Blondet, and Luis José Torres all commented that Law 141 was enacted without the consensus of investigative journalists, civil society organizations, and legal experts. They noted that, despite a long process of consultation and public engagement in the drafting the bill, the law did not reflect that process. Notwithstanding, Torres noted that faced with the limitations to the access to information created by the law, Proyecto de Acceso a la Información has engaged in strategic uses of law and litigation. For example, when Proyecto de Acceso a la Información considers a case that represents something of great public interest and in which

> the government does not want to deliver the information precisely because it knows that it will generate public discussion, because it has the potential to generate mobilization, we handle these cases outside Law 141. We presented a writ of mandamus, because these is the legal recourse that existed before Law 141. So, we always must be evaluating the type of case we have and how we are going to process it. Now, in terms of how cases are decided, I would not say that Law 141 has worsened, nor has it strengthened the right of access to information. It is not really the substantive component of the right of access to information. It is still, well, closed to that recognition of a constitutional right in *Soto*, of 1982. . . . Let's say that those general guidelines established by the Supreme Court have continued to be reiterated over the years, [and] they continue to control the adjudication in the courts.

These strategic uses of law described by Torres become clear when considering Proyecto de Acceso a la Información's litigation records. For example, since the enactment of Law 141 of 2019, Proyecto de Acceso a la Información has brought thirty cases against the PR government, of which fourteen have used the procedures established by the law, and sixteen have used the writ of mandamus or resorted to the courts to request that the PR government provide the documents requested.

In tandem with these mobilizations, the CPI and Carlos Ramos Hernández produced a report in October 2022, in which they demonstrated the systemic lack of governmental compliance with Law 141. The report evaluated the executive branch and its more than 120 agencies and looked at the 78 municipalities in their compliance with the law. The report also gathered data on the appointment and performance of the public records officers, the officials who are legally required to receive public records requests, process them, and facilitate access to them. It concludes that the PR government's implementation and execution is deficient and inconsistent.[50]

Carlos Ramos Hernández noted in our interview that institutional limitations created by the austerity measures implemented by the FOMB and the PR government curtailed the governmental compliance with the law. He argued that budgetary resources are needed to hire personnel and to put in place the necessary processes that guarantee the effective functioning of this law. He also noted that Law 141 faces limitations given the culture of opacity and the tendency of the local government to limit the access to information. Ramos Hernández stated:

> There is a culture of secrecy, of opacity. I believe that public institutions are so politicized that many public officials do not understand that they [access to documents] are owed to the people. And I think that also speaking of a colonial law, a state that has been very repressive, especially with leftist movements, with independence movements, that is tied to secrecy. A country that allowed *el Carpeteo* is a country that is wrong. And it is so ingrained in the culture of how the Puerto Rican police operated, particularly, that these things are passed from generation to generation a bit in how an agency operates, how the government operates.

Two important elements emerge from this quote: the culture of opacity and how Law 141 became inoperative.[51] Opacity and a "culture of opacity" in

PR was a common theme in my interviews, and many of my interviewees mentioned that it was a reason for their legal mobilizations. For example, Cecille Blondet pointed out that,

> We live in a culture of opacity where all the time we must go to court to request information, or where even with the technology that exists today, the information is not made available. And even information that I have access [to] is not made available to another person. We don't understand why. Well, because there is a n idea in the government that it must protect the information, and that is a mistake. The culture should be a culture of transparency. So, we try to make the public officials understand that their work is towards greater transparency, not towards putting [up] obstacles.

Blondet expanded on the tension between transparency and the culture of opacity and stated that "transparency is an ingredient of any democratic government." She continued, "to be transparent, a government must do it proactively. You must publish proactively, you must allow those who receive the information to also think, discuss, talk about what they receive. And decision-making must be open and there must be accountability."

In this understanding, the culture of opacity entails a moralized description of lack of compliance by the PR government. By articulating the rhetoric of culture, instead of colonial regime of permission, some of my interviewees developed a moralized narrative of the state, and its bureaucrats, that replicated some colonial instantiations and descriptions of the Puerto Rican government. This is not gratuitous, but rather demonstrates how anticorruption intervention in a colonial context constitutes a legalized and moralized common sense about corruption. Corruption narrative and anticorruption intervention thus become powerful devices in the Puerto Rican sociolegal and political imaginary.

Similarly, several of my interviewees offered descriptions and definitions of transparency aiming to go beyond the legalistic definition offered by Law 141 and by the PR government. For example, Oscar Serrano defined transparency as

> the exercise of responsibility and public power based on the right of the people to always know what their government is doing. Which in turn emanates from the constitutional principle that power really rests with the people and never leaves the people, and that constitutions are a trans-

> action where the people cede some powers to the government apparatus in pursuit of the common good. But it is giving up some rights, [and] not giving them up. And the condition for that to happen is that the people have the capacity to know what the government does with those funds and with its decisions.

In the same vein, Espacios Abiertos has defined transparency in terms of the right to access information and consistently emphasizes following these ten principles:

1. It is a human and constitutional right and not a governmental concession.
2. It is applicable to all public entities.
3. Any legislation or regulation must promote the maximum disclosure of information.
4. Any exception to access of information must be limited and justified.
5. Denial of public information must be justified by established legal principles.
6. Any refusal to supply information must be challenged through administrative and judicial means.
7. Laws should provide for fair and rapid processing of requests as well as for an equally rapid process of administrative and judicial review of the response to that request.
8. Clear, detailed, and updated information must be accessible to citizens through different means.
9. There must be clear protection for whistleblowers.
10. All legislation on access to information must promote open government.[52]

These principles are central to how the Transparency Network defines legality and how their members understand rights and rights consciousness. However, the principles do not convey or demonstrate how these organizations can challenge state power or the process of wealth extraction deployed by colonial legality. Rather, one could argue that these principles are deeply embedded in transnational discourses of good governance, compliance, and accountability. Thus, one ought to ask how and under what conditions these understandings of governance became the guiding principle for achieving state accountability.

The possible response that this chapter aims to articulate is that, under conditions of exploitation and subordination, such as those in PR, these principles could express a strategic response to, or an interruption of, the temporality of colonial legality. While the state of emergency normalizes lack of participation in the decision-making, requiring citizens' full obedience, and imposing punitive approaches to corruption, the demand for transparency and for access to information represent legal interruptions to the operativity of exceptionality.

This chapter has shown how legal mobilizations for access to information could reveal the structures of wealth extraction that are operating behind the logic of crisis, emergency, and anticorruption. By evidencing these processes, legal interruptions force colonial legality to reassert itself, reinstating and delimiting the space that is allowed for interaction and participation. Thus, these legal mobilizations produce an interruption or a rupture in the structure of exceptionality that colonial legality must address.

This became particularly clear in the wake of the US Supreme Court determination in *FOMB v. CPI* (2023), in which the court stated that the doctrine of sovereign immunity protects the FOMB from requests to access information under Law 141 and the PR Constitution. The FOMB has begun using this doctrine to deny access to information to civil society organizations. For example, on June 30, 2023, the FOMB denied the request for access to documents concerning the certified fiscal plan made by Espacios Abiertos on June 7, 2023.[53] In their letter of denial, the FOMB made clear that the constitutional right to access to information does not apply to them. This assumed a re-accommodation of the colonial state of exception to legal interruptions, and in which legal mobilizations were made ineffective by the US Supreme Court. Thus, one could assume that the Transparency Network and the civil society organizations will deploy other techniques to interrupt the colonial processes of exploitation and wealth extraction.

In asymmetrical power relations such as the colonial subordination of PR, the law, legal mobilizations, and the rights discourses become an effective device to resist and interrupt the exploitation. However, these mobilizations are not designed to transform and disrupt the colonial relation. For that, we ought to look at practices of colonial ruptures.

EPILOGUE

REIMAGINING

This book has underscored the legal structure of wealth extraction deployed by colonial legality in Puerto Rico—colonial legal structure that has manufactured the conditions for the multilayered crisis and systemically harmed the most vulnerable sectors of Puerto Rican society. In the face of colonial legality, civil society organizations have deployed a series of legal mobilizations and litigation strategies to interrupt the operations of this system of wealth extraction. These legal interruptions have been effective at evidencing and limiting the impact of colonial legality; however, the mobilizations are not able to disrupt the functioning of the colonial legality. For that, *a real state of exception* or *a radical process of rupture* with the colonial legality is needed.

As Benjamin reminds us in his Thesis VIII, the real state of exception is the sole means to confront the normalized state of exception. This real state of exception represents a radical rupture from the destructive cycle of legal violence enabled by the state of exception as structure and is an opening to the possibility of *justice*. The real state of exception serves as the entry point for the oppressed to engage in history, by bringing about a lasting transformation of the structure of domination. For Benjamin, the potential for justice always lies beyond the bounds of the law, necessitating a radical departure from legality. This rupture from the perpetual cycle of colonial legal violence can only be achieved through the real state of exception.

In this Epilogue, I explore the Summer of 2019 and #Wandalismo as the two mobilizations that effected temporary ruptures with the logic of colonial legality. The popular demand for Ricardo Rosselló's resignation and the uprising that took place between July 13 and August 2, of 2019,[1] constitute what Puerto Rican scholarship has termed the Puerto Rican Summer of 2019 (or *el Verano Boricua).*[2] This uprising was prompted by a series of corruption cases, brought to light by the Center for Investigative Journalism (CPI) after publishing the Telegram chat; the negligent management of the aftermath of Hurricanes Irma and María;[3] and the austerity measures imposed by the PR government and the FOMB. For the protestors, Rosselló was not only a corrupt politician, but his administration came to symbolize a larger context of state violence, colonial abandonment, and social harm manufactured by colonial legality. It is worth noting that this was the first time, since the Commonwealth of Puerto Rico or Estado Libre Asociado de Puerto Rico was established in 1952, that a governor resigned as a result of popular demonstrations. The two weeks of consecutive mobilizations and demonstrations constituted a significant rupture with the repetitive temporality of crisis and the logic of colonial legality.

Then, on January 23, 2020, thousands of Puerto Ricans marched on the streets of San Juan behind a banner that read: "Stop the Criminal Negligence. Resign Wanda!" The demonstration was part of a series of anticorruption mobilizations that took place after the discovery of a series of warehouses containing emergency supplies to help with the impact of Hurricane María as discussed in Chapter 4. On X (formerly Twitter), the hashtags #WandaRenuncia and #Wandalismo trended on January 25 and 26, 2020. #Wandalismo, a Spanish play on words, combines the first name of former Governor Wanda Vázquez with vandalism, aiming to convey that her administration, by not helping the affected communities, was engaging in vandalism against the people.

The Summer of 2019 and #Wandalismo were temporary ruptures and challenges to colonial legality. For instance, in their accounts of the demonstrations, Marisol LeBrón (2021) and Christopher Powers (2020) showed how the protests became not only spaces of resistance and mourning, but also life, joy, and pleasure. In the different accounts of the Summer of 2019, one can identify how these protests aimed at restoring life beyond the narrow strictures of colonial legality. Thus, these mobilizations can be understood as going beyond legal or legalistic conceptions of politics and operating through recognition, generosity, and the ability to feel with others. The practices of colonial ruptures, therefore, give preference to those who have been victims of colonial, racial, and gender violence, those who have been historically oppressed and subjugated to colonial governance. Colonial ruptures imply a broader understanding of the processes of reparations for colonial violence and its catastrophes.

In the context of the Summer of 2019, the practices of colonial ruptures can be understood as the opposition to the colonial corruption narratives and interventions assembled by the Trump administration, the FOMB, and the PR government. As shown in the previous chapters, anticorruption interventions imposed by the United States in PR, and the development of punitive approaches to anticorruption implemented by the PR government, prevented Puerto Ricans from accessing emergency relief in the aftermath of Hurricane María, the 2020 earthquakes, and during the COVID-19 pandemic. Similarly, these colonial policies denied Puerto Ricans their autonomy and self-determination and prevented them from actively participating in the solutions to the crisis. Colonial anticorruption intervention generates systemic social harms.

The Summer of 2019—in its complexity, multidimensionality, and diversity—crafted a richer interpretation of corruption.[4] The demonstrations emphasized the systemic and political operativity of corruption, giving new meaning to this concept—one that emphasized the corruption of the powerful. Demonstrators utilized the number 4,645 to memorialize those who died as a result of negligent management in the aftermath of Hurricane María.[5] This number served as a symbol of mourning, but also reflected the general understanding that Rosselló's administration, by not providing basic recovery aid in the wake of Hurricane María, was responsible for the deaths. Protestors also demanded that Rosselló's administration and members of the FOMB should resign due to their alleged corruption and harmful austerity measures. The protestors—demonstrating based on their belief of the corruption of every part of the Puerto Rican and US governments, or that these governments only serve the interests of the bondholders and hedge funds—radicalized the definitions and understandings of corruption. This is exemplified by the banner leading the massive march that took place on July 22, 2019,[6] which said "#RickyRenuncia #NiCorruptosNiCobardes" ("#Resign Ricky #Neither

Corrupt nor Cowards"). This banner clearly demonstrated that the Summer of 2019 identified corruption as the central dimension of their mobilizations.

These two examples display the mourning for those who died in the wake of Hurricane María and the resignification of corruption as a systemic part of colonial legality. Therefore, for the protestors, the problem was the colonial legal structure, the symbiotic relationship between the government and colonial capital, and the lack of transparency and democracy. This understanding of corruption explains why the rule of law and legality were not used as rhetorical devices during the Summer of 2019. Rather, the demonstrations emphasized a radical claim for the transformation of the government. For a two-week period, PR experimented with the suspension of the permanent state of emergency imposed by Rosselló's administration to manage every aspect of the multilayered crisis. The Summer of 2019 constituted a preliminary attempt to establish *a real state of exception*.

The call for Rosselló's resignation suspended legality and created a space in which the terms of the debate were not based on the constitutionality of the event, but on the popular claim for alternate ways of doing politics. Even when the Puerto Rican police engaged in excessive use of force and rioting under the justification that after 11 pm the demonstrations were no longer protected by the Constitution, protestors did not articulate their claims in terms of legality, but rather, in the terms of political demands.[7]

At least fifty-two people were affected by different types of interventions by law enforcement during the protests. As Kilómetro Cero (2019) reported, this number does not include the hundreds of people estimated to have suffered the effects of tear gas fired throughout the streets of Viejo San Juan on multiple occasions. Additionally, Kilómetro Cero argued that at least seventeen were arrested and twenty-seven were injured by the police's use of batons, rubber bullets, pepper spray, and tear gas, as well as beatings, property damage, and other assaults. Kilómetro Cero reported five complaints regarding crowd management, use of force by the police, and intimidation by law enforcement officers on social media. Even though these intimidations were made via social media, Kilómetro Cero reported that they still did not have the necessary documentation of them.

Despite intimidation and police violence, the Summer of 2019 ousted Ricardo Rosselló and his closer allies and created the conditions for a new understanding of accountability. Moreover, the Summer of 2019 also symbolized the convergence of multiple demands against corruption, austerity, environmental degradation, the transformation of PR into a tax haven, and more. These mobilizations, of course, did not take place in a vacuum; they are part of a long process of transformation that began with the mobilization against the US Navy in Vieques, radicalized in the context of the student strikes of 2010 and 2017, put in practice by the active opposition to PROMESA and the FOMB, and recovery efforts and self-organizing after María.[8] The Summer of 2019 operated as a concrete example of the beginning of a radical rupture with colonial legality.

However, the law and colonial legality again became the focus of social mobilization when Pedro Pierluisi was appointed secretary of state[9] and then assumed the governorship for a weekend.[10] The constitutionality of the appointment of Pierluisi went before the PR Supreme Court[11] on August 7, 2019, in the case of *Senate of Puerto Rico v. Pedro Pierluisi*. This legal capture was carried out, at the same time, by the local political parties, by commentators, and by some members of the legal academy who thought it necessary to return the debates and political activism to the framework provided by colonial legality. In other words, there was an urgency to return to the limited political imagination and conservative political space that has characterized colonial legality. Despite this neoliberal counter-revolutionary movement, the critiques of corruption of the powerful and the opposition to colonial legality continued.

For instance, the #Wandalismo demonstration of January 2020 implemented similar strategies as the Summer of 2019, demanding the elimination of PROMESA and the FOMB and the resignation of Wanda Vázquez. It is important to note that during the Summer of 2019 demonstrators also demanded Vázquez's resignation, when she actively thwarted investigations on the alleged corruption cases surrounding Rosselló's administration. It is precisely in this context that the use of criminal negligence and demands for Vázquez's resignation become important. For the demonstrators, her administration represented the continuation of the criminogenic and corrupt Rosselló administration.

Two important aspects emerged from the January 2020 demonstrations. First, they articulated creative and critical understandings of the earthquakes and the criminogenic role of the state in their management. The demonstrators coined #Wandalismo, referring to the corrupt management of the earthquakes and the lack of distribution of emergency supplies. #Wandalismo became the critical conceptualization of the criminal negligence that Puerto Ricans have been enduring.[12] Thus, Puerto Ricans questioned the role of the US and PR governments in the management of disasters and held the United States, the FOMB, and the PR government accountable for the lack of preparedness, the devastation generated by the earthquakes, and the lack of recovery and aid relief in the aftermath. #Wandalismo aimed to shame and blame the local government for the systemic harm that exacerbated the devastation.

The second aspect that emerged from the demonstrations against #Wandalismo is resistance to state and police violence. On January 23, shortly before 11 pm and after allegedly announcing that the crowd needed to disperse, the police declared the protest illegal and began launching tear gas and firing nonlethal ammunition at the protestors.[13] Despite these acts of state violence, protests continued with their political demands against #Wandalismo. In other words, they created an opening for building a more just PR and imagining alternate futures in opposition to systemic abandonment, colonial state crimes, crises, and disasters.

The Summer of 2019 and #Wandalismo, in their diversity and multiplicity, engaged in a systemic disruption of the repetitive temporality of the crisis constituted by colonial legality. Certainly, these demonstrations did not address or represent a solution to all the issues discussed through this book. Rather, they operated as specific instantiations of popular and political demonstrations against the rationality and systems of domination deployed by colonial legality. That is, they constituted a non-legal interruption, or a temporary rupture with the neoliberal rationality that has constituted the epistemic feedback loop in which every claim and demand must be articulated in terms of colonial legality. These demonstrations are important because they constructed and operated within a different epistemic regimen, one that goes beyond the limited legal framework defined by the US and PR governments. Hence, colonial ruptures.

These practices of colonial ruptures are embedded in the lived experiences of Puerto Ricans during the multilayered crisis; they can be found in demonstrations against the transformation of PR into a tax haven and in the demands for a just recovery (or the hashtag #NoLeDonenalGobierno) in the aftermath of Hurricane Fiona. Puerto Ricans have experienced a reconfiguration of politics that is not only defined by demonstrations, the uses of social media, and the articulation of anticorruption discourses, but by ruptures with the law and the legal system. However, these temporary ruptures remain in the terrain of possibilities and are not yet able to generate an anticolonial process. For PR to survive the brutal violence of colonialism, a real process of decolonization is needed. Although this process is yet to come, for now, we can identify the emergence of these colonial ruptures.

As PR continues under a colonial state of exception, characterized by ongoing dynamics of wealth extraction, *Crisis by Design* proposes an open-ended conclusion. Until there is a real process of decolonization in which the processes of wealth extraction are ended, only legal interruptions and temporary ruptures with colonial legality can disrupt the practices described in this book.

Crisis by Design has theorized the processes and dynamics through which law and exceptionality have operated and manufactured a colonial multilayered crisis. Moreover, this theorization can help us understand that seemingly unfinished task of law—capturing life in all instances, in all its fragments. To the margins, and in the fragments of what seems like an all-encompassing colonial system, life still strives.

NOTES

Introduction

1. When it made landfall in PR, Fiona was a Category 1 hurricane with 85 mph winds, leaving behind some 30 inches of rain (Diaz 2022).

2. Declet-Barreto 2022.

3. Garriga-López (2020) coined the concept of compounded disaster, while Bonilla (2020b) coined "swarm of disaster" to refer to this multiplicity of disasters affecting PR.

4. Public Law 114–187 of 2016.

5. Bonilla 2020a, 2020b; García-López 2020; Lloréns 2021; Morales 2019; Mulligan and Garriga-López 2020; Onís 2021; Rivera 2020; Tormos-Aponte et al. 2021.

6. Harman and Squires 2006.

7. The multilayered crisis affecting PR is also embedded in the climate crisis and racial violence. Therefore, I defined disaster as part of the structure of colonialism, to emphasize that these disasters are preventable, avoidable, and far from predetermined.

8. On crisis, see Desai (2023), Gilmore (2007), and Miller (2009).

9. I am following Go's (2008, 2016, 2023) theoretical approach to the anticolonial thought.

10. I am following Green and Ward's (2019) Gramscian conceptualization of civil society organizations as one of the forms of opposition to state crimes.

11. LeBrón 2021; Powers 2020, 2022.

12. Valentín and Minet 2019.

13. Puerto Rican scholars have engaged and analyzed the multilayered crisis from an array of approaches including sociology of disaster, anthropology, decolonial theory, public policy, feminist theory, ethnic studies, history, and economics.

14. Agamben 2005; Scheuerman 2000; Schmitt 2005. Recent studies in the field of

security studies, law, and public safety have engaged with Agamben's (2005) study of the normalization uses of the state of exception to address periods of crises (Bishai 2020; Gerstle and Isaac 2020; Neal 2019). Ellcessor (2022) has developed a critical analysis of emergency technologies, and Honing (2009) has developed a critique of the logic of exceptionalism.

15. Sarat 2010.

16. Alford 2017; Goitein 2019; Scheppele 2008, 2018; Scheuerman 2000, 2006, 2012.

17. J. Whyte 2013; Zartaloudis 2010.

18. This analysis is in tune with public law scholars such as Rossiter (2002), Scheuerman (2000, 2006), and Sheffer (1999).

19. Agamben's legal history of the state of exception in western democracies oversees the role of race, class, gender, and colonial power relationship (Durantaye 2012; Morton 2013; Rifkin 2012).

20. See also Arendt (1958), Davidson (2017), and Fitzpatrick (2008).

21. Cotula 2017; Greene 2015; Opitz and Tellmann 2015; Scheuerman 2000, 2006.

22. McCormack 2015.

23. Atiles 2018.

24. Ashton 2011; Bernat 2018; Mattei 2010; Ong 2006; Reynolds 2012; J. Whyte 2019.

25. On crisis as opportunity see Klein (2008, 2018).

26. Cooper and Whyte 2017.

27. Mbembe (2003), Hussain (2003), Morton (2013), Rajah (2023), Reynolds (2012, 2017), Saito (2020, 2021), Svirsky and Bignall (2012) among others have shown that colonial states have used the state of exception as a technique of colonial rule.

28. León 2020.

29. The only reference Agamben (2005) made to the uses of the state of exception in the colonial context is found when discussing the "Algerian crisis" in 1961 without any real discussion of the anticolonial wars, their impact in the development of French jurisprudence of emergency, and its racialized implications. Fanon (2004, 2008) has vividly described the ontological and epistemic implications of the Argelia anticolonial war and has demonstrated how the colony is structured through Manichean inclusive exclusion.

30. Benjamin 2021; Derrida 1992. On the connection between exceptionality, race, and violence, see Valdez et al. (2020).

31. Ophir et al. 2009.

32. The Insular Cases are a series of seminal rulings issued by the US Supreme Court between 1900 and 1922, setting the legal reality of PR and other unincorporated territories.

33. Camacho (2019) demonstrates how the state of exception is not an aberration of law, but rather the norm in Guam.

34. Thiong'o (2011, 2013) has extensively shown the effects of the British colonial state of emergency imposed on Kenya between 1952 and 1960.

35. Merry (2000), and Santos (2007, 2020, 2023) have shown how colonialism not only transformed the colony, but also transformed the law of the metropolis. See also Anghie (2006, 2009), Massoud (2013), and Tzouvala (2020).

36. On racialized dynamic of exceptionality, see Amarasinghe and Rajhans (2020) and Weheliye (2014).

37. Brabazon 2017; Golder and McLoughlin 2018; Johns 2015; Tzouvala 2018; J. Whyte 2019; Whyte and Wiegratz 2016.

38. Krever 2017; Slobodian 2018, 2023; Tzouvala 2018; Whyte and Wiegratz 2016.

39. Brown 2015, 2019.

40. Quiñones-Pérez and Seda-Irizarry 2020; Villanueva 2022; Villanueva et al. 2018.

41. OE-2023-09 (April 11, 2023)—to declare the state of emergency as a result of the effects of coastal erosion and to implement prevention, mitigation, and adaptation—became one of the latest developments of emergency powers to enact climate change policy.

42. There is an important tradition of examination of the uses of executive order as a legal measure to govern in liberal democracies (Curley and Federman 2020; Rudalevige 2021). David Whyte (2007) has shown how executive orders and the state of emergency created a liminal space for plunder, dispossession, and wealth extraction in Iraq.

43. On financialization, see Krippner (2011), Langley (2008), and Lapavitsas (2013).

44. On public debt, see Graeber (2011), Hager (2016), Lazzarato (2013), Marazzi (2011), and Merling et al. (2017).

45. Blalock 2022; Harris and Varellas 2020; Tzouvala 2022; J. Whyte 2019.

46. Barak 2012; Tombs 2016.

47. David Whyte (2007) shows how corruption is not the result of exogenous practices, but is rather intrinsically embedded in the neoliberal rationality, and is instrumental to US imperialism. This book suggest that corruption and state-corporate crimes have become routinized in colonial legality.

48. On state crime, see Barak (1991), Chambliss (1989), Chambliss et al. (2010), Kauzlarich and Kramer (1998), Green and Ward (2004, 2019), Lasslett (2012, 2014), and Rothe (2009).

49. On corporate crime, see Bittle (2012), Snider (2000), and Tombs and Whyte (2015). On state-corporate crimes, see Aulette and Michalowski (1993), Friedrichs and Rothe (2014), Lasslett (2018), Michalowski and Kramer (2006), and Rothe (2010).

50. Pearce 1976; Rothe and Kauzlarich 2022, D. Whyte 2009.

51. Agozino 2003, 2018; Atiles 2024.

52. Bernat and Whyte 2017; Ciocchini and Greener 2022; D. Whyte 2014.

53. Faust and Kauzlarich 2008.

54. Harcourt 2010; Wacquant 2009.

55. There is an initiative in PR called Red de Transparency (translated to Transparency Network) that aims to bring together different pro-transparency organizations, and it has had limited impact in legally accessing information. For the purpose of this book, I will be using the term "Transparency Network" to denote the five organizations described in this Introduction.

56. These organizations operate as counter-hegemonic agents challenging common sense and the narrative of the crisis constituted by colonial legality. On counter-hegemonic agents, see Ciocchini and Khoury (2018, 2021), Gramsci (1971), and Green and Ward (2019).

57. CPI was founded in 2008 by investigative journalists Omaya Sosa Pascual and Oscar Serrano with the key mission of promoting access to information. On the role of investigative journalists in fighting economic crimes and corruption, see Gottschalk (2021).

58. The PR Constitution recognizes, in its Bill of Rights, the right to access information (Article 11, Section 4). Additionally, in *Soto v. Secretary of Justice* (1982), the PR Supreme Court delimited the constitutional and legal parameters for the effective exercise of the right to access information (Ramos Hernández 2016; Rivera Ramos 1975).

59. Espacios Abiertos was established in 2014 and was initially funded by a grant from Open Society Foundation. In our interview, Cecille Blondet raised the issue of funding and the need for Espacios Abiertos and other NGOs or civil society organizations to remain independent and not accept funding from the US and PR governments. This has led to an important discussion on the role of funding institutions such as Filantropía Puerto Rico and Foundation for Puerto Rico.

60. My translation.

61. Moore 2018.

62. Law 2 of 2018.

63. I have been working with this organization and conducting participatory observation since 2021.

64. Liu 2020.

65. Chua 2012, 2019; McCann 2006.

66. Marshall and Hale 2014.

67. Chua and Engel 2019.

68. Canfield 2022; McCann 1994, 2006; Sarat and Scheingold 2006; Scheingold 2004.

69. Similarly, when the primary data—such as laws, executive orders, legislative reports, investigations, and news articles—are only available in Spanish, I have translated the specific section or quotes provided in this book.

70. On crimes of the powerful and methodology, see Alvesalo-Kuusi and Whyte (2018), Lasslett (2012, 2014, 2018), Rothe and Kauzlarich (2022), and Tombs and Whyte (2002).

71. https://www.estado.pr.gov/ordenes-ejecutivas

72. https://sutra.oslpr.org/osl/esutra/

73. https://oversightboard.pr.gov/documents/

74. Abel 2010; Calavita 2016; Cramer 2021; Ewick and Silbey 1998; Marshall and Barclay 2003; Silbey 2005; Silbey and Sarat 1987.

Chapter 1

1. *FOMB v. CPI* 598 U.S.__ (2023).

2. The legal doctrine that states that a government cannot be sued without its consent. See also Eleventh Amendment to the US Constitution.

3. The FOMB is an entity within the PR government—PROMESA, Sections 5 (19) (B) and 101 (C) (1)—which means that while seven members are appointed by the US president, they are not federal appointees, and they are not subjected to federal appointment clause.

4. Similar to the federal Freedom of Information Act (FOIA). The Puerto Rican

jurisprudence on transparency was established by the Puerto Rican Supreme Court ruling on *Soto v. Secretario Justicia* (1982).

5. CPI sued the FOMB in federal district court because Section 2126A of PROMESA channels all forms of litigation against the FOMB to federal courts (Mann 2023).

6. Chandler (2011) argues that it is largely accepted that common law sovereign immunity applies to the unincorporated territories, while constitutional sovereign immunity provided by the Eleventh Amendment does not apply to the territories.

7. Article 4, Section 3, Clause 2.

8. Blackhawk (2023) suggests that colonialism is not an externality of the US Constitution, but rather is a colonial document designed to reflect and legitimate the settler colonialism and colonial domination at large.

9. The opinion of the court was delivered by Justice Kagan. Justice Thomas filed a dissenting opinion.

10. The court made clear that it was not deciding whether Puerto Rico or the FOMB are entitled to sovereign immunity (Schwartz 2023).

11. The court explained that "PROMESA says nothing explicit about abrogating sovereign immunity" and stated that PROMESA did not satisfy the standard established in *Kimel v. Florida Board of Regents,* 528 U.S. 62, 120S. CT 631 (2000), which states that Congress's intent to abrogate sovereign immunity must be "unmistakably clear" (Schwartz 2023).

12. Ayala and Bernabe 2009; Merry 2000; Rivera Ramos 2001, 2007; Trías Monge 2007; Thompson 2010.

13. On the economic, political, and social reasons that led to the United States being involved in the war, see Go (2008), Lawson and Seidman (2004), Malavet (2004), G. Murphy (2005), L. Pérez (2008), Rivera Ramos (2007).

14. Mattei and Nader 2008; Tzouvala 2020.

15. The Treaty of Paris was signed on December 10, 1898, between the United States and Spain. As result Spain transferred sovereignty over PR, Guam, and the Philippines to the United States. Simultaneously, the United States had just acquired Hawaii on July 7, 1898 (Merry 2000), which meant that in 1898, the United States had finally expanded its territory to the Pacific and to the Caribbean.

16. Torruella (2018) coined the term "legal experiment" to describe the colonial governance of PR through the four organic laws approved by the US Congress between 1900 and 2016. Unlike Torruella, I proposed to describe these organic laws as exceptional laws, given that they framed the state of exception as a structure of colonial governance.

17. Foraker Act of April 12, 1900 (Public Law 56-191, 31 Stat. 77).

18. Estades (1999) and Rivera Ramos (2001) have shown that for the first two years, PR was under martial law. On the uses of martial law and the transition to civil government in the territories, see Blackhawk (2023).

19. In 1902 the Insular Government enacted the political code of PR. This code stipulates the internal administration structure, the division of powers, municipal and regional divisions and districts, the powers of the local judicial system, and the legislative system. This Political Code is still in force, even after the approval of the Constitution of the Commonwealth of PR in 1952.

20. Section 7 of the Foraker Act renamed the archipelago Porto Rico, and its inhabitants became citizens of Porto Rico. Puerto Rico was finally renamed on May 17, 1932, under the Hoover administration, by an amendment to the Jones Act of 1917. This change, which occurred after years of being requested by the Puerto Ricans, represents an example of how the law is articulated to constitute the legal reality of colonial subjects.

21. Burnett 2008.

22. The only reason for not applying Spanish colonial laws was when they did not conform to the US Constitution (Section 8).

23. Dietz 1986.

24. Ayala and Bernabe 2009.

25. Dietz 1986.

26. The four clearest examples of Insular Cases are *Downes v. Bidwell*, 182 U.S. 244 (1901), which concerns the uniformity clause; *Hawaii v. Mankichi*, 190 U.S. 197 (1903), which considers grand juries; *Dorr v. United States*, 195 U.S. 138 (1904), which discusses jury trials; and *Balzac v. Porto Rico*, 258 U.S. 298 (1922), which also concerns jury trials (Cepeda Derieux and Weare 2020).

27. There is significant scholarship on the Insular Cases that can be consulted: Atiles 2016; Burnett 2005, 2009; Burnett and Marshal 2001; Cabranes 1979; Erman 2018, 2022; López-Baralt 1999; Malavet 2004; Ponsa-Kraus 2022; Rivera Ramos 2001, 2007; Sparrow 2006, 2022; Torruellas 1988, 2007, 2018; Venator Santiago and Morera 2022.

28. Cepeda Derieux and Weare 2020.

29. Presided by Justice Melville W. Fuller (1889–1910), the court justified the colonial possession within the expansionist and racist jurisprudence of the nineteenth century. This includes jurisprudence emanating from Northwest Ordinance of 1787 (*Marbury v. Madison (*1803)); the Marshall Trilogy and the Domestic Dependent Nations; *Dred Scott v. Sanford (*1857); and the Guano Islands (*Jones v. United States* (1890)). This was the same court that ruled on *Plessy v. Ferguson* (1896) and several cases constitutive of the US state of exception. It is not surprising that the court that established the doctrine of racial segregation under the concept "separate but equal" extended exceptional relations and legal racism to PR.

30. Paraphrasing Merry's (1988) idea that law transformed the colonies, but colonialism also transformed the law.

31. As *Boumediene v. Bush* (2008) demonstrates, the precedents established by the Insular Cases would be used to grant the writ of habeas corpus for prisoners of Guantánamo Bay (Burnett 2009). On Guantánamo and exceptionality, see Agamben (2005), Aradau (2007), and Butler (2004). On torture and the legacy of Guantánamo, see Hajjar (2022, 2023).

32. The Jones-Shafroth Act of March 2, 1917 (Public Law 64-386, 39 Stat. 951).

33. On the different political processes and laws that led to the extension of the US citizenship to Puerto Ricans, see Venator Santiago (2018).

34. Merchant Marine Act of June 5, 1920 (Public Law 66-261, 41 Stat. 988).

35. Rodríguez 2010.

36. Ayala and Bernabe 2009; Dietz 1986; Irizarry 2011.

37. Dávila-Ruhaak 2020.

38. Caraballo-Cueto and Lara 2017.

39. Dietz 1986.

40. US Public Law 76–768, August 22, 1940.

41. Atiles 2019; Meléndez-Badillo 2024; Nieves Falcón 2009; Paralitici 2011, 2017.

42. Public Law 362 (61 Stat. 770, H.R. 3309, 18th Cong.).

43. Ayala and Bernabe 2009.

44. Article 4 states that except as provided in Section 5 of this act, the Jones Act of March 2, 1917, as amended, is hereby continued in force and effect, and may hereafter be cited as the "Puerto Rican Federal Relations Act."

45. The PR Constitution was approved by Congress with Public Law 447 of July 3, 1952, but not without making substantial modifications and deleting Sections 5 and 20 of Article 2 and Section 3 of Article 7.

46. *ELA* stems from the Spanish name Estado Libre Asociado de Puerto Rico or Free Associate State.

47. Constitution of PR of 1952, Article 6, Section 8.

48. Some examples are *Figueroa v. People of Puerto Rico* (1956) in which the US Court of Appeals for the First Circuit ruled that the ELA's constitution was not a mere congressional organic law, such as the Foraker Act and the Jones Act, and established that arguing otherwise was to accuse Congress of fraud. In *Hernández Agosto v. Romero Barceló* (1984) and *United States v. Quinones* (1985), the same court reiterated that ELA's constitution was not simply a federal statute and, therefore, could not be revoked unilaterally by Congress. In *United States v. Lopez Andino* (1987), the Court of Appeals for the First Circuit concluded once again that the ELA was a separate sovereignty of the United States.

49. For example, in *Harris v. Rosario* (1980), the US Supreme Court determined that, by virtue of its powers under the territorial clause of the US Constitution, Congress could treat PR differently from the rest of the states. In *United States v. Sánchez* (1993), the Court of Appeals for the Eleventh Circuit concluded that PR is still a US territory, and Congress may unilaterally revoke the Puerto Rican Constitution or Public Law 600 and replace it with laws or regulations of their choice.

50. Donald B. Verilli Jr. later joined the law firm Munger Rolles & Olson LLP, in which he was the attorney for the FOMB in *FOMB v. Aurelius* (2020).

51. The 2007 report by the president's task force on Puerto Rico's status reinforced the validity of the colonial condition and the absolute power of Congress over PR. Another report was produced in 2011, in which it was recognized that PR's status was not solved, and progress should be made in the direction of its resolution.

52. Santana (2023) has called these the New Insular Cases. These cases reassert US colonialism in PR by redefining the logic of exceptionality that defined the legal structure of domination defined by the original Insular Cases.

53. Discussions of the US colonial legal history and the role of law in imperialism have experienced a revival in recent years, as demonstrated by the publications on this issue in all major law reviews. See the conversation between Blackhawk (2023) and Chacón (2023).

54. The double jeopardy clause of the Fifth Amendment of the US Constitution.

55. Justice Kagan delivered the opinion of the court in a six to two decision. Justice Breyer filed a dissenting opinion, which Justice Sotomayor joined.

56. Ponsa-Kraus 2020.

57. Public Law 98–353, July 10, 1984.

58. Graham 2017.

59. This case was decided together with *Acosta-Febo v. Franklin California Tax-Free Trust*, 15–255.

60. Justice Thomas delivered the opinion of the court, in which Chief Justice Roberts and Justices Kennedy, Breyer, and Kagan joined. Sotomayor filed a dissenting opinion, which Justice Ginsburg joined. Alito recused himself given that his financial disclosure reports indicate that either he or his wife own shares in a Franklin fund that holds Puerto Rican municipal bonds (Stohr and Kaske, 2016).

61. Justice Kavanaugh delivered the opinion of the court (eight to one), in which Chief Justice Roberts and Justices Thomas, Breyer, Alito, Kagan, Gorsuch, and Barrett joined. Thomas and Gorsuch filed concurring opinions. Sotomayor filed a dissenting opinion.

62. Schwartz 2022.

63. Santana (2023) and Blackhawk (2023) have conducted similar analyses of Gorsuch's position regarding the Insular Cases in *Vaello-Madero*.

64. Currently, the Northern Mariana Islands is the only unincorporated territory to receive Supplemental Social Security benefits. https://www.cbpp.org/research/social-security/supplemental-security-income#:~:text=Among%20the%20U.S.%20Territories%2C%20only,and%20has%20stricter%20eligibility%20criteria

65. Santana 2023.

66. Dick (2015) provides a general discussion of taxation in the US colonial history in PR.

67. Eyermann 2016.

68. Marans 2016.

69. ACRE 2021.

70. Austin 2022.

71. On the political debates surrounding the enactment of PROMESA, see Lamba-Nieves et al. (2021), López-Santana (2022), Meléndez (2018a, 2018b), and Torruella (2018). Skeel (2019) provides a reflection on the enactment and implementation of PROMESA form the perspective of a member of the FOMB.

72. Cabán (2018) and Meléndez (2018a, 2018b), among others, have provided important contextualization and analysis of the law.

73. On the uses of financial control boards, see Cintrón Arbasetti and Minet (2017a).

74. Torruella 2018.

75. Law 82 of 2019, Law 90 of 2019, and Law 138 of 2019.

76. Law 29 of 2019 and Law 142 of 2020.

77. Law 176 of 2019; Law 181 of 2019; Law 82 of 2020; Law 195 of 2022.

78. Law 47 of 2019.

79. Law 80 2020 and Law 81 of 2020.

80. Law 41 of 2022.

81. https://ntc-prod-public-pdfs.s3.us-east-2.amazonaws.com/kCKT62I7tBfFlW_VIohtBr5X8pc.pdf

82. Lamba-Nieves et al. 2021.

83. The bankruptcy case is being held in the US District Court for the District of PR. The case is *Financial Oversight and Management Board for Puerto Rico*, 17-cv-01578, US District Court.

84. Santamaría 2021.

85. ACRE 2021.

86. Law 76 of 2000.

87. Lamba-Nieves et al. 2021.

88. Zamot had been paid a $325,000 annual salary.

89. Austin 2022.

90. https://www.kutakrock.com/newspublications/publications/2016/09/promesa-a-summary-of-the-puerto-rico-oversight-leg

91. Prohibits enacting or enforcing any law "that would impair or defeat the purposes of PROMESA," "as determined by" the FOMB.

92. Allows the FOMB to seek to nullify legislation that is "significantly inconsistent with" the FOMB's certified fiscal plan (a blueprint for the commonwealth's fiscal goals).

93. Atiles 2022b; LeBrón 2019, 2021.

94. UTIER stands for the Spanish acronym for Electrical Industry and Irrigation Workers Union.

95. In early 2017, during my time at UPRM, I engaged in participatory observation in the meetings and organizational sessions, leading to the APRUM joining this lawsuit. This participatory observation allowed me to engage in the process of decision-making and rationalization leading to mobilizing the law.

96. *FOMB v. Aurelius Investment*, 149 S. Ct. 1649 (2020).

97. Article 2, Section 2 of the US Constitution requires the president to nominate all officers, and then, with the advice and consent of Congress, to appoint the officers (Schwartz and Lewis 2020).

98. The opinion of the court was delivered by Justice Breyer, in which Chief Justice Roberts and Justices Ginsburg, Alito, Kagan, and Kavanaugh joined. Justices Thomas and Sotomayor filed concurring opinions.

99. Campbell 2022; Cepeda Derieux and Weare 2020; Ponsa-Kraus 2020, 2022.

100. Ponsa-Kraus 2020.

Chapter 2

1. Proyecto de la Cámara de Representantes 0515, of February 9, 2021.

2. Operate as the Puerto Rican version of the Public Law 94–412 of 1976: National Emergencies Act (NEA).

3. PIP: Partido Independentista Puertorriqueño.

4. MVC: Movimiento Victoria Ciudadana.

5. The law creates the PR Department of Public Safety and in its Article 5.10 it expands the governor's emergency powers.

6. The Spanish original is available here: https://sutra.oslpr.org/osl/SUTRA/anejos/137765/PC0515%20(Conferencia)%20(Veto%20Expreso).pdf

7. The Spanish original is available here: https://sutra.oslpr.org/osl/SUTRA/anejos/137765/PC0515%20(Conferencia)%20(Veto%20Expreso).pdf

8. For a heterodox conceptualization of subordinate financialization, see Bortz and Kaltenbrunner (2018) and Bonizzi et al. (2022).

9. Largely developed as export processing zones, PR serves as model for other territories and countries in the Global South such as Singapore (Slobodian 2023).

10. Austin 2016, 2022.

11. LeBrón 2019.

12. 26 US Code Section 936—Puerto Rico and possession tax credit.

13. Feliciano 2018.

14. PPD: Partido Popular Democratico.

15. PNP: Partido Nuevo Progresista.

16. Meléndez 2018b.

17. Bernabe 1998.

18. Meléndez 2018b.

19. Caraballo-Cueto and Lara 2017.

20. Public Law 104–188 of 1996 eliminated Section 936.

21. Ayala and Bernabe 2009.

22. Feliciano (2018: 31) argued that "[t]he elimination of Section 936 may be one of the most important factors contributing to the decline of the manufacturing industry in Puerto Rico" and to the economic crisis. Caraballo-Cueto and Lara (2017) have pointed out that the elimination of Section 936 did not bring significantly higher revenues to the US Treasury while it set the stage for the worst depression in PR's economy in more than a hundred years.

23. On austerity see Alsina et al. (2019), Blyth (2013), Hager (2016), and Lazzarato (2013).

24. Torres Asencio 2017.

25. This law was then amended by Law 32 of 2011 and by Law 19 of 2017.

26. Meléndez 2018b.

27. See for example the public hearing on Cerro Maravilla and Las Carpetas (Pérez Viera 2000).

28. On the Calderón administration's public safety policy, see LeBrón (2019).

29. Quiñones-Pérez and Seda-Irizarry 2020.

30. Caraballo-Cueto 2021.

31. As in the United States and Europe, CRAs play a key role in the PR economic and financial crisis (Cintrón Arbasetti 2016c). Particularly, in 2014, S&P, Moody's, and Fitch systemically downgraded the Puerto Rican government and its instrumentalities to the lowest levels. On the CRA role in the economic crisis, see White (2009, 2013). On how CRAs reproduced racialized and colonial dynamics in municipal bond markets, see Norris (2023). For an engagement with crime of the powerful, see Barak (2012), Snider (2011) and Will et al. (2013).

32. Caraballo-Cueto and Lara 2017.

33. Acevedo Vilá was indicted in federal court for money laundering, conspiracy, and lying to the FBI. A jury found him not guilty.

34. Pérez Lizasuain 2018.

35. Meléndez 2018a.

36. COFINA was created pursuant to Law 91 of 2006.

37. COFINA does not generate its own income, but rather it depends on the sales tax collections.

38. Austin 2016, 2022.

39. Comisión Ciudadana para la Auditoría Integral del Crédito Público (2019).

40. Newman and O'Brien 2011.

41. Mattei 2022.

42. Constitution of PR, Article 6, Section 2.

43. Austin 2022: 14.

44. Austin 2022.

45. Meléndez (2018b) shows that between 2006 and 2014, public corporations increased their total debt from $27.2 billion to $32.4 billion. By 2014, public corporation's share of PR's total debt reached 46.8 percent. The largest increase in public debt belongs to COFINA, at $16.3 billion, or 23.5 percent of the total debt. By 2014, the commonwealth's debt accounted for 20.7 percent of the public debt and the municipal debt for the remaining 6 percent. Between 2006 and 2014, banks, Wall Street, and the local government engaged in questionable financial practices that exacerbated the economic crisis.

46. Fortuño, like all the Puerto Rican governors since 2000, was in office for a single four-year term. It is important to note that since the Pedro Rosselló administration (1993–2000) no other governor have been able to win re-election for a second term, which in many ways has contributed to the multilayered crisis and/or is a manifestation of a deep political crisis.

47. On the role of CRAs in Fortuño's austerity measures, see Cintrón Arbasetti (2016c).

48. This policy was enacted by Law 29 of 2009.

49. When Fortuño left office, he joined the law firm Steptoe & Johnson LLP, from where he continued lobbying in US Congress in all issues related to the economic and financial crisis, including the enactment of PROMESA and the appointment of its members.

50. OE-2009–01 and OE-2009–04 of January 8, 2009. Additionally, Fortuño promulgated nine other executive orders concerning the economic crisis.

51. The Puerto Rican Supreme Court has consistently supported the uses of the state of emergency for crisis management. For example, on February 16, 2023, in *Amadeo Ocasio v. Pedro Pierluisi* (AC-2022–0070), the PR Supreme Court ruled in favor of Governor Pedro Pierluisi and his authority to issue executive orders to address periods of emergency such as the COVID-19 pandemic.

52. Meléndez (2018b) argued that during Fortuño's tenure, the total government employment (including in the municipalities) was reduced by 13.3 percent, from 297,300 to 257,700.

53. Atiles 2013, 2019, 2022b; Atiles and Whyte 2011; LeBrón 2019; Pérez Lizasuain 2018.

54. Public Law 111–5 of 2009.

55. Meléndez 2018b.

56. OE-2010–34. See Atiles (2016).

57. Law 32 of 2011, which amended Article 12 of Law 76 of 2000.

58. OE-2013–03.

59. OE-2013–14.

60. Meléndez 2018b.

61. Meléndez 2018b.

62. Cintrón Arbasetti 2016c. The role of the CRAs in the Puerto Rican debt crisis can be understood as a manifestation of state-corporate crimes.

63. *ASPPRO v. Secretario de Hacienda* (2015).

64. Krueger et al. 2015.

65. OE-2015–22.

66. The Puerto Rico Fiscal Oversight and Economic Recovery Organic Act (Law 208 of 2015) consolidates this working group.

67. OE-2015–46.

68. OE-2016–10; OE-2016–14; OE-2014–17; OE-2016–26; OE-2016–27; OE-2016–30; OE-2016–31.

69. The first, appointed by President Obama in 2016, were Chairman José Carrión III, Carlos M. García, José Ramon González, Arthur J. Gonzalez, David A. Skeel Jr., Anna Matosantos, and Andrew G. Biggs. After serving for over four years, José Carrión, Carlos Gonzalez, and Jose Gonzalez resigned from their positions in August 2020. President Trump then appointed Justin M. Peterson, Antonio Medina, Betty Rosa, and John Nixon to the FOMB. David Skeel became the chairman of the FOMB, and Arthur Gonzalez and Andrew Biggs remained in their position for another term. In January 2024, after the resignation of Justin Peterson and Antonio Medina in late 2023, the Biden administration appointed Juan Sabater to the vacant spot left by Peterson.

70. López-Santana 2022.

71. Hedge Clippers 2017a.

72. The covered entities required to submit a fiscal plan are the Commonwealth of PR, COFINA, PR Electric Power Authority (PREPA), PR Aqueduct and Sewer Authority, PR Highway and Transportation Authority, UPR, Government Developing Bank, Public Corporation for the Supervision and Insurance of Cooperatives, and Municipal Revenue Collection Center.

73. As ACRE (2021) has shown, the FOMB's first fiscal plan in 2018 called for a staggering $12.78 billion in spending cuts to be carried out between fiscal year (FY) 2018 and 2024. FOMB's FY2022 fiscal plan was $233 million less than the budget proposed by the PR government.

74. ACRE 2021.

75. Brusi and Godreau 2019; Soto-Vega 2022; Virella 2022.

76. Dennis 2019c.

77. Espacios Abiertos 2023.

78. https://public.tableau.com/app/profile/gabriel.rios1304/viz/Gastosfiscalesenel mundo/Gastosfiscalesenelmundo

79. https://public.tableau.com/app/profile/gabriel.rios1304/viz/GastosfiscalesenEs tadosUnidos/GastosfiscalesenEstadosUnidos

80. López-Santana 2022.

81. OE-2017–01; OE-2017–02; OE-2017–03; OE-2017–04; OE-2017–05; OE-2017–06.

82. OE-2017–01; OE-2017–31; OE-2017–76; OE-2018–23; OE-2018–53; OE-2019–30.

83. Originally, Law 5 provided for the extension of the state of fiscal emergency for three months. However, the Legislative Assembly enacted Law 46 of 2017, extending the fiscal emergency period until December 31, 2017. Additionally, Law 46 of 2017 amended Law 5 of 2017 providing that while the FOMB is constituted, the governor may extend the emergency period for six months or less through an executive order.

84. Created through Law 2 of 2017.

85. OE-2017–02.

86. OE-2017–11; OE-2017–14; OE-2017–15; OE-2017–16; OE-2017–18; OE-2017–19.

87. Law 4 of 2017 and Law 8 of 2017.

88. Law 13 of 2017.

89. Law 45 of 2018 and Law 46 of 2018.

90. Law 93 of 2017 and Law 94 of 2017.

91. The office was created through executive order OE-2017–04. The state of emergency regarding infrastructure used Law 76 of 2000, and it was extended by the Rosselló administration in four additional instances (OE-2017–38; OE-2018–02; OE-2018–25; OE-2019–01).

92. The law amending Law 29 of 2009, regulating public-private partnerships, which established the P3 office.

93. OE-2010–34.

94. As Ranganathan (2019) has consistently demonstrated, these infrastructure projects contribute to corruption and enable wealth extraction by local and international elites.

95. Created by Law 97 of 2017.

96. W. Murphy 2022.

97. The bill was introduced in the House of Representative as PC 1275 and in the Senate as PS 653.

98. OE-2019–66. This declaration was the sixth extension of the state of fiscal emergency since Law 5 of 2017 was enacted.

99. OE-2020–50; OE-2020–92.

100. During the Vázquez and Pierluisi administrations, new forms of state of emergency came into force, including the declaration of the state of emergency regarding gender violence (originally issued by OE-2021–13 and renewed by OE-2022–35, OE-2023–20, and OE-2023–39).

101. OE-2021–03; OE-2021–52; OE-2021–84; OE-2022–37; OE-2022–58; OE-2023–19; OE-2023–38.

102. Dennis 2019b.

103. Austin 2022.

104. OE-2021–18.

105. The privatization of PREPA took place in two stages. LUMA energy—which is jointly owned by the Houston-based corporation Quanta Services, the Canadian corporation ATCO, and the emergency management corporation IEM—acquired the transmission and distribution systems, customer service, and billing, among other key functions in 2021 (Onís and Lloréns 2021). Power generation was acquired in January 2023 by Genera PR, a subsidiary of the New York–based energy company New Fortress Inc. As Gustavo García-López (2022) has shown, the privatization of the PREPA by LUMA took place under a corrupt process, marked by political investments and revolving doors.

106. Gonzalez 2022.

107. Ruiz Kuilan 2023.

108. Gonzalez 2023. These meetings have become a pattern in the PR administration. For example, Cintrón Arbasetti (2016c) notes that García Padilla, Fortuño, and Rosselló all met with the CRAs at some point in their administrations to seek better ratings for the PR credit.

109. https://www.puertoriconow.com

110. González 2024.

111. García Pelatti 2024.

112. Cintrón Arbasetti 2021.

113. Bonilla 2018.

114. Bonilla 2018; Padilla 2021.

115. Padilla 2021.

116. Watlington 2019.

117. https://www.the2022actsociety.org. For more on how the 20/22 Act Society operates as a trade association or a political lobby, see Hedge Clippers (2024).

118. There is a series of reports on whether these acts in fact created the promised jobs. See, for example, Econometrika's report, in which the authors differ from Santos-Lozada (2021).

119. Valentín et al. 2021; Solá-Santiago 2021.

120. Dennis 2020a.

121. Atiles 2022a.

Chapter 3

1. US Public Law 117–82 of 2022.

2. PROMESA does not require compliance with Rule 2014 of the Federal Bankruptcy Procedures, which calls for disclosure of conflict of interest or any connection with the debtor, creditors, and any interested party in the bankruptcy process. According to Walsh (2018), the Treasury Department asked that the Obama administration leave out the disclosure provision of PROMESA, and no one considered the request controversial.

3. FOMB's members and employees have systemically failed to publish their financial disclosures and any possible conflict of interest as required by Section 109 of PROMESA (ACRE 2021).

4. There is no independent body that oversees the FOMB's conflicts of interest. However, the FOMB hired the firm GEC Risk Advisory as its ethics advisor. The consultancy firm reviews the financial reports of the FOMB— at $750 per hour—before they are published and determines if there are conflicts of interest.

5. Espacios Abiertos 2023.

6. Rice and Valentín 2019.

7. Atiles 2020, 2024; Lasslett 2012; Pearce 1976; Rothe and Kauzlarich 2022; D. Whyte 2009.

8. Aulette and Michalowski 1993; Green and Ward 2004, 2019; Michalowski and Kramer 2006; Tombs and Whyte 2015.

9. The Puerto Rican debt is a product of the political economy of colonialism and its capitalist sociolegal processes. Ontological considerations and their exoteric abstractions of the power dynamics involved in the process of indebtedness obscure and mystify the structural and material conditions that generate the debt, hindering our ability to comprehend such processes. Moreover, these ontological considerations often individualize the sociopolitical implications of debt and limit people's ability to articulate a collective response to the colonial dynamics inherent in the Puerto Rican debt. Thus, this chapter aims to demonstrate that, contrary to individualizing interpretations, debt is produced through sociolegal, political, and economic processes that can be resisted.

10. Bhatti and Sloan 2017b.

11. Bhatti and Sloan 2017c.

12. On the predatory nature of the payday loan, see Soederberg (2014).

13. CABs are like a negative amortization mortgage, in which the outstanding principal grows over time because the unpaid interest get tacked onto the amount owed (Bhatti and Sloan 2017d).

14. Bhatti and Sloan 2016a.

15. See Fraser's (2022) concept of cannibal capitalism.

16. Bhatti and Sloan 2016a.

17. Bhatti and Sloan 2017d.

18. Bhatti and Sloan 2017d.

19. The largest portion of these fees, an estimated $323 million, was for scoop and toss deals in which UBS was the lead underwriter (Bhatti and Sloan 2016b).

20. Bhatti and Sloan 2016b.

21. Pavlo 2017.

22. Bhatti and Sloan 2016b.

23. Bhatti and Sloan 2017d.

24. Bhatti and Sloan 2017d.

25. Bhatti and Sloan 2017a, 2017d.

26. Bhatti and Sloan 2017a.

27. Cintrón Arbasetti and Minet 2017b.

28. Bhatti and Sloan 2016a.

29. On hedge funds see Barak (2012), Neely (2022), Pistor (2019), Sassen (2014), Shaxson (2019), and Will et al. (2013).

30. Hedge Clippers 2015a, 2021b; Wolff 2016.

31. Dayen 2016.

32. Brigade Capital Management, Fir Tree, Perry Capital, Paulson and Co., and Goldman Sachs Asset Management each bought $120 million in bonds (Cintrón Arbasetti 2016a).

33. Cintrón Arbasetti and Minet 2017b. Hedge Clippers (2015a, 2015b) identified thirteen hedge funds buying substantial amounts of Puerto Rican debt in 2015. Among them were: Bluemountain Capital Management; Stone Lion Capital Partners L.P.; Paulson & Co.; Third Point; Centerbridge Partners; Appaloosa Management; Aurelius Capital; Fortress Investment Group; Apollo Global Management; Perry Capital; Fir Tree; Marathon Asset Management; Angelo Gordon.

34. Aronoff 2018.

35. Aronoff 2018.

36. Hedge Clippers 2021b.

37. Cintrón Arbasetti 2015.

38. Hedge Clippers 2015c.

39. Lazar, Citigroup, and Morgan Stanley made private presentations to investors in New York about PR bonds (Cintrón Arbasetti 2016a). On October 10, 2013, Lazar organized a marketing session with seventy-five hedge funds to promote debt investment opportunities in PR, in which former governor Luis Fortuño was the keynote speaker.

40. Cintrón Arbasetti 2016b.

41. Hedge Clippers 2021b.

42. Cintrón Arbasetti and Minet 2017b.

43. The group is comprised of Franklin Mutual Adviser, Oppenheimer Funds, Santander Securities (First Puerto Rico Family of Funds). Cintrón Arbasetti and Minet (2017d) explain that both Carlos García and José González liquidated their investment in Puerto Rican bonds made by First Puerto Rico Family Funds in October 2016, shortly after being appointed to the FOMB.

44. Goldman Sachs and UBS do not belong to any group.

45. Including Quinn Emanuel Urquhart & Sullivan. Some of the Puerto Rican law firms supporting US-based law firms were McConnel Valdés, Reichard & Escalera, O'Neill & Borges, Toro, Colón, Mullet, Rivera & Sifre law firm, and Goldman Antonetti & Cordova.

46. Hedge Clippers 2018b.

47. Cintrón Arbasetti and Minet 2017b; Hedge Clippers 2018b; Neely 2022; Wolff 2016.

48. Hedge Clippers 2018a.

49. Hedge Clippers 2017c.

50. Ambac, a municipal bond insurer with investment in COFINA, sought to capitalize on the Land Authority's farms and/or real estate owned by the PR government. Dennis (2021a) points out that Ambac hired Christiansen Commercial Real Estate to analyze the value of eighty-one properties owned by the PR government. Accordingly, Christensen valued these properties at over $1.3 billion. Christiansen also serves as the chief executive officer of PR Industrial Solutions Management, a joint venture founded in 2019 by Taconic Capital Advisors and Monarch Alternative Capital, two vulture funds investing in PR bonds and acquiring industrial properties (Dennis 2021a).

51. Doctrines of Champerty is an obscure legal theory with its roots in English common law from the Middle Ages, when wealthy landowners would buy up land for the purpose of collecting on court claims made against poor tenants whom they knew couldn't afford the rent (Aronoff 2018).

52. Dayen 2016.

53. Act 60 of 2019 kept these tax exemptions.

54. Dayen 2016.

55. Dennis 2020c, 2020e.

56. A third composition of the FOMB took office in June 2024, and was composed of the following members: Arthur Gonzalez (chairman), Andrew Briggs, Betty Rosa, Juan Sabater, Luis Ubiñas, and John Nixon. Hedge Clippers (2016, 2017a, 2017b, 2018c, 2018d) has produced a systemic analysis of the conflict of interest surrounding these three members of the FOMB. See also Dennis (2020f).

57. *CPI v. FOMB* (2017) was the first lawsuit brought by the CPI to gain access to information, and it's part of the legal dispute that led to *FOMB v. CPI* (2023).

58. Valentín and Cintrón Arbasetti 2018.

59. Gillette 2019, 2021.

60. Lamba-Nieves et al. 2021.

61. Gillette and Skeel 2016b.

62. Dennis 2019d, 2020f.

63. MSC is one of the larger Medicare Advantage providers in PR and also a commercial health insurance provider.

64. ACRE 2021.

65. ACRE 2021; Hedge Clippers 2018a, 2018b.

66. Hedge Clippers 2016.

67. Carlos García was also the chairman of Caribbean Financial Group and its payday loan business ComoLoco (Hedge Clippers 2016). ComoLoco has engaged in predatory lending, taking advantage of the underbanked, amidst the FOMB's imposed austerity measures that undermined the access to basic social services and other social protection. On December 2022 it was reported that Carlos García was the founder and CEO of Nave Bank, a newly created digital bank in PR.

68. Hedge Clippers 2018a.

69. Among them was Fernando L. Batlle, whose brother Juan C. Batlle became managing director of Santander Security (Hedge Clippers 2016). In 2011 Juan C. Batlle moved from a senior role at Santander to replace Carlos García as the head of the GDB while his brother Fernando left the GDB to become CEO of Santander Securities. This amounted to a revolving door of brothers, rotating between the bond's underwriter to the government agency charged with selecting bond underwriters. Fernando Battle was also executive director of COFINA, where he oversaw a $4.1 billion debt issuance in June 2009, the biggest issuance in PR history. Later, while Juan Batlle presided over the GDB, he authorized four bond emissions in COFINA that amounted $1.9 billion, and in which Santander was the underwriter. Hedge Clippers (2018a) explains that Juan and Fernando Batlle became senior managing director of Ankura Consulting Group in 2017. Only days after assuming this position, Ankura signed its first contract with the

GDB to work as its financial advisor for four months for a total of $1.6 million. Since, Ankura had eight other contracts with the GDB, three with PREPA, and four with FAFAA.

70. Hedge Clippers 2016.

71. Santander underwrote twenty CAB deals totaling $14.4 billion; $1.5 billion in capitalized payments; and $735 million went to pay for canceling interest rate swaps (Hedge Clippers 2016).

72. Hedge Clippers 2016.

73. Hedge Clippers 2018a.

74. Hedge Clippers 2021a.

75. DCI has ties to BlueMountin Capital Management, one of the largest bondholders of PREPA (Hedge Clippers 2021a). Peterson was an advisor of the ad hoc group of general obligation bondholders, which has evolved to include just two members, Aurelius Capital and Autonomy Capital. These two hedge funds had as much as $1.4 billion invested in general obligation bonds (Hedge Clippers 2019, 2021a). Autonomy Capital was one of the hedge funds that raised objections to any debt cancellation after Hurricane María.

76. Hedge Clippers 2021a.

77. https://www.linkedin.com/in/joseperezriera

78. Valentín 2018d.

79. Espacios Abiertos 2023.

80. A report issued by the fees examiner appointed by the Title III court in 2018 noted the following techniques of wealth extraction implemented by these law and consultancy firms: automatic rate increases, misjudgments, lack of details in the invoices, duplication of services (Valentín 2018a).

81. Citi Global Markets—a subsidiary of the bank that served as underwriter for the government in several debt transactions—advises on the debt-restructuring process and leads the privatization efforts of PREPA. The financial institution would receive $24 million once the private sector takes over PREPA.

82. Valentín 2018b, 2018e.

83. Mazzucato and Collington 2023.

84. Mazzucato and Collington 2023; Valentín 2018a.

85. Walsh 2018.

86. MIO stands for McKinsey Investment Officer Partners.

87. Compass CSS High Yield, Compass ESMA, and Compass TSMA (Walsh 2018).

88. Pandora Select is one of these firms, and as of 2016 it held money on behalf of McKinsey (Walsh 2018).

89. Austin 2022.

90. Rice and Valentín 2019.

91. In restructuring PREPA, the FOMB approved contracts with McKinsey and its subsidiaries. In 2018, the FOMB approved a $1.5 billion contract with NFEnergia to convert two PREPA power plants to natural gas. That company is a subsidy of New Fortress, owned by SoftBank Group Corporation, an undisclosed McKinsey client. Mean-

while, the FOMB passed another $1 billion in PREPA fuel contracts to Puma Energy, an undisclosed client of McKinsey. In June 2020 the FOMB approved a fifteen-year $1.5 billion concession to LUMA, a consortium jointly owned by McKinsey's client Quanta Services Inc.

92. The parties in the restructuring were: the ad hoc group of GDB Creditors; Bonistas del Patio; Alianza de Cooperativas; Grupo Encuentro Solidario; the GDB; the FAFAA. The Ad Hoc Group of GDB Creditors is composed by the following hedge funds: Avenue Capital, Brigade Capital Management, Fir Tree Partner, and Solus Alternative Asset Management.

93. Section 405 (automatic stay upon enactment) of Title IV of PROMESA provided for voluntary negotiation among creditors and debtors.

94. Hedge Clippers 2018a.

95. Hedge Clippers 2018a.

96. Hedge Clippers 2018c, 2018d.

97. Cintrón Arbasetti and Minet 2017c.

98. *CPI v. Alejandro García Padilla y Banco Gubernamental de Fomento* (2015).

99. Law 241 of 2018.

100. Connor 2018; Dennis and Connor 2018a, 2018b; Molinari 2020.

101. Ironically, former Governor Rosselló's key argument for eliminating the Commission for the Comprehensive Audit of the Public Credit in 2017 was that he didn't want to waste $2 or $3 million on an audit, Kobre & Kim's report cost $16 million to taxpayers (Connor 2018; Hedge Clippers 2020).

102. COFINA debt principal was reduced from $17.6 to $11.9 billion, or a 32 percent reduction—though overall, when interest payments are included, the total debt service will be $32.3 billion over forty years (Dennis and Connor 2018a).

103. Austin 2022.

104. Espacios Abiertos 2023.

105. According to Dennis and Connor (2018b) these hedge funds are: Aurelius Capital; Baupost Group; Canyon Capital; GoldenTree Asset Management; Old Bellows Partners; Scoggin Capital Management; Taconic Capital Advisors; Tilden Park Capital; and Whitebox Advisors. Collectively, these hedge funds were organized as the COFINA Senior Bondholders Coalition, and they were also involved in the renegotiation of the PR general obligations bonds.

106. The FOMB in conjunction with the Unsecured Creditors Committee sought to challenge the constitutionality of these emissions (Austin 2022; Dennis 2019a).

107. The Commission for the Comprehensive Audit of the Public Credit raised concerns about possible violations to PR's Constitution, as well as dubious accounting and disclosure practices by the underwriters (CCAPC 2017).

108. ACRE 2021.

109. Dennis 2019a, 2019b.

110. Hedge Clippers 2019; Dennis 2019e; Valentín 2018c; Walsh 2019.

111. Dennis 2019b.

112. Dennis 2020b.

113. ACRE 2021; Austin 2022; Dennis 2020d, 2020e.

114. The Martin Act grants New York's attorney general broad powers to investigate securities fraud, and unlike anti-fraud laws in other states and on the federal level, it does not require proof of intent to deceive (Hedge Clippers 2020).

115. ACRE 2021.

116. The worst cuts in the plan of adjustment fall on unsecure creditors (government vendors, public sector workers, and individuals with rulings against the state) with an estimated cut of 99.3 percent or less than a penny for every dollar (Dennis 2021b).

117. Dennis 2021b.

118. The plan of adjustment reduces the central government debt by 61 percent, from $18.8 billion to $7.4 billion, but if the $7 billion in cash granted to hedge funds were taken into consideration, the debt reduction would be only 23 percent. Additionally, 1.03 percent of the property tax collection taken from the Municipal Revenue Collection Center will be paid to the bondholders.

119. Canyon Capital, GoldenTree, Whitebox Advisors, and Taconic Capital, who were key players in the making of COFINA's debt adjustment plan, also profited from these pension cuts.

120. Under Act 60, IFEs can benefit from: 2–4 percent rates on income taxes; 6 percent tax on the distributions from earnings and profits derived from IFEs; 100 percent exemption from PR taxes on such dividends; 1.5 percent in municipal taxes; 100 percent exemption from all property taxes; a fifteen-year tax decree that is renewable for two additional fifteen-year periods.

121. Invest Puerto Rico, created under the Law 13 of 2017, has made great effort to bring "digital nomads" to PR by promoting the tax incentives and other benefits created under Act 60 of 2019.

122. Cintrón Arbsetti 2021.

123. Cohen and Pons 2019.

124. Valentín 2021.

125. Goldstein and Cave 2020.

126. Espacios Abiertos 2023.

Chapter 4

1. The government of PR estimated that the recovery could cost over $130 million (Lee et al. 2022).

2. García-López 2018.

3. UN Office of the High Commissioner on Human Rights (October 30, 2017). "Puerto Rico: Human Rights Concerns Mount in Absence of Adequate Emergency Response." https://www.ohchr.org/en/press-releases/2017/10/puerto-rico-human-rights-concerns-mount-absence-adequate-emergency-response

4. Cooper and Whyte 2017; Faust and Kauzlarich 2008; Green and Ward 2004, 2019; Tombs 2017, 2019.

5. There is important sociolegal scholarship studying law and disasters: Darian-Smith (2022); Downey (2021); Sarat and Lezaun (2009); Sterett (2015a, 2015b, 2023); Sterett and Mateczun (2020, 2022).

6. Agamben (2005) mentioned the use of the state of exception to deal with the aftermath of a series of earthquakes that, in 1908, devastated Calabria, Italy; he suggested that the declaration of the state of siege was used to suppress looting provoked by the disaster, and then he immediately moved to discuss whether necessity is the primary source of law. Agamben missed the opportunity to reflect on one of the key aspects of the management of disasters through the state of exception or through emergency powers: the militarization and punitive dynamic at play in the aftermath of the disaster.

7. Public Law 100–707 of November 1988.

8. For a legal discussion of the negligent role of FEMA in PR, see Murray (2019a, 2019b).

9. In the aftermath of disasters, we can also identify state crimes of omission: a specific confluence between systemic abandonment, criminal negligence, and inequality (Berger 2009; Faust and Carlson 2011).

10. Escaleras et al. 2007; Escaleras and Register 2016; Green 2004; Wei and Marinova 2016.

11. Collins (2014) engages in a similar analysis of the state crimes of omission and revictimization in the aftermath of the 2010 earthquake in Haiti.

12. In 2018, after Hurricane María devastated the archipelago, the emergency plan had not been disclosed by the government. As a result, on October 26, 2018, the CPI and Proyecto de Acceso a la Información sued the Department of Public Safety to made public the emergency plan.

13. Martinez Orabona et al. 2022.

14. Vélez-Vélez and Villarubia-Mendoza 2021.

15. Vélez-Vélez and Villarubia-Mendoza 2021.

16. Minet 2019.

17. These executive orders used Law 20 of 2017 as the basis for the declaration of the state of emergency.

18. OE-2017–45; OE-2017–47. OE-2017–48 imposes a price freeze and prohibited the sale of alcohol.

19. OE-2017–49.

20. OE-2017–50.

21. Kilómetro Cero (2018a) argued that this curfew and the arrests were illegal, given that Rosselló's administration used Law 211 of 1999—which have been derogated by Law 20 of 2017—as the emergency legal framework to issue these executive orders. All executive orders between OE-2017–47 and OE-2017–58 were issued under the legal framework of Law 211 of 1999, while OE-2017–59 to OE-2018–06 were all issued under the legal framework of Law 20 of 2017. This change is important and may validate Kilómetro Cero's argument that the decisions made during the first part of the Hurricane María response were following a legal framework that has been derogated, which illustrates the lack of preparedness and the questionable management of the emergency.

22. Kilómetro Cero 2023.

23. OE-2017–52 and OE-2017–54.

24. Law to Unify the Functions of Law Enforcement Agents in PR in the Case of an Emergency or Disaster Declaration.

25. This expansion of law enforcement agencies goes in tandem with what LeBrón (2019) describes as punitive governance.

26. OE-2017–62.

27. Cintrón Arbasetti 2017; García-López 2018.

28. OE-2017–51.

29. OE-2017–53. On December 8, 2017, this executive order was amended by OE-2017–72. This new executive order suspended Sections 1 and 3 (which provided for the deregulation of the contracting process). Also, this executive order amended Sections 4, 5, 6 of OE-2017–53, with the intention of clarifying and imposing some restrictions.

30. An example of the interwoven connection between militarization and privatization of the management of the hurricane is OE-2017–71 of December 5, in which Rosselló's administration allowed the US military, the US Army Corps of Engineers, and the telecommunication industry to use any measure they considered necessary to access telecommunication infrastructure.

31. OE-2017–56.

32. OE-2017–59.

33. OE-2017–68.

34. OE-2017–73.

35. OE-2017–60.

36. Martinez Orabona et al. 2022.

37. Murray 2019b.

38. Frontline 2018.

39. Rivera (2020) has called this process disaster colonialism, while Bonilla (2020a) and García-López (2020) have named it coloniality of disasters.

40. On the leptospirosis outbreak and the PR government inaction, see Sutter and Sosa Pascual (2018).

41. García-López 2018.

42. See the video posted by David Begnaud: https://www.youtube.com/watch?v=FGorE-MOMOI

43. Robles 2018.

44. Sosa Pascual and Valentín Ortiz 2019.

45. On September 28, 2022, Senator Mike Lee (R-UT) and Representative Nydia Velazquez (D-NY) introduced a bill entitled the Puerto Rican Recovery Act in both houses of Congress. This bill was aimed at requiring the US Coast Guard to provide temporary exemptions from certain Jones Act restrictions to vessels providing relief to PR after Hurricane Fiona. The exemptions were intended to be valid for one year or until the end of the major disaster declaration of September 22, 2022, whichever came first. The bill was never discussed in either house.

46. Colón-Ramos et al. 2019; Murray 2019b.

47. Martinez Orabona et al. 2022.

48. Sosa Pascual and Wiscovitch Padilla 2020b.

49. See the CPI special report "The Deaths of Hurricane María": https://periodismoinvestigativo.com/2018/09/the-deaths-of-hurricane-maria/

50. OE-2018–01.

51. Florido 2018.

52. Valentín and Minet 2019.

53. Powers 2020, 2022.

54. OE-2017–65 and OE-2017–69.

55. This agency was first created in 2009 by Law 29 of 2009. In January 2017, Rosselló's administration enacted Law 1 of 2017 with the intention to amend Law 29 of 2009. On the public-private partnerships and their implications in the neoliberal understanding of the state, see Grimsey and Lewis (2004).

56. The only prosecutions for fraud and corruption were Donald Ellison, the former president of Cobra Acquisitions, and Dr. Ahsha Tribble, who was the FEMA deputy regional administrator (Acevedo 2022).

57. Aronoff 2017.

58. OE-2018–02.

59. OE-2017–78; OE-2018–05.

60. OE-2018–11.

61. OE-2017–66. Unlike previous executive orders, Rosselló used the legal framework provided by Law 5 of 2017, Section 206(a), which grants the governor emergency power to take over the administration of any agency of the PR government.

62. García-López 2018.

63. Hedge Clippers 2018a, 2018b.

64. Disaster Solutions is a joint venture between AECOM and a subsidiary of SNC-Lavalin Group Inc.

65. Brock Pierce is one of the early investors in Bitcoin and founders of several crypto ventures (Bowles 2018; Strauss 2019; Watlington 2019).

66. Crandall 2019.

67. Atiles 2023a; US Commission on Civil Rights 2022. https://www.washingtonpost.com/politics/it-totally-belittled-the-moment-many-look-back-in-anger-at-trumps-tossing-of-paper-towels-in-puerto-rico/2018/09/13/8a3647d2-b77e-11e8-a2c5-3187f427e253_story.html

68. https://recovery.pr.gov/en. Similar transparency portals have been implemented in other US jurisdictions such as Louisiana, New Jersey, New York, and Texas following hurricanes.

69. https://espaciosabiertos.org/la-transparencia-del-portal-de-transparencia/

70. https://espaciosabiertos.org/espacios-abiertos-questions-the-work-of-cgi-technologies-contractor-for-the-governments-transparency-portal/

71. Ethics Global had a contract with COR3 (under P3) to provide "administrative consulting." The contract (2019-CR0039) amounted to $20,000 and lasted from February 18, 2019, to June 30, 2019.

72. Díaz Torres 2019.

73. Colón and Rodriguez 2019.

74. There have been significant efforts to amend this law by anticorruption organizations such as Sembrando Sentido, Somos Más, among others.

75. Flaherty and Ebbs 2019.

76. Willison et al. 2021.

77. Sommerfeldt 2020.

78. O'Donnell 2020.

79. The US federal government, through the Community Development Block Grant (CDBG), has two key programs: (1) CDBG-Disaster Recovery (CDBG-DR), focused on disaster recovery, and (2) CDBG-Mitigation (CDBG-MIT), which addresses risk mitigation to increase disaster resiliency. For an analysis of these funds, see Meléndez (2020a, 2020b), Molinari (2022) and Torres-Cordero (2020).

80. Lamba-Nieves and Santiago-Bartolomei 2018.

81. The USCCR (2022) strongly suggests that when hiring contractors, the search should begin by looking at local options. Relying on out-of-town contractors creates missed opportunities to provide employment, job training, and contracting opportunities to low-income local workers and small- and minority-controlled businesses, which are often in severe need of work due to the disruption to local business following a disaster.

82. Tormos-Aponte et al. 2022.

83. Bonilla 2022; Jones 2022; Tormos-Aponte 2022.

84. In its special series "María: The Money Trail," CPI have collected and indexed all the federal and state reports on the Hurricane María. These audits or investigations included: seven reports issued by GAO between 2018 and 2022; six reports issued by the Office of the Inspector General of the Department of Homeland Security; two reports issued by the Inspector General of HUD; one report issued by the Office of the Inspector General of the DoD; and one self-report issued by FEMA.

85. Murray 2019b.

86. See also Ivis García 2022.

87. Ivis García 2022; Godreau-Aubert 2022; Molinari 2022.

88. Molinari 2019.

89. Molinari 2019.

90. Katz 2020; Robles 2020.

91. As result of the lack of disaster relief and the distribution of economic assistant, over 10,000 families were at risk or have already lost their houses (Díaz Torres 2020).

92. Hinojosa 2020; Sierra 2020.

93. OE-2020–01.

94. OE-2020–02.

95. OE-2020–04; OE-2020–12.

96. OE-2020–03; OE-2020–13.

97. OE-2020–07; OE-2020–08; OE-2020–09.

98. OE-2020–10.

99. OE-2020–15; OE-2020–18; OE-2020–46.

100. OE-2020–14; OE-2020–16; OE-2020–19.

101. Sierra 2020.

102. Dennis 2020a.

103. Hedge Clipper 2018d.
104. Dennis 2020a.
105. Dennis 2020a.
106. Hinojosa 2020.
107. Santiago-Bartolomei and Lamba Nieves 2022; Suárez et al. 2022.
108. Rosa and Mazzei 2020.
109. Jackson 2020b.
110. The official acronym is NMEAD, which comes from its name in Spanish: Negociado Para el Manejo de Emergencias y Administración de Desastres. This agency is part of the Department of Public Safety created under the above discussed Law 20 of 2017.
111. O. Serrano 2020.
112. O. Serrano 2020.
113. Quintero 2020. The OPFEI is an autonomous agency that appoints special independent prosecutors to investigate and prosecute government officials who engage in criminal conduct. The office can be considered the PR version of the US Department of Justice Office of Special Counsel. The OPFEI was established by Law 2 of February 23, 1988, and it has been largely underfunded, which has impeded its ability to effectively address public corruption.
114. Hoyos and Corujo 2020.
115. Suárez and Tormos-Aponte 2022; Tormos-Aponte et al. 2022.
116. Tormos-Aponte et al. 2022.
117. Díaz Torres 2022.
118. As Rodríguez Vázquez (2022) has shown, floodings caused by Fiona in the southern region were worsened by the lack of investment in PREPA irrigation channels. Although FEMA allocated $62 million in recovery funds for permanent works on the irrigation channels, the works are not expected to start until 2024.
119. Tormos-Aponte et al. 2022.
120. Bonilla 2022.
121. Lee et al. 2022.
122. OE-2022–46.
123. OE-2022–47.
124. OE-2022–48.
125. OE-2022–49.
126. OE-2021–24; OE-2021–69; OE-2022–21; OE-2022–50; OE-2023–03; OE-2023–24; OE-2024-01. These declarations followed the legal framework of Act 76 of 2000.
127. Pierluisi issued an executive order OE-2023–04 (March 21, 2023) to create a strategic counsel to evaluate the adjudication of CDBG-MIT funds. This is part of an on-going process of re-regulation of the procedures to administer the recovery funds.
128. Tormos-Aponte et al. 2022.
129. Aronoff 2022.
130. The Puerto Rico Energy Public Policy Act, or Law 17 of 2019, set the goals for PR to meet 100 percent of its electricity needs with renewable energy by 2050.

131. Martínez 2022.

132. Encarnación et al. 2022.

133. Martínez 2022. The wholesalers included Shell, Total, Toral, Buckeye Partners, and Peerless.

134. Martínez 2022.

135. Valentín et al. 2022.

136. Maldonado et al. 2022.

137. The management and maintenance of the shelter have been subcontracted to a private corporation, and in this case the Public Housing Administration contracted JA Machuca & Associates to run the shelters.

138. Maldonado et al 2022.

139. Méndez Gonzalez 2022.

140. LeBrón 2019; Torres-Cordero 2024; Villarrubia-Mendoza and Vélez-Vélez 2020.

Chapter 5

1. Goitein 2021; Kipfer and Mohamud 2021; Sterett 2023.

2. Pérez et al. 2022.

3. C. García et al. 2021; Murphy Marcos 2024.

4. Atiles 2023b; Atiles and Whyte 2023; Parmet 2023; Sterett 2023.

5. 50 U.S.C. ch. 36 §1601 et seq.

6. 42 U.S.C. 5121 et seq. This statute enabled the creation of the Federal Emergency Management Agency (FEMA).

7. 50 U.S.C. §§4501 et seq.

8. 58 Stat. 682, ch. 373.

9. Courts have been at the center of scholarly and political debates during the pandemic (Mello and Parmet 2021; 2022; Parmet 2023). Particularly salient are the debates concerning the role of the US Supreme Court in reshaping the jurisprudence of a public health crisis established in *Jacobson v. Massachusetts*, 1905 (Parmet 2023).

10. Agamben 2021; Appadauri 2020; Atiles 2021, 2023b; Atiles and Whyte 2023; Greene 2020; Maitra 2020; Meierhenrich 2021; D. Whyte 2021.

11. OE-2020–20, of March 12, 2020.

12. The executive orders are: OE-2020–23; OE-2020–29; OE-2020–32; OE-2020–33; OE-2020–34; OE-2020–38; OE-2020–41; OE-2020–44; OE-2020–48; OE-2020–52; OE-2020–54; OE-2020–60; OE-2020–62; OE-2020–64; OE-2020–66; OE-2020–76; OE-2020–77; OE-2020–79; OE-2020–80; OE-2020–81; OE-2020–83; OE-2020–87.

13. The executive orders are: OE-2021–10; OE-2021–14; OE-2021–19; OE-2021–26; OE-2021–27; OE-2021–28; OE-2021–32; OE-2021–36; OE-2021–40; OE-2021–43; OE-2021–65; OE-2021–67; OE-2021–70; OE-2021–75; OE-2021–80; OE-2021–81; OE-2021–82; OE-2021–85; OE-2021–86; OE-2022–02; OE-2022–07; OE-2022–11; OE-2022–19; OE-2022–23; OE-2023–12; OE-2023–13.

14. Kilómetro Cero 2023.

15. In addition to Law 20 of 2017, the emergency powers jurisprudence in PR relies on

Law 76 of 2000; Law 69 of 1969, known as the Military Code of Puerto Rico; Law 62 of 1962; Law 81 of 1912 (Department of Health Act); and the US jurisprudence.

16. Martinez 2020; A. Serrano 2020; Valentín and Minet 2020.

17. Balmaceda 2020a, 2020b; Ostolaza et al. 2023.

18. Gelardi 2020.

19. S.3548–116th Congress (2019–2020) Coronavirus Aid, Relief, and Economic Security Act or the CARES Act.

20. OE-2020–22; OE-2020–28; OE-2020–81; OE-2020–83.

21. OE-2020–24.

22. OE-2020–27.

23. OE-2020–23.

24. OE-2021–36.

25. Florido 2020; Kilómetro Cero 2023.

26. Comision de Derecho Civiles 2020; Kilómetro Cero 2020b.

27. OE-2020–36.

28. Wiscovitch Padilla and Sosa Pascual 2020.

29. Dennis 2020c.

30. OE-2021–34.

31. Composed mainly of the PR Manufacturers' Association, the Pharmaceutical Industry Association of PR, and the Private Sector Coalition.

32. OE-2020–37; OE-2020–38.

33. Dennis 2020d; Kilómetro Cero 2023; Sosa Pascual and Wiscovitch Padilla 2020a, 2020b.

34. OE-2020–54.

35. OE-2020–66.

36. On October 1, 2020, OE-2020–76 eliminated the curfew, and fifteen days after on October 16, 2020, OE-2020–77 reimposed the curfew from 10 pm to 5 am, which continued with some variations until its elimination in May 2021.

37. OE-2021–01.

38. OE-2021–54.

39. OE-2020–51; OE-2021–28; OE-2021–37; OE-2021–40; OE-2022–09.

40. OE-2021–58; OE-2021–62; OE-2021–63; OE-2021–75.

41. OE-2021–63; OE-2021–64.

42. OE-2021–82; OE-2021–87; OE-2022–03; OE-2022–06; OE-2022–10.

43. OE-2022–15.

44. *CPI v. Carlos Mellado López* (2021), SJ2021CV00567.

45. OE-2021–80; OE-2020–85; OE-2022–02; OE-2022–07.

46. OE-2021–81; OE-2022–05.

47. OE-2021–82; OE-2021–87; OE-2022–03; OE-2022–06.

48. OE-2021–86.

49. OE-2022–23.

50. Quoted in Rieder 2020.

51. Mason and Shalal 2020.

52. Garcia and Beverley 2021.

53. The contract, at a cost of $650,000, started on June 15, 2020, and ended on July 17, 2020.

54. PR became 98 percent an opportunity zone after the enactment of the Tax Cuts and Jobs Act, which meant that the pharmaceutical industry could claim almost everywhere in PR.

55. On zombie capitalism, see Harman (2009) and Peck (2010).

56. Hedge Clippers 2022a.

57. Dennis 2020d.

58. Hedge Clippers 2022a.

59. Dennis 2020d.

60. The tax expenditure in billions is: $15.691 in 2017; $13.809 in 2018; $13.965 in 2019; $13.497 in 2020; $12.164 in 2021; $14.568 in 2022; $14.811 in 2023 (projected). See Puerto Rico Department of Treasury, "Puerto Rico Tax Expenditure Report for Tax Year 2023," https://hacienda.pr.gov/sites/default/files/tax_expenditure_report.pdf

61. Hedge Clippers 2022a.

62. Hedge Clippers 2022a.

63. D. Whyte 2020.

64. Such as ABM Industries, Fuller Group, and Securitas.

65. Dietrich 2013.

66. Tombs and Whyte 2008.

67. Hedge Clippers 2022a, 2022b.

68. Hedge Clippers 2022b.

69. Hedge Clippers 2022b.

70. US Code Title 42, ch. 85.

71. Dietrich 2013.

72. This is in addition to other environmental hazards such as those generated by Applied Energy System Coal Plant (Atiles and Rojas-Paez 2022; Onís 2021); years of military experimentations in Vieques and Culebra (Atiles 2014; Baver 2006); Monsanto and other seeds and GMO companies; and other forms of environmental degradation. PR has over 500 Superfund sites.

73. Hedge Clippers 2022b.

74. Baxter—a pharmaceutical company producing 50 percent of the US supply of saline in PR—announced that unlike in the aftermath of Hurricane María, there will not be a shortage and or delays, since it has invested billions in their own microgrid.

75. Knox and Whyte 2023.

76. Dennis 2020d.

77. Dennis 2020b.

78. Dennis 2020d: 6.

79. Valentín and Cintrón Arbasetti 2020.

80. Resolución de la Cámara de Representantes 1741, of June 29, 2020.

81. In May 2023, Wiscovitch Padilla and Sosa Pascual (2023) published an investigation on the ties between the Vázquez and Pierluisi administrations and a technology services corporation named SupportPR. This corporation, together with other tech-

nology and advising corporations that form what Wiscovitch Padilla and Sosa Pascual (2023) termed a "technology cartel," received millions of dollars in contracts from the Department of Health amidst the COVID-19 pandemic. The directors of these corporations are donors of the PNP and of Pierluisi's campaign, which attests to the dynamics of strategic accommodation deployed by the local elites to maintain the hegemonic position amidst crisis and disasters.

82. The government acquired test kits without taking the necessary precautions regarding their reliability, as the purchase of 50,000 test kits for $650,000 from Castro Business exemplifies. The Department of Health was unable to use the test kits since they did not have FDA approval. Castro Business used a series of intermediary corporations based in the United States, Australia, and China to acquire the test kits. Only 8,900 tests sold by Castro Business reached the Department of Health (Valentín and Cintrón Arbasetti 2020).

83. The PRHR report identified overpricing and the non-delivery of products. This is the case of Apex General Contractors, and the former governmental employee turned disaster entrepreneur Juan Maldonado, to whom the government paid, in advance, $38 million for 1 million test kits. The case of Juan Maldonado is an example of revolving doors and the symbiosis between the private and public sector, since he has been back and forth between the private sector and the government since 2009. Apex and Maldonado followed the same scheme as the other suppliers, only this time there were over seven intermediaries at the local and international level. Many intermediaries received tax incentives from the local and US government (Valentín and Cintrón Arbasetti 2020). Another example of overpricing is found in the purchase of test kits from Maitland 175, a corporation based in Florida. The Department of Health paid between 120 and 420 percent more that the market price for the test kits. Maitland 175 was also involved in alleged fraudulent dealings with the PRNG, which disbursed $4.3 million in emergency-related purchases between April and June 30 (Valentín and Cintrón Arbasetti 2020).

84. The PRHR report identified the mishandling of public funds. This involved two purchase orders for 100,000 test kits made by 313 LLC amounting to $3.6 million. Despite the corporation requiring prepayment of 60 percent of the amount owed, the government of PR paid 100 percent of the bill before receiving the test kits. 313 LLC promised that it would supply all the test kits (101,500) before April 6, 2020; however, it only delivered 1,000. The test kits did not have FDA approval, but the Department of Health distributed them to various hospitals. Although late, in mid-April 2020, 313 LLC attempted to deliver the remaining test kits, but the Department of Health declined to receive them until the initial purchase price was reduced. 313 LLC finally sued the government to force it to receive test kits without changing the terms of payment, since the delay was allegedly due to the FDA. 313 LLC and its president Ricardo Vázquez Hernández had received tax incentives and exceptions from the PR government in areas ranging from legal advice to the video games and electronics industry.

85. Atiles 2021.

86. The president of the Medical Task Force, Dr. Segundo Rodríguez, was the lead figure in the purchase order issued to Apex General Contractors. The PRHR report

argues that Rodríguez exceeded his powers, duties, and responsibilities, which were limited to strategic plans on the handling of the pandemic.

87. Wiscovitch Padilla and Sosa Pascual 2020.

88. https://www.sba.gov/funding-programs/loans/covid-19-relief-options/paycheck-protection-program

89. Public Law 116–136, March 16, 2020.

90. Griffin et al. 2023.

91. https://www.pandemicoversight.gov

92. Hrushka 2023.

93. First Bank Puerto Rico is a subsidiary of First Bancorp. In September 2020, First Bancorp acquired Banco Santander Puerto Rico, one of the key financial institutions that led PR to its current economic and financial crisis.

94. https://www.justice.gov/usao-pr/pr/44-individuals-indicted-federal-grand-jury-roles-multimillion-dollar-fraudulent-scheme

95. These are: PR Asset Portfolio Serving International, Zenus Bank International, Standard International Bank, Medici Bank International, WTC International Bank Corporation, and Fairwinds International Bank.

96. An amendment to Law 20 of 2017.

97. Law 66 of 2020 amended Law 35 of 2020, adding additional penalties and fines to the above-described offenses.

98. Kilómetro Cero 2020b, 2023.

99. Florido 2020.

100. Article 5.14 of Law 20 of 2017.

101. The benefits are calculated based on a formula established by the Disaster Unemployment Assistance Program in accordance with the Unemployment Insurance Program Letters issued by the US Department of Labor (Whittaker 2022).

102. https://www.pandemicoversight.gov

103. Collazo and De Jesús 2021.

104. Two DLHR employees helped me to disentangle the confusing and contrived bureaucratic operations of this department. The employees asked not to be included in this publication to avoid possible retaliation.

105. The DLHR amended in two instances its already existing contract with EVERTEC. The original contract, to provide technological consulting services. amounted to over $4 million dollars and was then amended to design the Fast PUA platform. The amendment was for an additional $1.1 million, signed on June 8, 2020.

106. Alvarez and Sepúlveda 2020; Sepúlveda 2020. EVERTEC worked with Fast Enterprises. Governor Pedro Pierluisi and former FOMB chairman José Carrión are connected to Banco Popular and EVERTEC. According to the database Little Sis, during his time at O'Neill & Borges (January 2017 to July 2019), Pedro Pierluisi served as an attorney and lobbyist for EVERTEC.

107. When the new platform started operating on August 25, 2020, all PUA beneficiaries had to re-register and submit all the information and documents they had previously submitted to the new platform (Soto Rodríguez 2020).

108. Tellado 2020.

109. Resolución de la Cámara de Representantes 1767, of May 11, 2020.

110. ENDI 2021.

111. OIG-QI-21–001 of July 24, 2020.

112. According to the investigation, an individual with connections in the DLHR managed to receive $126,000 in PUA assistance. Furthermore, the third report found that the DLHR may have disbursed more than $1 million in funds from the PUA program to nine addresses including residences, apartments, and post office boxes. In September 2022, the OIG reported that nine public employees received payments of PUA, even when they were fully employed.

113. https://fred.stlouisfed.org/series/PUAICPR

114. Case number: SJ2021CV05428 of August 24, 2021.

115. Law 141 of 2019.

116. Ruiz Kuilan 2022.

117. I requested information again on June 9, 2023, and received a response with limited information on June 26, 2023.

118. On March 24, 2022, local newspapers reported that the DLHR referred to the PRDJ and the FBI over 700 cases of fraud, 600 of which were from incarcerated individuals (Caro 2022).

119. Compare this case of fraud with $10.3 million and fifty individuals arrested between February 2023 and May 2023 by the FBI in PR for fraud to PPP loans.

120. Boricua 2021.

121. Between July 2020 and July 26, 2022, Fast Enterprises was awarded five contracts for technological services to the DLHR amounting to over $4 million.

Chapter 6

1. For a systemic study of transparency, see Donaldson and Kingsbury (2013), Koivisto (2022), Valdovinos (2022), and Viola and Laidler (2021).

2. On corruption narratives, see Ranganathan et al. (2023) and Villanueva (2019).

3. On how crisis and systemic corruption becomes moralized, see Whyte and Wiergratz (2016) and Vergara (2020).

4. Barak 2012; Tombs 2016.

5. Hetherington 2011; Sampson 2010, 2015; Zaloznaya 2013, 2017.

6. Valentín and Minet 2019.

7. Mazzei and Robles 2019.

8. I am following Benjamin's Thesis VIII and his distinction between the state of exception as rule and the real state of exception (Reynolds 2017; J. Whyte 2013).

9. On the relationship between corruption of the powerful and its normalization, see David Whyte (2007, 2014, 2015).

10. Atiles 2022c, 2023a.

11. Coloniality refers to longstanding patters of power that emerged as a result of colonialism, but that define culture, labor, intersubjectivity relations, and knowledge production well beyond the strict limits of colonial administration. Maldonado-Torres (2007: 257) develops the concept of coloniality of being, arguing that it appears in historical projects and ideas of civilization that advance colonial projects of various kinds

inspired or legitimized by the idea of race. The coloniality of being in turn produces the ontological colonial difference, deploying a series of fundamental existence characteristics and symbolic realities (Maldonado-Torres 2007: 252).

12. Mattei and Nader 2008; Saha 2013.

13. On the history of corruption in PR, see Atiles et al. (2022) and Villanueva (2022).

14. OE-2017–10 of 2017.

15. Law 8 of 2017 introduces a series of anticorruption policies in Section 6.8.

16. Law 15 of 2017. In my interview with Ivelisse Torres Rivera, the inspector general, she described the limitations and challenges faced by this new agency. For example, Torres Rivera was appointed as inspector general in 2019, two years after Law 15 was enacted, and she had to build the office anew. Torres Rivera noted that her office sought to amend Law 15 to guarantee the economic and fiscal independence of the office (Law 70 of 2019), which is important since it could guarantee the independence of the office for investigating members of the government without the risk of losing their funding.

17. Law 2 of 2018.

18. OE-2019–31.

19. Law 122 of 2019.

20. Law 141 of 2019.

21. The bill was initially sent by the Office of the Governor (Fortaleza) to the Legislative Assembly on November 29, 2017, just months after Hurricane María, and, in less than two months, had already been transformed into law.

22. Section 3.7; Title IV, Sections 4.2, 4.4, 4.5, 4.6; and Title V.

23. Law 144 of 2019, introduces additional legal protections for whistleblowers and guarantees that public employees and officials who report acts of corruption are offered free legal assistance. While I was conducting my participatory observation with the Transparency Network, these organization also drafted an amendment to this law.

24. This anticorruption measure has been in place since 1997, when it was first introduced by Law 119. Originally, Law 199 required the Puerto Rican Police Department (PRPD) to keep a registry of persons convicted of corruption. This law was amended by Law 141 of 2016, in which the registry was transferred to the PRDJ.

25. In PR the secretary of the PRDJ fulfills the duties of the US attorney general.

26. OE-2019–31. Unlike the registry of persons convicted of corruption, the registry of lobbyists (which is also administered by the PRDJ) includes no personal information and no financial disclosure. In total, the registry contains thirty corporations, law firms, and individuals that "voluntarily" provided information about their business with the Puerto Rican government.

27. Wanda Vázquez, former secretary of justice and former governor of PR, made every effort to conceal the legal implications of the corrupt acts discussed in the Telegram chat. For example, on November 24, 2020, the Office of the Independent Special Prosecutors of PR concluded that the Telegram chat did not provide enough evidence to prosecute Rosselló and members of his government.

28. During his last eight days in office, Rosselló signed eighty-six laws and executive orders (*NotiCel* 2019).

29. OE-2021–02.

30. OE-2021–29.

31. Atiles 2019.

32. Article 11, Section 4 of the PR Constitution.

33. Ramos Hernández 2016; Rivera Ramos 1975.

34. Atiles 2019; LeBrón 2017.

35. Case number K PE2010–1384 (mandamus) April 6, 2010.

36. Case number SJ2016CV00238 (mandamus) September 15, 2016.

37. Pagán 2016.

38. Case number SJ2019CV02706 (mandamus) March 18, 2019.

39. This is a common issue identified by transparency and access of information scholarship, and it is not limited to PR; see Chapman and Hunt (2006) and Porumbescu et al. (2022).

40. The lack of preservation of historical archives, together with the lack of access to information, is a recurrent issue for scholars studying PR. In my research I experienced the all-too-common challenges that scholars experience when conducting research on PR, including lack of accessibility, limited availability of the archives, unwillingness of public personnel to grant access to documents and information, and other institutional barriers that contribute to what the Transparency Network terms "the culture of opacity."

41. CPI 2021.

42. Valentín and Minet 2021.

43. Sosa Pascual 2016.

44. Valentín 2021.

45. Minet 2021.

46. Ackerman and Sandoval-Ballesteros 2006; Berliner 2014; Donaldson and Kingsbury 2013.

47. Berliner 2014.

48. Sharma 2013.

49. Hetherington 2011.

50. CPI 2022.

51. Carlos Ramos Hernández noted in our interview that, together with the CPI and other organizations, they have been in the process of amending Law 141. The process was initiated by Representative José Márquez, who co-authored Bill 1303 in April 2022.

52. https://espaciosabiertos.org/en/10-principios-para-el-acceso-a-la-informacion/

53. https://drive.google.com/file/d/1zzXyZUad4jpcrLAlJK-F2dPCzGQSJK5c/view

Epilogue

1. Mazzei and Robles 2019.

2. Cabán 2020; Colón Morera 2020; Cotto 2020; García-López 2020; LeBrón 2021; Powers 2020, 2022; Villanueva and LeBrón 2020.

3. Sosa Pascual and Valentín 2019.

4. My description of the Summer of 2019 is based on participatory observation con-

ducted during these demonstrations. From July 13 to August 2, 2019, I attended daily demonstrations in San Juan and the metropolitan area, including the massive march demanding the resignation of Rosselló on July 22, 2019, in San Juan. Besides San Juan, I also took part in demonstrations in Mayagüez and Cabo Rojo. Participation in these demonstrations provided me with a firsthand experience of the organizations, discussions, and understandings circulating among people involved in the Summer of 2019. This experience also allowed me to collect primary data on the meanings and understandings of corruption and anticorruption that were being developed during the demonstrations.

5. Powers 2020, 2022.

6. Allyn 2019.

7. Brusi 2019; LeBrón 2021.

8. Atiles 2019, 2022b.

9. The appointment took place on July 31, 2019, and with it a legal and political battle was unleashed over whether the nomination was constitutional.

10. Pierluisi assumed the governorship on Friday, August 2, 2019, after his nomination to secretary of state was approved by the House of Representatives of PR. For secretary of state of PR, it is required that both houses approve the nomination.

11. The Senate of PR and its president Thomas Rivera Schatz argued that Pierluisi's swearing in as governor was inadmissible since they understood that Law 7 of 2005 (to allow a secretary of state to become governor without having to be confirmed by both houses) was unconstitutional. That interpretation, in effect, was unanimously validated by the Supreme Court of PR.

12. On anticolonial performance in PR, see Ruiz (2019).

13. Kilómetro Cero (2020a).

BIBLIOGRAPHY

Abel, Richard. 2010. "Law and Society: Project and Practice." *Annual Review of Law and Social Science* 6: 1–23.

Acevedo, Nichole. 2022, May 19. "Ex-FEMA, Energy Company Officials Plead Guilty in Post-Hurricane Case in Puerto Rico." *NBC News*. https://www.nbcnews.com/news/latino/ex-fema-energy-company-officials-plead-guilty-post-hurricane-case-puer-rcna29502

Ackerman, John, and Irma Sandoval-Ballesteros. 2006. "The Global Explosion of Freedom of Information Laws." *Administrative Law Review* 58, no. 1: 85–130.

ACRE. 2021, September 15. "PROMESA Has Failed: How a Colonial Board Is Enriching Wall Street and Hurting Puerto Ricans." Center for Popular Democracy and Action Center on Race and the Economy. https://acrecampaigns.org/wp-content/uploads/2021/09/ENGLISH-PROMESA-Has-Failed-Report-CPD-ACRE-9-14-2021-FINAL.pdf

Agamben, Giorgio. 1998. *Homo Sacer: Sovereign Power and Bare Life*. Translated by Daniel Heller-Roazen. Stanford: Stanford University Press.

———. 2005. *State of Exception*. Translated by Kevin Attel. Chicago: University Chicago Press.

———. 2021. *Where Are We Now?: The Epidemic as Politics*. Translated by Valeria Dani. Lanham: Rowman & Littlefield.

Agozino, Biko. 2003. *Counter Colonial Criminology: A Critique of Imperialist Reason*. London: Pluto Press.

———. 2018. "Imperialism: The General Theory of Crime of the Powerful." In *Revisiting Crimes of the Powerful: Marxism, Crime and Deviance*, edited by Steven Bittle, Laura Snider, Steve Tombs, and David Whyte, 297–308. London and New York: Routledge.

Alford, Ryan. 2017. *Permanent State of Emergency: Unchecked Executive Power and the Demise of the Rule of Law*. Montreal: McGill-Queen's University Press.

Allyn, Bobby. 2019, July 22. "Thousands in Puerto Rico Seek to Oust Rosselló in Massive 'Ricky Renuncia March.'" *NPR*. https://www.npr.org/2019/07/22/744093831/thousands-in-puerto-rico-seek-to-oust-rossell-in-massive-ricky-renuncia-march

Alsina, Alberto, Carlo Favero, and Francesco Giavazzi. 2019. *Austerity: When It Works and When It Doesn't*. Princeton: Princeton University Press.

Alvarez, Yennifer, and Aixa Sepúlveda. 2020, May 8. "El Colapso de La Plataforma Del Desempleo Se Pudo Haber Evitado." *NotiCel*. https://www.noticel.com/gobierno/ahora/top-stories/20200508/el-colapso-de-la-plataforma-del-desempleo-se-pudo-haber-evitado/

Alvesalo-Kuusi, Anne, and David Whyte. 2018. "Researching the Powerful: A Call for the Reconstruction of Research Ethics." *Sociological Research Online* 23, no. 1:136–152.

Amarasinghe, Punsara, and Sanjay Rajhans. 2020. "*Agamben's Two Missing Factors*; Understanding State of Emergency Through Colonialism and Racial Doctrine." *Open Political Science* 3, no. 1: 34–46.

Anghie, Antony. 2006. "The Evolution of International Law: Colonial and Postcolonial realities." *Third World Quarterly* 27, no. 5: 739–753.

———. 2009. "Rethinking Sovereignty in International Law." *Annual Review of Law & Social Science* 5, no. 1: 291–310.

Appadaurai, Arjun. 2020. "The COVID Emergency." *Social Anthropology* 28, no. 2: 221–222.

Aradau, Claudia. 2007. "Law Transformed: Guantanamo and the 'Other' Exception." *Third World Quarterly* 28, no. 3: 489–501.

Arendt, Hannah. 1958. *The Origins of Totalitarianism*. New York: Meridian.

Aronoff, Kate. 2017, October 31. "There's a Shady Puerto Rico Contract You Didn't Hear About." *The Intercept*. https://theintercept.com/2017/10/31/puerto-rico-electric-contract-cobra/

———. 2018, September 28. "Vulture Funds Stand to Make Millions in Wake of Hurricane Maria." *The Intercept*. https://theintercept.com/2018/09/28/puerto-rico-hurricane-maria-recovery-funds/

———. 2022, September 20. "Puerto Rico Can Blame Its Total Blackout on Predatory Companies and Poor Decision in Washington." *New Republic*. https://newrepublic.com/article/167787/puerto-rico-fiona-blackout? . . . ocial&utm_campaign=EB_TNR&utm_source=Twitter#Echobox=1663689576-1

Ashton, Philip. 2011. "The Financial Exception and the Reconfiguration of Credit Risk in US Mortgage Markets." *Environment and Planning A: Economy and Space* 43, no. 8: 1796–1812.

Atiles, Jose. 2013. "Neoliberalism, Law, and Strikes." *Latin American Perspectives* 40, no. 5: 105–117.

———. 2014. "The Criminalization of Socio-Environmental Struggles in Puerto Rico." *Oñati Socio-Legal Series* 4, no. 1: 85–103.

———. 2016. *Apuntes Para Abandonar El Derecho: Estado de Excepción Colonial En Puerto Rico*. Cabo Rojo: Educación Emergente.

———. 2018. "State of Exception as Economic Policy: A Socio-Legal Analysis of the Puerto Rican Colonial Case." *Oñati Socio-Legal Series* 8, no. 6: 819–844.

———. 2019. *Jugando con el Derecho: Movimientos Anticoloniales Puertorriqueños y la Fuerza de Ley*. Cabo Rojo: Editora Educación Emergente.

———. 2020. "Exceptionality and Colonial State-Corporate Crime in the Puerto Rican Fiscal and Economic Crisis." *Latin American Perspectives* 47, no. 3: 49–63.

———. 2021. "The COVID-19 Pandemic in Puerto Rico: Exceptionality, Corruption and State-Corporate Crimes." *State Crime Journal* 10, no. 1: 104–125.

———. 2022a. "The Paradise Performs: Blockchain, Cryptocurrencies, and the Puerto Rican Tax Haven." *South Atlantic Quarterly* 121, no. 3: 612–627.

———. 2022b. "Punitive Governance and the Criminalization of Socioenvironmental, Anti-Austerity and Anticorruption Mobilizations in Puerto Rico." *Critical Criminology* 30: 961–981.

———. 2022c. "From Anti-Corruption to Decolonial Justice: A Sociolegal Analysis of the Puerto Rican Summer of 2019." *Centro Journal* 34, no. 2: 385-414.

———. 2023a. "*Coloniality of Anti-corruption*: Whiteness, Disasters and the US Anti-Corruption Policies in Puerto Rico." *Sociological Review* 71, no. 6: 1277–1298.

———. 2023b. "Emergency Powers, Anti-corruption, and Policy Failure During the COVID-19 Pandemic in Puerto Rico." *Law and Policy* 45, no. 3: 253–272.

———. 2024. "Crimes of the Powerful in Latin America and the Caribbean: Toward a Research Agenda." *Sociology Compass* 18, no 2: e13172.

Atiles, Jose, Gustavo García, and Joaquín Villanueva. 2022. "Beyond Corruption and Anticorruption Narrative: Introducing a Critical Research for Puerto Rican Studies." *Centro Journal* 34, no. 2: 7–24.

Atiles, Jose, and Gustavo Rojas-Paez. 2022. "Coal Criminals: Crime of the Powerful, Extractivism and Historical Harms in the Global South." *British Journal of Criminology* 62, no. 5: 1289–1304.

Atiles, Jose, and David Whyte. 2011. "Counter-Insurgency Goes to University: The Militarisation of Policing in the Puerto Rico Student Strikes." *Critical Studies on Terrorism* 4, no. 3: 393–404.

———. 2023. "Reproducing Crises: Understanding the Role of Law in the COVID-19 Global Pandemic." *Law and Policy Journal* 45, no. 3: 238–252.

Aulette, Judy, and Raymond Michalowski. 1993. "The Imperial Chicken Fire: States, Corporations, and Public Health." In *Political Crime in Contemporary America*, edited by Kenneth Tunnell, 171–206. New York: Garland Press.

Austin, Andrew. 2016, June 3. "Puerto Rico's Current Fiscal Challenges." *Congressional Research Service*. https://crsreports.congress.gov/product/pdf/R/R44095

———. 2022, May 2. "Puerto Rico's Public Debts: Accumulation and Restructuring." *Congressional Research Service*. https://sgp.fas.org/crs/row/R46788.pdf

Ayala, César, and Rafael Bernabe. 2009. *Puerto Rico in the American Century: A History Since 1898*. Chapel Hill: University of North Carolina Press.

Ayuda Legal. 2021, November 10. "Comunicado: Pleito acceso a información pública revela que el Departamento del Trabajo tenía mayor discresion para proteger a las madres sin cuido de menores durante la pandemia." https://www.ayudalegalpuertorico.org/2021/11/10/comunicado-pleito-de-acceso-a-informacion-dt/

Balmaceda, Javier. 2020a, May 7. "Long in Recession, Puerto Rico Needs More Than Just COVID-19 Relief to Overcome Its Crises." Center on Budget and Policy Priorities. https://www.cbpp.org/research/economy/long-in-recession-puerto-rico-needs-more-than-just-covid-19-relief-to-overcome-its

———. 2020b, July 28. "Without a Boost in Next COVID-19 Relief Bill, Puerto Rico Faces Deep Food Aid Cut." Center on Budget and Policy Priorities. https://www.cbpp.org/blog/without-boost-in-next-covid-19-relief-bill-puerto-rico-faces-deep-food-aid-cuts

Barak, Gregg, ed. 1991. *Crime by the Capitalist State: An Introduction to State Criminality*. Albany: SUNY Press.

———. 2012. *Theft of a Nation: Wall Street Looting and Federal Regulatory Colluding*. Lanham: Rowman & Littlefield.

Baver, Sherrie. 2006. "'Peace Is More Than the End of Bombing': The Second Stage of the Viequess Struggle." *Latin American Perspectives* 33, no. 1: 102–115.

Benjamin, Walter. 2003. *Selected Writings. Vol. 4: 1938–1940*. Cambridge, MA: Harvard University Press.

———. 2021. *Toward the Critique of Violence: A Critical Edition*. Edited by Peter Fenves and Julia Ng. Stanford: Stanford University Press.

Berger, Dan. 2009. "Constructing Crime, Framing Disaster." *Punishment & Society* 11, no. 4: 491–510.

Berliner, Daniel. 2014. "The Political Origins of Transparency." *Journal of Politics* 76, no. 2: 479–491.

Bernabe, Rafael. 1998. "Puerto Rico's La Huelga Del Pueblo." *Solidarity*. http://www.solidarity-us.org/site/node/1796

Bernat, Ignasi. 2018. "The Permanent State of Exception in the Southern Periphery of Europe." *Oñati Socio-Legal Series* 8, no. 6: 925–949.

Bernat, Ignasi, and David Whyte. 2017. "State-Corporate Crime and the Process of Capital Accumulation: Mapping a Global Regime of Permission from Galicia to Morecambe Bay." *Critical Criminology* 25: 71–86.

Bhatti, Saqib, and Carrie Sloan. 2016a. "Puerto Rico's Payday Loans: $33.5 Billion of the Island's Debt Is Actually Interest on Payday Loans." ReFund America Project. https://acrecampaigns.org/wp-content/uploads/2020/04/PuertoRicosPaydayLoans-Jun2016.pdf

———. 2016b. "Scooping and Tossing Puerto Rico's Future: Puerto Rico Borrowed $3.2 Billion to Pay Fees and Interest to Banks and Investors." ReFund America Project. https://acrecampaigns.org/wp-content/uploads/2020/04/ScoopingandTossingPuertoRicosFuture-Aug2016.pdf

———. 2017a. "Beware of Bankers Bearing Gifts: Wall Street Sold Puerto Rico Billions in Predatory Loans Disguised as Gifts." ReFund America Project. https://

acrecampaigns.org/wp-content/uploads/2020/04/BewareofBankersBearingGifts-Feb2017.pdf

———. 2017b. "Down the Wells: Wells Fargo's Payday Loans Have Left Puerto Rico Billions of Dollars in the Hole." ReFund America Project. https://acrecampaigns.org/wp-content/uploads/2020/04/DowntheWells-Apr2017.pdf

———. 2017c. "Goldman's Strong Man in Puerto Rico: Trump's Puerto Rico Policy Is a Back Door Bailout for Goldman Sachs." ReFund America Project. https://acrecampaigns.org/wp-content/uploads/2020/04/GoldmansStrongManinPuertoRico-Apr2017.pdf

———. 2017d. "Broken Promises: PROMESA Is a Mode for Undermining Democracy and Pushing Austerity Elsewhere in the U.S." ReFund America Project. https://acreinstitute.org/wp-content/uploads/2020/04/BrokenPromises-August2017.pdf

Bittle, Steven. 2012. *Still Dying for a Living. Corporate Criminal Liability After the Westray Mine Disaster.* Vancouver and Toronto: University of British Columbia Press.

Bishai, Linda, ed. 2020. *Law, Security and the State of Perpetual Emergency.* Cham, Switzerland: Palgrave Macmillan.

Blackhawk, Maggie. 2023. "The Constitution of American Colonialism." *Harvard Law Review* 137, no. 1: 2–152.

———. 2022. "Introduction: Law and the Critique of Capitalism." *South Atlantic Quarterly* 121, no. 2: 223–237.

Blyth, Mark. 2013. *Austerity: The History of a Dangerous Idea.* Oxford and New York: Oxford University Press.

Bonilla, Yarimar. 2018, February 28. "For Investors, Puerto Rico Is a Fantasy Blank Slate." *The Nation.* https://www.thenation.com/article/archive/for-investors-puerto-rico-is-a-fantasy-blank-slate/

———. 2020a. "The Coloniality of Disaster: Race, Empire, and the Temporal Logics of Emergency in Puerto Rico, USA." *Political Geography* 78: 102181.

———. 2020b. "The Swarm of Disaster." *Political Geography* 78: 102182.

———. 2022, October 22. "Why Must Puerto Ricans Always Be Resiliente?" *New York Times.* https://www.nytimes.com/2022/10/10/opinion/fema-fiona-puerto-rico.html

Bonilla, Yarima, and Marisol LeBrón. 2019. *Aftershocks of Disaster: Puerto Rico Before and After the Storm.* Chicago: Haymarket.

Bonizzi, Bruno, Annina Kaltenbrunner, and Jeff Powell. 2022. "Financialised Capitalism and the Subordination of Emerging Capitalist Economies." *Cambridge Journal of Economics* 46, no. 4: 651–678.

Boricua, Bosillo. 2021, December 7. "Miles podrías recibir cartas de recobro por el PUA a partir de enero." *Rayos X.* https://www.telemundopr.com/programas/rayos-x/miles-podrian-recibir-cartas-de-recobro-por-el-pua-a-partir-de-enero/2286016/

Bortz, Pablo, and Annina Kaltenbrunner. 2018. "The International Dimension of Financialization in Developing and Emerging Economies." *Development and Change* 49: 375–393.

Bowles, Nellie. 2018, February 2. "Making a Crypto Utopia in Puerto Rico." *New York*

Times. https://www.nytimes.com/2018/02/02/technology/cryptocurrency-puerto-rico.html

Brabazon, Honor, ed. 2017. *Neoliberal Legality: Understanding the Role of Law in the Neoliberal Project*. London and New York: Routledge.

Brown, Wendy. 2015. *Undoing the Demos: Neoliberalism's Stealth Revolution*. Princeton: Princeton University Press.

———. 2019. *In the Ruins of Neoliberalism*. New York: Columbia University Press.

Brusi, Rima. 2019, July 30. "Why Puerto Rico's Cops Ignore the Constitution at Night." *The Nation*. https://www.thenation.com/article/archive/puerto-rico-police-abuse/

Brusi, Rima, and Isar Godreau. 2019. "Dismantling Public Education in Puerto Rico." In *Aftershocks of Disaster: Puerto Rico Before and After the Storm*, edited by Yarimar Bonilla and Marisol LeBrón, 243–249. Chicago: Haymarket.

Burnett, Christina Duffy. 2005. "United States: American Expansion and Territorial Deannexation." *University of Chicago Law Review* 72, no. 3: 797–879.

———. 2008. "'They Say I Am Not an American . . .': The Noncitizen National and the Law of American." *Virginia Journal of International Law* 48, no. 4: 659–718.

———. 2009. "A Convenient Constitution? Extraterritoriality After Boumedine." *Columbia Law Review*, no. 109: 973–1046.

Burnett, Christina Duffy, and Burke Marshall, eds. 2001. *Foreign in a Domestic Sense: Puerto Rico, American Expansion, and the Constitution*. Durham: Duke University Press.

Butler, Judith. 2004. *Precarious Life: The Powers of Mourning and Violence*. London and New York. Verso.

Cabán, Pedro. 2018. "PROMESA, Puerto Rico and the American Empire." *Latino Studies* 16, no. 2: 161–184.

———. 2020. "Puerto Rico's Summer 2019 Uprising and the Crisis of Colonialism." *Latin American Perspectives* 47, no. 3: 103–116.

Cabranes, Jose. 1979. *Citizenship and the American Empire: Notes on the Legislative History of the United States Citizenship of Puerto Rico*. New Haven: Yale University Press.

Calavita, Kitty. 2016. *Invitation to Law and Society. An Introduction to the Study of Real Law*. Chicago: University of Chicago Press.

Camacho, Keith L. 2019. *Sacred Men: Law, Torture, and Retribution in Guam*. Durham: Duke University Press.

Campbell, James. 2022. *Aurelius*'s Article III Revisionism: Reimagining Judicial Engagement with the *Insular Cases* and "The Law of the Territories." *Yale Law Journal* 131, no. 8: 2542–2651.

Canfield, Matthew. 2022. *Translating Food Sovereignty: Cultivating Justice in an Age of Transnational Governance*. Stanford: Stanford University Press.

Caraballo-Cueto, Jose. 2021. "The Economy of Disaster? Puerto Rico Before and After Hurricane Maria." *Centro Journal* 1, no. 33: 66–88.

Caraballo-Cueto, Jose, and Juan Lara. 2017, December 20. "Deindustrialization and Unsustainable Debt in Middle-Income Countries: The Case of Puerto Rico." *Jour-*

nal of Globalization and Development 8, no. 2. https://doi.org/10.1515/jgd-2017-0009

Caro, Leysa. 2022, March 24. "El Departamento Del Trabajo Ha Referido Sobre 700 Posibles Casos de Fraude al PUA." *El Nuevo Día*. https://www.elnuevodia.com/noticias/locales/notas/el-departamento-del-trabajo-ha-referido-sobre-700-posibles-casos-de-fraude-al-pua/

CCAPC. 2017. "Pre-Audit Survey Report." Commission for the Comprehensive Audit of the Public Credit. https://periodismoinvestigativo.com/wp-content/uploads/2016/06/Informefinal.pdf

Center for Investigative Journalism (CPI). 2021, October 7. "Puntos Claves Sobre Los Pandora Papers." https://periodismoinvestigativo.com/2021/10/puntos-clave-los-pandora-papers/

———. 2022. "Transparency in Puerto Rico. Report on the Government's (Non)Compliance with Act 141 of 2019." https://periodismoinvestigativo.com/informe-de-cumplimiento-con-la-ley-141/

Cepeda Derieux, Adriel, and Neil Weare. 2020, November. "After *Aurelius*: What Future for the *Insular Cases*?" *Yale Law Journal Forum* 130: 284–307.

Césaire, Aimé. 2000. *Discourse on Colonialism*. Translated by Joan Pinkham. New York: Monthly Review Press.

Chacón, Jennifer. 2023. "Legal Borderlands and Imperial Legacies: A Response to Maggie Blackhawk's *The Constitution of American Colonialism*." *Harvard Law Review* 137 no. 1: 1–22.

Chambliss, William. 1989. "State-Organized Crime—The American Society of Criminology, 1988 Presidential Address." *Criminology* 27, no. 2: 183–208.

Chambliss, William, Raymond Michalowski, and Ronald Kramer, eds. 2010. *State Crime in the Global Age*. Hoboken: Taylor and Francis.

Chandler, Adam D. 2011, June. "Puerto Rico's Eleventh Amendment Status Anxiety." *Yale Law Journal* 120, no. 8: 2183–2197.

Chapman, Richard, and Michael Hunt, eds. 2006. *Open Government in a Theoretical and Practical Context*. Hampshire and Burlington: Ashgate.

Chua, Lynette. 2012. "Pragmatic Resistance, Law, and Social Movements in Authoritarian States: The Case of Gay Collective Action in Singapore." *Law & Society Review* 46, no. 4: 713–748.

———. 2019. "Legal Mobilization and Authoritarianism." *Annual Review of Law and Social Science* 15, no. 1: 355–376.

Chua, Lynette, and David Engel. 2019. "Legal Consciousness Reconsidered." *Annual Review of Law & Social Science* 15: 335–353.

Cintrón Arbasetti, Joel. 2015, December 9. "The Crisis in Puerto Rico Fills Politicians and Lobbyists' Pockets in the US." Center for Investigative Journalism. https://periodismoinvestigativo.com/2015/12/the-crisis-in-puerto-rico-fills-politicians-and-lobbyists-pockets-in-the-united-states/

———. 2016a, August 31. "275 Investment Firms Jumped on Puerto Rico's Junk Debt." Center for Investigative Journalism. https://periodismoinvestigativo.com/2016/08/275-investment-firms-jumped-on-puerto-ricos-junk-debt/

———. 2016b, November 2. "Bonistas y gobierno se enredan en laberinto de demandas." Center for Investigative Journalism. https://periodismoinvestigativo.com/2016/11/bonistas-y-gobierno-se-enredan-en-laberinto-de-demandas/

———. 2016c, December 27. "Casa Acreditadoras se cuelgan año tras año en evaluación federal." Center for Investigative Journalism. https://periodismoinvestigativo.com/2016/12/casas-acreditadoras-se-cuelgan-ano-tras-ano-en-evaluacion-federal/

———. 2017, October 10. "Masked and Armed with Rifles: Military Security Roam the Street od San Juan." Centro de Periodismo Investigativo. https://periodismoinvestigativo.com/2017/10/masked-and-armed-with-rifles-military-security-firms-roam-streets-of-san-juan/#

———. 2021, May 10. "Acts 20 and 22 Created a Class of Intermediaries Who Manage Tax Exemptions." Center for Investigative Journalism. https://periodismoinvestigativo.com/2021/05/acts-20-and-22-created-a-class-of-intermediaries-who-manage-tax-exemptions/

Cintrón Arbasetti, Joel, and Carla Minet. 2017a, June 1. "The Silent Expansion of Fiscal Control Boards in the US." Center for Investigative Journalism. https://periodismoinvestigativo.com/2017/06/the-silent-expansion-of-fiscal-control-boards-in-the-u-s/

———. 2017b, October 17. "The Dilemma of Rebuilding Puerto Rico or Paying the Debt." Center for Investigative Journalism. https://periodismoinvestigativo.com/2017/10/the-dilemma-of-rebuilding-puerto-rico-or-paying-the-debt/

———. 2017c, October 17. "Who Owns Puerto Rico's Debt Exactly? We've Tracked Down 10 of the Biggest Vulture Firms." *In These Times*. https://inthesetimes.com/article/who-owns-puerto-ricos-debt-exactly-weve-tracked-down-10-of-the-biggest-vult

———. 2017d, October 19. "The Highest Bidder in Puerto Rico's Bankruptcy." Center for Investigative Journalism. October 19. https://periodismoinvestigativo.com/2017/10/the-highest-bidders-in-puerto-ricos-bankruptcy/

Ciocchini, Pablo, and Stefanie Khoury. 2018. "A Gramscian Approach to Studying the Judicial Decision-Making Process." Critical Criminology 26, no. 1: 75–90.

———. 2021. "Thinking in a Gramscian Way: Reflections on Gramsci and Law." In *Research Handbook on Law and Marxism*, edited by Paul O'Connell and Umut Ozsu, 139–155. *Research Handbook on Law and Marxism*. Northampton: Edward Elgar.

Ciocchini, Pablo, and Joe Greener. 2022. "Regimes of Extreme Permission in Southeast Asia: Theorizing State-Corporate Crime in the Global South." *British Journal of Criminology 63, no. 5: 1309–1326.*

Cohen, Luc, and Corina Pons. 2019, April 18. "New York Fed Cracks Down on Puerto Rico Banks Following Venezuela Sanctions." Reuters. https://www.reuters.com/article/idUSKCN1RU2EI

Collazo, Valeria, and Adriana De Jesús. 2021. "Episode 11: El Fraude al PUA." *En que Quedó*. https://enquequedo.com/podcast/11-el-fraude-al-pua/

Collins, Victoria. E. 2014. "State Crime and the Re-Victimization of Displaced Populations: The Case of Haiti." In *Toward a Victimology of State Crime,* edited by Dawn Rothe and David Kauzlarich, 131–148. London and New York: Routledge.

Colón, Vanessa, and Rodríguez, Victor. 2019, August 22. "Puerto Rico's Former FEMA Chief Moves to a Firm That Advises the Island's Main Recovery Office." Center for Investigative Journalism. https://periodismoinvestigativo.com/2019/08/puerto-ricos-former-fema-chief-moves-to-a-firm-that-advises-the-islands-main-recovery-office/

Colón Morera, José Javier. 2020. "The Boricua Summer: Keys from a Human Rights Perspective." *Latin American Perspectives* 47, no. 3: 117–128.

Colón-Ramos, Uriyoán, et al. 2019. "Foods Distributed During Federal Disaster Relief Response in Puerto Rico After Hurricane María Did Not Fully Meet Federal Nutrition Recommendations." *Journal of the Academy of Nutrition and Dietetics* 119, no. 11: 1903–15.

Comisión Ciudadana para la Auditoría Integral del Crédito Público. 2019, January 15. COFINA: Deuda Ilegal e Ilegitima. https://ntc-legacy-assets.s3.amazonaws.com/document_dev/2019/01/17/Informe%20sobre%20COFINA%20enero%202019_1547740010072_30040005_ver1.0.pdf

Comisión de Derecho Civiles. 2020. "Declaraciones de La Comisión de Derechos Civiles En Torno a Las Órdenes Ejecutivas y El COVID-19." https://cdc.pr.gov/SalaPrensa/Documents/Declaraciones%20de%20la%20Comision%20de%20Derechos%20Civiles%20en%20torno%20a%20las%20Ordenes%20Ejecutivas%20y%20el%20COVID-19.pdf

Connor, Kevin. 2018, October 4. "Vulture Funds Profits Off of Puerto Rico's Debt Crisis While Debt Creators Get Immunity." Little Sis. https://news.littlesis.org/2018/10/04/vulture-funds-profit-off-of-puerto-ricos-debt-crisis-while-debt-creators-get-immunity/

Cooper, Victoria, and David Whyte, eds. 2017. *The Violence of Austerity*. London: Pluto Press.

———. 2018. "Grenfell, Austerity, and Institutional Violence." *Sociological Research Online* 27, no. 1: 207–216.

Cotula, Lorenzo. 2017. "The State of Exception and the Law of the Global Economy: A Conceptual and Empirico-Legal Inquiry." *Transnational Legal Theory* 8, no. 4: 424–454.

Cramer, Renée. 2021. *Birthing a Movement: Midwives, Law, and the Politics of Reproductive Care*. Stanford: Stanford University Press.

Crandall, Jillian. 2019. "Blockchains and the 'Chains of Empire': Contextualizing Blockchain, Cryptocurrency, and Neoliberalism in Puerto Rico." *Design and Culture* 11, no. 3: 279–300.

Curley, Cali, and Peter Stanley Federman. 2020. "State Executive Orders: Nuance in Restrictions, Revealing Suspensions, and Decisions to Enforce." *Public Administration Review* 80, no. 4: 623–628.

Darian-Smith, Eve. 2022. *Global Burning: Rising Antidemocracy and the Climate Crisis*. Stanford: Stanford University Press.

Davidson, Neil. 2017. "Crisis Neoliberalism and Regimes of Permanent Exception." *Critical Sociology* 43, no. 4–5: 615–634.

Dávila-Ruhaak, Sarah. 2020. "Protection of Vulnerable Communities: A Case of Coal-

Ash Disaster in Puerto Rico." *Michigan Journal of Environmental & Administrative Law* 9, no. 2: 379–432.

Dayen, David. 2016. "Vultures over Puerto Rico." *American Prospect* (Winter): 44–49. https://issuu.com/americanprospect/docs/tap_winter_2016

Declet-Barreto, Juan. 2022, September 28. "Puerto Ricans: We Won't Become Resilient Until We Have an Equitable and Just Recovery." *Union of Concerned Scientists*. https://blog.ucsusa.org/juan-declet-barreto/puerto-ricans-we-wont-become-resilient-until-we-have-an-equitable-and-just-recovery/

Dennis, Abner. 2019a, February 20. "Six Billion Reasons to Go After the Banks." Public Accountability Initiative. https://public-accountability.org/report/six-billion-reasons-to-go-after-the-banks/

———. 2019b, June 5. "Puerto Rico's Debt Battles: The Oversight Board Goes on a Suing Spree." Little Sis. https://news.littlesis.org/2019/06/05/puerto-ricos-debt-battles-the-oversight-board-goes-on-a-suing-spree/

———. 2019c, March 23. "The Puerto Rico Pension Heist: Hedge Fund Vultures and Revolving Door Bankers Are Trying to Loot Puerto Rico's Retirement System." Public Accountability Initiative. https://public-accountability.org/report/the-puerto-rico-pension-heist/

———. 2019d, August 5. "Pedro Pierluisi, the Vulture Governor." Little Sis. https://news.littlesis.org/2019/08/05/pedro-pierluisi-the-vulture-governor/

———. 2019e, October 16. "A Guide to Puerto Rico's Debt Adjustment Plan: Cuts for Pensioners and Payment on Allegedly Illegal Debt." Little Sis. https://news.littlesis.org/2019/10/16/a-guide-to-puerto-ricos-debt-adjustment-plan-cuts-for-pensioners-and-payments-on-allegedly-illegal-debt/

———. 2020a, January 22. "The Earthquake and Banco Popular: How Puerto Rico's Largest Bank Hinders a Just Recovery." Little Sis. https://news.littlesis.org/2020/01/22/the-earthquake-and-banco-popular-how-puerto-ricos-largest-bank-hinders-a-just-recovery/

———. 2020b, February 19. "A Tax Haven Called Puerto Rico." Little Sis. https://news.littlesis.org/2020/02/19/a-tax-haven-called-puerto-rico/

———. 2020c, April 9. "COVID-19 and the Collapse of Private Hospitals in PR." Little Sis. https://news.littlesis.org/2020/04/09/covid-19-and-the-collapse-of-private-hospitals-in-puerto-rico/

———. 2020d, July 30. "Pain and Profit: COVID-19 Profiteers in Puerto Rico." Hedge Clippers. http://hedgeclippers.org/pain-and-profit-covid-19-profiteers-in-puerto-rico/

———. 2020e, August 5. "The 21 Vulture Funds Stalking Puerto Rico's Central Government: Legal Challenges, Investments, Insider Trading." Public Accountability Initiative. https://public-accountability.org/report/the-21-vulture-funds-stalking-puerto-ricos-central-government-legal-challenges-investments-insider-trading/

———. 2020f, October 29. "Puerto Rico's Act 22 Investors Bet on a Pierluisi and Romero Government." Little Sis. https://news.littlesis.org/2020/10/29/puerto-ricos-act-22-investors-bet-on-a-pierluisi-and-romero-government/

———. 2021a, February 16. "Creditors Stalk Puerto Rico Government's Real Estate

Properties, Including the Land Authority's Farms." Little Sis. https://news.littlesis.org/2021/02/16/creditors-stalk-puerto-rico-governments-real-estate-properties-including-the-land-authoritys-farms/

———. 2021b, March 17. "$7 Billion in Cash for Vulture Funds in Oversight Board's New Debt Adjustment Plan." Little Sis. https://news.littlesis.org/2021/03/17/7-billion-in-cash-for-vulture-funds-in-oversight-boards-new-debt-adjustment-plan/

Dennis, Abner, and Kevin Connor. 2018a, November 19. "The COFINA Agreement, Part 1: The First 40 Years Plan." Little Sis. https://news.littlesis.org/2018/11/19/the-cofina-agreement-part-1-the-first-40-years/

———. 2018b, November 20. "The COFINA Agreement, Part 2: Profits for the Few." Little Sis. https://news.littlesis.org/2018/11/20/the-cofina-agreement-part-2-profits-for-the-few/

Derrida, Jacques. 1992. "Force of Law: The 'Mystical Foundation of Authority.'" In *Deconstruction and the Possibility of Justice*, edited by Drucilla Cornell, Michel Rosenfeld, and David Carlson, 3–67. New York and London: Routledge.

Desai, Manali. 2023. "An Eventful Critique of Crisis Language in Historical Sociology." *Social Science History* 47, no. 1: 1–9.

Diaz, Jaclyn. 2022, September 23. "5 Numbers That Show Hurricane Fiona's Devastating Impact on Puerto Rico." *NPR*. https://www.npr.org/2022/09/23/1124345084/impact-hurricane-fiona-puerto-rico

Díaz Torres, Rafael. 2019, September 16. "Impossible to Keep Track of All Recovery Contracts Granted by the Government of Puerto Rico." Center for Investigative Journalism. https://periodismoinvestigativo.com/2019/09/track-recovery-contracts-puerto-rico/

———. 2020, October 26. "Casi Diez Mil Familias Podrían Tener Sus Viviendas Afectadas a Diez Meses de Los Terremotos." Center for Investigative Journalism. https://periodismoinvestigativo.com/2020/10/casi-diez-mil-familias-podrian-tener-sus-viviendas-afectadas-a-diez-meses-de-los-terremotos/.

———. 2022, October 27. "Poor Conditions of Bridges in PT Raise Doubts on Ability to Withstand Future Cyclones." Center for Investigative Journalism. https://periodismoinvestigativo.com/2022/10/poor-conditions-of-bridges-in-puerto-rico-raise-doubts-on-ability-to-withstand-future-cyclones/.

Dick, Diane. 2015. "U.S. Tax Imperialism in Puerto Rico." *American University Law Review* 65, no. 1: 1–86.

Dietrich, Alexa. 2013. *The Drug Company Next Door: Pollution, Jobs, and Community Health in Puerto Rico*. New York: New York University Press.

Dietz, James L. 1986. *Economic History of Puerto Rico: Institutional Change and Capitalist Development*. Princeton: Princeton University Press.

Donaldson, Megan, and Benedict Kingsbury. 2013. "The Adoption of Transparency Policies in Global Governance Institutions: Justifications, Effects, and Implications." *Annual Review of Law and Social Science* 9, no. 1: 119–147.

Downey, Davia C. 2021. *Disasters and Economic Recovery*. London and New York: Routledge.

Durantaye, Leland. 2012. "The Paradigm of Colonialism." In *Agamben and Colonial-*

ism, edited by Marcelo Svirsky and Simone Bignall, 229–238. Edinburgh: Edinburgh University Press.

Ellcessor, Elizabeth. 2022. *In Case of Emergency: How Technologies Mediate Crisis and Normalized Inequality*. New York: New York University Press.

Encarnanción, José. 2020, December 6. "Dominican Mothers in Puerto Rico Face the Pandemic 'In the Shadows." Center for Investigative Journalism. https://periodismoinvestigativo.com/2020/12/dominican-mothers-in-puerto-rico-face-the-pandemic-in-the-shadows/

Encarnación, José, Rafael Díaz, and Wilma Maldonado. 2022, October 7. "LUMA Doesn't Follow Its Own Emergency Plan." Center for Investigative Journalism. https://periodismoinvestigativo.com/2022/10/luma-doesnt-follow-its-own-emergency-plan/

ENDI. 2021, May 24. "Esto es lo que debes hacer si tienes el punto controvertible 3F tras reclamar la ayudad por desempleo." *El Nuevo Día*. https://www.elnuevodia.com/noticias/locales/notas/esto-es-lo-que-debes-hacer-si-tienes-el-punto-controvertible-3f-tras-reclamar-la-ayuda-por-desempleo/

Erman, Sam. 2018. *Almost Citizens: Puerto Rico, the U.S. Constitution, and Empire*. Cambridge, UK: Cambridge University Press.

———. 2022. "Status Manipulation and Spectral Sovereigns." *Columbia Human Rights Law Review* 53, no. 3: 813–881.

Escaleras, Monica, Nejat Anbarci, and Charles A. Register. 2007. "Public Sector Corruption and Major Earthquakes: A Potentially Deadly Interaction." *Public Choice* 132, no. 1–2: 209–230.

Escaleras, Monica, and Charles Register. 2016, August 2. "Public Sector Corruption and Natural Hazards." *Public Finance Review* 44, no. 6: 746–768.

Espacios Abiertos. 2023, August. "Their Advisors, Your Money: Lack of Access to the Data That Have Informed the Restructuring Process in Puerto Rico. Policy Brief." https://drive.google.com/file/d/11Nw8yAtzLN74suGatdcMMyeLLNhOcGm9/view

Estades, María Eugenia. 1999. *La Presencia Militar de Estados Unidos En Puerto Rico 1898–1918: Intereses Estratégicos y Dominación Colonial*. Río Piedras: Huracán.

Ewick, Patricia, and Susan Silbey. 1998. *The Common Place of Law: Stories from Everyday Life*. Chicago: University of Chicago Press.

Eyermann, Craig. 2016, May 2. "Puerto Rico Officially Defaults on Its Debt." *MyGovCost*. http://www.mygovcost.org/2016/05/02/puerto-rico-officially-defaults-on-its-debt/

Fanon, Frantz. 2004. *The Wretched of the Earth*. New York: Grove Press.

———. 2008. *Black Skin, White Masks*. New York: Grove Press.

Fassin, Didier, and Mariella Pandolfi, eds. 2010. *Contemporary States of Emergency: The Politics of Military and Humanitarian Interventions*. New York: Zone Books.

Faust, Kelly, and Susan M. Carlson. 2011. "Devastation in the Aftermath of Hurricane Katrina as a State Crime: Social Audience Reactions." *Crime, Law and Social Change* 55, no. 1: 33–51.

Faust, Kelly, and David Kauzlarich. 2008. "Hurricane Katrina Victimization as a State Crime of Omission." *Critical Criminology* 16, no. 2: 85–103.

Feliciano, Zaida. 2018. IRS Section 936 and the Decline of Puerto Rico's Manufacturing. *Centro Journal* 30 no. 3: 30–42.

Fitzpatrick, Peter. 2008. *Law as Resistance: Modernism, Imperialism, Legalism*. London: Ashgate.

Flaherty, Anne, and Stephanie Ebbs. 2019, March 26. "Federal Watchdog Launches Investigation into Potential 'Interference' in Puerto Rico Aid." *ABC News*. https://abcnews.go.com/Politics/federal-watchdog-launches-investigation-potential-interference-distribution-millions/story?id=61957794/

Florido, Adrian. 2018, June 1. "An Impromptu Memorial to Demand That Puerto Rico's Hurricane Dead Be Counted." *NPR*. https://www.npr.org/2018/06/01/616216225/an-impromptu-memorial-to-demand-puerto-ricos-hurricane-dead-be-counted

———. 2020, April 30. "Advocate for the Poor in Puerto Rico Is Released After Arrest During Protest." *NPR*. https://www.npr.org/2020/04/30/848684061/puerto-rico-police-arrest-advocate-for-the-poor

Fraser, Nancy. 2019. *The Old Is Dying and the New Cannot Be Born: From Progressive Neoliberalism to Trump and Beyond*. London and New York: Verso.

———. 2022. *Cannibal Capitalism: How Our System Is Devouring Democracy, Care, and the Planet—and What We Can Do About It*. London and New York: Verso.

Friedrichs, David O., and Dawn L. Rothe. 2014. "State-Corporate Crime and Major Financial Institutions: Interrogating an Absence." *State Crime Journal* 3, no. 2: 146–162.

Frontline. 2018, May 1. "Blackout in Puerto Rico." *PBS*. https://www.pbs.org/wgbh/frontline/documentary/blackout-in-puerto-rico/

GAO. 2018, May. "Puerto Rico: Factors Contributing to the Debt Crisis and Potential Federal Actions to Address Them: A Report to Congressional Committees." *GAO*. https://www.gao.gov/assets/700/691675.pdf

———. 2022, September 15. "Update on FEMA's Disaster Recovery Efforts in Puerto Rico and the U.S. Virgin Islands." *GAO*. https://www.gao.gov/assets/gao-22-106211.pdf

García, Catherine, Fernando I. Rivera, Marc A. Garcia, Giovani Burgos, and María P. Aranda. 2021. "Contextualizing the COVID-19 Era in Puerto Rico: Compounding Disasters and Parallel Pandemics." *Journals of Gerontology: Series B: Psychological Sciences and Social Sciences* 76, no. 7: e263–267.

García, Ivis. 2022. "Deemed Ineligible: Reasons Homeowners in Puerto Rico Were Denied Aid After Hurricane María." *Housing Policy Debate* 32, no. 1: 14–34.

Garcia, Lynne, and Michael Beverley. 2021. "Reinvigorating Puerto Rico's Pharmaceutical Industry—A U.S. Security Imperative." *Centro Journal* 33, no. 2: 56–93.

García-López, Gustavo. 2018. "The Multiple Layers of Environmental Injustice in Contexts of (Un)Natural Disasters: The Case of Puerto Rico Post-Hurricane Maria." *Environmental Justice* 11, no. 3: 101–108.

———. 2020. "Reflections on Disaster Colonialism: Response to Yarimar Bonilla's 'The Wait of Disaster.'" *Political Geography* 78: 102170.

———. 2022. "Environmental Corruption and the Colonial Growth Machine in Puerto Rico." *Centro Journal* 2, no. 34: 177–206.

García Pelatti, Luisa. 2024, April 16. "FMI: La economía de Puerto Rico volverá a caer

0.2% este año y alcanzará crecimiento cero en 2025. *Sin Comillas*. https://sincomillas.com/fmi-la-economia-mundial-crecera-3-2-este-ano-y-el-proximo/

Garriga-López, Adriana. 2020. "Compounded Disasters: Puerto Rico Confronts COVID-19 Under US Colonialism." *Social Anthropology* 28, no. 2: 269–270.

Gelardi, Chris. 2020, April 9. "Colonialism Made Puerto Rico Vulnerable to Coronavirus Catastrophe." *The Nation*. https://www.thenation.com/article/politics/puerto-rico-coronavirus/?print=1www.thenation.com/article/politics/puerto-rico-coronavirus/?print=1

Gerstle, Gary, and Joel Isaac, eds. 2020. *States of Exception in American History*. Chicago: University of Chicago Press.

Gillette, Clayton. 2014. "Dictatorships for Democracy: Takeovers of Financially Failed Cities." *Columbia Law Review* 114, no. 6: 1373–1463.

———. 2019. "How Cities Fail—Service Delivery Insolvency and Municipal Bankruptcy." *Michigan State Law Review*, no. 5: 1211–1248.

———. 2021. "Saving Cities or Exploiting Creditors?—State Redirection of Municipal Assets." *Fordham Urban Law Journal* 48, no. 4: 753–799.

Gillette, Clayton, and David Skeel. 2016a. "Governance Reform and the Judicial Role in Municipal Bankruptcy." *Yale Law Journal* 125, no. 5: 1150–1237.

———. 2016b. "A Two-Step Plan for Puerto Rico." Faculty Scholarship at Penn Law. https://scholarship.law.upenn.edu/faculty_scholarship/1621/

Gilmore, Ruth Wilson. 2007. *Golden Gulag: Prisons, Surplus, Crisis, and Opposition in Globalizing California*. Oakland: University of California Press.

Go, Julian. 2008. *American Empire and the Politics of Meaning: Elite Political Cultures in the Philippines and Puerto Rico During the U.S. Colonialism*. Durham: Duke University Press.

———. 2016. *Postcolonial Thought and Social Theory*. New York and Oxford: Oxford University Press.

———. 2023. "Thinking Against Empire: Anticolonial Thought as Social Theory." *The British Journal of Sociology* 74, no. 3: 279–293. https://doi.org/10.1111/1468-4446.12993.

Godreau-Aubert, Ariadna. 2022. "Lawyering in Times of Peril: Legal Empowerment and the Relevance of the Legal Profession." *New York University Law Review* 6, no. 97: 1599–1630.

Goitein, Elizabeth. 2019, January–February. "What the President Could Do If He Declares a State of Emergency." *The Atlantic*. https://www.theatlantic.com/magazine/archive/2019/01/presidential-emergency-powers/576418/

———. 2021, March 29. "Reining in the President's Emergency Powers." *Brennan Center*. https://www.brennancenter.org/our-work/analysis-opinion/reining-presidents-emergency-powers

Golder, Ben, and Daniel McLoughlin, eds. 2018. *The Politics of Legality in a Neoliberal Age*. London and New York: Routledge.

Goldstein, Matthew, and Damien Cave. 2020, October 19. "Chasing Illicit Money, Global Officials Circle a Puerto Rican Firm." *New York Times*. https://www.nytimes.com/2020/10/19/business/puerto-rico-euro-pacific-investigation.html

González, Joanisabel. 2022, November 8. "Another Debt Restructuring Enters Home Stretch." *El Nuevo Día.* https://www.elnuevodia.com/english/news/story/another-debt-restructuring-enters-home-stretch/

———. 2023, February 16. "El gobierno rinde cuentas a las casas acreditadoras." *El Nuevo Día.* https://www.elnuevodia.com/negocios/economia/notas/el-gobierno-rinde-cuentas-a-las-casas-acreditadoras/

———. 2024, April 12. "En $51,100 millones el deficit acumulado del gobierno." *El Nuevo Día.* https://www.elnuevodia.com/negocios/economia/notas/en-51100-millones-el-deficit-acumulado-del-gobierno/

Gottschalk, Peter. 2021. "Filling the Gap in White-Collar Crime Detection Between Government and Governance: The Role of Investigative Journalists and Fraud Examiners." *Journal of White Collar and Corporate Crime* 2, no. 1: 36–46.

Graeber, David. 2011. *Debt: The First 5,000 Years.* Hoboken: Melville House.

Graham, Perry T. 2017. "Municipal Bankruptcy in the Oldest Colony in the World After *Puerto Rico v. Franklin California Tax-Free Trust* and PROMESA." *Loyola Law Review* 63: 179–205.

Gramsci, Antonio. 1971. *Selections from Prison Notebooks.* Edited by Quintin Hoare and Geoffrey Nowell Smith. London: Lawrence & Wishart.

Green, Penny. 2004. "Disaster by Design: Corruption, Construction, and Catastrophe." *British Journal of Criminology* 45: 528–546.

Green, Penny, and Tony Ward. 2004. *State Crime: Governments, Violence and Corruption.* London: Pluto Press.

———. 2019. *State Crime and Civil Activism: On the Dialectics of Repression and Resistance.* London and New York: Routledge.

Greene, Alan. 2015. "Questioning Executive Supremacy in an Economic State of Emergency." *Legal Studies* 35, no. 4: 594–620.

———. 2020. *Emergency Powers in a Time of Pandemic.* Bristol: Bristol University Press.

Griffin, John, Samuel Kruger, and Prateek Mahajan. 2023. "Did FinTech Lenders Facilitate PPP Fraud?" *Journal of Finance* 78, no. 3: 1777–1827.

Grimsey, Darrin, and Mervyn K. Lewis. 2004. *Public Private Partnerships: The Worldwide Revolution in Infrastructure Provision and Project Finance.* Cheltenham and Northampton: Edward Elgar.

Hager, Sandy Brian. 2016. *Public Debt, Inequality, and Power: The Making of a Modern Debt State.* Oakland: University of California Press.

Hajjar, Lisa. 2022. *The War in Court: Inside the Long Fight Against Torture.* Oakland: University of California Press.

———. 2023. "Guantanamo's Legacy." *Annual Review of Law and Social Science,* 19: 53–74.

Hall, Stuart, Chas Critcher, Tony Jefferson, John Clarke, and Brian Roberts. 2013. *Policing the Crisis: Mugging, the State and Law and Order.* London: Red Globe Press.

Harcourt, Bernard E. 2010. "Neoliberal Penalty." *Theoretical Criminology* 14, no. 1: 74–92.

Harman, Chris. 2009. *Zombie Capitalism: Global Crisis and the Relevance of Marx.* Chicago: Haymarket.

Harris, Angela, and Jay Varellas. 2020. "Law and Political Economy in a Time of Accelerating Crises." *Journal of Law and Political Economy* 1 no. 1: 1–27.

Hartman, Chester, and Gregory Squires, eds. 2006. *There Is No Such Thing as a Natural Disaster. Race, Class, and Hurricane Katrina*. New York: Routledge.

Hedge Clippers. 2015a, July 10. "Hedge Fund Vultures in Puerto Rico." Hedge Clippers. http://hedgeclippers.org/hedgepapers-no-17-hedge-fund-billionaires-in-puerto-rico/

———. 2015b, September 21. "New York City's Public Pension Vultures in Puerto Rico." Hedge Clippers. http://hedgeclippers.org/hedgepapers-no-20-new-york-citys-public-pension-vultures-in-puerto-rico/

———. 2015c, September 24. "The Antonio Weiss Files: Vulture, Bribes & Conflict of Interests in PR." Hedge Clippers. http://hedgeclippers.org/hedgepapers-no-21-the-antonio-weiss-files-vultures-bribes-conflicts-of-interest-in-puerto-rico/

———. 2016, December 16. "Pirates of the Caribbean." Hedge Clippers. http://hedgeclippers.org/pirates-of-the-caribbean-how-santanders-revolving-door-with-puerto-ricos-development-bank-exacerbated-a-fiscal-catastrophe-for-the-puerto-rican-people/

———. 2017a, March 21. "Puerto Rico: Pain and Profit." Hedge Clippers. http://hedgeclippers.org/puerto-rico-pain-and-profit/

———. 2017b, May 16. "The Looting of Puerto Rico's Infrastructure Fund." Hedge Clippers. https://hedgeclippers.org/partner-paper-no-5-the-looting-of-puerto-ricos-infrastructure-fund-carlos-m-garcias-destructive-fiscal-policies-hurt-puerto-rico-once-could-it-happen-again/

———. 2017c, December 19. "Private Equity and Puerto Rico." Hedge Clippers. http://hedgeclippers.org/report-no-53-private-equity-and-puerto-rico/

———. 2018a, January 23. "Hurricane Harvard and the Damage Done to Puerto Rico." Hedge Clippers. http://hedgeclippers.org/report-no-54-hurricane-harvard-and-the-damage-done-to-puerto-rico-how-the-universitys-endowment-investment-harms-the-island/

———. 2018b, May 22. "Pain and Profit After Maria." Hedge Clippers. http://hedgeclippers.org/pain-and-profit-after-maria/

———. 2018c, August 21. "The Golden Revolving Doors." Hedge Clippers. https://hedgeclippers.org/hedgepaper-no-61-the-golden-revolving-door/

———. 2018d, November 14. "Insurer to Profit: Conflict of Interest in the Career of José Carrión III." Hedge Clippers. https://hedgeclippers.org/hedge-paper-no-65-insured-to-profit-conflicts-of-interests-in-the-career-of-jose-carrion-iii/

———. 2019, August. "Pain and Profit: Rosselló Is Gone but Vultures Still Prey on Puerto Rico." Hedge Clippers. https://hedgeclippers.org/hedge-papers-no-68-pain-and-profit-rossello-is-gone-but-vultures-still-prey-on-puerto-rico/

———. 2020, March. "It's Time to Martin Act." Hedge Clippers. https://hedgeclippers.org/hedge-paper-71/

———. 2021a, March 17. "The New Oversight Lords." Hedge Clippers. https://hedgeclippers.org/puerto-rico-new-oversight-lords/

———. 2021b, December 15. "Pain and Profit in Sovereign Debt." Hedge Clippers. http://hedgeclippers.org/pain-and-profit-in-sovereign-debt-how-new-york-can-stop-vulture-funds-from-preying-on-countries/

———. 2022a, August 17. "Pharma's Failed Promise: How Big Pharma Hurts Workers, Dodges Taxes, and Extract Billions in Puerto Rico." Hedge Clippers. https://hedgeclippers.org/hedgepaper-67-pharmas-failed-promise-how-big-pharma-hurts-workers-dodges-taxes-and-extracts-billions-in-puerto-rico/

———. 2022b, October. "Pharma's Failed Promise: Exposing the Industry's Environmental Degradation in Puerto Rico." Hedge Clippers. https://www.populardemocracy.org/sites/default/files/%5BENGLISH%5D%20Hedge%20Papers%2077%20Pharmas%20Failed%20Promise%20Enviro%20Degradation%20CPD%20October%202022%20FINAL.pdf

———. 2024, April 10. "Pain & Profit: Act 22." Hedge Clippers. https://hedgeclippers.org/wp-content/uploads/2024/04/ENGLISH-PAIN-PROFIT_-ACT-22-Charities-that-Take-from-Puerto-Ricans-April-2024-FINAL.pdf

Hetherington, Kregg. 2011. *Guerrilla Auditors: The Politics of Transparency in Neoliberal Paraguay*. Durham: Duke University Press.

Hinojosa, Jennifer. 2020. "Puerto Rico's Earthquakes in the Southwest Region and Vulnerable Communities." *Centro Research Brief.* https://centropr-archive.hunter.cuny.edu/centrovoices/current-affairs/puerto-rico's-earthquakes-southwest-region-vulnerable-communities

Hinojosa, Jennifer, and Edwin Meléndez. 2018. "The Housing Crisis in Puerto Rico and the Impact of Hurricane María." *Centro Research Brief.* https://centropr-archive.hunter.cuny.edu/sites/default/files/data_briefs/HousingPuertoRico.pdf

Honing, Bonnie. 2009. *Emergency Politics: Paradox, Law, Democracy*. Princeton: Princeton University Press.

Hoyos, Joshua, and Cristina Corujo. 2020, July 7. "Puerto Rico Governor Facing Scrutiny After Firing Government Minister." *ABC News*. https://abcnews.go.com/US/puerto-rico-governor-facing-scrutiny-firing-government-minister/story?id=71642023

Hrushka, Anna. 2023, January 25. "Popular Bank to Pay $2.3 M over Alleged PPP Fraud." *Banking Dive*. https://www.bankingdive.com/news/federal-reserve-fines-popular-bank-2-point-3-million-ppp-loan-fraud-fintechs-sba/641202/

Hussain, Nasser. 2003. *The Jurisprudence of Emergency: Colonialism and the Rule of Law*. Ann Arbor: University of Michigan Press.

Irizarry, Edwin. 2011. *Economía de Puerto Rico*. D. F., México: McGraw-Hill.

———. 2020b, January 24. "Puerto Ricans Take over Old San Juan to Oust Another Corrupt Governor." *Remezcla*. https://remezcla.com/features/culture/puerto-ricans-take-over-old-san-juan-oust-governor/

Jiménez, Mónica. 2020."Puerto Rico Under the Colonial Gaze: Oppression, Resistance, and the Myth of the Nationalist Enemy." *Latino Studies* 18, no. 1: 27–44.

———. 2024. *Making Never-Never Land: Race and Law in the Creation of Puerto Rico*. Chapel Hill: University of North Carolina Press.

Johns, Fleur. 2015. "On Failing Forward: Neoliberal Legality in the Mekong River Basin." *Cornell International Law Journal* 48, no. 2: 347–383.

Jones, Benji. 2022, September 19. "How a Category 1 Hurricane Did So Much Damage in Puerto Rico." *Vox*. https://www.vox.com/energy-and-environment/2022/9/19/23360769/puerto-rico-hurricane-fiona-flooding

Katz, Jonathan. 2020, January 17. "Puerto Rico's Latest Man-Made Disaster." *Slate*. https://slate.com/news-and-politics/2020/01/puerto-rico-earthquakes-disaster.html

Kauzlarich, David, and Ronald C. Kramer. 1998. *Crimes of the American Nuclear State: At Home and Abroad*. Boston: Northeastern University Press.

Kilómetro Cero. 2018a. "Mi candado lo tranco yo." Kilómetro Cero. https://www.kilo-metroo.org/blog-desde-cero/2018/9/19/ov6mdpl5nknzg3c93lf26dj46iekuc

———. 2018b, December 4. "Skill over Force: A Critical Analysis of the Use-of-Force Statistics of the Puerto Rico Police Against the People." Kilómetro Cero. https://drive.google.com/file/d/0B3p2WlC_-VLibEJjc2pxZjZibWZvbGtBczNzdHVRS1JvNlU0/view

———. 2019. "Documentation on Interventions and Cases of Use of Force by the Puerto Rico Police Department During the #RickyRenuncia Protests." Kilómetro Cero. https://docs.google.com/document/d/1--lPFG_XwMppj71-v45EHeSe5QuIq0gRTXlWvDBGbg4/edit#heading=h.2et92p0

———. 2020a. "Documentación de Intervenciones y Casos de Uso de Fuerza de La Policía Durante Las Protestas Wanda Renuncia." Kilómetro Cero. https://docs.google.com/document/d/1FoPzYOVckahXGUl9MBba2QOzGcT3wblCouXNXxdGXXg/edit#heading=h.rgldnspa1ad3

———. 2020b. "No Más Criminalización En La Pandemia." Kilómetro Cero. https://www.kilometroo.org/blog-desde-cero/2020/3/15/kilmetro-cero-pide-garantas-para-personas-intervenidas-durante-toque-de-quedanbsp

———. 2023. "El Fracaso No Está En La Sábana: Lecciones de Seguridad Pública En Tiempos Pandemicos: Un Informe de Kilometro Cero." Kilómetro Cero. https://static1.squarespace.com/static/5af199815cfd796ad4930e20/t/640fe5017390bf23b4ef9521/1678763274871/3-digital

Kipfer, Stefan, and Jamilla Mohamud. 2021. "The Pandemic as Political Emergency." *Studies in Political Economy* 102, no. 3: 268–288.

Kishore, Nishant, et al. 2018. "Mortality in Puerto Rico After Hurricane Maria." *New England Journal of Medicine* 379, no. 17: e30.

Klein, Naomi. 2008. *The Shock Doctrine: The Rise of Disaster Capitalism*. New York: Picardo.

———. 2018. *The Battle for Paradise: Puerto Rico Takes on the Disaster Capitalists*. Chicago: Haymarket.

Knox, Robert, and David Whyte. 2023. "Vaccinating Capitalism: Racialized Value in the COVID-19 Economy." *Mortality* 28, no. 2: 329–345.

Koivisto, Ida. 2022. *The Transparency Paradox: Questioning an Ideal*. Oxford and New York: Oxford University Press.

Krever, Tor. 2017. "Law, Development, and Political Closure Under Neoliberalism." In *Neoliberal Legality: Understanding the Role of Law in the Neoliberal Project*, edited by Honor Brabazon, 22–42. London and New York: Routledge.

Krippner, Greta. 2011. *Capitalizing on Crisis: The Political Origins of the Rise of Finance*. Cambridge, MA: Harvard University Press.

Krueger, Anne. 2017. "The Puerto Rican Saga." *Intereconomics* 52, no. 5: 323–324.

Krueger, Anne, Ranjit Teja, and Andrew Wolfe. 2015, July 13. "Puerto Rico—A Way Forward." Also known as Krueger Report. Commonwealth of Puerto Rico. http://www.gdb-pur.com/documents/FinalUpdatedReport7-13-15.pdf

Lamba-Nieves, Deepak, Sergio M. Marxuach, and Rosanna Torres. 2021, June 29. "PROMESA: A Failed Colonial Experiment?" Center for a New Economy. https://grupocne.org/2021/06/29/promesa-a-failed-colonial-experiment/

Lamba-Nieves, Deepak, and Raúl Santiago-Bartolomei. 2018. "Transforming the Recovery into Locally Led Growth: Federal Contracting in the Post-Disaster Period." *Center for a New Economy*. https://grupocne.org/wp-content/uploads/2018/09/Federal_Contracts_FINAL_withcover-1.pdf

———. 2023. "Who Gets Emergency Housing Relief? An Analysis of FEMA Individual Assistance Data After Hurricane María." *Housing Policy Debate* 33, no. 5: 1146–1166. doi:10.1080/10511482.2022.2055612

Langley, Paul. 2008. *The Everyday Life of Global Finance: Saving and Borrowing in Anglo-America*. Oxford and New York: Oxford University Press.

Lapavitsas, Costas. 2013. *Profiting Without Producing: How Finance Exploits Us All*. London and New York: Verso.

Lasslett, Kristian. 2012. "State Crime by Proxy: Australia and the Bougainville Conflict." *British Journal of Criminology* 52, no. 4: 705–23.

———. 2014. *State Crime on the Margins of Empire: Rio Tinto, the War on Bougainville, and Resistance to Mining*. London: Pluto Press.

———. 2018. *Uncovering the Crimes of Urbanisation: Researching Corruption, Violence and Urban Conflict*. London. Routledge.

Lawson, Gary, and Guy Seidman. 2004. *The Constitution of Empire: Territorial Expansion and American Legal History*. New Haven and London: Yale University Press.

Lazzarato, Maurizio. 2013. *Governing by Debt*. Translated by Joshua David Jordan. Los Angeles: Semiotext(e).

Leandra, Victoria. 2020, July 30. "PR High School Students Defraud Unemployment System as Thousands Wait Desperately for Benefits." *The Americano*. https://theamericanonews.com/2020/07/30/unemployment-fraud-by-students-puerto-rico/

LeBrón, Marisol. 2017. "Carpeteo Redux." *Radical History Review*, no. 128: 147–172.

———. 2019. *Policing Life and Death: Race, Violence, and Resistance in Puerto Rico*. Oakland: University of California Press.

———. 2021. *Against Muerto Rico: Lessons from the Verano Boricua*. Cabo Rojo: Editora Educación Emergente.

Lee, Erica, Adam Levin, and Corrie Clark. 2022, November 14. "Hurricane Fiona Recovery: Context and Challenges." *Congressional Research Service*. https://www.everycrsreport.com/reports/IN12044.html

León, Kenneth Sebastian. 2020. *Corrupt Capital: Alcohol, Nightlife, and Crimes of the Powerful*. New York and London: Routledge.

Liu, Sida. 2020. "Between Social Spaces." *European Journal of Social Theory* 24, no. 1: 123–139.

Lloréns, Hilda. 2021. *Making Livable Worlds: Afro-Puerto Rican Women Building Environmental Justice*. Seattle: University of Washington Press.

López-Baralt, José. 1999. *The Policy of the United States Towards Its Territories with Special Reference to Puerto Rico.* San Juan: Editorial de la Universidad de Puerto Rico.

López-Santana, Mariely. 2022. "Financial Oversight Boards in the U.S. Federal System: Insights from the Puerto Rican Debt Crisis." *Publius: The Journal of Federalism* 53, no. 2: 201–226.

Maitra, Ani. 2020, March 30. "COVID-19 and the Neoliberal State of Emergency." *Common Dreams.* https://www.commondreams.org/views/2020/03/30/covid-19-and-neoliberal-state-emergency

Malavet, Pedro. 2004. *America's Colony: The Political and Cultural Conflict Between the United States and Puerto Rico.* New York: New York University Press.

Maldonado-Torres, Nelson. 2007. "On the Coloniality of Being." *Cultural Studies* 21, no. 2–3: 240–270.

———. 2019. "Afterword: Critique and Decoloniality in the Face of Crisis, Disaster, and Catastrophe." In *Aftershocks of Disaster: Puerto Rico Before and After the Storm*, edited by Yarimar Bonilla and Marisol LeBrón, 332–344. Chicago: Haymarket.

Maldonado, Wilma, Tatiana Díaz, and Jose Encarnación. 2022, September 27. Hurricane Shelters Without Water and Electricity Don't Comply with the Law." Center for Investigative Journalism. https://periodismoinvestigativo.com/2022/09/hurricane-shelters-without-water-and-electricity-dont-comply-with-the-law/

Mann, Ronald. 2023, January 10. "A Fight over Public Records in Puerto Rico Hinges on Financial Board's Claim of Sovereign Immunity." *SCOTUS Blog.* https://www.scotusblog.com/2023/01/a-fight-over-public-records-in-puerto-rico-hinges-on-financial-boards-claim-of-sovereign-immunity/

Marans, Daniel. 2016, January 2. "Puerto Rico Is in Serious Trouble. Here's What You Need to Know." *HuffPost.* http://www.huffingtonpost.com/entry/puerto-rico-debt-default-explained_us_56870c25e4b0b958f65bca7a

Marazzi, Christian. 2011. *The Violence of Financial Capitalism.* Translated by Kristina Lebedeva. Los Angeles: Semiotext(e).

Márquez, Denis. 2020a, May 11. "Informe de la Delegación del Partido Independentista Puertorriqueño en torno a la Resolución de la Camara 1741."

———. 2020b, July 7. "Segundo Informe de la Delegación del Partido Independentista Puertorriqueño en torno a la Resolución de la Camara 1741."

Marshall, Anna Maria, and Scott Barclay. 2003. "Symposium Introduction: In Their Own Words: How Ordinary People Construct the Legal World." *Law & Social Inquiry* 28, no. 3: 617–628.

Marshall, Anna-Maria, and Dale Hale. 2014. "Cause Lawyering." *Annual Review of Law and Social Science*, no. 10: 301–320.

Martinez, Elivan. 2020, May 4. "Puerto Rico Never Set up an Information Network to Gather Data on COVID-19." Center for Investigative Journalism. https://periodismoinvestigativo.com/2020/05/puerto-rico-never-set-up-an-information-network-to-gather-data-on-covid-19/

———. 2022, December 13. "Puerto Rico, the Island Most Vulnerable to Disaster, Lacks an Energy Assurance Plan." Center for Investigative Journalism. https://periodis

moinvestigativo.com/2022/12/puerto-rico-the-island-most-vulnerable-to-disasters-lacks-an-energy-assurance-plan/

Martinez Orabona, Annette, Luis Avilés, Marinilda Rivera Díaz, and Luis Jose Torres Asencio. 2022. "Sin Información ante el desastre: Gestion de la información para el manejo de riesgos socioambientales en Puerto Rico." *Centro de Periodismo Investigativo.* https://periodismoinvestigativo.com/lcdm-informe/

Martínez-Roman, Adi. 2022, September 26. "Demanding Accountability in Puerto Rico's Energy Crisis." *City Limits.* https://citylimits.org/2022/09/26/opinion-demanding-accountability-in-puerto-ricos-energy-crisis/

Mason, Jeff, and Andrea Shalal. 2020, August 6. "Trump Signs Executive Order to Boost US Drug Manufacturing." Reuters. https://www.reuters.com/article/us-health-coronavirus-usa-drugs/tru . . . signs-executive-order-to-boost-u-s-drug-manufacturing-idUSKCN2521ZP

Masses, Issel. 2022, October 4. "5 Years After Hurricane Maria, No Lessons: When Corruption Trumps Reconstruction in Puerto Rico." Open Contracting Partnership. https://www.open-contracting.org/2022/10/04/5-years-after-hurricane-maria-no-lessons-when-corruption-trumps-reconstruction-in-puerto-rico/

Massoud, Mark Fathi. 2013. *Law's Fragile State: Colonial, Authoritarian, and Humanitarian Legacies in Sudan*. Cambridge and New York: Cambridge University Press.

Mattei, Clara. 2022. *The Capital Order: How Economists Invented Austerity and Paved the Way to Fascism*. Chicago: University of Chicago Press.

Mattei, Ugo. 2010. "Emergency-Based Predatory Capitalism: The Rule of Law, Alternative Dispute Resolution and Development." In *Contemporary States of Emergency: The Politics of Military and Humanitarian Interventions*, edited by Didier Fassin and Mariella Pandolfi, 89–105. New York: Zone Books.

Mattei, Ugo, and Laura Nader. 2008. *Plunder: When the Rule of Law Is Illegal*. London: Blackwell.

Mazzei, Patricia, and Frances Robles. 2019, July 24. "Ricardo Rosselló, Puerto Rico's Governor, Resigns After Protests." *New York Times*. https://www.nytimes.com/2019/07/24/us/rossello-puerto-rico-governor-resigns.html/

Mazzucato, Mariana, and Rosie Collington. 2023. *The Big Con: How the Consulting Industry Weakens Our Businesses, Infantilizes Our Governments, and Warps Our Economies*. New York: Penguin Press.

Mbembe, Achille. 2003. "Necropolitics." *Public Culture* 15, no. 1: 11–40.

McCann, Michael. 1994. *Rights at Work: Pay Equity and the Politics of Legal Mobilization*. Chicago: University of Chicago Press.

———. 2006. "Law and Social Movements: Contemporary Perspectives." *Annual Review of Law and Social Science* 2, no. 1: 17–38.

McCormack, Derek. 2015. "Governing Inflation—Price and Atmospheres of Emergency." *Theory, Culture & Society* 32, no. 2: 131–154.

Meierhenrich, Jens. 2021. "Constitutional Dictatorship from Colonialism to COVID-19." *Annual Review of Law and Social Science* 17: 411–439.

Meléndez, Edwin. 2018a. "The Politics of PROMESA." *Centro Journal* 30, no. 3: 43–71.

———. 2018b. "The Economics of PROMESA." *Centro Journal* 30, no. 3: 72–103.

———. 2020a. "Post-Disaster Recovery in Puerto Rico and Local Participation—Introduction." *Centro Journal* 32, no. 3: 4–38.

———. 2020b. "Puerto Rico Housing and Community Development Industry's Capacity for Disaster Recovery." *Centro Journal* 32, no. 3: 118–156.

Meléndez-Badillo, Jorell. 2024. *Puerto Rico: A National History*. Princeton: Princeton University Press.

Mello, Michelle, and Wendy Parmet. 2021. "Public Health Law After Covid-19." *New England Journal of Medicine* 385, no. 13: 1153–1155.

———. 2022. "U.S. Public Health Law—Foundations and Emerging Shifts." *New England Journal of Medicine* 386, no. 9: 805–808.

Méndez Gonzalez, Luis. 2022, December 13. "Post-Maria Law, Aimed at Providing Diesel to Radio Stations in an Emergency, Is Useless." Center for Investigative Journalism. https://periodismoinvestigativo.com/2022/12/post-maria-law-aimed-at-providing-diesel-to-radio-stations-in-an-emergency-is-useless/

Merling, Lara, Kevin Cashman, Jake Johnston, and Mark Weisbrot. 2017, July. "Life After Debt in Puerto Rico: How Many More Lost Decades?" *Center for Economic and Policy Research*. https://cepr.net/images/stories/reports/puerto-rico-2017-07.pdf

Merry, Sally Engle. 1988. "Legal Pluralism." *Law and Society Review* 22, no. 5: 869–896.

———. 1991. "Law and Colonialism." *Law & Society Review* 25, no. 4: 889–922.

———. 2000. *Colonizing Hawai'i: The Cultural Power of Law*. Princeton: Princeton University Press.

Michalowski, Raymond, and Ronald Kramer, eds. 2006. *State-Corporate Crime*. New Brunswick: Rutgers University Press.

Miller, Ruth. 2009. *Law in Crisis. The Ecstatic Subject of Natural Disasters*. Stanford: Stanford University Press.

Minet, Carla. 2019. "María's Death Toll: On the Crucial Role of Puerto Rico's Investigative Journalist." In *Aftershocks of Disaster: Puerto Rico Before and After the Storm*, edited by Yarimar Bonilla and Marisol LeBrón, 75–79. Chicago: Haymarket.

———. 2021, April 13. "Current Transparency and Open Data Laws in Puerto Rico Should Have Never Been Approved." Center for Investigative Journalism. https://periodismoinvestigativo.com/2021/04/current-transparency-and-open-data-laws-in-puerto-rico-should-have-never-been-approved/

Molinari, Sarah. 2019. "Authenticating Loss and Contesting Recovery: FEMA and the Politics of Colonial Disaster Management." In *Aftershocks of Disaster: Puerto Rico Before and After the Storm*, edited by Yarimar Bonilla and Marisol LeBrón, 285–297. Chicago: Haymarket.

———. 2020. "The Public Reckoning: Anti-Debt Futures After #RickyRenuncia." *Society and Space*. https://www.societyandspace.org/articles/the-public-reckoning-anti-debt-futures-after-rickyrenuncia

———. 2022. "Disaster Fraud Prevention by Exclusion: Property, Homeownership, and Individual Housing Repair Aid in Puerto Rico." *Centro Journal* 2, no. 34: 327–351.

Moore, Sarah. 2018. "Towards a Sociology of Institutional Transparency: Openness, Deception and the Problem of Public Trust." *Sociology* 52, no. 2: 416–430.

Morales, Ed. 2019. *Fantasy Island: Colonialism, Exploitation, and the Betrayal of Puerto Rico.* New York: Bold Type Books.

Morton, Stephen. 2013. *States of Emergency: Colonialism, Literature and Law*, Liverpool: Liverpool University Press.

Mulligan, Jessica, and Adriana Garriga-López. 2020. "Forging *Compromiso* After the Storm: Activism as Ethics of Care Among Health Care Workers in Puerto Rico." *Critical Public Health* 31, no. 2: 214–225.

Murphy, Gretchen. 2005. *Hemispheric Imaginings: The Monroe Doctrine and Narratives of U.S. Empire.* Durham: Duke University Press.

Murphy, Wendy W. 2022. "Accounting for Justice: Citizen Public Debt Audits and the Case of Puerto Rico." *Studies in Social Justice* 16, no. 1: 182–199.

Murphy Marcos, Coral. 2024, April 10. "Puerto Rico's Unnatural Disaster." *The Nation.* https://www.thenation.com/article/world/puerto-rico-healthcare-crisis/

Murray, Yxta M. 2019a. "What FEMA Should Do After Puerto Rico—Toward Critical Administrative Constitutionalism." *Arkansas Law Review* 72, no. 1: 165–220.

———. 2019b. "'Fema Has Been a Nightmare'— Epistemic Injustice in Puerto Rico." *Willamette Law Review* 55, no. 2: 321–394.

Neal, Andrew W. 2019. *Security as Politics: Beyond the State of Exception.* Edinburgh: Edinburgh University Press.

Neely, Megan Tobias. 2022. *Hedged Out: Inequality and Insecurity on Wall Street.* Oakland: University of California Press.

Newman, Katherine, and Rourke O'Brien. 2011. *Taxing the Poor: Doing Damage to the Truly Disadvantaged.* Oakland: University of California Press.

Nieves Falcón, Luis. 2009. *Un siglo de represión política en Puerto Rico 1898–1998.* San Juan: Ediciones Puerto.

Norris, Davon. 2023, December. "Embedding Racism: City Government Credit Ratings and the Institutionalization of Race in Markets." *Social Problems* 70, no. 4: 914–934, https://doi.org/10.1093/socpro/spab066

NotiCel. 2019. "Saldo Rosselló Nevares: 86 Leyes Firmadas En 8 Días." *NotiCel.* https://www.noticel.com/gobierno/ahora/legislatura/20190806/saldo-rossello-nevares-86-leyes-firmadas-en-8-dias/

O'Donnell, Katy. 2020, January 15. "Trump to Lift Hold on $8.20B in Puerto Rico Disaster Aid." *Politico.* https://www.politico.com/news/2020/01/15/trump-to-lift-hold-on-82b-in-puerto-rico-disaster-aid-099139

Ong, Aihwa. 2006. *Neoliberalism as Exception: Mutations in Citizenship and Sovereignty.* Durham: Duke University Press.

Onís, Catalina. 2021. *Energy Islands: Metaphors of Power, Extractivism, and Justice in Puerto Rico.* Oakland: University of California Press.

Onís, C., and H. Lloréns. 2021. "Fuera LUMA": Puerto Rico Confronts Neoliberal Electricity System Takeover amid Ongoing Struggles for Self-Determination." *Georgetown Journal of International Affairs.* https://gjia.georgetown.edu/2021/06

/21/fuera-luma-puerto-rico-confronts-neoliberal-electricity-system-takeover-amid-ongoing-struggles-for-self-determination/

Ophir, Adi, Michal Givoni, and Sari Hanafi, eds. 2009. *The Power of Inclusive Exclusion: Anatomy of Israeli Rule in the Occupied Palestinian Territories.* New York: Zone Books.

Opitz, Sven, and Ute Tellmann. 2015. "Future Emergencies—Temporal Politics in Law and Economy." *Theory, Culture & Society* 32, no. 2: 107–129.

Ostolaza, César, Carla Rosas, Ana María García-Blanco, Joel Gittelsohn, and Uriyoán Colón-Ramos. 2023. "Impact of the COVID-19 Pandemic on Food Insecurity in Puerto Rico." *Journal of Hunger & Environmental Nutrition* 18, no. 3: 380–395.

Padilla, Andrew. 2021, February 26. "The Road to U.S. Statehood for Puerto Rico Is Paved with Austerity and Settler Colonialism." *Daily Beast.* https://www.thedailybeast.com/the-horrific-colonialist-costs-of-puerto-rican-us-statehood

Pagán, Fabiola. 2016, October 8. "Victoria a Medias Para Documentalista Que Solicito Grabaciones Policiacas de La Huelga UPR." *Pulso Estudiantil.* https://pulsoestudiantil.com/victoria-a-medias-para-documentalista-que-solicito-grabaciones-policiacas-de-la-huelga-upr/

Paralitici, Jose. 2011. *La represión contra el independentismo puertorriqueño: 1960–2010.* Río Piedras: Ediciones Gaviota.

———. 2017. *Historia de la lucha por la independencia de Puerto Rico.* Río Piedras: Publicaciones Gaviota.

Parmet, Wendy E. 2023. *Constitutional Contagion: COVID, The Courts, and Public Health.* Cambridge and New York: Cambridge University Press.

Pavlo, Walter. 2017, November 2. "Puerto Rico Debt Crisis: Lawsuit Claims UBS Scammed Island Residents." *Forbes.* https://www.forbes.com/sites/walterpavlo/2017/11/02/puerto-rico-debt-crisis-lawsuit-claims-ubs-scammed-island-residents/?sh=3ec956357264

Pearce, Frank. 1976. *Crime of the Powerful: Marxism, Crime and Deviance.* London: Pluto Press.

Peck, Jamie. 2010. "Zombie Neoliberalism and the Ambidextrous State." *Theoretical Criminology* 14, no. 1: 104–110.

Pérez, José, Adriana Garriga-López, and Carlos Rodríguez-Díaz. 2022, April 1. "How Is Colonialism a Sociostructural Determinant of Health in Puerto Rico?" *AMA Journal of Ethics* 24, no. 4: E305–312.

Pérez, Louis. 2008. *Cuba in the American Imagination: Metaphor and the Imperial Ethos.* Chapel Hill: University of North Carolina Press.

Pérez Lizasuain, César. 2018. *Rebelión, No-Derecho y Poder Estudiantil: La Huelga de 2010 En La Universidad de Puerto Rico.* Cabo Rojo: Editora Educación Emergente.

Pérez Vargas, Luis. 2021, January 19. "Por Qué Una Reforma a La Ley de Ética Gibernamental?" *El Nuevo Día.* https://www.elnuevodia.com/opinion/punto-de-vista/por-que-una-reforma-a-la-ley-de-etica-gubernamental/

Pérez Viera, Edgardo. 2000. *El Juicio de la Historia: Contra Insurgencia y Asesinato Político en Puerto Rico.* San Juan: Editorial Cultural.

Pistor, Katharina. 2019. *The Code of Capital: How the Law Creates Wealth and Inequality*. Princeton: Princeton University Press.

Ponsa-Kraus, Christina. 2020. "Political Wine in a Judicial Bottle: Justice Sotomayor's Surprising Concurrence in *Aurelius*." *Yale Law Journal* 130: 101–131.

———. 2022. "The Insular Cases Run Amok: Against Constitutional Exceptionalism in the Territories." *Yale Law Journal* 131, no. 8: 2449–2541

Porumbescu, Gregory, Stephen Grimmelikhuijsen, and Albert Meijer. 2022. *Government Transparency: State of the Art and New Perspectives*. Cambridge: Cambridge University Press.

Powers, Christopher. 2020. *4645*. Cabo Rojo: Editora Educación Emergete.

———. 2022. "'What Do the Doves Say?' The Revolt Against Colonial Corruption in the Verano Boricua." *Centro Journal* 2, no. 34: 381–401.

Pozen, David E., and Kim Lane Scheppele. 2020. "Executive Underreach, in Pandemics and Otherwise." *American Journal of International Law* 114, no. 4: 608–617.

Prados Rodríguez, Eva. 2019. "Puerto Rico's Fight for a Citizen Debt Audit: A Strategy for Public Mobilization and a Fair Reconstruction." In *Aftershocks of Disaster: Puerto Rico Before and After the Storm*, edited by Yarimar Bonilla and Marisol LeBrón, 250–256. Chicago: Haymarket.

Puerto Rico Commission for the Comprehensive Audit of the Public Credit. 2016. "Second Interim Pre-Audit Survey." https://periodismoinvestigativo.com/wp-content/uploads/2016/06/Informefinal.pdf

Quiñones-Pérez, Argeo, and Ian J. Seda-Irizarry. 2020. "The Self-Inflicted Dimensions of Puerto Rico's Fiscal Crisis." *Latin American Perspectives* 47, no. 3: 87–102.

Quintero, Laura. 2020, July 8. "Denisse Longo Signed the Referrals After She Was Asked to Resign." *El Nuevo Día*. July 8. https://www.elnuevodia.com/english/news/story/dennise-longo-signed-the-referrals-after-she-was-asked-to-resign/

Rajah, Jothie. 2023. *Discounting Life: Necropolitical Law, Culture and the Long War on Terror*. Cambridge and New York: Cambridge University Press.

Ramos Hernández, Carlos. 2016. "Acceso a La Información, Transparencia y Participación Política." *Revista Juridica de La Universidad de Puerto Rico* 4, no. 81: 1015–1068.

———. 2022. "Transparency in Puerto Rico. Report on the Government (Non)Compliance with Act 141 of 2019." Center for Investigative Journalism. https://periodismoinvestigativo.com/informe-de-cumplimiento-con-la-ley-141/

Ranganathan, Malini. 2019. "Empire's Infrastructures: Racial Finance Capitalism and Liberal Necropolitics." *Urban Geography* 41, no. 4: 492–96.

Ranganathan, Malini, David Pike, and Sapana Doshi. 2023. *Corruption Plots: Stories, Ethics, and Publics of the Late Capitalist City*. Ithaca: Cornell University Press.

Reynolds, John. 2012. "The Political Economy of State of Emergency." *Oregon Review of International Law* 14, no. 1: 85–130.

———. 2017. *Empire, Emergency, and the International Law*. Cambridge: Cambridge University Press, 2017.

Rice, Andrew, and Luis Valentín. 2019, April 17. "The McKinsey Way to Save an Island.

Why Is a Bankrupt Puerto Rico Spending More Than a Billion Dollars on Experts Advice?" *Intelligencer*. https://nymag.com/intelligencer/2019/04/mckinsey-in-puerto-rico.html

Rieder, Rem. 2020, October 14. "Trump's Exaggerated Claims on Biden and Pharma in Puerto Rico." *Fact Check*. https://www.factcheck.org/2020/10/trumps-exaggerated-claims-on-biden-and-pharma-in-puerto-rico/

Rifkin, M. 2012. "Indigenising Agamben: Rethinking Sovereignty in Light of the 'Peculiar' Status of Native Peoples." In *Agamben and Colonialism,* edited by Marcelo Svirky and Simone Bignall, 77–108. Edinburgh: Edinburgh University Press.

Rivera, Danielle. 2020. "Disaster Colonialism: A Commentary on Disasters Beyond Singular Events to Structural Violence." *International Journal of Urban and Regional Research* 46, no. 1: 126–135.

Rivera Ramos, Efrén. 1975. "La Libertad de Informacion: Necesidad de Su Reglamentacion En Puerto Rico." *Revista Juridica de la Universidad de Puerto Rico* 44, no.1–2: 67–112.

———. 2001. *The Legal Construction of Identity: The Judicial and Social Legacy or American Colonialism in Puerto Rico.* Washington, DC: American Psychological Association.

———. 2007. *American Colonialism in Puerto Rico: The Judiciary and the Social Legacy.* Princeton: Markus Wiener.

———. 2023, May 15. "El Tribunal Supremo de Estados Unidos avala el gobierno secreto." *El Nuevo Día.* https://www.elnuevodia.com/opinion/punto-de-vista/el-tribunal-supremo-de-estados-unidos-avala-el-gobierno-secreto/?r=59046

Robles, Frances. 2018, August 10. "Containers of Hurricane Donations Found Rotting in Puerto Rico Parking Lot." *New York Times.* https://www.nytimes.com/2018/08/10/us/puerto-rico-aid.html

———. 2020, March 1. "Month After Puerto Rico Earthquakes, Thousands Are Still Living Outside." *New York Times.* https://www.nytimes.com/2020/03/01/us/puerto-rico-earthquakes-fema.html

Rodríguez, Manuel. 2010. *A New Deal for the Tropics: Puerto Rico During the Depression Era, 1932–1935.* Princeton: Markus Wiener.

Rodríguez Vázquez, Victor. 2022, July 30. "Más Atrasos En El Proceso de Recuperación Tras El Huracán María Debido a Señalamientos Federales." Center for Investigative Journalism. https://periodismoinvestigativo.com/2020/07/mas-atrasos-en-el-proceso-de-recuperacion-tras-el-huracan-María-debido-a-senalamientos-federales/

———. 2022, September 29. "No Solutions to Prevent Blockages in Irrigation Channels During Severe Floods in PR." Center for Investigative Journalism. https://periodismoinvestigativo.com/2022/09/no-solutions-to-prevent-blockages-in-irrigation-channels-during-severe-floods-in-puerto-rico/

Rosa, Alejandra, and Patricia Mazzei. 2020, January 20. "Video Reveals Unused Earthquake Aid in Puerto Rico: 'We Are Outraged.'" *New York Times.* https://www.nytimes.com/2020/01/20/us/puerto-rico-protests-emergency-supplies.html

Rossiter, Clinton. 2002. *Constitutional Dictatorship: Crisis Government in the Modern Democracies.* Los Angeles: Transaction.

Rothe, Dawn. 2009. *State Criminality*. Lanham: Lexington Books.

———. 2010. "Facilitating Corruption and Human Rights Violations: The Role of International Financial Institutions." *Crime, Law and Social Change* 53, no. 5: 457–476.

Rothe, Dawn, and David Kauzlarich. 2022. *Crimes of the Powerful: White-Collar Crime and Beyond*. London and New York: Routledge.

Rudalevige, Andrew. 2021. *By Executive Order: Bureaucratic Management and the Limits of Presidential Power*. Princeton: Princeton University Press.

Rudalevige, Andrew, and Victoria E. Yu. 2020. "The Law Pandemics and Presidential Power: A Taxonomy." *Presidential Studies Quarterly* 50, no. 3: 690–715.

Ruiz, Sandra. 2019. *Ricanness: Enduring Time in Anticolonial Performance*. New York: New York University Press.

Ruiz Kuilan, Gloria. 2022, July 31. "El gobierno devuelve $85.2 millones en fondos federales para la ayuda en pagos de Vivienda, agua y luz." *El Nuevo Día*. https://www.elnuevodia.com/noticias/gobierno/notas/el-gobierno-devuelve-852-millones-en-fondos-federales-para-la-ayuda-en-pagos-de-vivienda-agua-y-luz/

———. 2023, January 20. "Fiscal Plan 2024 Without Austerity Measures." *El Nuevo Día*. https://www.elnuevodia.com/english/news/story/fiscal-plan-2024-without-austerity-measures/

Saha, Jonathan. 2013. *Law, Disorder, and the Colonial State. Corruption in Burma c. 1900*. New York: Palgrave.

Saito, Natsu Taylor. 2020. *Settler Colonialism, Race, and the Law: Why Structural Racism Persists*. New York: New York University Press.

———. 2021. Indefinite Detention, Colonialism, and Settler Prerogative in the United States. *Social & Legal Studies* 30(1): 32–65.

Sampson, Steven. 2010. "The Anti-Corruption Industry: From Movement to Institution." *Global Crime* 11, no. 2: 261–278.

———. 2015. "The Anti-Corruption Package." *Ephemera: Theory & Politics in Organization* 15, no. 2: 435–443.

Santana, Willie. 2023. "The New Insular Cases." *William & Mary Journal of Race, Gender & Social Justice* 29, no. 2: 435–462

Santamaría, Daniel. 2021, February 10. "Denuncian Que Propuesta de La Junta Para Pagar La Deuda Dejaría a La Isla Sin Efectivo En 8 Años." *Metro*. https://www.metro.pr/pr/noticias/2021/02/10/denuncian-que-propuesta-de-la-junta-para- pagar-la-deuda-dejaria-a-la-isla-sin-efectivo-por-8-anos.html

Santiago-Bartolomei, Raúl, and Deepak Lamba-Nieves. 2022, December 12. "The Impact of Short-Term Rentals in Puerto Rico: 2014–2020." *Center for a New Economy*. https://grupocne.org/2022/12/12/the-impact-of-short-term-rentals-in-puerto-rico-2014-2020/#conclusion

Santos, Boaventura de Sousa. 2007. "Beyond Abyssal Thinking: From Global Lines to Ecologies of Knowledges." *Review Fernand Braudel Center* 1, no. 30: 45–89.

———. 2020. *Toward a New Legal Common Sense: Law, Globalization, and Emancipation*. Cambridge University Press.

———. 2023. *Law and the Epistemologies of the South*. Cambridge and New York: Cambridge University Press.

Santos-Lozada, Alexis. 2021. "The Effect of Capital Gains Tax Exemptions in Non-Agricultural Private Employment in Puerto Rico." *SocArXiv Papers*. https://doi.org/doi:10.31235/osf.io/jgdf8

Sarat, Austin, ed. 2010. *Sovereignty, Emergency, Legality*. New York: Cambridge University Press.

Sarat, Austin, and Javier Lezaun. 2009. *Catastrophe: Law, Politics, and the Humanitarian Impulse*. Amherst and Boston: University of Massachusetts Press.

Sarat, Austin, and Stuart Scheingold, eds. 2006. *Cause Lawyers and Social Movements*. Stanford: Stanford University Press.

Sassen, Saskia. 2014. *Expulsions: Brutality and Complexity in the Global Economy*. Cambridge, MA: Harvard University Press.

Scheingold, Stuart. 2004. *The Politics of Rights: Lawyers, Policy, and Political Change*. Ann Arbor: University of Michigan Press.

Scheppele, Kim Lane. 2008. "Legal and Extralegal Emergencies." In *The Oxford Handbook of Law and Politics*, edited by K. Wittington, D. Kelemen, and G. Caldeira, 165–188. Oxford and New York: Oxford University Press.

———. 2018. "Autocratic Legalism." *University of Chicago Law Review* 85, no. 2: 545–584.

Scheuerman, William E. 2000. "The Economic State of Emergency." *Cardozo Law Review* 21: 1869–1894.

———. 2006. "Emergency Powers." *Annual Review of Law & Social Science* 2, no. 1: 257–277.

———. 2012. "Emergencies, Executive Power, and the Uncertain Future of US Presidential Democracy." *Law & Social Inquiry* 37, no. 3: 743–767.

Schmitt, Carl. 2005. *Political Theology*. Translated by George Schwab. Chicago: University of Chicago Press.

Schwartz, Mainon. 2022, April 28. "Equal Protection Does Not Mean Equal SSI Benefits for Puerto Rico Residents, Says Supreme Court." *Congressional Research Service*. https://crsreports.congress.gov/product/pdf/LSB/LSB10737

———. 2023, May 16. "SCOTUS Rules That PROMESA Does Not Abrogate Puerto Rico Oversight Board's Sovereign Immunity—If It Has Any." *Congressional Research Service*. https://crsreports.congress.gov/product/pdf/LSB/LSB10965

Schwartz, Mainon, and Kevin Lewis. 2020, November 23. "Puerto Rico's Financial Oversight and Management Board: The Supreme Court's Analysis and What It Means for Congress." *Congressional Research Service*. https://crsreports.congress.gov/product/pdf/LSB/LSB10555

Sembrando Sentido. 2021. "Contracting in Recovery: Strengths and Weaknesses in Procurement Processes with CDBG-DR Funds." https://drive.google.com/file/d/1zdqYIa22dSocToVfEUw4KEUvbLAeHE_z/view

———. 2022. "Evaluation of Public Procurement Processes in Puerto Rico." https://drive.google.com/file/d/1eGBlol-HCieJGEkObto-ooTxiIG_RpBN/view

Sepúlveda, Aixa. 2020, May 8. "EVERTEC No Facturará Por La Plataforma de PUA." *NotiCel*. https://www.noticel.com/ahora/top-stories/gobierno/20200508/evertec-no-facturara-por-la-plataforma-de-pua/

Serrano, Angelica. 2020, May 29. "PR Department of Health Still Has Problems Producing Correct and Updated COVID-19 Data." Center for Investigative Journalism. https://periodismoinvestigativo.com/2020/05/pr-department-of-health-still-has-problems-producing-correct-and-updated-covid-19-data/

Serrano, Oscar. 2020, December 18. "OPFEI Exoneró a Un Funcionario Que Mintió al Tribunal y Quien Ahora Es Juez." Center for Investigative Journalism. https://periodismoinvestigativo.com/2020/12/opfei-exonero-a-un-funcionario-que-mintio-al-tribunal-y-quien-ahora-es-juez/

———. 2021, March 7. "Demandan Para Que Se Divulge Registro de Convictos Por Corrupción, Que Se Supone Fuera Público Desde 2018." *NotiCel*. https://www.noticel.com/tribunales/ahora/top-stories/20210307/demandan-para-que-se-divulgue-registro-de-convictos-por-corrupcion-que-se-supone-fuera-publico-desd/

Sharma, Aradhana. 2013. "State Transparency After the Neoliberal Turn-—The Politics, Limits, and Paradoxes of India's Right to Information Law." *PoLAR: Political & Legal Anthropology Review* 36, no. 2: 308–325.

Shaxson, Nicholas. 2019. *The Financial Curse: How Global Finance Is Making Us All Poorer*. New York: Grove Press.

Sheffer, Martin. 1999. *The Judicial Development of Presidential War Powers*. Westport: Praeger.

Sheller, Mimi. 2020. *Island Futures: Caribbean Survival in the Anthropocene*. Durham: Duke University Press.

Sierra, Gretchen. 2020, May 7. "Don't Hold Puerto Rico Hostage: Pass the Earthquake Supplemental." *The Hill*. https://thehill.com/opinion/finance/496679-dont-hold-puerto-rico-hostage-pass-the-earthquake-supplemental-act#.XrVxLFg1Czk.twitter

Silbey, Susan S. 2005. "After Legal Consciousness." *Annual Review of Law and Social Science* 1: 323–368.

Silbey, Susan, and Austin Sarat. 1987. "Critical Tradition in Law and Society Research." *Law & Society Review* 21, no. 1: 165–174.

Skeel, David. 2019. "Notes from the Puerto Rico Oversight (Not Control) Board." *Delaware Journal of Corporate Law* 43: 529–549.

Slobodian, Quinn. 2018. *Globalists: The End of Empire and the Birth of Neoliberalism*. Cambridge, MA, and London: Harvard University Press.

———. 2023. *Crack-Up Capitalism. Market Radicals and the Dream of a World Without Democracy*. New York: Metropolitan Books.

Snider, Laureen. 2000. "The Sociology of Corporate Crime: An Obituary (or Whose Knowledge Claims Have Legs?)." *Theoretical Criminology* 4, no 2: 196–206.

———. 2011. "The Conundrum of Financial Regulation: Origins, Controversies, and Prospects." *Annual Review of Law and Social Science* 7, no. 1: 121–137.

Soederberg, Susanne. 2014. *Debtfare States and the Poverty Industry: Money, Discipline and the Surplus Population*. Oxon and New York: Routledge.

Solá-Santiago, Frances. 2021, May 3. "What Logan Paul's Move to Puerto Rico Means—Beyond the Tax Breaks." *Refinery29*. https://www.refinery29.com/en-us/2021/05/10391555/logan-paul-moving-puerto-rico-millionaires-tax-break

Sommerfeldt, C. 2020, January 9. "Trump Administration Refuses to Release All Available Aid to Puerto Rico Despite Earthquakes, Citing 'Corruption' Concerns." *New York Daily News*. https://www.nydailynews.com/news/politics/ny-trump-refuses-aid-puerto-rico-earthquakes-20200109-leu5ushanzcnlehtnqucr6btze-story.html/

Sosa Pascual, Omaya. 2016, April 4. "Where Does Daddy Yankee's Money End Up?" Center for Investigative Journalism. https://periodismoinvestigativo.com/2016/04/where-does-daddy-yankees-end-up/

Sosa Pascual, Omaya, and Luis Valentín Ortiz. 2019, July 19. "The Pillage of Public Funds in PR Going on Behind the Chat." Center for Investigative Journalism. https://periodismoinvestigativo.com/2019/07/the-pillage-of-public-funds-in-puerto-rico-going-on-behind-the-chat/

Sosa Pascual, Omaya, and Jeniffer Wiscovitch Padilla. 2020a, March 14. "Millones a Diestra y Siniestra En Salud Para Vinculados a Los Estrategas de Campana de Rosselló Nevares." Center for Investigative Journalism. https://periodismoinvestigativo.com/2020/03/millones-a-diestra-y-siniestra-en-salud-para-vinculados-a-los-estrategas-de-campana-de-rossello-nevares/

———. 2020b, June 11. "More Death in Puerto Rico Than Announced During the Pandemic." *Centro de Periodismo Investigativo*. https://periodismoinvestigativo.com/2020/06/more-deaths-in-puerto-rico-than-announced-during-the-pandemic/

Soto Rodríguez, Miladys. 2020, August 25. "Todos los beneficiaries de PUA tendrán que registrarse en la nueva Plataforma." *Metro*. https://www.metro.pr/pr/noticias/2020/08/25/todos-los-beneficiarios-de-pua-tendran-que-registrarse-en-la-nueva-plataforma.html

———. 2022. "The Imperious Rule of Julia Keleher: Gender, Race, and Colonialism in the Corruption of Public Education in Puerto Rico." *Centro Journal* 34, no. 2: 123–144.

Sparrow, Bartholomew. 2006. *The Insular Cases and the Emergence of American Empire*. Lawrence: University of Kansas Press.

———. 2022. "The Undying Dead: Why a Century After *Balzac v. Porto Rico* the Insular Cases Are as Important as Ever." *Centro Journal* 34, no.1: 189–225.

Sterett, Susan. 2015a. "Disaster, Displacement, and Casework: Uncertainty and Assistance After Hurricane Katrina." *Law & Policy* 37, no. 1–2: 61–92.

———. 2015b. "Disaster Assistance and Legal Accountability: Care and Surveillance." *Studies in Law, Politics & Society* 68: 95–123.

———. 2023. *Litigating the Pandemic. Disaster Cascades in Court*. Philadelphia: University of Pennsylvania Press.

Sterett, Susan M., and Laura K. Mateczun. 2020. "Displacement, Legal Mobilization, and Disasters: Trial Courts and Legal Process." *Risk, Hazards & Crisis in Public Policy* 11, no. 4: 348–376.

———. 2022. "Legal Claims and Compensation in Climate-Related Disasters." *Political Science Quarterly* 137, no. 2: 293–330.

Stohr, Greg, and Michelle Kaske. 2016, March 21. "Scalia, Alito Court Absences Shape Puerto Rico Debt-Relief Bid." *Bloomberg*. https://www.bloomberg.com/

news/articles/2016-03-21/scalia-alito-court-absences-shape-puerto-rico-debt-relief-bid#xj4y7vzkg

Strauss, Neil. 2019, July 26. "Brock Pierce: The Hippie King of Cryptocurrency." *Rolling Stone*. https://www.rollingstone.com/culture/culture-features/brock-pierce-hippie-king-of-cryptocurrency-700213/

Suárez, Carlos, and Fernando Tormos-Aponte. 2022, September 21. "Puerto Rico's Vulnerability to Hurricanes Is Magnified by Weak Government and Bureaucratic Roadblocks." *The Conversation*. https://theconversation.com/puerto-ricos-vulnerability-to-hurricanes-is-magnified-by-weak-government-and-bureaucratic-roadblocks-190953

Suárez, Damaris, Victor Rodriguez, and Omaya Sosa Pascual. 2022, December 9. "A Nightmare for Puerto Ricans to Find a Home, While Others Accumulate Properties." Center for Investigative Journalism. https://periodismoinvestigativo.com/2022/12/a-nightmare-for-puerto-ricans-to-find-a-home-while-others-accumulate-properties/

Sutter, John, and Omaya Sosa Pascual. 2018, July 3. "Records Suggest Puerto Rico Saw a Leptospirosis Outbreak After Hurricane Maria—But Official Won't Call It That." Center for Investigative Journalism. https://periodismoinvestigativo.com/2018/07/records-suggest-puerto-rico-saw-a-leptospirosis-outbreak-after-hurricane-maria-but-officials-wont-call-it-that/

Svirsky, Marcelo, and Simone Bignall, eds. 2012. *Agamben and Colonialism*. Edinburgh: Edinburgh University Press.

Tax Justice Network. 2021, November 16. "The State of Tax Justice 2021." https://taxjustice.net/reports/the-state-of-tax-justice-2021/

Tellado, Rut. 2020, May 13. "Departamento de Trabajo Procesa Reclamaciones de PUA de Manera Manual." *El Nuevo Día*. https://www.elnuevodia.com/negocios/economia/notas/departamento-del-trabajo-procesa-reclamaciones-de-pua-de-manera-manual/

Thiong'o, Ngungi Wa. 2011. *Dreams in a Time of War: A Childhood Memoir*. London: Vintage Books.

———. 2013. *In the House of the Interpreter: A Memoir*. London: Vintage Books.

Thompson, Lanny. 2010. *Imperial Archipelago: Representation and Rule in the Insular Territories Under U.S. Dominion After 1898*. Honolulu: University of Hawai'i Press.

Tombs, Steve. 2012. "State-Corporate Symbiosis in the Production of Crime and Harm." *State Crime Journal* 1, no. 2: 170–195.

———. 2016. "'After' the Crisis: Morality Plays and the Renewal of Business as Usual." In *Neoliberalism and the Moral Economy of Fraud*, edited by David Whyte and J. Wiegratz, 31–43. New York: Routledge.

———. 2017. *Social Protection After the Crisis: Regulation Without Enforcement*. Bristol: University of Bristol Press.

———. 2019. "Grenfell: The Unfolding Dimensions of Social Harm." *Justice, Power and Resistance* 1, no. 3: 61–88.

Tombs, Steve, and David Whyte. 2002. "Unmasking the Crimes of the Powerful." *Critical Criminology* 11: 217–236.

———. 2008. *Safety Crimes*. New York: Routledge.

———. 2015. *The Corporate Criminal: Why Corporations Must Be Abolished*. Oxon: Routledge.

Tormos-Aponte, Fernando. 2022, October 1. "Neoliberal Disaster Management Is Forcing Puerto Ricans to Create Their Own Recovery." *Jacobin*. https://jacobin.com/2022/10/puerto-rico-fiona-neoliberalism-colonialism/

Tormos-Aponte, Fernando, Gustavo García-López, and Mary Painter. 2021. "Energy Inequality and Clientelism in the Wake of Disasters: From Colorblind to Affirmative Power Restoration." *Energy Policy* 158: 112550.

Tormos-Aponte, Fernando, Wendy Prudencio, Mary Painter, and Brevin Franklin. 2022. "Clientelism and Corruption in the Wake of Disasters." *Centro Journal* 2, no. 34: 305–325.

Tormos-Aponte, Fernando, Mary Painter, and Sameer Shah. 2022, September 28. "Puerto Rico's Electricity Problems Go Beyond Maria and Fiona." *Washington Post*. https://www.washingtonpost.com/politics/2022/09/28/puerto-ricos-electricity-problems-go-beyond-mara-fiona/

Torres Asencio, Luis. 2017, February 17. "Law Ley 76–2000 y Nuestro Estado Permanente de Emergencia." *80 Grados*. https://www.80grados.net/la-ley-76-2000-y-nuestro-estado-permanente-de-emergencia/

Torres-Cordero, Ariam. 2020. "What Is Possible? Policy Options for Long-Term Disaster Recovery in Puerto Rico." *Centro Journal* 32, no. 3: 199–223.

———. 2024. "Bomba Planning and the Pursuit of a Just Recovery." *Planning Theory*. https://doi.org/10.1177/14730952231225816

Torruella, Juan. 1988. *The Supreme Court and Puerto Rico: The Doctrine of Separate and Unequal*. Río Piedras: Editorial de la Universidad de Puerto Rico.

———. 2007. "The Insular Cases: The Establishment of a Regimen of Political Apartheid." *University of Pennsylvania Journal of International Law* 29, no. 2: 283–347.

———. 2018. "Why Puerto Rico Does Not Need Further Experimentation with Its Future: A Reply to the Notion of Territorial Federalism." *Harvard Law Review* 131, no. 3: 65–104.

Trías Monge, José. 2007. *Puerto Rico: Las Penas de La Colonia Mas Antigua Del Mundo*. San Juan: Editorial de la Universidad de Puerto Rico

Tzouvala, Ntina. 2018. "Neoliberalism as Legalism: International Economic Law and the Rise of the Judiciary." In *The Politics of Legality in a Neoliberal Age*, edited by Ben Golder and Daniel McLoughlin, 116–134. Abingdon and New York: Routledge.

———. 2020. *Capitalism as Civilisation: A History of International Law*. Cambridge and New York: Cambridge University Press.

———. 2022. "International Law and (the Critique of) Political Economy." *South Atlantic Quarterly* 121, no. 2: 297–320.

UN Office of the High Commissioner on Human Rights (UNCHR). October 30, 2017. "Puerto Rico: Human Rights Concerns Mount in Absence of Adequate Emergency Response." https://www.ohchr.org/en/press-releases/2017/10/puerto-rico-human-rights-concerns-mount-absence-adequate-emergency-response

US Commission on Civil Rights (USCCR). 2022. "Civil Right and Protections During the Federal Response to Hurricanes Harvey and María." https://www.usccr.gov/reports/2022/civil-rights-and-protections-during-federal-response-hurricanes-harvey-and-maria

Valdez, Inés, Mat Coleman, and Amna Akbar. 2020. "Law, Police Violence, and Race: Grounding and Embodying the State of Exception." *Theory & Event* 23, no. 4: 902–934.

Valdovinos, Jorge. 2022. *Transparency and Critical Theory: Becoming Transparent of Ideology*. Cham, Switzerland: Palgrave-Macmillan.

Valentín, Luis. 2018a, August 1. "Puerto Rico's Fiscal Control Board: Parallel Government Full of Lawyers and Consultants." Center for Investigative Journalism. https://periodismoinvestigativo.com/2018/08/puerto-ricos-fiscal-control-board-parallel-government-full-of-lawyers-and-consultants/

———. 2018b, August 18. "Puerto Rico Government Spends More Than Fiscal Control Board in Bankruptcy Lawyers and Financial Consultants." Center for Investigative Journalism. https://periodismoinvestigativo.com/2018/08/puerto-rico-government-spends-more-than-fiscal-control-board-in-bankruptcy-lawyers-and-financial-consultants/

———. 2018c, October 21. "Last in Line in Puerto Rico's Bankruptcy fight for Everything." Center for Investigative Journalism. https://periodismoinvestigativo.com/2018/10/last-in-line-in-puerto-ricos-bankruptcy-fight-for-everything/

———. 2018d, November 1. "Broken Island, Costly Bankruptcy." Center for Investigative Journalism. https://periodismoinvestigativo.com/2018/11/broken-island-costly-bankruptcy/

———. 2018e, December 13. McKinsey: Puerto Rico Bondholder and Fiscal Board's Lead Adviser. Center for Investigative Journalism. https://periodismoinvestigativo.com/2018/12/mckinsey-puerto-rico-bondholder-and-fiscal-boards-lead-adviser/#

———. 2021, October 5. "Pequeños Bancos Internacionales de Puerto Rico se Asoman en los Pandora Papers." Center for Investigative Journalism. https://periodismoinvestigativo.com/2021/10/pequenos-bancos-internacionales-de-puerto-rico-se-asoman-en-los-pandora-papers/

Valentín, Luis, and Joel Cintrón Arbasetti. 2018, November 28. "Emails Expose Federal Government Influence over Puerto Rico's Fiscal Board." Center for Investigative Journalism. https://periodismoinvestigativo.com/2018/11/emails-expose-federal-govt-influence-over-puerto-ricos-fiscal-board/

———. 2020, July 23. "Salud compró equipo médico a sobreprecio a contacto referido por la Guardia Nacional." Center for Investigative Journalism. https://periodismoinvestigativo.com/2020/07/salud-compro-equipo-medico-a-sobreprecio-a-contacto-referido-por-la-guardia-nacional/#

Valentín, Luis, Joel Cintrón Arbasetti, and Dalila Olmo. 2021, June 25. "Puerto Rico Act 22 Tax Incentive Fails." Center for Investigative Journalism. https://periodismoinvestigativo.com/2021/06/puerto-rico-act-22-fails/

Valentín, Luis, Wilma Maldonado, and Arelis Hernandez. 2022, December 8. "Puerto Rico Was Promised Billions for Safe Water. Taps Are Still Running Dry." Center for Investigative Journalism. https://periodismoinvestigativo.com/2022/12/puerto-rico-was-promised-billions-for-safe-water-taps-are-still-running-dry/

Valentín, Luis, and Carla Minet. 2019, July 13. "The 889 Pages of the Telegram Chat Between Rosselló Nevares and His Closest Aides." Center for Investigative Journalism. https://periodismoinvestigativo.com/2019/07/the-889-pages-of-the-telegram-chat-between-rossello-nevares-and-his-closest-aides/

———. 2020, April 18. "Puerto Rico Health Department's COVID-19 Math is wrong." Center for Investigative Journalism. https://periodismoinvestigativo.com/2020/04/puerto-rico-health-departments-covid-19-math-is-wrong/

———. 2021, October 5. "De Chayanne a Constratistas del Gobierno: Los Puertorriqueños en los Pandora Papers." Center for Investigative Journalism. https://periodismoinvestigativo.com/2021/10/de-chayanne-a-contratistas-del-gobierno-los-puertorriquenos-en-los-pandora-papers/

Vélez-Serrano, Mayra. 2018. "A Long History of Wall Street Bailouts and How Puerto Rico Will Not Be Different." *World Review of Political Economy* 9, no. 2: 265–288.

Vélez-Vélez, Roberto, and Jacqueline Villarubia- Mendoza. 2021, September 7. "Mobilizing Solidarity: Hurricane María as Structural Opening for Mutual Aid." *Sociological Review*. https://thesociologicalreview.org/magazine/september-2021/new-solidarities/mobilizing-solidarity/

Venator Santiago, Charles. 2006. "From the Insular Cases to Camp X-Ray: Agamben's State of Exception and United States Territorial Law." *Studies in Law, Politics, and Society* 39: 15–55.

———. 2015. *Puerto Rico and the Origins of US Global Empire: The Disembodied Shade*. Routledge.

———. 2018. "A Note on the Territorial Government and Incorporation Bills for Puerto Rico Introduced in Congress, 1898–2018." *Centro Journal* 30, no. 3: 313–31.

Venator Santiago, Charles, and Jose Javier Morera. 2022. "Introduction—Back to the Future: The Implications of Balzac One Hundred Years Later." *Centro Journal* 1, no. 34: 5–19.

Vergara, Camila. 2020. *Systemic Corruption: Constitutional Ideas for an Anti-Oligarchic Republic*. Princeton: Princeton University Press.

Verrilli, Donald. 2015. "Brief for the United States as Amicus Curiae Supporting Responders, in the Case of Commonwealth of 'Puerto Rico v. Sánchez Valle et Al." *SCOTUS Blog*. http://www.scotusblog.com/wp-content/uploads/2015/12/US-amicus-brief-in-Valle-15-108.pdf

Villanueva, Joaquín. 2019. "Corruption Narratives and Colonial Technologies in Puerto Rico." *NACLA Report on the Americas* 51, no. 2: 188–193.

———. 2022. "The Criollo Bloc: Corruption Narratives and the Reproduction of Colonial Elites in Puerto Rico, 1860–1917." *Centro Journal* 2, no. 34: 27–50.

Villanueva, Joaquín, Martín Cobián, and Félix Rodríguez. 2018. "San Juan, the Fragile City: Finance Capital, Class, and the Making of Puerto Rico's Economic Crisis." *Antipode* 50, no. 5: 1415–1437.

Villanueva, Joaquín, and Marisol LeBrón. 2020. "The Decolonial Geographies of Puerto Rico's 2019 Summer Protest." *Society and Space* 37, no. 4. https://www.societyandspace.org/forums/the-decolonial-geographies-of-puerto-ricos-2019-summer-protests-a-forum

Villarrubia-Mendoza, Jacqueline, and Roberto Vélez-Vélez. 2020. "Centros de Apoyo Mutuo: reconfigurando la asistencia en tiempos de desastre." *Centro Journal* 32, no. 3: 89–117.

Viola, Lora Anne, and Paweł Laidler, eds. 2021. *Trust and Transparency in an Age of Surveillance.* Abingdon and New York: Routledge.

Virella, Patricia. 2022. "Framing Corruption: The Ley de Reforma Educativa and Puerto Rico's Education Scandal." *Centro Journal* 2, no. 34: 95–121.

Wacquant, Loïc. 2009. *Punishing the Poor: The Neoliberal Government of Social Insecurity.* Durham: Duke University Press.

Walsh, Mary. 2018, September 26. "McKinsey Advises Puerto Rico on Debt. It May Profit on the Outcome." *New York Times.* https://www.nytimes.com/2018/09/26/business/mckinsey-puerto-rico.html

———. 2019, May 2. "Puerto Rico Seeks to Have $9 Billion in Debt Ruled Unconstitutional." *New York Times.* https://www.nytimes.com/2019/05/02/business/puerto-rico-debt-banks.html

Watlington, Chloe. 2019, January–February. "Tales from the Cryptos: Blockchain Visionaries and Old Colonial Scams in Puerto Rico." *The Baffler*, no. 43: 16–23.

Weheliye, Alexander. 2014. *Habeas Viscus: Racializing Assemblages, Biopolitics, and Black Feminist Theories of the Human.* Durham and London: Duke University Press.

Wei, Jiuchang, and Dora Marinova. 2016. "The Orientation of Disaster Donations: Differences in the Global Response to Five Major Earthquakes." *Disasters* 40, no. 3: 452–475.

White, Lawrence. 2009. "The Credit-Rating Agencies and the Subprime Debacle." *Critical Review* 21, no. 2–3: 389–399.

———. 2013. "Credit Rating Agencies: An Overview." *Annual Review of Financial Economics* 5, no. 1: 93–122.

Whittaker Julie. 2022. "Disaster Unemployment Assistance (DUA)." *Congressional Research Service.* https://crsreports.congress.gov/product/pdf/RS/RS22022

Whyte, David. 2007."The Crimes of Neo-Liberal Rule in Occupied Iraq." *British Journal of Criminology* 47, no. 2: 177–195.

———. 2009. *Crimes of the Powerful: A Reader.* London: Open University Press.

———. 2010. "The Neo-Liberal State of Exception in Occupied Iraq." In *State Crime in the Global Age*, edited by William Chambliss, Ray Michalowski, and Ronald Kramer, 134–51. Hoboken: Taylor and Francis.

———. 2014. "Regimes of Permission and State-Corporate Crime." *State Crime Journal* 3, no. 2: 237–246.

———, ed. 2015. *How Corrupt Is Britain?* London: Pluto.

———. 2020. *Ecocide: Kill the Corporation Before It Kills Us.* Manchester: Manchester University Press.

———. 2021, March 31. "COVID-19 Vaccines Are a Victory for Public Research, Not 'Greed' and 'Capitalism.'" *The Conversation.* https://theconversation.com/covid-19-vaccines-are-a-victory-for-public-research-not-greed-and-capitalism-158164

Whyte, David, and Jörg Wiegratz, eds. 2016. *Neoliberalism and the Moral Economy of Fraud.* London and New York: Routledge.

Whyte, Jessica. 2013. *Catastrophe and Redemption: The Work of Giorgio Agamben.* Albany: SUNY Press.

———. 2019. *The Morals of the Market: Human Rights and the Rise of Neoliberalism.* London: Verso.

Will, Susan, Stephen Handelman, and David C. Brotherton. 2013. *How They Got Away with It: White Collar Criminals and the Financial Meltdown.* New York: Columbia University Press.

Willison, Charley, et al. 2021. "How Do You Solve a Problem Like Maria? The Politics of Disaster Response in Puerto Rico, Florida, and Texas." *World Medical & Health Policy* 14, no. 3: 490–506.

Wiscovitch Padilla, Jeniffer, and Omaya Sosa Pascual. 2020, July 24. "Puerto Rico's Chronically Ill Health System Blocks Effective COVID-19 Response." *Centro Periodismo Investigativo.* https://periodismoinvestigativo.com/2020/07/puerto-ricos-chronically-ill-health-system-blocks-effective-covid-19-response/

Wiscovitch Padilla, Jeniffer, and Omaya Sosa Pascual. 2023. El Cartel de la technología que impera en el Departamento de Salud. Center for Investigative Journalism. May 16. https://periodismoinvestigativo.com/2023/05/cartel-de-tecnologia-impera-departamento-salud/

Wolff, Jennifer. 2016. "Debtors' Island." *New Labor Forum* 25, no. 2: 48–55.

Zaloznaya, Marina. 2013. "Beyond Anti-Corruptionism: Sociological Imagination and Comparative Study of Corruption." *Comparative Sociology* 12, no. 5: 705–751.

———. 2017. *The Politics of Bureaucratic Corruption in Post-Transitional Easter Europe.* Cambridge and New York: Cambridge University Press.

Zambrana, Rocío. 2021. *Colonial Debts: The Case of Puerto Rico.* Durham: Duke University Press.

Zartaloudis, T. 2010. *Giorgio Agamben: Power, Law, and the Uses of Criticism.* New York: Routledge.

INDEX

The authorized representative in the EU for product safety and compliance is:
Mare Nostrum Group
B.V Doelen 72
4831 GR Breda
The Netherlands

www.ingramcontent.com/pod-product-compliance
Lightning Source LLC
Chambersburg PA
CBHW020457270326
41926CB00008B/641

* 9 7 8 1 5 0 3 6 4 1 1 7 4 *